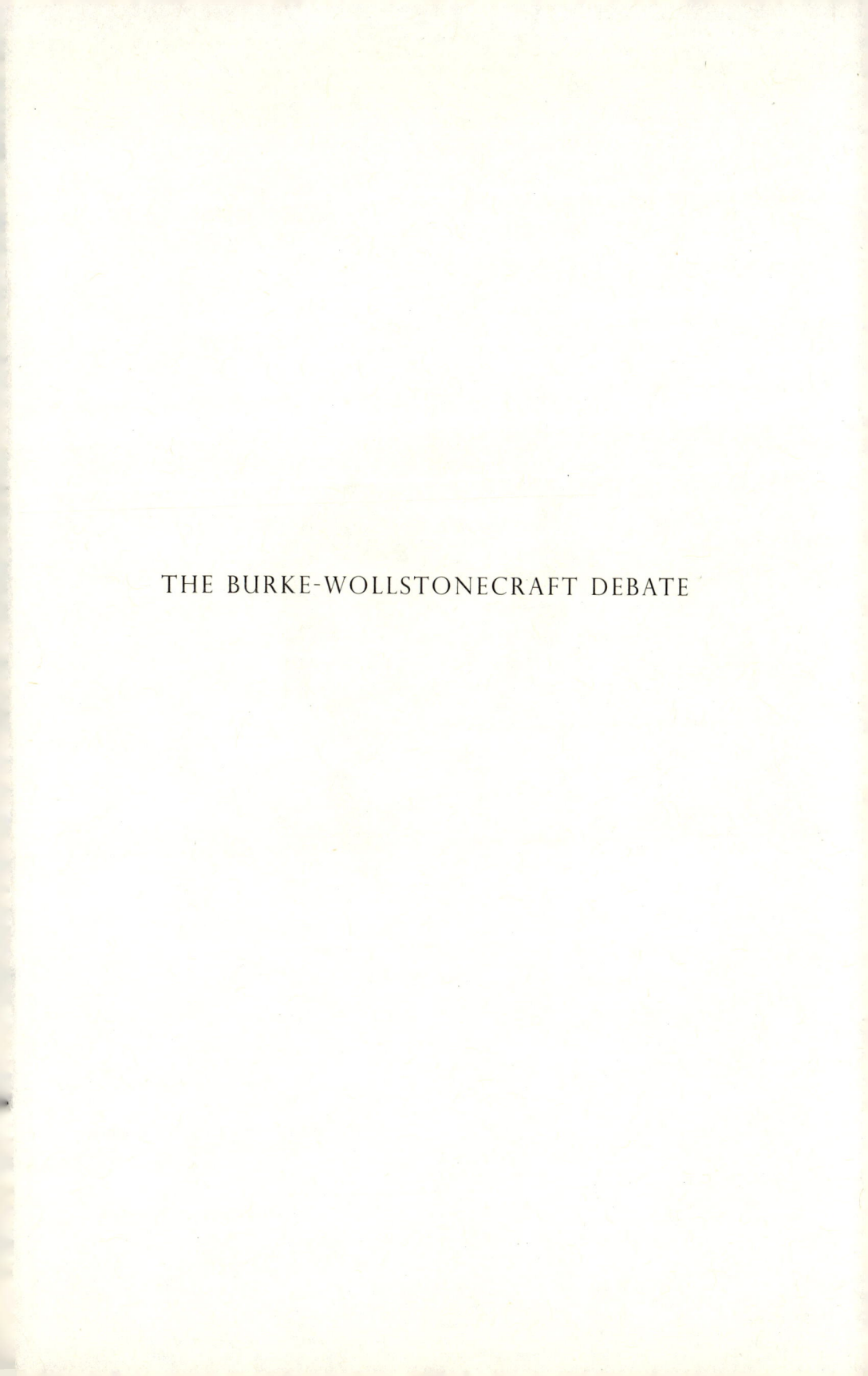

THE BURKE-WOLLSTONECRAFT DEBATE

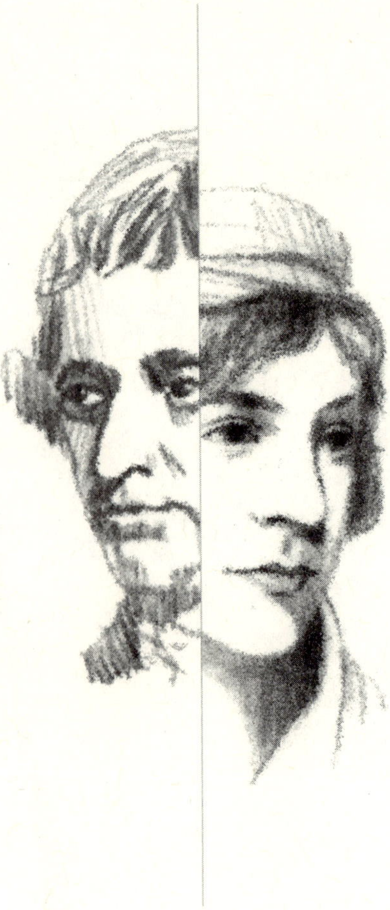

THE
BURKE-WOLLSTONECRAFT
DEBATE

SAVAGERY, CIVILIZATION, AND DEMOCRACY

DANIEL I. O'NEILL

THE PENNSYLVANIA STATE UNIVERSITY PRESS
UNIVERSITY PARK, PENNSYLVANIA

Library of Congress Cataloging-in-Publication Data

O'Neill, Daniel I., 1967–
The Burke-Wollstonecraft debate : savagery, civilization, and democracy / Daniel I. O'Neill.
p.   cm.
Includes bibliographical references (p.   ) and index.
ISBN 978-0-271-03201-6 (cloth : alk. paper)
1. Burke, Edmund, 1729–1797.
2. Wollstonecraft, Mary, 1759–1797.
3. France—History—Revolution, 1789–1799—Causes.
4. Enlightenment—Scotland.
I. Title.

JC176.O54 2007
306.2—dc22
2007002104

Copyright © 2007
The Pennsylvania State University
All rights reserved
Printed in the United States of America
Published by The Pennsylvania State University Press,
University Park, PA 16802-1003

The Pennsylvania State University Press is a member of the Association of American University Presses.

It is the policy of
The Pennsylvania State University Press
to use acid-free paper. This book is printed on Natures Natural, containing 50% post-consumer waste, and meets the minimum requirements of American National Standard for Information Sciences—Permanence of Paper for Printed Library Material, ANSI Z39.48–1992.

FOR ANASTASIA,
always

CONTENTS

ACKNOWLEDGMENTS IX

Introduction 1

1 The Scottish Enlightenment, the Moral Sense, and the Civilizing Process 21

2 Burke and the Scottish Enlightenment 51

3 Wollstonecraft and the Scottish Enlightenment 89

4 "The Most Important of All Revolutions" 125

5 Vindicating a Revolution in Morals and Manners 157

6 Burke on Democracy as the Death of Western Civilization 195

7 Wollstonecraft on Democracy as the Birth of Western Civilization 227

Conclusion 257

BIBLIOGRAPHY 263

INDEX 277

ACKNOWLEDGMENTS

This book has been a very long time in the making. It bears little resemblance to its first formulation as a dissertation, and I daresay that I can mark major moments in my adult life—personally, professionally, and geographically—by recalling what phase of reading, writing, or revision the project was in at the time. Over the course of nearly a decade, I have come to owe so many people so much that it would overburden an already long book by naming them all one by one, especially since I would inevitably leave people out of the accounting, despite my best efforts. Here, then, I reckon only the most important of my debts, both intellectual and personal.

The first of my scholarly debts is undoubtedly to my dissertation advisor at UCLA, Carole Pateman. Carole took a fellow working-class, first-generation student under her wing and refused to let me look back. I have benefited in equal measure from her immense learning on feminism and democracy and her friendship over the years. I will always consider myself very lucky to have been her student, and will never forget the day she asked me why on earth I would ever refer to Mary Wollstonecraft as a "liberal feminist." Indeed.

UCLA during the 1990s was a great place to be doing work at the nexus between political theory, history, and literature. Whatever merit this book has also owes a great deal to what I learned from Victor Wolfenstein and Brian Walker. In his seminar on Nietzsche and thereafter, Victor was a mentor who taught me how to really think about theory for the first time. Both he and Brian were careful readers of the dissertation, as well as great undergraduate teachers in whose classrooms, as a teaching assistant, I learned much that found its way, if only indirectly, into the book. Throughout this project, I have tried to construct mentally what the late, brilliant Richard Ashcraft would have said about its argument. While I'm sure it would not have fully satisfied him, it is no doubt much better than it would have been had I never taken his graduate seminars. Anne K. Mellor helped assure me that my necessary forays into the foreign terrain of English literary criticism were not wholly off base. Scott Bowman, Jason Caro, Andrew Lister, and Danise Kimball, in particular, provided the collegiality, friendship, and keen insight into theory that reminded me why the professoriate is a good profession, after all. Michael Goodhart did all that, and also patiently listened to my successive iterations of the project with his customary wit and wisdom in the ensuing years.

Toward the end of my time at UCLA, I benefited greatly from the arrival of Kirstie McClure. Kirstie's extraordinary erudition, joyously agonistic spirit, and tremendous generosity helped to transform the dissertation. After her reading and comments, the project was immeasurably better, and I will always be thankful to her for encouraging me to ascertain what my work was *really* about. Kirstie was also instrumental in bringing J. G. A. Pocock to UCLA to teach a seminar from which I learned an extraordinary amount, as I did by presenting a portion of my work on Wollstonecraft at a conference at the Clark Library in Los Angeles that she organized, and in which Pocock and others participated.

In my new home at the University of Florida, I have been blessed with fantastic colleagues. I owe special thanks to Leslie Paul Thiele, who read the entire manuscript with painstaking care and made innumerable valuable suggestions concerning everything, from the most overarching intellectual argument to the smallest detail. Peggy Kohn challenged me to articulate some of my ideas by writing the material on Burke for our coauthored piece in *Political Theory*. That exercise helped clarify my thinking immensely, and some of what I wrote at her prompting found its way into the book. I thank Dan Smith, my neighbor in Anderson Hall, for his sound professional advice and patience, and for the hotly contested basketball games in his office.

I owe thanks to two historians in particular. The first is Zephyr Frank of Stanford University, with whom I have shared the great joys of intellectual life since graduate school. Zephyr read the entire manuscript with his razor-sharp intellect and enviable literary gifts. The second is Mary Catherine Moran of Columbia University, who generously shared her work on the Scottish Enlightenment and gender with me while it was still in manuscript form. Her work helped to make Chapter 3 of this book much better than it would otherwise have been.

I am deeply indebted to Sandy Thatcher at Penn State University Press. I cannot imagine a better editor. Like many books he has published over the last thirty-plus years, this one owes its existence in large measure to his faith in it. Among many other things he did, Sandy procured two first-rate outside readers, Isaac Kramnick and Virginia Sapiro. They were ideal reviewers for a book on Burke and Wollstonecraft, and I thank them for their insightful comments and encouragement, which improved the manuscript greatly.

A number of institutions have provided financial support for this project over the years, without which it could not have come to fruition. I am grateful to the University of California for an Office of the President Dissertation Year Fellowship, to the UCLA Department of Political Science for several quarter-long fellowships, to the College of Liberal Arts and Sciences at the University of Florida for two Humanities Scholarship Enhancement Awards, and to the UF Department of Political Science for a summer research grant. I have also benefited from the interest and intellect of a large number of students at the institutions where I have taught, including Pepperdine University, California State University, Los Angeles, and the University of Southern California, as well as UCLA and Florida.

My greatest personal debts are, of course, to my family. My father instilled in me a love of learning in general and a passion for eighteenth-century radical ideas in particular, from a very early age. I will always remember him reading Thomas Paine aloud to me as a child. My mother gave me the great gift of academic discipline and dedicated herself to ensuring that I could attend college if that was what I wanted to do.

To my brother, the historian Johnathan O'Neill, I owe tremendous thanks for a lifetime of rich conversation about matters ranging from the profound to the prosaic, and a shared tapestry of experiences that unite us inevitably, despite the mutual intellectual incomprehension with which we often confront each other these days. I doubt we will ever convince each other, but despite the divergent paths our minds have taken, we both know that in the end our lives are equally far from Green Street.

To my wife, Anastasia, I owe more than words can convey. She has been there for me since graduate school, and has always proved herself the rock of stability, whatever storms might come. She has read every word and edited every version of this book in ways I always stubbornly resisted at first but invariably came to see were exactly right. She rescued the dissertation from a laptop hard drive ten minutes before the whole computer cooked down to oblivion, heard more job talk rehearsals than it is fair to make any human being endure, and knows more about Burke and Wollstonecraft than she ever wished to. In short, without her, neither this project nor my scholarly life would have been possible, and it is for this reason that the book is dedicated to her. To our two children, Cassidy and Jack, I owe continuing thanks for their daily reminders of what is most important in my life.

Portions of this work have been published previously, and were aided by the comments of numerous conference participants prior to publication, as well as by feedback from anonymous manuscript reviewers. I acknowledge the following journals for granting permission to reproduce my earlier work.

Sections of Chapter 7 and very small portions of the Introduction and Chapter 1 include lightly reworked material drawn from "Shifting the Scottish Paradigm: The Discourse of Morals and Manners in Mary Wollstonecraft's *French Revolution*," *History of Political Thought* 23, no. 1 (2002): 90–116. I thank the editors of the *History of Political Thought* and Imprint Academic for allowing me to use this material.

Sections of Chapters 4 and 6 are lightly revised versions of material previously published as "Burke on Democracy as the Death of Western Civilization," *Polity* 36, no. 2 (2004): 201–25. I thank Palgrave Macmillan for allowing me to reproduce this material.

A section of Chapter 2 and a small portion of Chapter 4 were previously published in "A Tale of Two Indias: Burke and Mill on Empire and Slavery in the West Indies and America," co-authored with Margaret Kohn, *Political Theory* 34, no. 2 (2006): 192–228, for which I wrote all the material on Burke. I thank Sage Publications for allowing me to use this material.

Thanks also to the Pierpont Morgan Library, Department of Printed Books and Bindings, New York, for permission to use a detail from William Blake's *The Marriage of Heaven and Hell* (1790) for the cover art.

INTRODUCTION

For more than two centuries, conservatism and feminism have been driving ideological forces in Western political thought. What concerns initially animated these two powerful modern theoretical perspectives? That is the fundamental question at the heart of this book. It is one that has proved very easy to ask and profoundly difficult to answer. This is not because I am the first to ask the question, of course; there has been no lack of discussion of these ideologies. Indeed, early on in the project I found that shelf upon shelf of anthologies, general histories, and textbooks were filled with ready responses to this basic query, all of them founded upon certain certainties. I soon realized, however, that any convincing approach to the problem would require a beginner's mind, one emptied of prefabricated answers and willing to return afresh to the earliest texts of modern feminism and conservatism.

Accordingly, this book focuses on the debate between Edmund Burke (1729–97) and Mary Wollstonecraft (1759–97) over the French Revolution. One leading scholar has rightly concluded that, from a contemporary perspective, Burke's writings and speeches constitute "the bible, and he the prophet" and "enduring philosopher of conservatism."[1] Similarly, the author of a landmark study on Wollstonecraft notes simply that "she has become western feminism's leading heroine."[2] Nevertheless, while we have an extensive literature on the so-called Burke-Paine controversy,[3]

---

1. Isaac Kramnick, "Introduction," in *The Portable Edmund Burke*, ed. Isaac Kramnick (New York: Penguin Books, 1999), ix, xi.
2. Barbara Taylor, *Mary Wollstonecraft and the Feminist Imagination* (Cambridge: Cambridge University Press, 2003), 9.
3. The long history of Burke versus Paine was captured as far back as forty years ago, in Ray Browne, ed., *The Burke-Paine Controversy: Texts and Criticism* (New York: Harcourt, Brace & World, 1963), and is the subject of R. R. Fennessy, *Burke, Paine, and the Rights of Man: A Difference of Political Opinion* (The Hague: Martinus Nijhoff, 1963); and Robert B. Dishman, *Burke and Paine on Revolution and the Rights of Man* (New York: Scribner, 1971).

this is the first book-length account of the clash between Burke and Wollstonecraft.

I am well aware that the attempt to answer my overarching question by framing the encounter between Burke and Wollstonecraft as one featuring canonical exemplars of "conservatism" and "feminism" is itself to invite censure on certain fronts. For one thing, both of these terms are, at the very least, linguistically anachronistic.[4] In addition, by party affiliation Burke was of course a Whig, not a Tory, and Wollstonecraft wrote at a time when no social movement existed to which she could affix her ideas. I am also deeply cognizant of the small library of scholarship, past and present, that rejects the label "conservative" as applied to Burke in favor of some other preferred nomenclature on more substantive grounds. So, too, there is a large body of literature on Wollstonecraft that, even when it identifies her as a feminist, subsumes her arguments under the rubric of some more conventional mode of interpretation, usually (though not exclusively) liberalism.[5]

Having acknowledged these historicist caveats, I want to explain why I am not overly troubled by them. Burke and Wollstonecraft may have *become* conservative and feminist icons only in the twentieth century, but that they *have* become such, indeed that this is the overwhelmingly predominant way of referring to them, is beyond dispute. Furthermore, as Conal Condren has argued, there are quite good reasons why thinkers like Burke and Wollstonecraft become canonical figures and their texts assume "classic" status, and why they subsequently march under occasionally anachronistic banners. Burke and Wollstonecraft wrote works spurred by a great political controversy, the French Revolution, and their writings were effectively deployed by contemporaries as resources in that political controversy. This deployment in turn led their authors to be recognized as authorities whose names and works were capable of being similarly used by successive generations of interpreters engaged in the political struggles of their own present. Finally, the rich ambiguity of such texts not only continues to make them fertile ground for exploitation in political debate, it also ensures that no particular interpretation of a given canonical authority can definitively close the hermeneutic circle, or foreclose future interpreters deploying the works for very different

---

4. The term "conservative" did not enter into Anglophone political discourse until the nineteenth century, and "feminist" only achieved popular currency in the twentieth.

5. For a discussion of this scholarship, see Chapters 2 and 5 in particular.

ends.[6] For these reasons, it is no wonder that Burke became a utilitarian liberal in the nineteenth century, a natural law conservative in the midtwentieth, and in the early twenty-first century seems well on his way, in some academic circles, to becoming an anti-imperial defender of cultural pluralism and difference. Similarly, it is not surprising that Wollstonecraft was long considered (and often still is) a "liberal feminist"—a term of ideological derision to those influenced by Marx or poststructuralism and of adulation to liberals themselves. In still other incarnations she has been read as a republican feminist, for both celebratory and damning purposes. Such are the predictable vicissitudes of political and ideological battles. My point is simply that, whether loved or hated, Burke is today predominantly understood *as* a conservative, and Wollstonecraft *as* a feminist of some sort, and their canonical names and classic texts are marshaled accordingly, within the framework of a given interpreter's own political interests, just as surely as they were initially forged as weapons in an epic political struggle more than two centuries ago.

In making this last claim, I follow scholars like Condren, Sheldon Wolin, Richard Ashcraft,[7] and numerous others in the assumption that political theory emerges most poignantly and powerfully from great political controversy and conflict. If this is so, it is little wonder that the debate between Burke and Wollstonecraft gave rise to what we now understand as conservatism and feminism. After all, their disagreement focused on the meaning of the French Revolution, the conflict that scholars regard as foundational for the emergence of political modernity itself. As one historian of political thought has recently put it:

> The French Revolution has been regarded by subsequent generations as the emergence of the modern political world. It comprised a paradigm shift that irrevocably changed the way in which we think about, speak of and therefore conduct our politics.... Conceptions of political legitimacy, human agency, historical

---

6. See Conal Condren, *The Status and Appraisal of Classic Texts: An Essay on Political Theory, Its Inheritance, and the History of Ideas* (Princeton: Princeton University Press, 1985), chapter 9, especially 255–62, where Condren makes specific reference to the shifting modes of Burke interpretation to illustrate his general point.

7. See especially Sheldon S. Wolin, *Politics and Vision: Continuity and Innovation in Western Political Thought*, exp. ed. (Princeton: Princeton University Press, 2006); and Richard Ashcraft, *Revolutionary Politics and Locke's "Two Treatises of Government"* (Princeton: Princeton University Press, 1986).

process and even time itself were fundamentally restructured by this cataclysmic event.... [But] ... the Revolution did not exert this influence through establishing any agreed truths about politics: on the contrary, it generated—and continues to generate—heated opposition and disagreement.[8]

As the effective touchstone of modernity, the French Revolution has always been highly controversial and evocative of the deepest political passions, from joyous affirmation to unbounded fear and hatred. That this was true from the beginning can be seen by considering the immediate and enormous ripple effect it had on its neighbor, Great Britain. The "Revolution controversy,"[9] which provided the historical context for Burke and Wollstonecraft's debate, was the occasion for what Alfred Cobban referred to as "perhaps the last real discussion of the fundamentals of politics" in Britain.[10] This discussion included such basic issues as the role of popular sovereignty, the legitimacy of monarchy, the desirability of private property, the theoretical basis and practical status of individual rights, and the relationship between religion and politics.

The British pamphlet war that took up the fundamental questions raised by the French Revolution lasted no more than a decade. It began shortly after the French adopted the *Declaration of the Rights of Man and the Citizen* in August 1789. A few months later, in November, Richard Price, the well-known Dissenting preacher, political reformer, and friend to Wollstonecraft, gave his famous speech to the Revolution Society in London, entitled *A Discourse on the Love of our Country*. In that speech Price attempted to defend the French Revolution chiefly by comparing its principles to those of Britain's Glorious Revolution of 1688. Burke's *Reflections on the Revolution in France*, in part a response to Price, appeared in 1790. Burke's famous essay was the match that ignited the tinderbox, sparking a furious flurry of rejoinders from such thinkers as Paine, Joseph Priestley, James Mackin-

---

8. Iain Hampsher-Monk, ed., *The Impact of the French Revolution: Texts from Britain in the 1790s* (Cambridge: Cambridge University Press, 2005), 1–2.
9. See especially Marilyn Butler, ed., *Burke, Paine, Godwin, and the Revolution Controversy* (Cambridge: Cambridge University Press, 1984); Mark Philp, ed., *The French Revolution and British Popular Politics* (Cambridge: Cambridge University Press, 1991); H. T. Dickinson, *British Radicalism and the French Revolution, 1789–1815* (New York: Blackwell, 1985); Albert Goodwin, *The Friends of Liberty: The English Democratic Movement in the Age of the French Revolution* (Cambridge: Harvard University Press, 1979); and Alfred Cobban, ed., *The Debate on the French Revolution, 1789–1800* (London: Nicholas Kaye, 1950), as well as Hampsher-Monk, *Impact of the French Revolution*.
10. Cobban, *Debate on the French Revolution*, 31.

stosh, and Catharine Macaulay. The first published reply to the *Reflections*, however, was Wollstonecraft's *A Vindication of the Rights of Men, in a Letter to the Right Honorable Edmund Burke* (1790), which was available less than a month after Burke's essay appeared.

Burke never formally responded to any of his critics; instead, he replied through numerous public texts and private letters designed to expand, clarify, and refine his position. These included *A Letter to a Member of the National Assembly* (1791), *An Appeal from the New to the Old Whigs* (1791), *Letters on a Regicide Peace* (1795–97), and *Letter to a Noble Lord* (1796), wherein his sworn enemies, including both Wollstonecraft and Paine, were specifically named. Burke also found support for his arguments in such journals as *The Antijacobin*. More important, his position gained a powerful ally in the British state, which became increasingly alarmed at the scope and depth of radical reforming zeal as the 1790s progressed, especially after Great Britain and France went to war in 1793. In 1794 twelve radicals, including John Horne Tooke, John Thelwall, and Thomas Hardy, a founding member and secretary of the London Corresponding Society, were arrested for high treason. In 1795 the Treasonable and Seditious Practices and Unlawful Assemblies Acts were passed, criminalizing certain public meetings and political discussions. In 1799 the LCS and other associations deemed dangerously radical were proscribed, and habeas corpus was suspended.[11]

These actions effectively put an end to the "Revolution controversy" and made Burke its posthumous de facto winner. Before the dissent was stifled, however, the radicals produced an extraordinary array of texts. These ranged from high-minded philosophical treatises like *Political Justice* (1793), written by Wollstonecraft's future husband, William Godwin, to popular weeklies edited by Thomas Spence and Daniel Isaac Eaton, which took fiercely anti-Burkean positions. These works advocated a dizzying variety of political and economic reforms.[12]

Like Burke, Wollstonecraft also expanded and sharpened her theoretical arguments as the French Revolution unfolded during the 1790s, until she died in 1797, the same year as Burke. Moreover, there is a fundamental continuity of themes between Wollstonecraft's direct reply to Burke in the first *Vindication* and the argument of *A Vindication of the Rights of Woman*

---

11. See Hampsher-Monk, *Impact of the French Revolution*, 2n3, 263–64, 316–17.
12. For a measure of the achievement of the popular radical pamphleteers, see Olivia Smith, *The Politics of Language, 1791–1819* (Oxford: Oxford University Press, 1984), chapters 1–4.

(1792), considered one of the cornerstones of modern feminism.[13] Thus, while the second *Vindication* was not written directly in response to Burke, insofar as it represents a deepening and broadening of the arguments first articulated in her earlier text, and addressed as it was to the French revolutionary, Talleyrand, in an endeavor to hold the French to what she understood as their theoretical principles, it can be read profitably as the second installment of her debate with Burke. Finally, it also makes good theoretical sense to read Wollstonecraft's little known *An Historical and Moral View of the Origin and Progress of the French Revolution; and the Effect It Has Produced in Europe* (1794), as a contribution to the Revolution controversy and as a theoretical counterpoint to Burke's views about the genesis and trajectory of the Revolution. The text was written about the events of 1789 but from the perspective of one on the ground in Paris during the Terror of 1793. As such, it takes up precisely the same figures and events as the *Reflections*, yet it interprets them in light of subsequent history and thus attempts to explain the violent course of the Revolution in a way that mirrors Burke's later writings. As a counternarrative of the same events Burke interprets, aimed instead at defending the principles of the Revolution, which formed in part the foundation for the changes she advocated in the two *Vindications*, Wollstonecraft's *French Revolution* can be read as part of an ongoing dialogue, the final installment in a three-part reply to Burke. This is true irrespective of any narrowly construed understanding of Wollstonecraft's authorial intentions (or, for that matter, Burke's).

Against this backdrop, I began the present project with a deceptively simple set of questions, or perhaps even the same question asked in slightly different ways. First, what was the basis for Burke and Wollstonecraft's fundamental disagreement over the French Revolution? Second (or put differently), why had Burke so vehemently opposed the Revolution, even long before the Terror, and why had Wollstonecraft so steadfastly supported it, even during the Terror? Third (or yet again), what did the Revolution seem to *signify* in Burke and Wollstonecraft's theoretical imaginations, such that the man conventionally regarded as the founding father of modern conservatism would dedicate his life to stopping its spread, whereas the woman seen as the most important early feminist would literally risk hers to defend it?

13. In making this claim, I agree with Butler, who writes: "Wollstonecraft's [second *Vindication*] is not always seen as strictly a part of the Revolution controversy, yet its arguments clearly relate to the egalitarian and radical case she had already advanced against Burke" (*Burke, Paine, Godwin*, 74).

Little did I know that the attempt to answer these questions, which entailed the inevitable three-sided conversation between reader, primary text, and secondary literature, would lead into a vast interpretive wilderness from which I would emerge only after humbling lessons of dispossession. It was as if Burke and Wollstonecraft were conducting an argument about the French Revolution in a language in which they were both fluent but whose idioms remained foreign to my ears. Repeated attempts to unlock the meaning of their texts by recourse to the conventional theoretical skeleton keys on offer (e.g., Burke as a natural law theorist, Wollstonecraft as a liberal feminist) left me feeling frustrated.

Foremost, then, this book is an attempt to translate the language of political argumentation that I think most fundamentally structures the conflict between Burke and Wollstonecraft over the meaning of the French Revolution, with the goal of opening up the meaning of their debate for us. Nevertheless, the pages that follow make no claim to show *the* political philosophy of Burke confronting *the* political philosophy of Wollstonecraft. I readily accept that there are multiple ways of reading these two thinkers, and multiple contexts for framing their works. Similarly, it is not my intention to provide a synoptic overview of everything that Burke and Wollstonecraft ever wrote, or to synthesize the various strands of their work under the flag of coherentism. This book has very little to say, for example, on the question of Burke's writings on India, and engages Burke on Ireland and America only insofar as these writings directly intersect, in my view, with his interpretation of events in France. So, too, I do not provide an analysis of Wollstonecraft's early novels and pedagogical works, or the later travelogue of her experiences in Scandinavia and her unfinished novel, *Maria*.

While what follows does not seek to establish itself as the only legitimate way of reading Burke and Wollstonecraft, then, or even of reading Burke and Wollstonecraft against each other, neither is it an arbitrary interpretation. As J. G. A. Pocock has argued, the political languages that become matters of theoretical interest to later interpreters are not confections; rather, they must be established empirically, that is to say, with evidence.[14] In one sense, this means that historians of political thought act

---

14. See J. G. A. Pocock, "Languages and Their Implications: The Transformation of the Study of Political Thought," in Pocock, *Politics, Language, and Time: Essays on Political Thought and History* (Chicago: University of Chicago Press, 1989), 25–26; and Pocock, "The Concept of a Language and the *métier d'historien:* Some Considerations on Practice," in *The Languages of Political Theory in Early-Modern Europe*, ed. Anthony Pagden (Cambridge: Cambridge University Press, 1987), 19–38.

like archaeologists, uncovering and recovering various linguistic contexts in which previous political arguments were conducted. As interpreters of such conversations, however, they must also be attuned to the complex interaction between discursive contexts and individual uses of language. The goal is not simply to be a linguistic archaeologist, but rather to find ways of understanding how particular deployments of political language modified the contexts they were originally situated within, and how some of those modifications led to the creation of entirely new languages of politics. That is to say, we have to recognize how some "moves" within a discursive context may not have simply modified the old linguistic paradigm but revolutionized it in unanticipated ways.[15]

Following such methodological advice, this book argues that the Burke-Wollstonecraft debate is best understood as an extended argument articulated within the unique linguistic parameters established by the thinkers of the Scottish Enlightenment. Of course, like "conservatism" or "feminism," "Scottish Enlightenment" is an ex post facto term of art that serves as shorthand for a complex intellectual movement; it was a term first coined in 1900, not one used during the eighteenth century.[16] However, while Adam Smith, David Hume, Adam Ferguson, William Robertson, John Millar, Lord Kames, James Beattie, James Fordyce, Dr. John Gregory, and the rest only earned the moniker "Scottish Enlightenment" posthumously, there is no question that they saw themselves as a coherent group engaged in a common intellectual project, that of articulating a "Science of Man" based on a broadly unified, self-consciously shared set of theoretical presuppositions that culminated in a distinctive political language.[17]

As this book demonstrates more thoroughly than has been done to date, Burke was a fellow traveler in this effort, and both the Scots and Burke recognized that they were taking part in a shared intellectual endeavor. At the same time, while it is clear that Wollstonecraft did not identify these thinkers as a coherent group, I show that she was very well acquainted with their arguments, had a profound understanding of their intellectual project and the language it was articulated in, and was deeply influenced by it. Thus, while we frequently have to guess at what Wollstonecraft dis-

---

15. Pocock, "Concept of a Language," 21, 30–31, 34.
16. See Alexander Broadie, "Introduction," in *The Cambridge Companion to the Scottish Enlightenment* (Cambridge: Cambridge University Press, 2003), 3.
17. See ibid., 1–2, and N. T. Phillipson, "The Scottish Enlightenment," in *The Enlightenment in National Context*, ed. Roy Porter and Mikuláš Teich (Cambridge: Cambridge University Press, 1981), 19–40, especially 20–21.

cussed with Price, Priestley, or the other members of the radical Dissenting circles in which she moved, proof of the imprint of Scottish Enlightenment ideas on her thinking is marked by deep and abundant empirical tracks in her texts.[18]

Specifically, my argument is that the clash between Burke and Wollstonecraft over the meaning of the French Revolution developed from a Scottish Enlightenment language of politics structured broadly around "moral sense" philosophy and the closely connected historical narrative of a "civilizing process" in which the Scots understood that moral sense to be embedded. The Scottish Enlightenment's approach to the topics of moral philosophy and history produced a distinctive, clearly identifiable language that provided the discursive scaffolding for the Burke-Wollstonecraft debate.

Lest there be any misunderstanding, I am not saying that Edmund Burke and Mary Wollstonecraft were simply mouthpieces for Scottish Enlightenment ideas. Rather, I am arguing that both thinkers took certain Scottish Enlightenment arguments as their clay, and transformed that clay in very distinct and idiosyncratic ways in the course of developing their own theoretical constructs. Both writers freely adapted, melded, criticized, and fundamentally transformed certain broadly shared Scottish Enlightenment ideas and the language in which they were articulated, from their own theoretical perspectives and for their own particular political ends, which were those of repudiating or defending the French Revolution.

My central contention is that viewing Burke's and Wollstonecraft's texts about the French Revolution from the perspective of their appropriation, deployment, and transformation of a language of politics specific to the Scottish Enlightenment enables us to uncover the stakes of their debate. To put this suggestively, perhaps it is only by showing the depth of Burke's and Wollstonecraft's debt to the Scottish Enlightenment, and making clear how both thinkers fundamentally transformed that language of politics for their own purposes, that we can really understand what they ultimately disagreed *about*.

Thus my answer to the series of questions with which I began the project, which takes here the form of a promissory note that the rest of the book aims to make good: the debate between Burke and Wollstonecraft about the French Revolution rested on what was ultimately a profound

---

18. At the same time, I argue that the extent to which Price, Priestley, and others known to Wollstonecraft were themselves familiar with Scottish Enlightenment ideas, and thus represented an additional conduit for those ideas to reach her, has been overlooked by most scholars. See Chapter 3.

disagreement about the relationship between democracy and civilization. For Burke, I argue, the French Revolution spelled the birth of a thoroughgoing democracy that encompassed both public and private spheres, a development that he interpreted literally as the end of Western civilization and its reversion to savagery. For Wollstonecraft, conversely, only such thoroughgoing democracy as she believed was promised by the French Revolution could mark the transition from savagery to civilization; for her, democratization was inseparable from, indeed analogous to, the civilizing process itself. If I am right, this means that modern conservatism and feminism emerged out of dialogic disagreement about deep democracy and whether it was synonymous with "savagery" or "civilization." Modern conservatism was born in white-hot hostility to deep democracy, understood as the end of civilization, whereas modern feminism was not simply about the extension of the "rights of man" to women in the public sphere, but rather about the spread of democracy into all aspects of human existence, which was equivalent to the spread of civilization.

The thinkers of the Scottish Enlightenment originated and developed the idea that history was a story of stadial movement in which all societies naturally passed through four stages—hunting, herding, farming, and commerce—a developmental process that simultaneously tracked a cultural arc from "savagery," through "barbarism," to "civilization." "Civilization" was not just a marker of material improvement for the Scots but also a normative judgment about the moral progress of society. Pocock has described the Scots' perception of society as a developmental process culminating in polite modes of social interaction, or civilized manners, as perhaps "the greatest change wrought by Enlightenment in the field of social and historical thought." "Manners" were the linguistic key to the Enlightenment historical narrative, in which eighteenth-century writers detailed the fate of the Latin provinces after the decline and fall of Rome, through the long, dark Christian millennium of "barbarism and religion," into the light of modernity. The fundamental theme of this new Enlightenment historiography was precisely the emergence of a shared civilization of manners and commerce, from which sovereign European states grew.[19]

19. See J. G. A. Pocock, *Barbarism and Religion*, vol. 2, *Narratives of Civil Government* (Cambridge: Cambridge University Press, 1999), 1–2, 19–20, 24 (quotation at 19); and Pocock, "Virtues, Rights, and Manners: A Model for Historians of Political Thought," in his *Virtue, Commerce, and History: Essays on Political Thought and History, Chiefly in the Eighteenth*

Chapter 1 provides a basic sketch of the central approach, themes, and conclusions drawn by Scottish Enlightenment historiography. It also articulates the Scots' equally important commitment to what can broadly be called "moral sense" philosophy and stresses its connection to the Scots' historical narrative. The opening chapter is not meant to be a synoptic overview of every aspect of the Scottish Enlightenment, a tremendously complex intellectual movement that has been the subject of any number of scholarly monographs in intellectual and social history. Rather, it functions heuristically as a means of orienting the reader to the Scots' central concerns with respect to two areas in particular, moral philosophy and history, and especially to the vocabulary in which those concerns were expressed. If we want to understand the debate between Burke and Wollstonecraft, I submit that we must first become broadly conversant with Scottish Enlightenment discourse on these two topics, which provided the linguistic ammunition for their clash.

The rest of the book examines the Burke-Wollstonecraft debate in an alternating, dialogic fashion. Chapters 2, 4, and 6 focus on Burke's arguments, while Chapters 3, 5, and 7 take up Wollstonecraft's. In the remainder of this Introduction, I want to give the reader an overview of my argument concerning each of these thinkers.

With respect to Burke, I stress his reliance on, and simultaneous transformation of, Scottish Enlightenment historiography for his understanding of the French Revolution. As Pocock has previously shown, Burke did not simply adopt the Scots' historical narrative in its entirety as a means of interpreting the Revolution's significance; rather, he modified their four-stages thesis in crucial ways.[20] Rightly or wrongly, Burke interpreted his Scottish friends as arguing that the mode of economic production *drove* the progressive development of natural moral sentiments and their expression in increasingly refined social manners. Against this, Burke offered an idealist and institutional inversion of the four-stages account. In Burke's

---

Century (Cambridge: Cambridge University Press, 1985), 37–50. See also Karen O'Brien, *Narratives of Enlightenment: Cosmopolitan History from Voltaire to Gibbon* (Cambridge: Cambridge University Press, 1997).

20. For Pocock's view of Burke, see "The Political Economy of Burke's Analysis of the French Revolution," in his *Virtue, Commerce, and History*, 193–212; his introduction to Burke's *Reflections on the Revolution in France* (Indianapolis: Hackett, 1987), vii–lvi; and his "Edmund Burke and the Redefinition of Enthusiasm: The Context as Counter-Revolution," in *The French Revolution and the Creation of Modern Political Culture*, vol. 3, ed. François Furet and Mona Ozouf (Oxford: Pergamon Press, 1989), 19–43.

view, modes of economic production were necessarily embedded in a rich soil of natural moral sentiment that was nurtured by two institutions, the nobility and the church.[21]

At this point, however, my argument fundamentally diverges from Pocock's, who stops short of developing a critical line of inquiry with respect to Burke. Specifically, why did Burke focus on the nobility and the church, and the worldview that they perpetuated, with its emphasis on the "spirit of nobility" and the "spirit of a gentleman"? And how exactly did Burke believe that these two institutions nurtured natural moral sentiments in such a way as to civilize the masses?

To answer these questions, one must grapple with the close connections between Burke's historical analysis of the French Revolution and his moral theory, especially as the latter was set forth some thirty years earlier in *A Philosophical Enquiry into the Origin of our Ideas of the Sublime and Beautiful* (1757) and other writings from that period. These are texts that Pocock wholly neglects in his often brilliant reading of Burke. Nevertheless, the need to discuss the relationship between Burke's aesthetics[22] and the broader epistemological presuppositions of his moral theory[23] for his interpretation

---

21. See Pocock's introduction to Burke's *Reflections*, xxxii–xxxiii; his "Political Economy of Burke's Analysis," 197–99; and his "Burke and the Redefinition of Enthusiasm," 31–34.

22. The first attempt to relate Burke's aesthetic and political thought was Neal Wood, "The Aesthetic Dimension of Burke's Political Thought," *Journal of British Studies* 4, no. 1 (1964): 41–64. An important early statement is found in Isaac Kramnick, *The Rage of Edmund Burke: Portrait of an Ambivalent Conservative* (New York: Basic Books, 1977). More recently, see especially Linda M. G. Zerilli's excellent *Signifying Woman: Culture and Chaos in Rousseau, Burke, and Mill* (Ithaca: Cornell University Press, 1994); and Stephen K. White, *Edmund Burke: Modernity, Politics, and Aesthetics* (Thousand Oaks, Calif.: Sage Publications, 1994). Iain Hampsher-Monk, "Rhetoric and Opinion in the Politics of Edmund Burke," *History of Political Thought* 9, no. 3 (1988): 455–84, discusses Burke's aesthetics in conjunction with the classical rhetorical tradition. Recent years have seen an explosion of work on Burke from the perspective of literary criticism. See especially Frans De Bruyn, *The Literary Genres of Edmund Burke: The Political Uses of Literary Form* (Oxford: Oxford University Press, 1996); Ronald Paulson *Representations of Revolution, 1789–1820* (New Haven: Yale University Press, 1983); Steven Blakemore, *Burke and the Fall of Language: The French Revolution as Linguistic Event* (Hanover: University Press of New England, 1988); and Terry Eagleton, "Aesthetics and Politics in Edmund Burke," *History Workshop Journal* 28 (1989): 53–62.

23. For the importance of Scottish Enlightenment moral philosophy for Burke, see especially Rodney W. Kilcup, "Reason and the Basis of Morality in Burke," *Journal of the History of Philosophy* 17, no. 3 (1979): 271–84; and Frans De Bruyn, "Edmund Burke's Natural Aristocrat: The 'Man of Taste' as a Political Ideal," *Eighteenth-Century Life* 11, no. 2 (1987): 41–60. See also the introductory essay in Burke, *Edmund Burke: Pre-Revolutionary Writings*, ed. Ian Harris (Cambridge: Cambridge University Press, 1993); Burleigh Taylor Wilkins, *The Problem of Burke's Political Philosophy* (Oxford: Clarendon Press, 1967), 50–71; and Frederick

of the French Revolution has become increasingly apparent. But scholars who have discussed Burke's early writings on aesthetics and moral philosophy have not placed them in the context of his reinterpretation of the Scottish Enlightenment historical thesis.[24]

Just as striking, little attention has been given to the arguments of Burke's *Abridgment of the English History* (1758) and *Account of the European Settlements in America* (1757),[25] or the ways in which these two texts resonate with both his overarching moral theory and narrative of history and thus with his later understanding of the French Revolution. Yet, if we want to understand Burke's interpretation of that event, I think we must focus our attention in a new way on the intersection of Burke's moral and aesthetic categories and his unique revision of Scottish Enlightenment historiography. These interpretive modalities meet most profoundly in

---

Dreyer, "The Genesis of Burke's *Reflections,*" *Journal of Modern History* 50 (September 1978): 462–79. The initial work connecting Burke to Scottish Enlightenment moral theory was John A. Lester Jr., "An Analysis of the Conservative Thought of Edmund Burke" (Ph.D. diss., Harvard University, 1942).

24. For a valuable exception, see Luke Gibbons, *Edmund Burke and Ireland: Aesthetics, Politics, and the Colonial Sublime* (Cambridge: Cambridge University Press, 2003). As the title suggests, however, its focus is only tangentially on the French Revolution. Moreover, Gibbons offers a very different, and highly sympathetic, reading of the interconnected role of Burke's aesthetics and historical imagination in his political theory, to which the present book might be seen as counterpoint. See also Tom Furniss, *Edmund Burke's Aesthetic Ideology: Language, Gender, and Political Economy in Revolution* (Cambridge: Cambridge University Press, 1993), which takes its lead from Burke's aesthetics and touches lightly on the Scots' historical narrative. Furniss's book is a fascinating reading of the *Enquiry* against the *Reflections* using Derridean deconstructive tools for the purpose of offering a complex rendering of Burke in the vein of Marx, that is, as a "bourgeois ideologist." This methodological approach and set of theoretical investments are very different from my own. For an argument that begins with Adam Smith's political economy, follows Pocock in connecting Burke to Scottish Enlightenment historiography, and discusses the connection between Burke's aesthetic and moral theory and Smith, see Donald Winch, *Riches and Poverty: An Intellectual History of Political Economy in Britain, 1750–1834* (Cambridge: Cambridge University Press, 1996). It should be noted that while Winch and Furniss broadly work the same intellectual turf, their conclusions are very different. More important, as their titles indicate, both scholars are centrally interested in Burke's relationship to political economy; for reasons I make clear throughout this book, I am not.

25. The chief exceptions concerning the latter text are F. P. Lock's outstanding biography, *Edmund Burke*, vol. 1, *1730–1784* (Oxford: Oxford University Press, 1998), chapter 5; C. P. Courtney, *Montesquieu and Burke* (Oxford: Basil Blackwell, 1963); T. O. McLoughlin, "Edmund Burke's *Abridgment of English History,*" *Eighteenth-Century Ireland* 5 (1990): 45–59; and Michel Fuchs, *Edmund Burke, Ireland, and the Fashioning of the Self* (Oxford: Voltaire Foundation, 1996). Regarding the former, see in particular Gibbons, *Edmund Burke and Ireland*, chapter 7; as well as Lock, *Edmund Burke*, chapter 5; and Fuchs, *Edmund Burke*, chapter 4, which also connect the *Account* to its Scottish Enlightenment context in their own ways.

Burke's assessment of the nobility and church's importance and the consequences of their respective demise, including the steps subsequently taken by the revolutionaries to democratize the moral and political landscape.

In this light, Chapter 2 seeks to recover the roots of Burke's moral philosophy and theory of history and demonstrate their connection to the Scottish Enlightenment. By looking at the broader historical context, as well as considering Burke's private correspondence and book reviews for the *Annual Register*, I begin by showing that he was a friend to, or acquaintance of, several of the leading Scots and demonstrate his explicit commitment to their broadly shared moral philosophy, historiography of a civilizing process, and overarching goal of establishing a "Science of Man." I focus particularly on Burke's epistemological presuppositions in *A Philosophical Enquiry into the Origin of our Ideas of the Sublime and Beautiful* and his other early writings, and their relation to Adam Smith's *Theory of Moral Sentiments*, James Beattie's philosophy of "common sense," and the links between Burke, William Robertson, and Adam Ferguson.

In Chapter 2, I also show that as early as the *English History* and *Account of the European Settlements in America*, Burke was already developing a unique and dynamic understanding of historical change, the central focus of which was the noneconomic bases for the cultivation and transformation of innate "morals" into civilized "manners" over the course of European history. In Burke's narrative of history, too, one moves from savagery, through barbarism, to civilization. Unlike the Scots' story, however, Christianity and feudal chivalry, and their institutional guarantors the church and nobility, play the central roles in the civilizing process. The remaining two chapters on Burke describe *how* he believed the nobility and church transformed natural moral sentiments into historically developed manners in a way that culminated in European civilization, and *why*, in turn, he believed that civilization came completely undone with the French Revolution and devolved into morally, politically, and socially repugnant "savagery."

Chapter 4 offers an interpretation of Burke's most famous work, the *Reflections on the Revolution in France*, in light of the previous contextual rereading of his moral theory and understanding of history. I argue that the *Reflections* represents an extraordinary weaving together of the moral philosophy, social theory, and historical arguments of the Scottish Enlightenment with the themes Burke had articulated in the *Enquiry*, *History*, and *Account*. In the *Reflections*, Burke argued that the church and nobility were the institutional purveyors of fear, on the one hand, and voluntary acquiescence in inequality and servitude, on the other. Together, by acting as the institutional embodiments of the principles of the "sublime" and "beautiful," respectively, Burke believed that these two institutions provided for the polishing of natural moral sentiments into appropriately deferential political and social manners, and created the requisite level of "habitual social discipline" necessary for "a people" to emerge, a beneficent "natural aristocracy" to govern, and civilization to flourish. By destroying these two institutions, the French revolutionaries obliterated the balanced alchemy of fear and love, sublimity and beauty, that had underwritten European civilization, and unleashed in their stead a world of fearless, untamed savagery.

In Chapter 6, I focus on the substantive nature of the "savagery" that Burke saw ensuing in the wake of the old European regime's collapse. In particular, I chart Burke's apocalyptic post-*Reflections* vision of democracy as a social, sexual, and cultural revolution aimed at leveling natural distinctions. Like the Scottish Enlightenment thinkers, Burke was convinced of the validity of a "moral sense" traceable to human nature and vital to the continuing progress of civilization. He therefore dreaded the threat to civilization posed by a total revolution that perverted and destroyed this instinctive affective sense and the various hierarchical relations derived from it. I show that Burke, in his later writings, decried what he saw as the revolutionaries' systematic attempt to break down natural authority relations within the family and to promote adultery and sexual promiscuity, a skyrocketing divorce rate, the legal equality of nontraditional families and their offspring, and an explosive growth in popular entertainment of all sorts, especially via the print medium. At the same time, I demonstrate how Burke drew explicit connections between this egalitarian revolution in morals and manners, the advent of political democracy, and the collapse of "civilization" into "savagery."

Burke consistently maintained that the French revolutionaries were introducing a new system of democratic manners precisely to accommodate and support their new scheme of democratic politics. Thus the collapse of civilization was signified for Burke by a politically engaged hoi polloi, ranging from tavern keepers and clerks to liberated women. His was a vision in which the masses had torn themselves free from their fealty to the natural aristocracy and lost all habitual social discipline, a nightmare vision of political equality echoed and reinforced by willful social, sexual, and cultural leveling in the private sphere. For Burke, it was thus thoroughgoing democracy that was synonymous with savagery and signaled the literal end of Western civilization.[26]

Mary Wollstonecraft's argument precisely inverted Burke's. Wollstonecraft simultaneously engaged in her own attempt to transform Scottish Enlightenment moral philosophy and historiography, but in an effort to defend the French Revolution as the first step toward thoroughgoing democracy and thus true civilization. While Wollstonecraft's links to the Scots have been partially developed, especially in an important piece by Jane Rendall, no scholar has established this relationship systematically. Moreover, Wollstonecraft's entire body of work on the French Revolution has yet to be read as an extended reply to Burke formulated in the reworked idiom of the Scottish Enlightenment language of politics.[27] My goal is to

26. As I make clear in Chapter 6, this conclusion also makes my interpretation of Burke fundamentally different from Pocock's. My conclusion shares most in common with Don Herzog's outstanding book on the rise of modern conservatism, *Poisoning the Minds of the Lower Orders* (Princeton: Princeton University Press, 1998). However, while I am very much in agreement with Herzog's broad thesis about the historical relation between conservatism and democracy, I disagree with him on crucial issues of interpretation with respect to Burke. Herzog wants to explain what he suggests is a basic difference in the types of theoretical arguments Burke made before and after the outbreak of the French Revolution: "Before 1789, Burke is a child of the Scottish enlightenment, devoted to free trade, a quaintly mechanistic psychologist devoted to unpacking the principles generating our judgments of the sublime and the beautiful; after 1789, he discards such lines of argument" (22). Herzog maintains that for Burke, these types of arguments represented "the sort of early enlightenment sentiment that he ruthlessly squelched after 1789" (46). It should be clear where we differ. My view is that Burke not only remained a child of the Scottish Enlightenment, as it were, but recast the Scots' historical thesis as his chief means of interpreting the French Revolution's meaning. Moreover, he did so specifically from the standpoint of his own earlier arguments concerning the sublime and the beautiful.

27. The first discussion to connect Wollstonecraft's *Historical and Moral View of the Origin and Progress of the French Revolution* to Scottish Enlightenment historiography is Jane Rendall's excellent article, "'The grand causes which combine to carry mankind forward': Wollstonecraft, History, and Revolution," *Women's Writing* 4, no. 2 (1997): 155–72. On Wollstonecraft's historical narrative and the Scots, see also Anna Neill, "Civilization and the Rights of Woman: Liberty and Captivity in the Work of Mary Wollstonecraft," *Women's Writing* 8, no. 1 (2001): 99–119, reprinted in *Mary Wollstonecraft and the Critics, 1788–2001*, ed. Harriet Devine Jump, 2 vols. (New York: Routledge, 2003), 2:418–35. For a suggestive precursor, see Gordon Spence, "Mary Wollstonecraft's Theodicy and Theory of Progress," *Enlightenment and Dissent* 14 (1995): 105–27, especially 124. The first discussion of Wollstonecraft's relationship to Scottish Enlightenment moral philosophy is Carol Kay, "Canon, Ideology, and Gender: Mary Wollstonecraft's Critique of Adam Smith," *New Political Science* 15 (1986): 63–76. Other scholars have suggested, but not developed, Wollstonecraft's links to the Scots. See G. J. Barker-Benfield's monumental *Culture of Sensibility: Sex and Society in Eighteenth-Century Britain* (Chicago: University of Chicago Press, 1992); Sylvana Tomaselli's introduction to *A Vindication of the Rights of Men and A Vindication of the Rights of Woman* (Cambridge: Cambridge University Press, 1995); Gary Kelly, *Revolutionary Feminism: The*

establish Wollstonecraft's links to both Scottish historiography and moral philosophy, and, more important, to examine the theoretical relevance of Wollstonecraft's revolutionary transformation of Scottish Enlightenment arguments.

In Chapter 3, I argue that Wollstonecraft engaged in a sustained critique of Scottish Enlightenment moral theory, particularly of the central theoretical role the Scots allocated to women in their effort to define and defend the emerging eighteenth-century "culture of sensibility." In this chapter I look at the Scots' view of women, as articulated by writers like James Fordyce, John Gregory, and other popular moralists, as well as by Adam Smith and David Hume, all of whom Wollstonecraft criticized extensively. I contend that Wollstonecraft's critique hinged on denying the Scots' assumption of the naturalness of the moral sentiments and the social manners derived from them, together with her denial of the historical role the Scots saw women as playing based on their natural aptitude for "common sense," or sensibility. The chapter also shows that it was Wollstonecraft's extensive work for Joseph Johnson's *Analytical Review*, from 1788 to 1792, that led her fundamentally to reevaluate her initial understanding of the discourse of common sense or sensibility, as well as the broad historical narrative within which the Scots had embedded it.

In Chapter 5, I consider both of Wollstonecraft's *Vindications*. I argue that in her direct reply to Burke's *Reflections*, her *Vindication of the Rights of Men* (1790), Wollstonecraft attempted to deconstruct Burkean moral theory, the historical arguments used to justify it, and the defense of church and nobility adduced to buttress it, by using the discursive tools that she had derived from the Scottish Enlightenment and reinterpreted. Wollstonecraft linked Burke's *Reflections* to the moral theory of his earlier *Philosophical Enquiry*, which she rightly understood as built upon the moral intuitionism of "sympathy," "common sense," and "sensibility." Her critique of Burke's *Enquiry* was therefore also a basic reevaluation of Scottish moral philosophy, one that stressed the socially constructed nature of both morals and manners. In this way Wollstonecraft contested Burke's reification of the old European regime. She argued to the contrary that

---

Mind and Career of Mary Wollstonecraft (London: Macmillan, 1992); and Chris Jones, "Mary Wollstonecraft's *Vindications* and Their Political Tradition," in *The Cambridge Companion to Mary Wollstonecraft*, ed. Claudia L. Johnson (Cambridge: Cambridge University Press, 2002), 42–58.

the *ancien régime*'s system of manners was an artificial and pernicious code of social mores developed in an oppressive, hierarchical institutional context fatal to the development of reason and thus to moral and civic virtue. Wollstonecraft took issue with Burke's conviction that social, political, sexual, and other inequalities were part of the natural order of things, and argued that all such hierarchies had to be wholly razed and reconstructed on the basis of democratic equality.

In *A Vindication of the Rights of Woman* (1792), Wollstonecraft turned her attention specifically to how the old European system of manners had affected women, and urged a "revolution in female manners" as part of what she saw as the democratic emancipatory potential of the French Revolution. Wollstonecraft used the tools of critical reason and eighteenth-century associational psychology to analyze the social construction of womanhood under the hierarchical institutions governing Europe. The plight of women appeared to her a particularly onerous example of an immoral system of manners, an aristocracy of sex in which men dominated the church, the nobility, the family, and educational institutions. She argued that all of these institutions acted together to produce and reproduce the artificial hierarchies and gross inequalities that oppressed women but were nevertheless defended as the products of moral "nature" and civilized manners by Burke and others. Far from arguing simply for an extension of standard liberal rights to women, Wollstonecraft's "revolution in female manners" necessitated the thorough democratization of political, economic, social, and gender relations. Virtue in both the public and private spheres for women and men alike, and thus real civilization, could be achieved in no other way.

Even in the wake of the Terror, Wollstonecraft sought to defend the French Revolution as a positive step forward in the civilizing process. I take up her argument to that effect through a reading of *An Historical and Moral View of the Origin and Progress of the French Revolution; and the Effect It Has Produced in Europe* (1794), the focus of Chapter 7. Armed with a firm belief in the social construction of character and a political commitment to democratic equality, Wollstonecraft rewrote the Scottish Enlightenment's entire history of manners in a way that denied their theoretical and historical connection to supposedly natural moral sentiments. She fundamentally refashioned the Scots' arguments by denying the central claim of the four-stages historical thesis, that the "polished" state of European manners that had accompanied the advent of commercial society marked an advance over earlier stages of the civilizing process. In this way

Wollstonecraft fully transformed the Scottish Enlightenment language of politics into a democratic defense of the French Revolution and a rejoinder to Burke.

Wollstonecraft's argument was complex. While she denied the Scottish and Burkean naturalization of the political, social, and economic status quo, Wollstonecraft agreed with the Scots that beneficial intellectual and technological progress had occurred with the advent of commercial society. Wollstonecraft went much further, however, and argued that the development of rational egalitarian principles, combined with the technological means of their transmission, could be used to radically transform the Old Regime in Europe.

Like Burke, Wollstonecraft was not surprised that the French Revolution produced the Terror, and she expected that the radical democratic transformation it foretold would not proceed peacefully. Rather than blame "nature," however, Wollstonecraft explained the Revolution's violent turn as the outcome of the radical inequality that prevailed in France and throughout Europe and was fatal to moral and civic virtue. Wollstonecraft believed that equality was the necessary prerequisite for developing the distinctively human capacity for reason sufficiently to control the passions and develop virtuous character. Consequently, she explained the French Revolution's violence, while refusing to justify it, as the predictable consequence of underdeveloped character in the context of the *ancien régime*'s many artificial social hierarchies. But she remained steadfast in her belief that intellectual and technological progress could eventually reshape both the public and private spheres on the basis of equality, the tragic violence of the Terror notwithstanding.

In my reading, then, Wollstonecraft's writings on the French Revolution were themselves truly revolutionary, insofar as they transformed elements of an already existing language of politics for her own, fundamentally different, theoretical purposes. By placing her writings in the context of their relationship to Scottish Enlightenment moral philosophy and history, we can see precisely how Mary Wollstonecraft made one of the most consistent arguments for the radical extension of democratic equality in the history of Western political thought.[28]

---

28. My conclusion here about Wollstonecraft's commitment to deep democracy is broadly consonant with that of Virginia Sapiro, in her pathbreaking work on Wollstonecraft as a political theorist, *A Vindication of Political Virtue: The Political Theory of Mary Wollstonecraft* (Chicago: University of Chicago Press, 1992), a book to which I am greatly indebted, as well as with that of Barbara Taylor. However, the paths Taylor, Sapiro, and I take to this broadly

Thus I argue that if modern feminism began with Mary Wollstonecraft, it began in an attempt to link the progress of civilization with the march of democracy. Moreover, Wollstonecraft made this revolutionary claim to counter the argument of the father of modern conservatism, Edmund Burke, that democracy and savagery were synonymous.

---

shared conclusion about Wollstonecraft's understanding of the relationship between feminism and democracy are very different. Taylor emphasizes the religious context of Wollstonecraft's thought; conversely, I am stressing the role of the secular in Wollstonecraft's moral philosophy and historical narrative, and I rest my analysis directly upon those secular sources. More recently, however, Taylor has briefly suggested the importance of Scottish Enlightenment moral theory for Wollstonecraft in "Feminists Versus Gallants: Manners and Morals in Enlightenment Britain," in *Women, Gender, and Enlightenment*, ed. Sarah Knott and Barbara Taylor (New York: Palgrave Macmillan, 2005), 30–52. Sapiro does not discuss the Scottish Enlightenment at all.

1 THE SCOTTISH ENLIGHTENMENT, THE MORAL SENSE, AND THE CIVILIZING PROCESS

In the past thirty years, a number of scholars have demonstrated the unique intellectual contribution made by a group of like-minded eighteenth-century Scots who were closely affiliated, both personally and professionally, and self-consciously unified around an identifiable theoretical project. The basic goal of the Scottish Enlightenment was to establish what David Hume, one of its leading lights, termed a "Science of Man" applicable to the increasingly complex commercial societies of Europe. The Scots sought a scientific understanding of individual ideas and beliefs as the key to understanding their social world and its historical development.[1] They aimed,

---

1. See especially N. T. Phillipson, "The Scottish Enlightenment," in *The Enlightenment in National Context*, ed. Roy Porter and Mikuláš Teich (Cambridge: Cambridge University Press, 1981), 19–40, especially 20; see also Phillipson, "Towards a Definition of the Scottish Enlightenment," in *City and Society in the Eighteenth Century*, ed. Paul Fritz and David Williams (Toronto: Hakkert, 1973), 125–47. In addition to a wide variety of primary sources, what follows intentionally relies on works that provide a broad overview of Scottish Enlightenment ideas, in order to elaborate the general conclusions scholars have drawn with respect to the Scots' thinking about moral philosophy and history. In this regard, I am deeply indebted to Christopher J. Berry, *Social Theory of the Scottish Enlightenment* (Edinburgh: Edinburgh University Press, 1997). Other general studies from which I have benefited include Gladys Bryson, *Man and Society: The Scottish Inquiry of the Eighteenth Century* (Princeton: Princeton University Press, 1945); Jane Rendall, ed., *The Origins of the Scottish Enlightenment, 1707–1776* (New York: St. Martin's Press, 1978); Louis Schneider, ed., *The Scottish Moralists on Human Nature and Society* (Chicago: University of Chicago Press, 1967); Alexander Broadie, ed., *The Cambridge Companion to the Scottish Enlightenment* (Cambridge: Cambridge University Press, 2003); Broadie, *The Scottish Enlightenment: The Historical Age of the Historical Nation* (Edinburgh: Birlinn, 2001); Broadie, ed., *The Scottish Enlightenment: An Anthology* (Edinburgh: Canongate Books, 1997); Broadie, *The Tradition of Scottish Philosophy: A New Perspective on the Enlightenment* (Savage, Md.: Barnes & Noble 1990); Ronald L. Meek, *Social Science and the Ignoble Savage* (Cambridge: Cambridge University Press, 1976); Anand C. Chitnis, *The Scottish Enlightenment: A Social History* (Totawa, N.J.: Rowman and Littlefield, 1976); David Spadafora, *The Idea of Progress in Eighteenth-Century Britain* (New Haven: Yale University Press, 1990); Ronald Hamowy, *The Scottish Enlightenment and the Theory of Spontaneous Order* (Carbondale: Southern Illinois University Press, 1987); R. H. Campbell and Andrew S. Skinner, eds., *The Origins and Nature of the Scottish Enlightenment* (Edinburgh: John Donald Publishers, 1982); Peter Jones, ed., *The 'Science of Man' in the Scottish Enlightenment: Hume, Reid, and Their Contemporaries* (Edinburgh: Edinburgh University Press, 1989); M. A. Stewart, ed., *Studies in the Philosophy of the Scottish Enlightenment* (Oxford: Oxford University Press, 1990); George E. Davie, *The Scottish Enlightenment and Other Essays* (Edinburgh:

that is, to provide an empirical account of human mental processes as the first step in analyzing human social arrangements and their development over time.[2] Various scholars have described this project as an attempt to study "man and society," "human nature and society," or "social man."[3] Such phrases suggest the Scots' shared commitment to studying moral philosophy as the essential prerequisite for any full-fledged narrative of social interactions and the ways in which these interactions changed over time.[4]

This chapter provides a broad sketch of the Scots' approach to two closely entwined issues, moral philosophy and social history, the two components of the Scottish Enlightenment that would do the most to create the Scots' distinctive language of politics and thus the most important for Edmund Burke and Mary Wollstonecraft. What follows, therefore, moves along two closely related but analytically separable axes, the first focused on the Scots' understanding of individual moral psychology and the second on the ways in which they understood social interaction over the course of history. These twin concerns provided the basic linguistic building blocks that Burke and Wollstonecraft would appropriate and meld into radically antithetical interpretations of the French Revolution.

"Moral Sense" Philosophy

When it came to the study of moral philosophy, the thinkers of the Scottish Enlightenment began with John Locke and Isaac Newton. In his *Essay Concerning Human Understanding* (1690), Locke had systematized sensationalist psychology by denying the existence of innate ideas and conceiving the human mind instead as a *tabula rasa*, a blank slate, on which impressions were stamped. This argument in turn rested on Newtonian assumptions, a fact that Sir Isaac is said to have recognized by famously declaring Locke the first Newtonian philosopher. Like Locke's *Essay*, Newton's own *Optics* (1704), which offered an empirical account of the physiology of perception, proved highly influential in the eighteenth century. Unlike his earlier *Principia* (1687), which was written in Latin and remained untrans-

---

Polygon, 1991); Hugh Trevor-Roper, "The Scottish Enlightenment," *Studies on Voltaire and the Eighteenth Century* 58 (1967): 1635–58; and Arthur Herman, *How the Scots Invented the Modern World* (New York: Three Rivers Press, 2001).

2. See Phillipson, "Scottish Enlightenment," 20–21.
3. The phrases are those of Bryson, Schneider, and Chitnis, respectively.
4. See Rendall, *Origins of the Scottish Enlightenment*, especially chapter 3, 96–101.

lated for forty years, the *Optics* was in English, and readily accessible to a wider audience. Consequently, Newton's notion of the "sensorium," or the termination of all nerve endings in the brain, together with Locke's theory of the blank slate, revolutionized a number of fields in the eighteenth century, and set the parameters of debate on moral philosophy for the Scottish Enlightenment.[5]

Early on in this story, the third earl of Shaftesbury (1671–1713), grandson of Anthony Ashley Cooper, felt compelled to respond to the far-reaching implications of Locke's ideas. In the wake of his son's degenerative illness, Cooper, who was Locke's political patron, had charged Locke with the education of his grandson. But the young Shaftesbury rebelled against the philosophy of the man he called his foster father, believing that the early eighteenth century was endangered by a moral relativism that threatened social order and from which Lockean epistemology offered no escape. What Shaftesbury attempted to provide was a naturalistically grounded or nontheological basis for ascertaining moral certitude.[6]

In the revised version of *Characteristics of Men, Manners, Opinions and Times* (1714), published the year after his death, Shaftesbury bequeathed to the eighteenth century a response to this problem that would have tremendous influence: the notion of an innate moral sense. At the same time, Shaftesbury's insistence on a common human nature had the unintended consequence of effectively universalizing this sense, enabling it to inhabit those outside the aristocracy, to whom he had originally intended to limit it.[7]

Shaftesbury's idea of an inner faculty responding to moral phenomena, much as other senses perceived physical phenomena, became extremely important for Francis Hutcheson (1694–1746), who, along with Andrew Fletcher of Saltoun and Gershom Carmichael, Hutcheson's teacher and predecessor at Glasgow, is often referred to as the father of the Scottish Enlightenment.[8] Hutcheson developed Shaftesbury's response to Lockean sensationalist psychology by combining it with the teachings of Carmichael

---

5. See G. J. Barker-Benfield, *The Culture of Sensibility: Sex and Society in Eighteenth-Century Britain* (Chicago: University of Chicago Press, 1992), 2–6; and Berry, *Social Theory of the Scottish Enlightenment*, 4. For a general discussion, see Roy Porter, *The Creation of the Modern World: The Untold Story of the British Enlightenment* (New York: W. W. Norton, 2000).

6. See Barker-Benfield's discussion of Shaftesbury in his *Culture of Sensibility*, 105–19. For a detailed discussion, see Lawrence E. Klein, *Shaftesbury and the Culture of Politeness* (Cambridge: Cambridge University Press, 1994).

7. See Barker-Benfield, *Culture of Sensibility*, 105–19.

8. On Hutcheson, see T. D. Campbell, "Francis Hutcheson: 'Father' of the Scottish Enlightenment," in Campbell and Skinner, *Origins and Nature of the Scottish Enlightenment*,

in an effort to counter Thomas Hobbes's and Bernard Mandeville's arguments that all human action was a form of ethical egoism. Hutcheson set forth his conclusions in such works as *An Inquiry into the Origin of our Ideas of Beauty and Virtue* (1725), *Short Introduction to Moral Philosophy* (1747), and *A System of Moral Philosophy* (1755).

Hutcheson built upon Shaftesbury's basic idea by arguing that human beings took immediate pleasure in certain behaviors and exhibitions of character that afforded them no advantage, and that their will was not involved in this process. As a corollary to this nonconsequentialist claim, Hutcheson maintained that the evaluation of moral qualities could not rest principally on reason, since in his view reason could point only to causal relations; it could not provide the basic rules of moral approval or disapproval. Rather, the mind had a number of "senses," or affective predispositions to accept certain ideas, that operated independent of human will and the utilitarian categories of pleasure and pain.[9] He believed that among these was, as Shaftesbury had argued, a "moral sense" by which people perceived virtue and vice in themselves and others. By such arguments, Hutcheson's system of ethics placed morality on a nonrational, instinctive footing rooted in a constant and uniform human nature.[10]

This last point became one of the central presuppositions on which the Scottish Enlightenment was based. Internal variations notwithstanding, the Scots all followed Hutcheson in building their moral philosophy on the assumption that human beings shared a common nature. Scholars have insisted on the pervasiveness of this view within the Scottish Enlightenment, and its fundamental importance to the Scots' theorizing. Indeed, it is difficult to overstate the importance of the fact that all of the social theorists of the Scottish Enlightenment believed in the constancy of human nature.[11]

There was a great deal of internal wrangling among the Scots on other fundamental epistemological questions, however, seen clearly in the ideas

---

167–85; and James Moore, "The Two Systems of Francis Hutcheson: On the Origins of the Scottish Enlightenment," in Stewart, *Studies in the Philosophy of the Scottish Enlightenment*, 37–59.

9. See Campbell, "Francis Hutcheson," 167–70; and Berry, *Social Theory of the Scottish Enlightenment*, 158–60.

10. See Broadie, *Tradition of Scottish Philosophy*, 92–95; Schneider, *Scottish Moralists*, xxi–xxii; and Berry, *Social Theory of the Scottish Enlightenment*, 158–59.

11. See Berry, *Social Theory of the Scottish Enlightenment*, especially 68–70; Broadie, "What Was the Scottish Enlightenment?" in his *Scottish Enlightenment: An Anthology*, 19–22; Bryson, *Man and Society*, 114–47; Schneider, *Scottish Moralists*, xxi–xxv; and Rendall, *Origins of the Scottish Enlightenment*, 96–101.

of one of the two central figure of the Scottish Enlightenment, David Hume (1711–76). It is impossible to do justice here to the complexity of Hume's moral philosophy, its enormous influence, or the library of secondary literature it has spawned. My goal is simply to point out certain of its leading features in order to understand Hume's importance for establishing the central terms of debate for much of the rest of eighteenth-century philosophical argument, and for the Scottish Enlightenment in particular.[12]

Whereas Hutcheson had attempted empirically to ground a revamped form of Christianity on the concept of an innate moral sense, Hume used the same empiricist tools to reach very different conclusions. In both cases, the goal of establishing a science of morality based on the assumed uniformity of human nature was the same. So too was the ostensible method; as the subtitle of Hume's *Treatise of Human Nature* (1739–40) indicated, his was "an attempt to introduce the experimental method of reasoning into moral subjects." Hume differed from Hutcheson, however, in the unprecedented extent to which he was willing to press that method, and in his unwillingness to transcend the narrow compass of its conclusions. Hume analyzed such fundamental concepts as the existence of an external world, cause and effect, and an individuated self, from a ruthlessly experiential perspective. In each case he found reason impotent, and he argued that on close empirical inspection human certainty dissolved, proving in the end to be nothing more than the effect of an association of ideas upon the imagination and the accumulated weight of custom and habit.[13] Of course, for Hume, as for the rest of the Scots, the very universality of human nature nevertheless made human behavior predictable, or amenable to scientific understanding, and he famously argued in *An Enquiry Concerning Human Understanding* (1748) that history's chief use was as a record of the universal propensities of said nature.[14] In this sense Hume's aim remained that of understanding the underlying forces that animated human conduct, notwithstanding the fact that in the process the irrational roots of such behavior were exposed by the harsh winds of skepticism.[15]

As all dabblers in philosophy know, Immanuel Kant later claimed that Humean skepticism had awakened him from his dogmatic slumber. To

---

12. A useful starting point, in addition to the material on Hume in the general overviews I have cited, is N. T. Phillipson, *Hume* (New York: St. Martin's Press, 1989).

13. See ibid., 35–52; Berry, *Social Theory of the Scottish Enlightenment*, 58–60; Bryson, *Man and Society*, 121–30; Rendall, *Origins of the Scottish Enlightenment*, 96–101.

14. See especially Broadie, *Scottish Enlightenment: Historical Age*, 61–64.

15. Broadie, "What Was the Scottish Enlightenment?" 3–31, especially 20–21; and Berry, *Social Theory of the Scottish Enlightenment*, 68–70.

Kant, Hume seemed to have dispensed not simply with any innate moral sense as the basis for knowing God's will, and the obligations derived from it, but with God himself. If Hutcheson, despite his intentions, might be accused of tending toward Deism, Hume appeared to be an outright infidel and atheist, one who undermined universally valid moral principles entirely in his purportedly scientific examination of morality.

Enter the second leading figure of the Scottish Enlightenment, Adam Smith (1723–90). Smith was a fellow traveler in the attempt to develop a science of morals as a branch of the science of man. He was also a good friend of Hume's, a former student of Hutcheson, and the author of *The Theory of Moral Sentiments* (1759).

Smith's argument in *The Theory of Moral Sentiments* was in large part built upon a fundamental disagreement with his friend Hume over the question of the source of our moral obligations.[16] Like Hutcheson, Hume had argued that benevolence was one of the animating passions in human nature. Unlike Hutcheson, however, Hume believed that it was a mistake to see benevolent action as the product of an innate moral sense. Instead, Hume explained moral approval as an expression of our ability sympathize with, or take part simultaneously with others in, the happiness generally following from benevolent action. Thus virtue was a matter of artifice and rested upon the ability of individuals to take sympathetic pleasure in the happiness of society at large. Hume's view was utilitarian, because sympathy, as the source of moral approval or disapproval, was ultimately linked to the pleasure or pain, and thus the aggregate social happiness or unhappiness, resulting from a given action.[17]

Like Hume, Smith focused on the concept of sympathy as the key to moral philosophy, but his view of it was very different from Hume's. As T. D. Campbell reminds us, in order to understand their disagreement we would do well to recognize Smith's goals in writing *The Theory of Moral Sentiments* as they relate to the broader Scottish Enlightenment project of establishing a science of man. Smith's argument was indeed a reply to Hume, but not of the sort moral philosophers have come to expect. Smith did not set out to devise an answer to what we, in retrospect, would see as

16. See D. D. Raphael and A. L. Macfie, eds., "Introduction," in Adam Smith, *The Theory of Moral Sentiments* (Indianapolis: Liberty Fund, 1984), 10.
17. Ibid., 11–13; and Berry, *Social Theory of the Scottish Enlightenment*, 160–65. As with Hume, so with Smith—the secondary literature is vast. I have benefited particularly from T. D. Campbell, *Adam Smith's Science of Morals* (Totowa, N.J.: Rowman and Littlefield, 1971). More recently, see especially Charles L. Griswold Jr., *Adam Smith and the Virtues of Enlightenment* (Cambridge: Cambridge University Press, 1999).

the most pressing philosophical problem Hume left to the eighteenth century, namely, the need to establish a nontheological basis for defending moral judgments. Rather, Smith, like the rest of the Scots (including Hume himself), was attempting to ground social morality scientifically by examining its roots. From this perspective, *The Theory of Moral Sentiments* was an attempt empirically to analyze human nature with the goal of explaining the origin and function of *existing* moral rules. If we bear this in mind, we will not make the mistake of confusing Smith's goal of describing the process of making moral judgments with an argument principally aimed at defending specific moral judgments against others. In other words, we will not confuse Smith's attempt to describe what "is" with an attempt to define what "ought" to be morally binding. While this is never an absolute distinction, Smith's chief concern in the *Moral Sentiments* was with the origin and function of moral judgments, not the criticism of certain moral judgments as opposed to others. His "scientific" aim was to explain as wide a variety of social phenomena as possible with the smallest number of explanatory concepts; like a contemporary social scientist, Smith sought a parsimonious theory, and sympathy proved to be the independent variable that yielded it.[18]

How did this process occur, according to Smith? "By the imagination," he argued, "we place ourselves in [another's] situation...we enter as it were into his body, and become in some measure the same person with him." Sympathy was thus predicated on the ability of human beings to change places with others through an act of imagination.[19] As Campbell explains, for Smith sympathy was a type of feeling *with* another that gave rise to a feeling *for* him or her. It is important not to confuse the latter feeling, which Smith called "sentiment," with sympathy itself, which is the condition that gives rise to it; moral sentiments derive from sympathy, not vice versa. Smithian sympathy refers to the prior act of an agent putting him- or herself in the place of another and imaginatively feeling what the other feels.[20]

Smith's disagreement with Hume concerned the origin and function of sympathy in the formation of existing moral judgments. Contrary to Hume, Smith defined sympathy very broadly as "our fellow-feeling with any passion whatever," and insisted that it depended first and foremost not on the *consequences* of particular actions but rather on our understanding of the

18. See Campbell, *Adam Smith's Science of Morals*, 18–22, 87–89.
19. Smith, *Theory of Moral Sentiments*, I.i.1.2, p. 9.
20. See Campbell, *Adam Smith's Science of Morals*, 94–97.

motives of the actors involved. The point here is the role played by affect in providing the fundamental basis for shared sympathetic response, and thus (as Smith would have it) for the common moral sentiments of approval and disapproval. Smith believed that uniform affective responses were woven into the fabric of a universal human nature. For this reason, "whatever is the passion which arises from any object in the person principally concerned, an analogous emotion springs up, at the thought of his situation, in the breast of every attentive spectator." As opposed to Hume, then, for Smith utilitarian consequentialism gave way to what was innate or natural as the ultimate arbiter of morality and justice. Originally, people approved of another's moral judgment and the action derived from it to the extent that it was seen "not as something useful, but as right, as accurate, as agreeable to truth and reality: and it is evident that we attribute those qualities to it for no other reason but because we find that it agrees with our own." In sharp contrast, "the idea of the utility of all qualities of this kind, is plainly an after-thought, and not what first recommends them to our approbation."[21]

Smith believed that the source of social morality was universally shared passions activated by external sensations.[22] Conversely, he argued that "it is altogether absurd and unintelligible" to believe "that the first perceptions of right and wrong can be derived from reason." To the contrary:

> These first perceptions, as well as all other experiments upon which any general rules are founded, cannot be the object of reason, but of immediate sense and feeling. It is by finding in a vast variety of instances that one tenor of conduct constantly pleases in a certain manner, and that another as constantly displeases the mind, that we form the general rules of morality. But reason cannot render any particular object either agreeable or disagreeable to the mind for its own sake.... Nothing can be agreeable or disagreeable for its own sake, which is not rendered such by immediate sense and feeling.[23]

---

21. Smith, *Theory of Moral Sentiments*, I.i.1.4–5, p. 10, and I.i.4.4, p. 20. For Smith's explicit rejection of Hume's notion that utility is the ultimate cause of sympathetic response, see part IV. See also Raphael and Macfie, "Introduction," 13–14; and Campbell, *Adam Smith's Science of Morals*, 116–19.

22. On the pervasiveness of this theme for the Scots, see John Dwyer, *The Age of the Passions: An Interpretation of Adam Smith and Scottish Enlightenment Culture* (East Lothian: Tuckwell Press, 1998).

23. Smith, *Theory of Moral Sentiments*, VII.iii.2.7, p. 320.

It is not that reason is nonexistent or without purpose; it simply cannot form the basis of moral judgments, which are rooted in affect.

This point is fundamental to the understanding of Smith's moral theory. As Smith put it, while man was "naturally endowed with a desire of the welfare and preservation of society," it was nevertheless the case that "the Author of nature has not entrusted it to his reason to find out that a certain application of punishments is the proper means of attaining this end; but has endowed him with an immediate and instinctive approbation of that very application which is most proper to attain it." Thus, when it came to promoting her "favorite ends," nature has "endowed mankind... with an appetite for the means by which alone this end can be brought about, for their own sakes, and independent of their tendency to produce it." Specifically, Smith informed his readers, "self-preservation, and the propagation of the species, are the great ends which Nature seems to have proposed in the formation of all animals."[24]

Smith's focus on the primacy of affect over reason was a fundamental feature of Scottish Enlightenment thinking about moral philosophy more generally. Even Hume, who disagreed entirely with Hutcheson's notion of a moral sense, was unmistakably in agreement with both Hutcheson and Smith on the weakness of reason relative to the passions. In *A Treatise of Human Nature*, he famously quipped that "reason is, and ought only to be the slave of the passions, and can never pretend to any other office than to serve and obey them."[25] This shows the very great extent to which the Scots not only shared a commitment to applying the experimental or empirical method to moral philosophy and the belief in the uniformity of human nature, but also agreed on the relative weakness of human reason.[26]

Furthermore, one might say that while Smith's response to Hume ostensibly rejected the notion of a God-given moral sense as urged by Hutcheson, Smith nevertheless managed to reach a conclusion strikingly similar to that of his former teacher. In Smith's account, innate feelings were the necessary prerequisites for shared sympathetic response. Without such natural responses to conditions, human beings would be incapable of feeling what others felt, and (by definition) sympathetic fellow feeling could

---

24. Ibid., II.i.5.10, p. 77.
25. David Hume, *A Treatise of Human Nature*, ed. L. A. Selby-Bigge (Oxford: Clarendon Press, 1896), II.iii.3, p. 415.
26. See, for example, Rendall, *Origins of the Scottish Enlightenment*, 99–100; Berry, *Social Theory of the Scottish Enlightenment*, 156–57; and Schneider's introduction to *Scottish Moralists*, xvii.

not occur. So, while Smith denied Hutcheson's moral sense in favor of sympathy, sympathy, in the end, rested not on Humean utility but rather found its way back to nature and the instinctive responses of ordinary individuals to moral phenomena. For Smith, the mutual sympathy or "concord" sufficient for achieving "the harmony of society" thus emerged from a complex social interaction rooted in affect, in which the individual actor and the social spectator sought common ground. The actor, or the person immediately affected, could "only hope to obtain this by lowering his passion to that pitch, in which the spectators are capable of going along with him"; that is, the actor must "flatten" the "sharpness" of the passion's "natural tone." Simultaneously, "the spectator must, first of all, endeavor, as much as he can, to put himself in the situation of the other, and to bring home to himself every little circumstance of distress which can possibly occur to the sufferer" in order to "render as perfect as possible, that imaginary change of situation upon which his sympathy is founded."[27] For Smith, this simultaneous lifting and flattening of natural affect between actor and spectator jointly produced shared communal mores and moral codes.[28]

In terms of the Scottish Enlightenment, there was one other historically important response to Hume's heretical *Treatise of Human Nature*. This was the so-called common sense school of moral philosophy, which we might profitably see as the high-water mark of the Scots' general recourse to instinct and feeling over reason. The idea of common sense was initially articulated by Lord Kames (1696–1782) in his *Essays on the Principles of Morality and Natural Religion* (1751) and was later developed by him at some length in his *Sketches of the History of Man* (1774). In the *Essays* Kames argued that Hume's utilitarian version of sympathy was too weak a principle to control human appetites and passions. At the same time, he insisted that human beings had a moral sense that could not be reduced to Hutche-

---

27. Smith, *Theory of Moral Sentiments*, I.i.4.6–8, pp. 21–22.
28. Particularly in the much-revised third part of the 1790 edition of *The Theory of Moral Sentiments*, Smith's "attentive spectator" was transformed from an external to an internal phenomenon, the "impartial spectator" or "man within the breast." This character was not a flesh-and-blood human being with real interests but a disembodied ideal type who manifested the "normal" reactions of an "ordinary" person upon observing the behavior of others. Nonetheless, the spectator was empirical in the sense that he represented the internalization of the correct social consensus concerning the moral propriety or impropriety of a given action when viewed by those with a sufficient degree of self-command. See Campbell, "The Impartial Spectator," in his *Adam Smith's Science of Morals*, 127–45.

sonian benevolence, a disposition that Kames argued was incapable of explaining the necessity of justice. Rather, Kames argued in his *Sketches*, human beings have a common moral sense of justice.[29]

The leading intellectual light of Scottish common sense philosophy was Thomas Reid (1710–96), who in 1764 replaced Smith as chair of moral philosophy at Glasgow. Its two other leading figures, Dugald Stewart (1753–1828) and (especially) James Beattie (1735–1803), would do much to popularize Reid's thought.

Hume was the dominant figure in Reid's intellectual world, and the specific task Reid set himself was to refute Hume's *Treatise of Human Nature*. To this end, in 1764 he published the complex and technical *Inquiry into the Human Mind on the Principles of Common Sense*, which he had begun in 1739, the year Hume's *Treatise* was published.

Reid's theory began with sensations, which he argued were natural signs, and the role they played in perception. Individuals might misread signs, Reid argued, in which case their perceptions might be false; but the signs themselves were unfailingly accompanied by a notion or conception of the object's existence. This argument in turn was accompanied by a belief that objects existed, although they might be misperceived. Experience might therefore lead one to have a false understanding of a sensation, but this was very different from doubting, as Hume did, that the external world existed at all. In a manner similar to Hutcheson's, Reid attempted to show that our various beliefs about the existence of the self, the external world, and God were in some sense shared by all people and embodied in all languages. He concluded that such shared ideas could not possibly be explained in Humean terms simply as the products of experience. Although Reid admitted that some human powers were habits acquired by use, exercise, and study, he believed that the most important were natural and universal, or rooted in a shared "common sense." He concluded that the intuitive transhistorical truth of common sense provided the basis for morality, science, and religion.[30]

29. Berry, *Social Theory of the Scottish Enlightenment*, 161–62, 167–69.
30. For an in-depth philosophical study, see S. A. Grave, *The Scottish Philosophy of Common Sense* (Oxford: Clarendon Press, 1960). For more general treatments, see especially Broadie, "The Common Sense Reaction," in his *Tradition of Scottish Philosophy*, 105–18. See also Davie, "The Social Significance of the Scottish Philosophy of Common Sense," in his *Scottish Enlightenment and Other Essays*, 51–85; Bryson *Man and Society*, especially 130–36; Phillipson, "Scottish Enlightenment," 37–40; and Rendall, *Origins of the Scottish Enlightenment*, 98–99.

Reid's work offered a serious and complex answer to Hume. Through his student Dugald Stewart, it would exert a great deal of influence in both Scotland and America in the nineteenth century. In the event, however, Reid's answer to Hume proved too esoteric and cumbersome to carry much popular weight, besides which Reid was notoriously gracious and respectful to his adversary, and this alone could be seen as giving the patina of legitimacy to what many saw as blasphemous and dangerous ideas.

It would be left to James Beattie, professor of moral philosophy and logic at Marischal College, Aberdeen, to answer Hume in the vigorous manner required to uphold religious orthodoxy. Beattie popularized Reid in an attempt to counter the fears of moral anarchy raised by Humean skepticism. For him, it was an all-out literary war with his nemesis, the revolt of the provincial from Aberdeen against the urbane Edinburgh intellectual.[31] The vehicle for this frontal assault was Beattie's *Essay on the Nature and Immutability of Truth: in Opposition to Sophistry and Skepticism* (1770).

Beattie was accused not simply of popularizing Reid's work but of vulgarizing it in an ad hominem attack on Hume; indeed, this is the prevailing scholarly opinion of his contribution to the history of ideas.[32] Despite this assessment, however, Beattie's *Essay* was enormously popular. He became one of Scotland's most famous thinkers, read in salons throughout Britain and beyond, studied by students at university, celebrated by churchmen and even by the king and queen themselves. He received a large royal pension, an honorary degree from Oxford, and an allegorical painting by Reynolds that was apparently his most valued possession. It portrayed Beattie as the defender of truth against the twin devils of Hume and Voltaire—all of this notwithstanding the fact that Beattie considered metaphysical inquiry, and in fact the whole process of analytical thought, both painful and morally counterproductive. He believed that such endeavors tended to undermine men's most deeply held beliefs, sow the seeds of doubt and anxiety, and make them incapable of decisive action.[33]

---

31. On Beattie in particular, in addition to the material previously cited, see N. T. Phillipson, "James Beattie and the Defense of Common Sense," in *Festschrift für Rainer Gruenter*, ed. Bernhard Fabian (Heidelberg: Carl Winter Universitätsverlag, 1978), 145–54. Phillipson's piece gives a vivid sense of the combination of personal animosity and fear of intellectual inferiority animating Beattie's attack on Hume (see especially 150–52).

32. See Grave, *Scottish Philosophy of Common Sense*, 5; Phillipson, "Beattie and the Defense of Common Sense," 151–52; Bryson, *Man and Society*, 134; and Rendall, *Origins of the Scottish Enlightenment*, 99.

33. See especially Phillipson, "Beattie and the Defense of Common Sense," 145, 151, 153–54. See also Rendall, *Origins of the Scottish Enlightenment*, 99.

The Scottish Enlightenment Historical Narrative: From "Savagery" to "Civilization"

Sociable Presuppositions

Scottish Enlightenment moral philosophy led inevitably to an investigation of human social interaction. As Christopher Berry argues, Scottish social theory can be understood, in large part, as a critique of the natural jurisprudential approach, with its associated concept of a state of nature.[34] Adam Ferguson's (1723–1816) *Essay on the History of Civil Society* (1767) in particular is often singled out as important for understanding Scottish Enlightenment social theory. As Ferguson, the erstwhile chair of moral philosophy at Edinburgh, put the Scots' fundamental claim, "Mankind are to be taken in groups, as they have always subsisted."[35] While this is a view that goes back to the ancients, the Scots would ultimately use it as the basis for a new historical thesis with profound theoretical implications.

Ferguson argued that while some philosophers, like Hobbes and Rousseau, imagined the departure of mankind from some presocial state of nature, this was entirely specious. The principles of science required one to proceed from the empirical observation of normal phenomena, and in the case of human beings, society *was* their natural state and always had been. Scottish Enlightenment thinkers believed that the evidence on this score was overwhelming. They also used empiricism introspectively as a basis for their social theory (just as they had for their moral theory), and their assumption that human nature was uniform likewise validated introspection as evidence of human beings' innate sociability.[36]

That people had always lived in groups implied, for Ferguson, that if one were asked where the state of nature was to be found, one could answer that it was here, there, and everywhere.[37] It was therefore absurd to speak of artifice as distinguished from nature. Since man "has in himself a principle

---

34. Berry, *Social Theory of the Scottish Enlightenment*, 23.
35. Adam Ferguson, *An Essay on the History of Civil Society*, ed. Fania Oz-Salzberger (Cambridge: Cambridge University Press, 1995), 10.
36. See Bryson, *Man and Society*, 44; and Berry, *Social History of the Scottish Enlightenment*, 23–24.
37. "We may answer, It is here; and it matters not whether we are understood to speak in the island of Great Britain, at the Cape of Good Hope, or the Straits of Magellan. While this active being is in the train of employing his talents, and of operating on the subjects around him, all situations are equally natural...the highest refinements of political and moral apprehension, are not more artificial in their kind, than the first operations of sentiment and reason." Ferguson, *Essay on the History of Civil Society*, 14.

of progression, and a desire for perfection, it appears improper to say, that he has quitted the state of his nature, when he has begun to proceed; or that he finds a station for which he was not intended, while, like other animals, he only follows the disposition, and employs the powers that nature has given."[38]

The task that Ferguson and the Scots set themselves, then, was to trace how human beings in such natural social groups developed a second nature in the move from "rude" to "civil" society, the latter state in some sense a convention, but a convention that was entirely natural to human beings, as "art itself is natural to man."[39] Broadly speaking, this aim was shared by all of the social theorists and historians of the Scottish Enlightenment. They rejected contractarian notions of an asocial state of nature as both empirically false and unduly individualistic. Since the natural condition of human life was social, it simply would not do to adduce some extrasocial or extratemporal fiction as a means of establishing political legitimacy. Likewise, the Scots believed that "natural rights" had to be discussed within the context of natural sociability; they could not be divorced either conceptually or normatively from social existence.[40]

Hume articulated this view in *A Treatise of Human Nature*, where he responded to contractrarian assumptions regarding individualism and voluntary consent as the bases for political legitimacy by retorting that all existing governments were in fact the products of force legitimized by the accretion of time. Such "prescription," or habitual acceptance of power, filtered through imagination, custom, and habit, gave just title alike to confiscated property and governments originally founded on violence and usurpation. Social and political arrangements and their history thereby enabled a second nature to emerge, from which moral and political obligations as well as ideas of justice were derived.[41] Over time, Hume argued, the passions that provided the blunt impulse to enter societies were molded into virtue, an artificial construct that made for political and social stability, and could be judged by the ultimate standard, utility.[42] In this way Hume's philosophical skepticism gave way to historically rooted utilitarianism and in no way implied political radicalism, but rather a quietist, "skeptical" Whiggism.[43]

38. Ibid., 14.
39. Ibid., 14, 12.
40. See Berry, *Social Theory of the Scottish Enlightenment*, 30–33.
41. Ibid., 33–37.
42. See Phillipson, *Hume*, 35–52, and his "Scottish Enlightenment," 29–31.
43. See Duncan Forbes, *Hume's Philosophical Politics* (Cambridge: Cambridge University Press, 1975).

Indeed, while scholars have subsequently come to associate political conservatism most closely with Hume, Smith's politics were very close to Hume's,[44] and the political thought of the Scottish Enlightenment as a whole was decidedly not radical. There were, of course, some who favored moderate reform, particularly John Millar (1735–1801)[45] and even the notable exception in Dugald Stewart, the great chronicler and popularizer of Scottish Enlightenment ideas.[46] As with Hume and Smith, however, the Scots' largely unified defense of existing social and political arrangements was based on a number of broadly shared theoretical presuppositions about their philosophical meaning and purpose that largely buttressed the status quo.

In this regard, Ronald Hamowy has argued that the most important sociological contribution made by Scottish Enlightenment thinkers to the history of ideas was the notion of "spontaneously generated social orders."[47] The Scots argued that the social arrangements under which human beings lived were of such complexity that they simply could not have resulted from deliberate rational planning. They arose, instead, as the unintended consequence of innumerable individual actions that evolved slowly over many generations. These individual actions were themselves driven largely by instinct, friendship, loyalty, and habit. As Hamowy argues, the idea that enormously intricate social arrangements were not the conscious products of rational human agency and planning was revolutionary. It is most frequently identified with Adam Smith's "invisible hand" and the unfettered market economy, but this is somewhat misleading. In fact, the Scots did not limit the notion of spontaneously generated social order to economic life, but used it to describe systems of morals, language, legal systems, and governments themselves.

Ferguson wrote, concerning the last of these, "No constitution is formed by concert, no government is copied from a plan." Rather, "every step and every movement of the multitude, even in what are termed enlightened ages, are made with equal blindness to the future; and nations stumble

---

44. See Donald Winch, *Adam Smith's Politics: An Essay in Historiographic Revision* (Cambridge: Cambridge University Press, 1978), especially 170–71, 175–77. See also Duncan Forbes, "Sceptical Whiggism, Commerce, and Liberty," in *Essays on Adam Smith*, ed. Andrew S. Skinner and Thomas Wilson (Oxford: Clarendon Press, 1975), 179–201.

45. For Millar as a Foxite "New Whig," see especially Donald Winch, *Riches and Poverty: An Intellectual History of Political Economy in Britain, 1750–1834* (Cambridge: Cambridge University Press, 1996), 191–97; for the ways in which this ultimately distinguished him from Smith, see Duncan Forbes, "'Scientific' Whiggism: Adam Smith and John Millar," *Cambridge Journal* 7, no. 11 (1954): 643–70.

46. See Herman, *How the Scots Invented the Modern World*, 270–73.

47. See Hamowy, *Scottish Enlightenment*.

upon establishments, which are indeed the result of human action, but not the execution of any human design."[48] Such remarks led Ronald Meek to conclude that Ferguson's writings were easily the most theoretically advanced formulation of the law of unintended consequences in the second half of the eighteenth century.[49] While most clearly formulated by Ferguson, and most memorably applied by Smith, this emphasis on unintended consequences and the demotion of "purposive rationality" was fundamental to the Scottish Enlightenment writ large.[50]

The Four-Stages Historical Thesis: From "Savage" to "Civilized" Manners

The Scots' study of human sociability led inevitably to the study of history, understood as the record of innately social human beings interacting over time, shaping their moral sentiments in the process. That individual moral judgments and social arrangements were not predominantly the products of reason did not imply that social and historical development was incapable of explanation. To the contrary, the purpose of Scottish Enlightenment historiography was precisely to provide a "scientific" explanation of progress in individual moral capacities, and to unravel the developmental puzzle of human societies. The Scots asked how the complex and unintended machinery of human relationships changed over time, and they pondered the consequences of these changes at both the individual and the social levels. In their account, history evinced patterns amenable to explanation; history was a narrative of cause and effect, reason and consequence, rooted in contiguity, relations of temporal priority, and constant conjunction, a tale of moral as well as material progress.[51] The most important Scottish historians engaged in unraveling these patterns, apart from Hume, Smith, and Ferguson, were William Robertson (1721–93), principal of the College of Edinburgh from 1762 until the time of his death, John Millar, professor of civil law at Glasgow University for forty years, Lords Monboddo (1714–99) and Kames, and Dugald Stewart.

Like their moral theory, the Scots' historical views rested on the Newtonian bases of empiricism and comparison. On both counts they were heavily influenced by the relatively recent interaction of Europeans with other

---

48. Ferguson, *Essay on the History of Civil Society*, 120, 119.
49. Meek, *Social Science and the Ignoble Savage*, 150.
50. See Berry, *Social Theory of the Scottish Enlightenment*, 39–47.
51. Berry's discussion of these themes is outstanding. Ibid., chapter 3.

cultures, a process that had commenced in earnest during the fifteenth and sixteenth centuries. The Scots had at their disposal new evidence from missionaries, the travel logs of Cook and other European adventurers, and the experience of colonists to aid their own historical research. Their goal was to chart a comprehensive theory of history by tracing the stages of human development through a comparative analysis of differently situated contemporary societies. Their investigations were often breathtaking in scope and sometimes involved searching for a race of men with tails (Monboddo) and pondering whether orangutans had the faculty of speech. In every case, however, the Scots believed that their analyses would demonstrate the pattern of cause and effect on human nature and that their avowedly scientific research would surpass earlier historical studies, which they saw as rudimentary and limited in scope.[52]

In focusing on the comparative method, the Scots quite consciously took their lead from Montesquieu. When it came to the study of history and society, Millar regarded Montesquieu as akin to Lord Bacon, who pointed out the appropriate road, whereas Adam Smith was analogous to Sir Isaac Newton, who put theory into practice.[53] Montesquieu shared with the Scots the notion of a uniform human nature, and they greatly admired his attempt to relate government and laws to climate, economy, social institutions, and "manners," or modes of social interaction, through comparative analysis, a fact Dugald Stewart noted admiringly in his discussion of *The Spirit of the Laws* (1748).[54]

But Montesquieu's method was also somewhat different from the Scottish historians', and they believed that their work marked an improvement over his. For one thing, they argued, Montesquieu put far too much emphasis on the role of purely physical factors like climate in the historical process. For another, Montesquieu was not interested enough in the changes that took place in societies over time and never developed a specific, dynamic, progressive historical analysis of the engines driving those changes.[55] "Progress" for Montesquieu meant something akin to the simple passage of time, whereas the concepts of dynamism and normative progress animated Scottish historical inquiry.

52. See Rendall, *Origins of the Scottish Enlightenment*, 123–27; Bryson, *Man and Society*, 78–113; and Berry, *Social Theory of the Scottish Enlightenment*, 52–73.

53. See Chitnis, *Scottish Enlightenment*, 93. For the importance of Bacon to the Scots, see also Berry, *Social Theory of the Scottish Enlightenment*, 52–54.

54. See Bryson, *Man and Society*, 90–92.

55. See Berry, *Social Theory of the Scottish Enlightenment*, 78–82; Rendall, *Origins of the Scottish Enlightenment*, 124; Chitnis, *Scottish Enlightenment*, 95–96; Spadafora, *Idea of Progress*, 266.

Their strong claims to scientific method notwithstanding, in many instances the evidence required to fill in the gaps of a fully empirical theory of history was lacking. In these cases the Scots relied on educated guesswork, which is why their approach is often called "natural," "philosophical," or (as Stewart most revealingly dubbed it) "theoretical" or "conjectural" history. The Scots believed that history, as a branch of the science of man, could be based on certain fundamental and unvarying principles, or a minimum set of explanatory variables. Since human nature was assumed to be constant, the Scots were free to extrapolate across cultural contexts and to spin a narrative tale of social development over time and space. Understood in this way, lack of evidence was not an insurmountable impediment. Stewart insisted that travelers' reports should serve as landmarks to speculation, and that sometimes *a priori* conclusions could confirm seemingly incredible facts.[56] For example, Ferguson argued that in Arab clans and Native American tribes one could "behold, as in a mirror, the features of our own progenitors; and from thence we are to draw our conclusions with respect to the influence of situations, in which, we have reason to believe, our fathers were placed." Such "rude nations" provided a "representation of past manners, that cannot, in any other way, be recalled."[57]

The Scots' theoretical problem, of course, was how to account for widespread contemporaneous social and cultural variation in a manner consistent with their fundamental theoretical presupposition about human nature and their implicit denial of cultural relativism. Their solution to this problem was to argue that comparative empirical analyses, when combined with *a priori* conjecture, yielded the conclusion that human social development occurred in stages.[58] Specifically, human societies passed through four distinct phases of development: the primitive, the pastoral, the agricultural, and the commercial—or hunting, herding, farming, and commerce. At the same time, these four stages tracked an arc of cultural development that passed through three phases of "manners," or modes of social interaction, from savagery, through barbarism, to civilization.[59]

The first published version of the four-stages theory in Scotland was Sir John Dalrymple's *Essay Towards a General History of Feudal Property in*

56. See especially Broadie, "What Was the Scottish Enlightenment?" 25–28; see also Broadie, *Scottish Enlightenment: Historical Age*, 67–75; and Bryson, *Man and Society*, 83–92.
57. Ferguson, *Essay on the History of Civil Society*, 80.
58. See Berry, *Social Theory of the Scottish Enlightenment*, 74–90.
59. On the four-stages theory, see especially Meek, *Social Science and the Ignoble Savage*. See also Berry, *Social Theory of the Scottish Enlightenment*, 91–119; and Rendall, *Origins of the Scottish Enlightenment*, 123–27.

Great Britain (1757). This was followed shortly by an elaboration in Lord Kames's second edition of *Essays on the Principles of Morality and Natural Religion* (1758) and his *Historical Law Tracts* (1758), and would later be fully developed in his *Sketches of the History of Man* (1774). But both Dalrymple and Kames were members of Adam Smith's circle, and moreover, as Ronald Meek has shown, a strong case can be made that the thesis actually originated in Scotland with Smith himself, and that Dalrymple and Kames got their ideas from him.[60] At any rate, it is with Smith that the theory received its most thorough articulation.

From contemporaneous student notes, we know that Smith propounded a sophisticated version of the four-stages argument in his lectures on jurisprudence to moral philosophy classes at Glasgow in 1762–63.[61] He introduced the theory in his discussion of the origin of property rights. Before anything else about property relations could be discussed, Smith maintained, "it will be proper to observe that the regulations concerning them must vary considerably according to the state or age society is in at that time." Smith then went on to discuss the nature of the four stages and the processes that led from one to another. As the mode of subsistence changed, he argued, so did the "laws and regulations with regard to property," as well as the form of government. Smith even went so far as to claim that "in a certain view of things all the arts, the sciences, law and government, wisdom, and even virtue itself tend all to this one thing, the providing meat, drink, raiment, and lodging for men."[62] Smith would fully develop this argument in *The Wealth of Nations*, in essence an extended discussion of the actual functioning of a society that had reached the commercial age, the fourth stage of development, with the highest level of social complexity.

One need only remember Smith's critical remarks concerning the division of labor in *The Wealth of Nations* to be reminded that the Scots did not uncritically embrace commercial society. But Smith's position was representative of the Scottish Enlightenment's overall understanding of this relationship, inasmuch as he believed that on balance commercial society was a highly beneficial development, both economically and morally. As concerns the latter, this can be seen as far back as *The Theory of Moral*

---

60. See Meek, *Social Science and the Ignoble Savage*, 99–130; and Rendall, *Origins of the Scottish Enlightenment*, 125.

61. See Adam Smith, *Lectures on Jurisprudence*, ed. R. L. Meek, D. D. Raphael, and P. G. Stein (Indianapolis: Liberty Fund, 1982).

62. Ibid., i.27, p. 14; i.33, p. 16; vi.20, p. 338.

Sentiments, as can the nascent textual formulation of the four-stages argument itself.

In that earlier work, Smith argued that "the style of manners which takes place in any nation, may commonly upon the whole be said to be that which is most suitable to its situation."[63] An inattentive reader might conclude that Smith's position was a form of uncritical historicism *cum* cultural relativism, but he was actually far from a position of such "scientific" detachment in the face of widely varying social and cultural forms. Smith went on to argue that while moral sentiments were inflected by particular customs in such a way that custom could warp natural human instincts, it could not entirely "pervert" them. However, it was precisely the difference between rude peoples (savages and barbarians) on the one hand, and the polite, civilized, or polished peoples of commercial society on the other, that particular social customs or manners in the former groups sometimes sanctioned conduct that, when considered from the more elevated plane of the present, was "destructive of good morals," and "shock[ed] the plainest principles of right and wrong." That is, the normative problem with savages and barbarians, from Smith's perspective, was that they sometimes exhibited "manners" that perversely cut against the grain of the natural moral sentiments. In fact, one of Smith's criticisms of his own time was that while such practices as the abandonment of infants might have begun "in times of the most savage barbarity," where they were "more pardonable," they were sometimes inappropriately carried forward into later historical stages, thereby retarding the civilizing process in important respects. While such a practice "prevails among all savage nations," Smith concluded that it was ultimately immoral, socially dangerous, and unacceptable: "When custom can give sanction to so dreadful a violation of humanity, we may well imagine that there is scarce any particular practice so gross which it cannot authorize."[64]

Smith developed his normative defense of economic progress more fully in *The Wealth of Nations*. In this work he famously connected the advent of commercial society with overall material improvement, arguing that commerce was a rising tide that lifted all boats. He did this in part through striking comparisons between "civilized" Europeans and their "barbarian" and "savage" counterparts in other parts of the world. Smith argued that "the poverty of the lower ranks of people in China far surpasses

63. Smith, *Theory of Moral Sentiments*, V.2.13, p. 209.
64. See ibid., V.2.14–15, pp. 209–10.

that of the most beggarly nations in Europe." Indeed, the Chinese in port cities were "eager to fish up the nastiest garbage thrown overboard from any European ship. Any carrion, the carcass of a dead dog or cat, for example, though half putrid and stinking, is as welcome to them as the most wholesome food to the people of other countries." Elsewhere he remarked approvingly, in an echo of Locke, that a common day laborer in Britain had a more luxurious life than an American Indian sovereign or "an African king, the absolute master of the lives and liberties of ten thousand naked savages."[65]

As these remarks suggest, Smith saw the effects of commercial society as far more than simply material. At the most basic level, of course, Smith maintained that moderate wealth was normatively preferable to poverty; people ought to prefer it and embrace it, given the choice. While the material benefits of commercial society were desirable, however, they were not its principal beneficial consequence. More important, with respect to Europe, Smith argued, "commerce and manufactures gradually introduced order and good government, and with them, the liberty and security of individuals." Smith called these "by far the most important of all their effects."[66]

At other points in *The Wealth of Nations*, even while arguing against the immoral violence and economic folly attending the colonial conquest of the Aztec and Inca by Spanish *conquistadors*, Smith concluded that these imperial adventures did indeed have civilizing effects upon the people who endured them: "In spite of the cruel destruction of the natives which followed the conquest, these two great empires are, probably, more populous now than they ever were before: and the people are surely very different; for we must acknowledge, I apprehend, that the Spanish creoles are in many respects superior to the ancient Indians." Before their contact with commercial societies, Smith contended, "it seems impossible, that either of those empires could have been so much improved or so well cultivated as at present, when they are plentifully furnished with all sorts of European cattle, and when the use of iron, of the plough, and of many of the arts of Europe, has been introduced among them. But the populousness of every country must be in proportion to the degree of its improvement and cultivation."[67] In Smith's view, then, in the case of both the

---

65. See Adam Smith, *An Inquiry into the Nature and Causes of the Wealth of Nations*, ed. R. H. Campbell and A. S. Skinner, 2 vols. (Indianapolis: Liberty Fund, 1981), I, I.viii.24, pp. 89–90, and I, I.i.11, p. 24.
66. Ibid., I, III.iv.4, p. 412.
67. Ibid., II, IV.vii.b.7, pp. 568–69.

Aztec and Inca, the introduction of commercial society, albeit violent, marked an important advance in the civilizing process in several respects, not the least of which was population density, understood not simply in numerical terms but as a marker of normative progress.[68]

As Ronald Meek has shown, there is a good deal of evidence in the work of Smith's fellow Scottish Enlightenment thinkers to support the conclusion that they were the most important theoretical forerunners of historical materialism.[69] Unlike Karl Marx, however, the Scots saw the stages of history as evincing both intellectual *and* moral, as well as material, progress. They lauded the progressive steps from "rudeness" to "refinement" in the passage of societies from "infancy" to "maturity," which they viewed as a move to a more "polished" state of civilized existence.

In "A View of the Progress of Society in Europe," for example, the long opening essay in the *History of the Reign of the Emperor Charles V* (1769), William Robertson explicitly connected commercial society and refined manners, and specifically located them at the end point of a history of moral progress that led societies from benighted savagery, through barbarism, to the promised land of civilization. Robertson argued that "the progress of commerce had considerable influence in polishing the manners of the European nations, and in leading them to order, equal laws, and humanity."

> Commerce tends to wear off those prejudices, which maintain distinction and animosity between nations. It softens and polishes the manners of men. It unites them, by one of the strongest of all ties, the desire of supplying their mutual wants. It disposes them to peace, by establishing in every state an order of citizens bound by their interest to be the guardians of public tranquility.... In proportion as commerce made its way into the different countries of Europe, they successively turned their attention to those objects, and adopted those manners, which occupy and distinguish polished nations.[70]

---

68. Thus Broadie concludes: "There is no doubt that Smith believed that the four stages were stages in progress or improvement in the lives of people, where what is at issue is not just material progress but also progress in terms of the cultural values that are embodied in our lives." *Scottish Enlightenment: Historical Age,* 76.

69. See Meek, *Social Science and the Ignoble Savage;* see also Spadafora, *Idea of Progress,* 270–320; and Chitnis, *Scottish Enlightenment,* chapter 5.

70. Published as William Robertson, *The Progress of Society in Europe,* ed. Felix Gilbert (Chicago: University of Chicago Press, 1972), 63, 67. Some scholars have argued, against

For Robertson, then, commercial society brought with it not only material prosperity but also peace between nations, internal political stability and order, fairer laws, and, ultimately, progressive refinements in human relations, or polished manners.

Likewise, N. T. Phillipson has emphasized that although Hume's historical work did not rely on the four-stages thesis per se, his thinking about the development of civilization was shaped by a deep belief in the civilizing powers of commerce that were in the process of transforming western Europe. Hume held that commerce naturally tended to promote social order, dispel factiousness and warfare, stimulate refinements in the arts, and increase sociability and gentility. But in order for commerce to flourish, there had to be a prerequisite level of social stability. Having rejected the idea that either reason or the moral sense could be the basis for civilization, Hume instead saw political power, as embodied in constitutional authority, as the guarantor of property and security. Only when society allowed people to take political authority for granted would respect for property and a system of justice become habitual, thus enabling commerce, and ultimately civilization, to evolve and flourish.[71] Therefore, despite disagreement in the realm of moral philosophy, for Hume as for the other Scots, the development of commercial society was inextricably linked to the taming of the passions and the promotion of socially acceptable and beneficial moral standards.

This is no doubt why, in *The Wealth of Nations*, Smith acknowledged the influence of Hume's arguments about the relationship between commerce and manufacture, on the one hand, and good government and individual liberty and security, on the other.[72] Indeed, Hume argued that with the advent of commercial society an insensible moral revolution had taken place, whose parameters he discussed in his essay "Of Refinement in the Arts" (1752). Hume contended in this essay that *"industry, knowledge,* and *humanity,* are linked together by an indissoluble chain, and are found ... to be peculiar to the more polished and, what are commonly denominated,

---

Meek, that the Scots gave no particular cause priority in their discussion of social change; others have denied that Adam Smith (for example) was a materialist at all, while still others have gone so far as to maintain that the Scots were essentially idealists. Such criticisms are briefly canvassed in Berry, *Social Theory of the Scottish Enlightenment*, 117nn15–16, and his chapter 8, "Reading the Scottish Enlightenment," 185–99. I have tried to bear these criticisms of Meek in mind in what follows.

71. Phillipson, *Hume*, especially 15–16, 32–34, 48–52.
72. Smith, *Wealth of Nations*, I, III.iv.4, p. 412.

the more luxurious ages." In the broadest sense, "knowledge in the arts of government naturally begets mildness and moderation" in social behavior, or manners, thereby producing greater "humanity." According to Hume, such humanity was "the chief characteristic which distinguishes a civilized age from times of barbarity and ignorance." Conversely, "treachery and cruelty, the most pernicious and most odious of all vices, seem peculiar to uncivilized ages." Hume held it a moral truism that "every man would think his life or fortune much less secure in the hands of a MOOR or TARTAR, than in those of a FRENCH or ENGLISH gentleman, the rank of the men the most civilized in the most civilized nations."[73]

Similarly, and despite his fear that modern commercial society would undermine civic virtue (especially in the martial sense), Adam Ferguson clearly believed that the successive stages of social development were part of a positive natural progression, analogous to that of an individual human being as he passed from infancy to maturity. "In the human kind, the species has a progress as well as the individual." Ferguson saw this progress as the work of many ages, the accumulated effect of humans' unique capacity for intellectual development, whereby they "tend to a perfection in the application of their faculties, to which the aid of long experience is required, and to which many generations must have combined their endeavors."[74]

Ferguson's paternalism and social anthropomorphism were hardly unique among the Scots, though he gave them perhaps their best-known expression. They are clearly evident, for example, in Robertson's *History of America*, where he writes:

> As the individual advances from the ignorance and imbecility of the infant state to vigor and maturity of understanding, something similar to this may be observed in the progress of the species. With respect to it, too, there is a period of infancy, during which several powers of the mind are not unfolded, and all are feeble and defective in their operation. In the early stages of society, while the condition of man is simple and rude, his reason is but little exercised, and his desires move within a very narrow sphere. Hence arise two remarkable characteristics of the human mind in

---

73. David Hume, "Of Refinement in the Arts," in Hume, *Political Essays*, ed. Knud Haakonssen (Cambridge: Cambridge University Press, 1998), 107, 109, 112–13.
74. Ferguson, *Essay on the History of Civil Society*, 10.

this state. Its intellectual powers are extremely limited; its emotions and efforts are few and languid. Both these distinctions are conspicuous among the rudest and most unimproved of the American tribes.[75]

Both Phillipson and Karen O'Brien contend that Robertson's unfinished depiction of European empire in the Americas was one that wed stadial history to a particular providential theoretical understanding, such that humanity would eventually become unified under the auspices of new networks of commerce and communications emanating outward from Europe.[76] Robertson's study of empire in the New World was a story of how Europe had achieved the "commercial-imperial stage," and how superior European minds had exported themselves to other parts of the globe.[77] For this reason, it has been powerfully argued that in the unfinished portion of his manuscript dealing with North America, Robertson's unwavering commitment to inexorable stadial progress supported the later European conclusion that the Native Americans faced a brutal choice—assimilate or perish.[78] Such a stark dichotomy leads J. G. A. Pocock to conclude, "It is necessary, therefore, to read the *History of America* as a classical text in what we used to call 'imperialism' and presently term 'colonialism.'"[79]

Finally, the close connection between commercial society and the progressive improvement of natural morals into increasingly refined social manners is starkly evident in the work of John Millar, who was a student in Smith's moral philosophy classes at Glasgow.[80] In the revised edition of *The Origin of the Distinction of Ranks* (1779), Millar set forth a largely materialist approach to the question of social development and traced how

---

75. Robertson, *History of America*, in *Works*, ed. Dugald Stewart (Edinburgh, 1840), 819, quoted in Berry, *Social History of the Scottish Enlightenment*, 92.

76. See N. T. Phillipson, "Providence and Progress: An Introduction to the Historical Thought of William Robertson," in *William Robertson and the Expansion of Empire*, ed. Stewart J. Brown (Cambridge: Cambridge University Press, 1997), 55–73; and Karen O'Brien, "Robertson's Place in the Development of Eighteenth-Century Narrative History," ibid., 74–91.

77. Karen O'Brien, *Narratives of Enlightenment* (Cambridge: Cambridge University Press, 1997), 163.

78. See Bruce Lenman, "'From Savage to Scot' via the French and the Spaniards: Principal Robertson's Spanish Sources," in Brown, *Robertson and the Expansion of Empire*, 209.

79. J. G. A. Pocock, *Barbarism and Religion*, vol. 4, *Barbarians, Savages, and Empires* (Cambridge: Cambridge University Press, 2005), 190.

80. See Meek's discussion of Millar in *Social Science and the Ignoble Savage*, 160–73. For Millar's relationship to Smith, see 107–8.

changes in the mode of production influenced manners, laws, and government. Then, in a passage of extraordinary clarity, Millar summed up the general findings of the historians of the Scottish Enlightenment.

> When we survey the present state of the globe, we find that, in many parts of it, the inhabitants are so destitute of culture, as to appear little above the condition of brute animals; and even when we peruse the remote history of polished nations, we have seldom any difficulty in tracing them to a state of the same rudeness and barbarism. There is, however, in man a disposition and capacity for improving his condition, by the exertion of which, he is carried on from one degree of advancement to another; and the similarity of his wants, as well [as] of the faculties by which those wants are supplied, has every where produced a remarkable uniformity in the several steps of his progression.... By such gradual advances in rendering their situation more comfortable, the most important alterations are produced in the state and condition of a people: their numbers are increased; the connections of society are extended; and men, being less oppressed with their own wants, are more at liberty to cultivate the feelings of humanity: property, the great source of distinction among individuals, is established; and the various rights of mankind, arising from their multiplied connections, are recognized and protected: the laws of a country are thereby rendered numerous; and a more complex form of government becomes necessary, for distributing justice, and for preventing the disorders which proceed from the jarring interests and passions of a large and opulent community.... There is thus, in human society, a natural progress from ignorance to knowledge, and from rude to civilized manners, the several stages of which are usually accompanied with peculiar laws and customs.[81]

This was the essential Scottish Enlightenment arc of historical progress: from the rudeness and simplicity of savagery, through barbarism, to the polished and complex world of refined manners and civilized social arrangements. The advent of commercial society led to material improvement in the lives of individuals, the rise of personal and political liberty, justice

---

81. John Millar, *The Origin of the Distinction of Ranks*, 3d ed. (London: J. Murray, 1779), 3–5.

under the rule of law, and normatively preferable modes of social interaction, or refined manners. The division of labor drove material advances, and freedom to choose one's occupation arose as an unintended but positive consequence of the move from feudal agrarianism to urban commerce. So, too, laws became abstract and universal, first in the service of securing a stable commercial environment, by guaranteeing the validity of promises between strangers through the enforcement of contracts, the extension of credit, and uniform tax and tariff policies. The effect was to create a legal code that was less capricious and variable, and on the whole more just, than that of feudal agrarian society. On balance, then, the Scots saw commercial society as the normative as well as the material culmination of the civilizing process.[82]

The Scottish Enlightenment's historical narrative was in turn based on a broadly Lockean empirical psychology in which individuals and societies were seen as moving from the concrete and narrow to the abstract and complex. The story of the progressive development of property relations was therefore also the story of development in human thinking and emotional sensitivity, as well as in social complexity. The hunter-gatherer, focused on mere survival, had a limited range of experiences and consequently a limited range of ideas. So too the ideas formed among primitive herdsmen, who had crudely developed notions of property at best, were much simpler than those of the agrarian stage, where the earth was cultivated and property rights in land and its produce were claimed. In short, the ideas of "savages" and "barbarians" were necessarily narrower, predicated as they were on few external stimuli. As modes of production changed, experiences broadened, notions of property and other ideas became more abstract and sophisticated, a system of ranks built on fortune and birth emerged, and a government of impartial justice and an impersonal rule of law developed to protect liberty and property.[83] All of these changes broadened the range of human experience and enabled what most Scots (apart from Hume) saw as some form of a moral sense to be tamed and refined into modes of social interaction, or "manners," that became increasingly "civilized" over the course of the four stages.

82. Here and in the paragraph that follows, my conclusions are particularly indebted to Berry, *Social Theory of the Scottish Enlightenment*, chapter 5.

83. Berry argues that in this sense the mode of subsistence and its connection to immediacy or abstraction were fundamental for the Scots. While the Scots nowhere said that the mode of production was the *sole* cause of the specific form of social institutions, it was clearly the manner in which property was organized that gave coherence to the formal organization of power in law and government, and to social interaction as evidenced by manners. Ibid., 114.

The political theory of the Scottish Enlightenment has become a central focus of the so-called Cambridge school in general[84] and of J. G. A. Pocock in particular,[85] whose own interpretation has culminated in several chapters on Scottish historiography in his multivolume work on Gibbon, *Barbarism and Religion*.[86] Perhaps the most compelling aspect of Pocock's work is its insistence on the fundamental importance of the language of manners to the eighteenth century, and of the key role played by the Scots in defining and defending the discourse within which that term was central. According to the argument, the basic problem for eighteenth-century political thinkers was how property in land should be related to property in goods or capital. Defenders of the republican or civic humanist tradition assumed that landed property was the necessary prerequisite for the autonomy and leisure that enabled citizens to cultivate moral and civic virtue. So long as it was conceptualized in this purely classical sense, however, older, public-spirited "virtue" could not be reconciled with the new world of self-interested "commerce."[87]

Into this breach stepped the philosophers of the Scottish Enlightenment, whose goal, according to Pocock, was to reconcile commercial society and a redefined concept of virtue with the aid of the new notion of "manners." In this view, the Scots reconciled wealth and virtue by arguing that the ancient citizen was a morally underdeveloped being on at least two counts. While relying on the unpaid work of slaves or serfs because he lacked the credit and cash to pay wage laborers, he was simultaneously deprived of the multiple social relationships that only an advanced commercial society could deliver. However, because of the Scots' epistemological presuppositions concerning the necessary relationship between manifold experiences and complex ideas, they believed that it was precisely the rich web of social relationships created by commercial society that progressively tamed, transformed, and refined the "savage" (and later, "barbarian")

---

84. See especially Istvan Hont and Michael Ignatieff, eds., *Wealth and Virtue: The Shaping of Political Economy in the Scottish Enlightenment* (Cambridge: Cambridge University Press, 1983).

85. The best short discussion is J. G. A. Pocock, "Cambridge Paradigms and Scotch Philosophers: A Study of the Relations Between the Civic Humanist and the Civil Jurisprudential Interpretation of Eighteenth-Century Social Thought," in Hont and Ignatieff, *Wealth and Virtue*, 235–52.

86. See especially volume 2 of *Barbarism and Religion, Narratives of Civil Government* (Cambridge: Cambridge University Press, 1999).

87. See especially Pocock, "Virtues, Rights, and Manners: A Model for Historians of Political Thought," in his *Virtue, Commerce, and History: Essays on Political Thought and History, Chiefly in the Eighteenth Century* (Cambridge: Cambridge University Press, 1985), 37–50.

natural moral sentiments into softer, more "polished," more "polite" modes of social interaction—what they called the manners of civilized society. Pocock thus cast the Scots' four-stages historical thesis as a remarkable reworking of old republican themes that marked the creation of a brand of "commercial humanism" in which, at long last, virtue and commerce could be reconciled, so long as virtue could be redefined as the practice and refinement of civilized manners.[88]

Over the course of the following chapters, we will see the great extent to which Edmund Burke and Mary Wollstonecraft were familiar with the Scottish Enlightenment discursive paradigm that envisioned this particular relationship between natural moral sentiments and their expression in historically evolving systems of manners that became increasingly civilized over time. Indeed, I will argue that both Burke and Wollstonecraft began their respective interpretations of the French Revolution by taking up the Scottish Enlightenment argument that European societies should be understood as animated by naturally occurring moral sentiments moving in an ever more civilized direction. Of course, what each took the Revolution to signify was profoundly different. In order to understand why this should be the case, we will need to focus simultaneously on Burke's and Wollstonecraft's fundamental reshaping of Scottish historiography, as well as on their deep familiarity with, and opposite reactions to, Scottish moral philosophy. This is the project of the next two chapters.

88. Ibid., 48–50.

2 BURKE AND THE SCOTTISH ENLIGHTENMENT

When it comes to reading Edmund Burke, there are an astonishing number of preexisting theoretical frameworks in the secondary literature. There is, to be sure, a good deal to be learned from all of these readings. We have had Burke as a liberal of the nineteenth-century utilitarian[1] and anti-imperial[2] variety, Burke as a prophet of modernity's perils,[3] Burke as a republican,[4] Burke as a proto-romantic,[5] and Burke as a bourgeois ideologue.[6]

1. This was the dominant view for the first hundred years after his death, one that stressed Burke's formative role within the Whig interpretation of history. For examples, see Henry Buckle, *A History of Civilization in England*, 2 vols. (London: J. W. Parker and Son, 1857–61); John Morley, *Edmund Burke: A Historical Study* (1867; New York: Knopf, 1924); Leslie Stephen, *History of English Thought in the Eighteenth Century*, 2 vols. (1876; New York: Harcourt, Brace & World, 1963); and William Lecky, *A History of England in the Eighteenth Century*, 8 vols. (London: Longmans, Green, 1883–90). In the twentieth century this interpretation waned, but it still persists in Sir Philip Magnus's *Edmund Burke* (London: John Murray, 1939). Its best recent expression is J. R. Dinwiddy, "Utility and Natural Law in Burke's Thought: A Reconsideration," *Studies in Burke and His Time* 16, no. 2 (1974–75): 105–28, which views Burke as a utilitarian in the broadest sense possible, if not exactly as a liberal.

2. See especially Uday Singh Mehta, *Liberalism and Empire: A Study in Nineteenth-Century British Liberal Thought* (Chicago: University of Chicago Press, 1999); and Frederick G. Whelan, *Edmund Burke and India: Political Morality and Empire* (Pittsburgh: University of Pittsburgh Press, 1996), both of which focus on Burke's pursuit of Warren Hastings and the East India Company. For similar sympathetic views of Burke on the British Empire in the Irish and broader colonial context, see Luke Gibbons, *Edmund Burke and Ireland: Aesthetics, Politics, and the Colonial Sublime* (Cambridge: Cambridge University Press, 2003); and Michel Fuchs, *Edmund Burke, Ireland, and the Fashioning of the Self* (Oxford: Voltaire Foundation, 1996).

3. For examples, see Stephen K. White, *Edmund Burke: Modernity, Politics, and Aesthetics* (Thousand Oaks, Calif.: Sage Publications, 1994); Conor Cruise O'Brien, *The Great Melody: A Thematic Biography of Edmund Burke* (Chicago: University of Chicago Press, 1992); David Bromwich, *A Choice of Inheritance: Self and Community from Edmund Burke to Robert Frost* (Cambridge: Harvard University Press, 1989); and Michael Mosher, "The Skeptic's Burke," *Political Theory* 19, no. 3 (1991): 391–418. For a good discussion of the Left's historical fascination with Burke, see Isaac Kramnick, "The Left and Edmund Burke," *Political Theory* 11, no. 2 (1983): 189–214.

4. See Bruce James Smith, *Politics and Remembrance: Republican Themes in Machiavelli, Burke, and Tocqueville* (Princeton: Princeton University Press, 1985).

5. See especially Alfred Cobban, *Edmund Burke and the Revolt Against the Eighteenth Century* (1929; London: Allen & Unwin, 1960).

6. For an influential reading of Burke as a thinker torn between defending the Old Regime aristocracy and embracing the rising bourgeoisie, see Isaac Kramnick, *The Rage of Edmund Burke: Portrait of an Ambivalent Conservative* (New York: Basic Books, 1977). For the

Some scholars have been interested in extracting from Burke's work a general theory of political representation,[7] political parties and statesmanship,[8] or radicalism and revolution,[9] while others have focused more on Burke's particular relation to standard eighteenth-century Whig politics.[10] A still more general approach takes Burke as a repository of timeless wisdom capable of saving us from our own "present discontents."[11] And, finally, there is the dominant school of postwar Burkean interpretation that argues, with a greater or lesser degree of stridency, that Burke should be seen as the father of modern conservatism, a statesman whose political theory is deeply rooted in Thomism and the Scholastic tradition of natural law.[12]

---

erasure of all ambivalence, see C. B. Macpherson's unreconstructed *Burke* (Oxford: Oxford University Press, 1980). Macpherson follows the lead of Marx himself, who categorized Burke as "a vulgar bourgeois through and through"; see Marx, *Capital: A Critique of Political Economy*, vol. 1, trans. Ben Fowkes (New York: Vintage Books, 1977), 926n13.

7. See James Conniff, *The Useful Cobbler: Edmund Burke and the Politics of Progress* (Albany: State University of New York Press, 1994).

8. See Harvey C. Mansfield Jr., *Statesmanship and Party Government: A Study of Burke and Bolingbroke* (Chicago: University of Chicago Press, 1965).

9. See Michael Freeman, *Edmund Burke and the Critique of Political Radicalism* (Oxford: Basil Blackwell, 1980).

10. Most recently, see J. C. D. Clark's introduction to his edition of Burke's *Reflections on the Revolution in France* (Stanford: Stanford University Press, 2001), 23–111. See also John Brewer, "Rockingham, Burke, and Whig Political Argument," *Historical Journal* 18, no. 1 (1975): 188–201; Frederick Dreyer, *Burke's Politics: A Study in Whig Orthodoxy* (Waterloo, Ontario: Wilfrid Laurier University Press, 1979); and Frank O'Gorman, *Edmund Burke: His Political Philosophy* (Bloomington: Indiana University Press, 1973).

11. The argument is that of Jim McCue, *Edmund Burke and Our Present Discontents* (London: Claridge Press, 1997). It is also to be found in Gerald W. Chapman, *Edmund Burke: The Practical Imagination* (Cambridge: Harvard University Press, 1967), as well as in Ian Crowe, ed., *The Enduring Edmund Burke: Bicentennial Essays* (Wilmington, Del.: Intercollegiate Studies Institute, 1997).

12. The notion that Burke adheres to a neo-Aristotelian/Thomist conception of natural law goes back to Ernest Barker's *Essays on Government* (Oxford: Oxford University Press, 1945). The idea also finds early expression in Russell Kirk, "Burke and Natural Rights," *Review of Politics* 13, no. 4 (1951): 441–56. However, most arguments in the natural law vein generally trace their lineage back to Leo Strauss's *Natural Right and History* (Chicago: University of Chicago Press, 1953). On Strauss's reading of Burke, see Steven J. Lenzner, "Strauss's Three Burkes: The Problem of Edmund Burke in *Natural Right and History*," *Political Theory* 19, no. 3 (1991): 364–90. The Straussian thesis is amplified and most vociferously defended by Peter Stanlis; see especially his *Edmund Burke and the Natural Law* (Ann Arbor: University of Michigan Press, 1958), and his *Edmund Burke: The Enlightenment and Revolution* (New Brunswick, N.J.: Transaction Publishers, 1991). See also Charles Parkin, *The Moral Basis of Burke's Political Thought* (Cambridge: Cambridge University Press, 1956); Francis Canavan, *The Political Reason of Edmund Burke* (Durham: Duke University Press, 1960); Canavan, *Edmund Burke: Prescription and Providence* (Durham, N.C.: Carolina Academic Press and Claremont Institute for the Study of Statesmanship and Political Philosophy, 1987); and

In contrast to these various interpretive pathways, I am interested in stressing Burke's close connection to the Scottish Enlightenment's dominant intellectual concerns, specifically questions of epistemology in philosophy and moral theory and the attempt to develop a broadly systematic scientific study of history. My argument is that it was Burke's basic affinity for the Scots' approach to these problems, which he reworked from the perspective of his own early writings on moral philosophy and history, that would ultimately provide the framework for his overarching critique of the French Revolution. It is the aim of this chapter to articulate the scope and nature of Burke's connection to the Scottish Enlightenment language of politics, as well as to demonstrate the ways in which he took issue with and transformed that discourse in an idiosyncratic fashion from the time of his earliest writings.

Biography

At the biographical level, we have very strong evidence of Burke's links to the Scottish Enlightenment. In 1759, as many scholars have pointed out, Burke carefully read Adam Smith's *Theory of Moral Sentiments*. Burke's copy of the book was a gift from a mutual acquaintance, David Hume. In April 1759 Hume wrote to Smith that he had given the book to "such of our Acquaintance as we thought good Judges, and proper to spread the Reputation of the Book." These included "Burke, an Irish Gentleman, who wrote lately a very pretty Treatise on the Sublime."[13] Writing from London a few months later, Hume informed Smith that he was "very well acquainted" with Burke, "who was much taken with your Book," and noted that Burke had asked him for Smith's address so that he could write to him, which Burke did shortly thereafter, a letter of glowing praise for *The Theory of Moral Sentiments*.[14] For his part, Smith, then professor of moral philosophy at Glasgow, is said to have remarked that the author of the

---

Burleigh Taylor Wilkins, *The Problem of Burke's Political Philosophy* (Oxford: Oxford University Press, 1967). The natural law position is now defended by a new generation of scholars, e.g., Bruce Frohnen, *Virtue and the Promise of Conservatism: The Legacy of Burke and Tocqueville* (Lawrence: University Press of Kansas, 1993); and Joseph L. Pappin III, *The Metaphysics of Edmund Burke* (New York: Fordham University Press, 1993).

13. See Hume to Smith, 12 April 1759, in Adam Smith, *Correspondence of Adam Smith*, ed. E. C. Mossner and I. S. Ross (Indianapolis: Liberty Fund, 1987), 33.

14. See Hume to Smith, dated 28 July 1759, ibid., 42–43. Burke agreed that he knew Hume very well, and that in the early years of their acquaintance they were friends. See F. P. Lock's splendid biography, *Edmund Burke*, vol. 1, *1730–1784* (Oxford: Oxford University

Enquiry would be worthy of a university chair in philosophy.[15] Burke's letter to Smith, discussed below, initiated a long correspondence and friendship between the two men.

Of course, Burke never pursued the career Smith suggested for him, though in 1784 he did travel to Scotland to be installed as lord rector of the University of Glasgow, one of the two centers of the Scottish Enlightenment. The position of rector was generally reserved for distinguished or politically influential Scotsmen, and the choice of Burke, an Irishman, was without precedent.[16] During his trip, in April 1784, Burke spent a few days in Edinburgh sightseeing and dining with Smith, who was his constant companion. He also spent a good deal of time with Dugald Stewart, the great chronicler and popularizer of Scottish Enlightenment ideas. Burke and Smith then went on to Glasgow, where they dined with an acquaintance and sometime correspondent of Burke's, John Millar. The next day Burke accepted his new post, with Smith, Stewart, Millar, and the ever-present James Boswell in attendance, describing his election as rector as "by much the greatest honor I ever received." After a trip to Loch Lomond with Smith and others on Easter Sunday, and a few more days of socializing and sightseeing with his Scottish friends, Burke returned to Edinburgh for a final dinner with Adam Smith before returning to England.[17]

The next year, Burke went back up to Scotland for his reinstallation as rector. It was Professor Millar who was charged with writing to encourage him to accept a second term at Glasgow. Burke spent about a month in the country this time, including a week in Edinburgh socializing, marked by a visit with another old friend and correspondent, the eminent historian William Robertson.[18] During this period Burke also received the freedom of the city of Glasgow and election to the Royal Society of Edinburgh, the latter upon Adam Smith's nomination.[19]

Press, 1998), 187; and the editors' introduction to Adam Smith, *The Theory of Moral Sentiments*, ed. D. D. Raphael and A. L. Macfie (Indianapolis: Liberty Fund, 1984), 26–28.

15. See Burke, *The Correspondence of Edmund Burke*, ed. Thomas W. Copeland, 10 vols. (Chicago: University of Chicago Press, 1958–78) (hereafter *Correspondence*), 1:129.

16. See Lock, *Edmund Burke*, 536.

17. See Burke, *Correspondence*, 5:136–40, 142; Carl B. Cone, *Burke and the Nature of Politics: The Age of the French Revolution* (Lexington: University of Kentucky Press, 1964), 146–47; and Lock, *Edmund Burke*, 536–38 (Burke quoted at 537–38).

18. For the text of Millar's letter, see William C. Lehmann, *John Millar of Glasgow, 1735–1801* (New York: Arno Press, 1979), 399. For the letter from Robertson pursuant to his visit with Burke, see Burke, *Correspondence*, 5:221–22.

19. See Cone, *Age of the French Revolution*, 148; and Burke, *Correspondence*, 5:221.

We also have very strong evidence for Burke's connection to the thinkers and ideas of the Scottish Enlightenment through his association with Robert Dodsley's *Annual Register*, which Burke founded in 1758, serving as editor-in-chief until at least 1764, with the last volume under his editorship most probably appearing in 1765. As F. P. Lock points out, Burke remained a consultant to the *Register* long after that date, as his successor there was his friend Thomas English, who was responsible for the journal until 1795. English was aided by "other friends and followers of Burke, while Burke himself was occasionally consulted." Thus Lock concludes that well after 1765 the *Register* "continued to reflect his interests and point of view."[20]

The *Annual Register* was replete with book reviews praising the work of Burke's Scottish friends and acquaintances. He probably wrote many, if not all, of those that appeared before 1765, when he was sole editor of the venture, and perhaps others after that date, although this is impossible to confirm absolutely. Books reviewed in the *Annual Register* included Smith's *Theory of Moral Sentiments* (1759) and *Wealth of Nations* (1776); Robertson's *History of Scotland* (1759), *History of the Reign of the Emperor Charles V, with a View of the Progress of Society in Europe* (1769) and *History of America* (1777); Hume's *History of England* (1761); Adam Ferguson's *Essay on the History of Civil Society* (1767); and James Beattie's *Essay on the Nature and Immutability of Truth* (1770). Given that the journal reviewed only between four and seven books a year, and only those it thought highly of, the space devoted to Scottish thinkers was highly significant. This is particularly so as the book review section of the *Register* was the place where, more directly than anywhere else, Burke could express his own opinions.[21]

It is clear from this evidence that Burke was closely associated, both personally and professionally, with the most significant thinkers of the Scottish Enlightenment. The question becomes whether we can ascertain a shared intellectual basis underlying these associations, and whether we can trace the ways in which Burke blended the Scots' ideas with his own. I think that the answer to these questions is a resounding *yes*. In order to make this case, we will need to consider Burke's own early writings on moral

---

20. See Lock, *Edmund Burke*, 165–67, quoted at 166. As with many eighteenth-century journals, the editor of the *Annual Register* remained technically anonymous. For an argument that Burke was responsible for volumes after 1765, see T. O. McLoughlin, *Edmund Burke and the First Ten Years of the 'Annual Register,' 1758–1767* (Salisbury: University of Rhodesia, 1975).

21. See Lock, *Edmund Burke*, 175–78.

philosophy and history, his specific response to Scottish Enlightenment arguments on these two counts, and the uniquely Burkean theoretical standpoint that emerges from this interaction.

Burke's Moral Theory and the Moral Sense Philosophy of the Scottish Enlightenment

The Text

Burke never wrote a purely theoretical work on politics, responding instead to the controversies of his day in pamphlets, in correspondence, and from his seat in Parliament. His youthful work on aesthetics, *A Philosophical Enquiry into the Origin of our Ideas of the Sublime and Beautiful* (1757) was the only formal philosophical treatise Burke ever attempted.[22] As Stephen K. White reminds us, however, the very term "aesthetics" is a neologism that did not appear in English until around 1800; thus it is anachronistic to impute our present narrow understanding of that term to what was, in the eighteenth century, a much broader field of inquiry.[23] Andrew Ashfield and Peter de Bolla reinforce this point when they insist that the eighteenth century had no theory of aesthetics in the modern sense of that term. Rather, the approach taken to judging works of art was entwined with questions concerning the nature of human experience more broadly. Aesthetics was not primarily about art but about the formation of human identity and how individuals went about making sense of their experience.[24] In the eighteenth century the issue of aesthetic judgment opened out onto a much wider range of theoretical inquiry that went to fundamental issues of moral philosophy and political theory.

At the rhetorical level, at least, all interpreters of the *Enquiry* recognize that Burke's approach is rooted in the empiricist tradition of Newton and Locke. At a broad enough level of abstraction, then, scholars seem to agree

---

22. Edmund Burke, *A Philosophical Enquiry into the Origin of our Ideas of the Sublime and Beautiful*, ed. James T. Boulton (1757; Notre Dame: University of Notre Dame Press, 1968). All citations below refer to this edition. As Boulton notes in his valuable introduction, the second edition of 1759 contained several changes made in response to the book's reception. These included, most notably, the addition of an entirely new essay, "On Taste," and the new section "Power." Although it went through several subsequent editions in London, Burke made no revisions to the treatise after 1759.

23. See White, *Edmund Burke*, 5.

24. See Andrew Ashfield and Peter de Bolla, eds., *The Sublime: A Reader in Eighteenth-Century Aesthetic Theory* (Cambridge: Cambridge University Press, 1996), 2.

with James T. Boulton's point that Burke contended with the typical philosophical problems bequeathed to the eighteenth century. The *Enquiry* finds him searching in Newtonian fashion for the immutable laws thought to govern human life and, like Locke, analyzing the response of the human mind to experience. As Boulton points out, Burke was convinced of the existence of such general laws, and he arrived at this conclusion from "an uncompromising sensationist standpoint."[25] Even the Strauss-influenced natural law interpretations of Burke seem to accept this view.[26] Yet this raises an obvious and fundamental question: how do Burke's epistemological presuppositions relate to his broader moral and political theory? The natural law Burkeans, in particular, have failed to provide a convincing response to this question.[27] Indeed, one of the major shortcomings of the natural law interpretation is the short shrift it gives to the solution that Burke himself provided to this question, part of their failure to address the importance of the position he explicitly adopted for his moral and political theory writ large.

The first clue to understanding Burke's moral theory can be found in the *Enquiry*, when he writes: "When I say, I intend to enquire into the efficient cause of sublimity and beauty, I would not be understood to say, that I can come to the ultimate cause. I do not pretend that I shall ever be able to explain, why certain affections of the body produce such a distinct emotion of mind, and no other; or why the body is at all affected by the mind, or the mind by the body. A little thought will show this to be impossible."[28] Burke believed that reaching an empirically grounded understanding of the efficient, or instrumental, workings of our passions

---

25. Boulton, "Introduction," in Burke's *Enquiry*, xxxv–xxxvi.

26. Stanlis writes that Burke "utilized Locke's *Essay Concerning Human Understanding* for examples of the initial part played by the senses in experiencing aesthetic pleasure" (*Edmund Burke and the Natural Law*, 170). Likewise, Canavan concedes: "That [Burke] wrote the work in terms of Locke's psychology and epistemology is quite plain" (*Political Reason of Edmund Burke*, 38).

27. Stanlis, for example, seems to be on the right track when he declares that "a first-hand knowledge of his *On the Sublime and the Beautiful* is therefore prerequisite to an understanding of Burke's moral philosophy" (*Edmund Burke and the Natural Law*, 169). Yet Stanlis devotes only a few pages to discussing the *Enquiry*, the chief importance of which is said to lie in its "ethical dualism" and its rejection of the "pleasure-pain calculus" supposedly at the utilitarian heart of Locke's, as well as Hobbes's, philosophy—i.e., in Burke's belief "that pleasure and pain are each intrinsically real, that neither is merely the absence of the other" (169–70). Leaving Locke aside, this is a peculiar assessment of the *Enquiry's* main argument and its role in Burke's thought, as well as its relation to the broader universe of eighteenth-century ideas.

28. Burke, *Enquiry*, 129.

was all that one could hope to achieve. He thus tells his readers that when Newton attempted to go beyond working out the narrow functioning of gravitational laws to an assessment of their ultimate causes, he was incapable of doing so, because "that great chain of causes, which linking one to another even to the throne of God himself, can never be unravelled by any industry of ours. When we go but one step beyond the immediately sensible qualities of things, we go out of our depth."[29]

Burke reiterates his position that human beings are rationally incapable of comprehending ultimate causality, as it stands beyond the compass of sense experience, at several critical junctures in the text. In his discussion of beauty, for example, he concluded that when "our Creator intended that we should be affected with any thing, he did not confide the execution of his design to the languid and precarious operation of our reason." Instead, God imbued the particular object with "properties that prevent the understanding, and even the will, which seizing upon the senses and imagination, captivate the soul before the understanding is ready either to join with them or to oppose them."[30]

It is also vitally important to recognize that for Burke, as for his friend Adam Smith, "sympathy"—the most important of what he referred to as the three "principal links" in the "great chain of society"—functioned wholly "antecedent to any reasoning, by an instinct that works us to its own purposes, without our concurrence." Indeed, Burke's discussion of sympathy gives us an essential insight into his broader epistemological presuppositions. Burke argues against earlier writers who had mistakenly moved from sensations that arose from "the mechanical structure of our bodies, or from the natural frame and constitution of our minds, to certain conclusions of the reasoning faculty on the subjects presented to us."[31]

In short, Burke concluded in the *Enquiry* that irrational passions induced people to enter society and largely determined their particular interactions

---

29. Ibid., 129–30.
30. Ibid., 107.
31. Ibid., 44–46. The same emphasis on affect is characteristic of Burke's description of the other two links in the great chain of society, imitation and ambition. "We have a pleasure in imitating ... without any intervention of the reasoning faculty, but solely from our natural constitution, which providence has framed in such a manner as to find either pleasure or delight according to the nature of the object, in whatever regards the purposes of our being." So, too, we find that "God has planted in man a sense of ambition, and a satisfaction arising from the contemplation of his excelling his fellows in something deemed valuable amongst them" (49–50).

with others once there. The very foundations of human social interaction were not, in Burke's view, the products of reason, let alone of Thomistic or neo-Aristotelian "right reason," as the natural law interpretation would have it. Rather, Burke's aesthetic treatise was underpinned by his frequently stated belief in the power of irrational instincts implanted within us by the Creator and in the weakness of reason.[32]

Rodney Kilcup points out that when we read the *Enquiry* alongside Burke's other early writings, we find strong support for the conclusion that instinct plays the preeminent role in Burke's moral theory.[33] Like the aesthetic treatise, these pieces date to Burke's early years in England, before he became actively engaged in political life. One of the chief sources of this material is the so-called *Note-Book* Burke kept with his good friend (and perhaps distant relation) Will Burke, which came to light in the 1950s.[34]

In an essay in the *Note-Book* dealing with religion, Burke made several important statements about the relative importance of instinct over reason in the process of forming moral, religious, and political judgments. Among these, he wrote,

> *God has been pleased to give Mankind an Enthusiasm to supply the want of Reason; and truly, Enthusiasm comes nearer the great and comprehensive Reason in its effects, though not in the Manner of Operation,* than the Common Reason does; which works on confined, narrow,

---

32. For a similar argument about the *Enquiry*, see Vanessa L. Ryan, "The Physiological Sublime: Burke's Critique of Reason," *Journal of the History of Ideas* 62, no. 2 (2001): 265–79. Ryan notes that Burke's "physiologism" is "at the heart of his aesthetic theory: it provides the basis for his most fundamental assumption that the manner in which man is affected is uniform. It also leads him to minimize mental activity: his insistence on looking to the physical to explain the internal, psychological effects of the sublime breaks with a well-established assumption that the sublime is allied with an elevation of the mind. Reducing the role of conscious and reflective mental activity, Burke's turn to the physical sharply contrasts with Kant's later analytic of the sublime" (270).

33. See Rodney W. Kilcup, "Reason and the Basis of Morality in Burke," *Journal of the History of Philosophy* 17, no. 3 (1979): 271–84. Kilcup's piece provides the best single assessment of the roles of reason and instinct in Burke's thought and connects him to the Scottish Enlightenment. For more on this, see below.

34. See Burke, *A Note-Book of Edmund Burke*, ed. H. V. F. Somerset (Cambridge: Cambridge University Press, 1957). As the *Note-Book* contains essays written by both Will and Edmund, I have relied only on those pieces that are either definitively attributable to Edmund Burke (by initials or signature) or that Somerset has placed in the category of "almost certainly by Edmund Burke." In both instances I have followed the rules of attribution laid out by Somerset in his introduction (3–18). All scholars who have relied on this source have accepted these guidelines.

common, and therefore plausible, Topics.... The latter is common; and fit enough for common affairs—to buy and sell, to teach Grammar and the like; but is utterly unfit to meddle with Politics, Divinity and Philosophy. *But Enthusiasm is a sort of Instinct, in those who possess it, that operates, like all Instincts, better than a mean Species of Reason.*[35]

Burke's explicit affirmation of religious "enthusiasm," the great eighteenth-century antipode to rationality, as the specific solution to reason's weakness is clear evidence of the disproportionate weight he placed on the former over the latter in the formation of moral and political judgments. In Burke's view, human beings' weak reasoning capacity was compensated for by an affective response that enabled them to come closer to realizing God's purposes, albeit through explicitly irrational means. In the essay entitled "Religion," Burke consequently concluded that "Metaphysical or Physical Speculations neither are, or ought to be, the Grounds of our Duties; because we can arrive at no certainty in them. They have a weight when they concur with our own natural feelings; very little when against them."[36] Clearly Burke believed that reason, philosophy, and rational speculation of various sorts were all sources of delusion, deception, and obfuscation. Natural feelings were our only proper guides in matters concerning moral, religious, and political obligation.

In the *Note-Book* Burke insisted that when the Supreme Being wanted to communicate to his children, he left little room for doubt. "The best Proofs of such a Design are such acts of Power as can leave us no Doubt of their coming from God; for thus is it we know that he exist[s] and that he is all powerful and all-wise."[37] Likewise, in the *Enquiry*, Burke argued that we are "bound by the condition of our nature" to reach intellectual ideas of the Deity only after they have been passed through the medium of our senses. As a result, God's attributes necessarily form "a sort of sensible image," which first affects the imagination. And, to the imagination, God's "power is by far the most striking" of his attributes; indeed, "to be struck with his power, it is only necessary that we should open our eyes."[38] Demonstrations of power that reach us on the affective level are thus first

35. Ibid., 68. Emphasis added.
36. Ibid., 71.
37. Ibid., 74.
38. Burke, *Enquiry*, 68.

and foremost how God communicates with us, not through rationally ascertainable principles, as St. Thomas Aquinas would have it.

The arguments of the *Enquiry* and the *Note-Book* are echoed in Burke's famous spoof of Lord Bolingbroke, *A Vindication of Natural Society* (1756). Bolingbroke's tracts constituted a defense of Deism and an attack on religious institutions and divine revelation as irrational. As Burke, who wrote the pamphlet anonymously, explained in a preface added to the second edition, his purpose was to show through satire that the same techniques used to lampoon religion might just as easily be employed to subvert any number of social arrangements.[39] That is, the use of reason as a critical tool could be turned, with little effort, upon government and human relationships of all sorts, with disastrous consequences. When the reasoning mind was set free with "no Restraint from a Sense of its own Weakness," everything excellent and venerable could become the target of seemingly plausible attacks, including creation itself; such is the danger of examining the "divine Fabrics by our Ideas of Reason and Fitness." But, Burke scoffed, this was truly the "Fairy Land of Philosophy."[40]

All of which is to say that rather than advocating the use of our rational capacities to ascertain the "divine Fabrics," Burke rejected this endeavor as patently absurd and downright dangerous. To the contrary, the proper response when we departed from the sphere of our ordinary, empirically derived ideas was to be "sensible of our Blindness. And this we must do, or we do nothing, whenever we examine the Result of a Reason which is not our own. . . . What would become of the World if the Practice of all moral Duties, and the Foundations of Society, rested upon having their Reasons made clear and demonstrative to every Individual?"[41] The answer to this rhetorical question, of course, is nothing good. It is worth noting, against the natural law school, that it was precisely the attempt to judge the most basic religious, social, and political institutions and our obligations to them by the standard of reason that was the problem for Burke, not the solution to the problem.

Burke argued in the fashion of eighteenth-century empiricism, inoculated from Humean skepticism by a belief in instinct and affect. We know narrow and limited things through our senses, and reason can determine

---

39. See Burke, *The Writings and Speeches of Edmund Burke*, ed. Paul Langford, 8 vols. to date (Oxford: Oxford University Press, 1981–) (hereafter *Writings and Speeches*), 1:134.
40. Ibid., 1:135.
41. Ibid., 1:136.

only efficient, never ultimate, causality. The latter is impossible to determine by any reasoning process, Burke insisted, just as it is impossible to say why the body is at all affected by the mind, or the mind by the body. Reason is fit for common affairs—for buying and selling, for teaching subjects like grammar; but it is entirely unfit to guide us in matters of politics, divinity, or philosophy. In no case did Burke assert that reason could tell us what human relationships *ought* to be like. Rather, he argued consistently that God's will was embodied in natural human instincts and could only be apprehended affectively.[42]

Burke's early writings thus make clear that the central idea underlying a good deal of postwar Burkean interpretation—the notion that his thought is ultimately rationalist and based on the Scholastic concept of natural law derived from the exercise of right reason—is seriously in error.[43] In fact, a careful examination of Burke's early work shows just the opposite: that affect, or instinct activated via sensation, serves as the foundational touchstone for his moral, social, and political theory.

In short, the natural law school ignores the epistemology that Burke explicitly endorsed in its search for his supposedly implicit metaphysical commitments, which are themselves then simply assumed to rest necessarily on a rationalist epistemological base.[44] This approach gets Burke's con-

42. As F. P. Lock notes, in the *Enquiry*, "Burke searches for explanations that do not require the exercise of reason or reflection." Lock points out that this is because Burke consistently held to the view that "feeling is more reliable than reason." Lock concludes that the elevation of feeling over reason and the privileging of the supposedly natural was "a characteristic Burkean theme" that played "an important part not only in the *Enquiry*, but in Burke's later political writings" (*Edmund Burke*, 102, 97).

43. While natural law interpreters make much of Burke's early writings' illustrating his antipathy to *abstract* individual rationality of the type that they see as leading to the French Revolution, this conclusion ultimately obscures more than it clarifies.

44. For example, in *The Metaphysics of Edmund Burke*, Joseph L. Pappin III writes that his goal is "to demonstrate that Burke's political philosophy is grounded in a realist metaphysics, one that is basically consonant with the Aristotelian-Thomistic tradition.... In large part, the thrust of this work has been to make explicit the implicit metaphysical core of Burke's political thought" (170–71). For Father Canavan and the natural law school, however, "it is doubtful that Burke's epistemology, as it appears in his early writings, was compatible with the metaphysic implied in his moral and political theory." Thus Canavan concludes that, "to the extent that he subordinated speculation even in the properly theoretical order to practical norms, Burke weakened the foundations of his own thought, and must be said to have had an attitude toward speculative reason not fully compatible with the metaphysic which was implicit in his moral and political theory" (Canavan, *Political Reason of Edmund Burke*, 45, 53). Elsewhere, in response to Kilcup's assertion that Burke accepted the modern view of reason as a strictly limited process dependent on sensory impressions, Canavan argues that "it might be more accurate to say that he was handicapped by it but in revolt against it" (*Edmund Burke: Prescription and Providence*, 63).

servative political theory right, but it does so at the cost of getting the philosophical commitments underlying that theory wrong. Moreover, the natural law position clearly rests on an *a priori* set of ideological assumptions about what constitutes the proper relationship between speculative Scholastic right reason, the "properly theoretical order," and a supposedly true metaphysics in the first instance.[45] But wishing that Burke's epistemological commitments were more like those of Aquinas, a medieval thinker who preceded him by half a millennium, does not make it so, as the textual evidence clearly demonstrates.[46] More important, such an approach not only ignores what is explicit in Burke's texts, it also ignores or seriously neglects the compelling contextual evidence that links Burke's arguments in the *Enquiry* and elsewhere much more closely to his own century, place, and life, and thereby directly to his friends and acquaintances in the Scottish Enlightenment.

Burke's Moral Theory in Scottish Enlightenment Context

It was Adam Smith's *Theory of Moral Sentiments*, buttressed by James Beattie's popularized version of the Scottish philosophy of common sense, that proved most influential on Burke's political theory, largely because their arguments were so close to the views Burke had already articulated in his own early work.[47] To understand Burke's connection to Smith and Beattie, we must return to his correspondence and the book reviews he wrote for the *Annual Register*.

Scholars are well acquainted with the ringing letter of endorsement Burke wrote to Adam Smith in 1759 concerning *The Theory of Moral Sentiments*, in which he embraced Smith's approach to moral philosophy as well

---

45. For example, Canavan laments, "in eighteenth-century Britain there were few indeed who had kept a grasp on the concept of noetic intelligence, the ability of the mind to 'see into'... the nature of a thing and, in particular, the nature of man." *Edmund Burke: Prescription and Providence*, 63.

46. My critique of the natural law approach has focused on epistemological issues. For a range of different criticisms, see James Conniff, *Useful Cobbler*, 37–48.

47. On this theme, in addition to the aforementioned article by Kilcup, see especially Frans De Bruyn, "Edmund Burke's Natural Aristocrat: The 'Man of Taste' as a Political Ideal," *Eighteenth-Century Life* 11, no. 2 (1987): 41–60. See also Morton J. Frisch, "Burke on Theory," *Cambridge Journal* 7, no. 5 (1954): 292–97; Mario Einaudi, "The British Background of Burke's Political Philosophy," *Political Science Quarterly* 49, no. 4 (1934): 576–98; the introductory essay in Burke, *Edmund Burke: Pre-Revolutionary Writings*, ed. Ian Harris (Cambridge: Cambridge University Press, 1993); and Wilkins, *Problem of Burke's Political Philosophy*, 50–71. Wilkins's book is by far the most moderate produced by the natural law school.

as his broad conclusions.[48] This allegiance makes obvious sense, as Smith's arguments in the *Moral Sentiments* were extremely close to those Burke was drawing at roughly the same time in the *Enquiry*. Burke's letter was followed by a similarly laudatory review of Smith's book in the *Annual Register*.

In *The Theory of Moral Sentiments*, as we know, Smith argued that when it came to making moral judgments, it was absurd to suppose that the first perceptions of right and wrong could be derived from reason. Smith and Burke agreed that such notions could be drawn only from a combination of immediate sensations and the instinctive feelings evoked by them. For both thinkers, it was by finding affectively that, as Smith put it, one type of conduct constantly pleased and another constantly displeased the mind, that the general rules of morality were formed.[49] As we have seen, Burke argued in the *Enquiry* in a precisely analogous fashion. For both men the focus of these instinctive, affective experiences was the two principal ends of human existence, which Burke referred to, in terms virtually identical to those Smith used, as "self-preservation" and "society."[50]

Of course, the key to Smith's moral theory was sympathy. Even before he had read *The Theory of Moral Sentiments*, Burke too had concluded that sympathy was one of the three "principal links" that formed "the great

---

48. See Burke, *Correspondence*, 1:129–30. The letter, dated 10 September 1759, reads in part:

> I am not only pleased with the ingenuity of your Theory; I am convinced of its solidity and Truth.... I have ever thought that the old Systems of morality were too contracted and that this Science could never stand well upon any narrower Basis than the whole of Human Nature.... A theory like yours founded on the Nature of man, which is always the same, will last, when those that are founded on his opinions, which are always changing, will and must be forgotten. I own I am particularly pleased with those easy and happy illustrations from common Life and manners in which your work abounds more than any I know by far. They are indeed the fittest to explain those natural movements of the mind with which every Science relating to our Nature ought to begin. But one sees, that nothing is less used, than what lies directly in our way. Philosophers therefore very frequently miss a thousand things that might be of infinite advantage.... It seems to require that infantine simplicity which despises nothing, to make a good Philosopher, as well as to make a good Christian.

49. For Smith, "the Author of nature has not entrusted it to his reason to find out that a certain application of punishments is the proper means of attaining this end," but rather "has endowed him with an immediate and instinctive" feeling of moral approval or disapproval with regard to "self-preservation" and the "propagation of the species," the two "great ends which Nature seems to have proposed in the formation of all animals." Rather than "the slow and uncertain determinations of our reason ... Nature has directed us to the greater part of these by original and immediate instincts." See Smith, *Theory of Moral Sentiments*, II.i. 5.10, pp. 77–78, and Chapter 1 of this volume.

50. Burke, *Enquiry*, 38, 40.

chain of society." So too Burke described sympathy exactly as Smith did, as "a sort of substitution, by which we are put into the place of another man, and affected in many respects as he is affected."[51] The crucial concept of sympathy, as understood by both men, was identical.[52]

In fact, Burke's letter to Smith and the review that followed enable us to place him quite specifically with respect to internal Scottish Enlightenment squabbles regarding moral philosophy. In the *Enquiry* Burke had rejected the relation between beauty and virtue, thereby implicitly denying Francis Hutcheson's thesis in *An Inquiry into the Origin of our Ideas of Beauty and Virtue*. In so doing, he also resisted the Hutchesonian formulation of a "moral sense." What would lead Burke to take this step? As Ian Harris argues, by linking beauty with virtue, Hutcheson, following Shaftesbury, had inadvertently made ethics relatively autonomous and independent of theology. If man had an innate, natural moral sense that enabled him to discern right from wrong, whence the need for divine revelation and orthodox religion? Virtue could be explained without direct reference to God.[53] This implication was totally unacceptable to Burke. Smith's theory, however, focusing as it did on instinctive sympathetic response and avoiding any direct reference to a "moral sense," could be squared easily with Burke's religious convictions, especially in that Smith specifically identified sympathy as a God-given instinct.

Because of these shared assumptions, Burke agreed with Smith that "common Life and manners," or existing social and cultural mores embodied in normalized codes of conduct, were the best instruments "to explain those natural movements of the mind with which every Science relating to our Nature ought to begin."[54] Social manners, that is to say, were, for both Burke and Smith, a natural outgrowth and empirical crystallization of moral instincts. Both thinkers believed that "manners" captured the innate moral responses of the mind and reflected them in socially acceptable modes of human interaction. By making this connection, Burke, like Smith and all of the thinkers of the Scottish Enlightenment, inseparably entwined moral theory with the study of society and history.

Like the Scots, Burke held that social interaction was the embodiment of universal human nature as reflected in manners, and saw history as the

---

51. Ibid., 44.
52. On this point, see Boulton's introduction to Burke's *Enquiry*, xlii.
53. See Burke, *Burke: Pre-Revolutionary Writings*, 58–61; see also Lock, *Edmund Burke*, 93–94, 98–100; and White, *Edmund Burke*, 25–26.
54. Burke, *Correspondence*, 1:130.

record of evolution in manners over time. As we know, it was this broadly cohesive moral theory that formed the basis of the Scots' theorizing on society and history and necessarily extended their science of man to a broad range of social arrangements, both past and present. This would hold equally true for Burke.

At this point, it is worth pondering from a political, as opposed to a merely philosophical, perspective why Burke might find such a position appealing. The Scots' "scientific" set of presuppositions led to a rather quiescent political conclusion: what "ought" to be morally binding upon individuals was largely subsumed by an empirical account of what actually "is" morally binding in a given society. The leading implication of Scottish moral philosophy in the eighteenth century was its tendency to normalize, naturalize, and reify existing social morality as the supposed embodiment of human instinct. Burke concurred. The most compelling aspect of *The Theory of Moral Sentiments* was that it sought "the foundation of the just, the fit, the proper, the decent, in our most common and most allowed passions." Smith had effectively made social approval and disapproval the yardstick for measuring obligation and obedience by asserting that these responses were based on nature, in the form of sympathetic fellow feeling. Burke found this approach entirely convincing and called Smith's treatise "in all its essential parts just, and founded on truth and nature." By "making approbation and disapprobation the tests of virtue and vice, and showing that those are founded on sympathy," Burke wrote, Smith "raises from this simple truth, one of the most beautiful fabrics of moral theory, that has perhaps ever appeared."[55]

The second source of Scottish Enlightenment influence on Burke's moral theory came from the common sense reaction to David Hume. For Burke, when a thinker like Bolingbroke attempted to base moral, political, social, or religious obligations on reason alone, the results were an inevitable

---

55. *Annual Register* (1759): 485. In *Virtuous Discourse: Sensibility and Community in Late Eighteenth-Century Scotland* (Edinburgh: John Donald Publishers, 1987), John Dwyer argues that by the time of the sixth edition of *The Theory of Moral Sentiments*, in 1790, Smith had transformed the basis of moral approval or disapproval from an essentially social phenomenon rooted in public opinion, to a principally individual one; that is, the basis of Smithian morality changed from "the man without" (a mirror of communal attitudes) to "the man within" (a fully individualized conscience, or an "impartial spectator" of one's own actions). See especially chapter 7. There is much to this argument, but it did not affect Burke, who reviewed only the first edition of Smith's treatise and lauded it precisely for its commitment to socially aggregated natural moral sentiments in the form of public opinion. For Burke, as the letter and review make clear, this was the chief marker of Smith's genius.

slide into anarchy.[56] Reason's power was ultimately corrosive; it could raise fundamental questions, but it could not answer them satisfactorily. Moreover, as we have seen, Burke believed that extending the role of empiricism beyond the level of efficient causality—that is, bringing it to bear on the most fundamental questions of moral and political philosophy—was impossible. In fact, there is abundant evidence in the pages of the *Annual Register* that Burke saw Humean skepticism as a mirror image of the descent into moral, political, and social anarchy that necessarily followed from Bolingbroke's rationalism. There is good reason to believe that Burke's endorsement of Smith's response to Hume was strengthened by his reading of James Beattie's popularized version of Thomas Reid's "common sense" philosophy.[57]

In the 1771 issue of the *Annual Register*, Beattie's *Essay on the Nature and Immutability of Truth in Opposition to Sophistry and Skepticism* was the subject of a long review that featured lengthy excerpts and extraordinary praise for Beattie's tract. While Thomas Copeland has argued that Burke almost certainly wrote this review,[58] we cannot be absolutely sure that this is the case, as it appeared well after Burke had ceased to be sole editor of the journal. Nevertheless, as Lock maintains, it is quite clear that the *Register* continued to reflect Burke's interests and point of view throughout this period.

The review shows the *Register* wholeheartedly allied with Beattie in his war on Humean skepticism in a way that fits perfectly with Burke's early work and is clearly compatible with Smith's modification of Hutchesonian moral theory. Indeed, defending Beattie's version of "common sense" would have enabled Burke to receive all the argumentative benefits of proceeding as if a moral sense actually existed (retooled now as God-given common

---

56. On this theme, see also Isaac Kramnick, "Skepticism in English Political Thought: From Temple to Burke," *Studies in Burke and His Time* 12, no. 1 (1970): 1627–60.

57. This view is broadly consonant with Kilcup, "Reason and the Basis of Morality in Burke," as well as with the earliest statement of Burke's connection to Scottish Enlightenment moral philosophy, John A. Lester Jr., "An Analysis of the Conservative Thought of Edmund Burke" (Ph.D. diss., Harvard University, 1942).

58. See Thomas W. Copeland, "Edmund Burke and the Book Reviews in Dodsley's *Annual Register*," *Publications of the Modern Language Association* 57, no 2 (1942): 446–68. Copeland lists the review of Beattie's *Essay* as one of the half-dozen cases after 1764 for which "Burke's authorship is supported by evidence full enough or striking enough to be almost completely convincing." In this instance, Copeland gives that evidence as "Burke's acquaintance with Beattie; with his book; striking parallel between review and Burke's known opinion of the book" (467). See more on this below.

sense), while combining it with instinctive sympathy and traditional orthodoxy in religion. Professors of philosophy might not be satisfied with this eclectic synthesis, but Burke was not an academic, and this particular concoction served his catholic theoretical propensities well.

The reviewer maintains that the discovery of truth is the goal of all superior intellects, notwithstanding the fact that the admitted weakness of the human mind has led some skeptics to doubt that such a thing is possible.[59] According to the reviewer, such skeptical thinkers have espoused two very different, but equally pernicious, ends—fanaticism and infidelity—both of which hold out the possibility of social dissolution.[60] Skepticism was both dangerous and groundless, and it was a sign of the times. Beattie's outstanding merit was to destroy this sophistry with such force that "the systems he explodes will be remembered only in his refutation."[61]

It is instructive to consider those sections of Beattie's *Essay* that the reviewer singled out as especially meritorious and worthy of reproduction in the pages of the *Register*. The first pertains to Beattie's development of the term "common sense." The reviewer writes, "The author establishes the standard of Truth in *Common Sense*, into which all reasoning is ultimately resolved. The tenor and idea of this primitive and fundamental standard of all Truth, he distinguishes and defines in a manner the most clear and precise."[62]

The reviewer also singles out an ad hominem attack on skeptics in general and Hume in particular as particularly illustrative of Beattie's intellec-

---

59. The reviewer writes, "Not contented with showing, what is but too evident, the narrowness and imbecility of the human understanding, they have denied that it is at all calculated for the discovery and comprehension of truth; or, what amounts to the same, that no fixed order existed in the world, so correspondent to our ideas, as to afford the least ground for certainty in any thing." *Annual Register* (1771): 252.

60. The reviewer writes, "It is evident too, that morality must share the fate of knowledge, and every duty of life become precarious, if it be impossible for us to know that we are bound to any duties, or that the relations which gave rise to them have any real existence." Ibid.

61. Ibid., 252–53.

62. Ibid., 253. Beattie defines common sense as "that power of the mind which perceives truth, or commands belief, not by progressive argumentation, but by an instantaneous, instinctive, and irresistible impulse; derived neither from education nor from habit, but from nature; acting independently on our will, whenever its object is presented, according to an established law, and therefore properly called *Sense*; and acting in a similar manner upon all, or at least upon a great majority of mankind, and therefore properly called *Common Sense*." Beattie hammers home the sharp distinction between reason and common sense; in fact, he "cannot discern any necessary connection" between them. To the contrary, "we believe an intuitive principle, without being able to assign any other reason for our belief than this, that the law of our nature determines us to believe it, even as the law of our nature determines us to see a color when presented to our open eyes at noon-day." Furthermore,

tual powers. In it, Beattie claimed that if an inhabitant from another planet were to read Hume's *Treatise of Human Nature*, he could only conclude that Hume was a tasteless and heartless metaphysician who knew nothing of his subject.[63] In contrast to Hume, Beattie argued that true genius required "sensibility of heart" and was not "consistent with a disproportionate strength of the reasoning powers above those of taste and imagination." Minds in which the faculties exist in just relation "trust to their own feelings, which are strong and decisive, and leave no room for hesitation or doubts about their authenticity. They see through moral subjects at one glance; and what they say, carries both the heart and the understanding along with it." Such minds exist in "men of taste."[64]

Beattie's conclusion about the importance of "taste" was in keeping with that Burke had drawn in his short essay "On Taste," which he added to the second edition of the *Enquiry*.[65] Unlike Beattie's nemesis Hume, who had also written on the topic, Burke was convinced that a basic, universal standard of taste could be determined. In fact, Burke thought that taste was probably "the same in all human creatures," in order for "the ordinary correspondence of life" to be maintained. Taste was rooted in "imagination," which in turn was ultimately based on sensory perceptions and the natural sympathetic responses those perceptions evoked. Like Smith, Burke argued that "by the force of natural sympathy" such responses "are felt in all men without any recourse to reasoning, and their justness recognized in every breast."[66] And, like Burke, Beattie concluded that "a little knowledge of one small part of the mental system, is all that any man

---

"common sense, like other instincts, arrives at maturity with almost no care of ours." A genius in reasoning may be totally deficient in common sense. Such are skeptics like Hume, who are legitimately answered with recourse to "original undisguised feelings" and the retort, "'I am confuted, but not convinced'" (253–55).

63. After listing Hume's catalog of absurdities, Beattie writes, "What a strange detail! does not the reader exclaim? Can it be that any man should ever bring himself to think, or imagine that he could bring others to think, so absurdly! What a taste, what a heart must he possess, whose delight it is, to represent nature as a chaos, and man as a monster; to search for deformity and confusion, where others rejoice in the perception of order and beauty, and to seek to embitter the happiest moments of human life, namely those we employ in contemplating the works of creation, and adoring their Author, by this suggestion, equally false and malevolent, that the moral, as well as the material world, is nothing but darkness, dissonance, and perplexity!" Ibid., 258.

64. Ibid., 256, 259.

65. The issue of taste was taken up by Hume, Voltaire, D'Alembert, and Montesquieu, among numerous others. See Boulton's introduction to the *Enquiry*, xxx–xxxi. For its importance to Burke, see especially De Bruyn, "Edmund Burke's Natural Aristocrat."

66. Burke, *Enquiry*, 11, 16–17, 22.

can be allowed to have, who is defective in imagination, sensibility, and the other powers of taste."[67]

Such were the views of James Beattie, heartily endorsed by the journal Edmund Burke founded, and which reflected his point of view for at least a generation. We know that the admiration was reciprocated, for Beattie was heavily indebted to Burke's *Enquiry*, whose author he described as one of the "best critics."[68] In fact, the two men met in London in 1773, an event memorialized in Beattie's diary, with Burke warmly receiving Beattie and showering praise upon his *Essay*. Beattie wrote in his diary, "Mr. Burke gave me as kind a reception as I ever received from any body, and paid me many compliments in the genteelest manner. Says that my post-script [to the *Essay*] is one of the most manly & most masterly pieces of eloquence he has ever seen."[69] This assessment of the postscript is virtually identical to a line from the *Annual Register*'s review of Beattie's work, and bolsters the argument that Burke was its writer.[70] At the very least, Burke knew the *Essay* well, and he apparently took his warm appreciation of Beattie on his one and only trip to France, which occurred later in 1773, where he defended Beattie's work in Paris against what were no doubt the sneers of freethinking protorevolutionaries.

Burke's Theory of History and the Scottish Enlightenment

From Montesquieu to the Scottish Enlightenment—and Idiosyncrasy: Burke's English History

In 1757, the same year in which his *Enquiry* first appeared, Burke also agreed with his publisher Dodsley to write a one-volume work, *An Essay towards an Abridgment of the English History*. In the event, Burke wrote only a portion of that history, down to the year 1216, covering the period

---

67. Beattie concludes, "what true religion and true philosophy dictate of God, and providence, and man, is so charming, so consonant with all the finer and nobler feelings in human nature, that every man of taste who hears of it, must wish it to be true: and I never yet heard of one person of candor, who wished to find the evidence of the gospel satisfactory, and did not find it so." *Annual Register* (1771): 259.
68. Beattie quoted in Boulton's introduction to Burke's *Enquiry*, lxxxv.
69. See Lock, *Edmund Burke*, 343–44, Beattie quoted at 344.
70. The reviewer notes that "Dr. Beattie [had] an occasion for adding a postscript in his vindication to the second edition of his work. This postscript is one of the finest pieces of writing we remember to have seen." *Annual Register* (1771): 253.

from the Roman invasion of Britain to the reign of King John. The reasons Burke chose to leave the field of history remain somewhat unclear, although conventional wisdom holds that he terminated the project owing to his increasing involvement in politics, and to the great success of David Hume's *History of England*.[71]

At any rate, Burke's *English History* remains an unfinished fragment, published only posthumously, in 1812, and has been the subject of relatively little scholarly attention. This is in spite of the fact that it is roughly the same length as the *Reflections on the Revolution in France*.[72] The British historian G. M. Young dismissed it as written in bad English that was clearly a translation from French, but at least one famous commentator, Lord Acton, held the work in very high esteem.[73] For our purposes, Burke's *English History* is fundamentally important because it is close kin to the *Enquiry*; just as the latter provides the most straightforward evidence concerning Burke's beliefs about moral philosophy, the former is invaluable in delineating the forces he considered most important in the historical process.[74]

As C. P. Courtney has argued, the chief historical influence on Burke's *English History* was clearly Montesquieu.[75] In fact, Burke refers in the text to Montesquieu as "the greatest genius, which has enlightened this age."[76] As we know, the Scots also regarded Montesquieu as their intellectual forefather. Indeed, one of the reasons Burke would later be so favorably disposed toward Scottish Enlightenment historiography was that both he and the great Scottish historians lauded Montesquieu. Courtney has also noted, however, that the use Burke made of Montesquieu (like the use he would later make of the Scots) was essentially a "free adaptation for his own purpose" of certain of the French historian's general principles that often departed from him on important matters of interpretation.[77]

71. See Lock, *Edmund Burke*, 143–44; Carl B. Cone, *Burke and the Nature of Politics: The Age of the American Revolution* (Lexington: University of Kentucky Press, 1957), 30–33.
72. For exceptions in addition to Lock (141–64), see especially C. P. Courtney, *Montesquieu and Burke* (Oxford: Basil Blackwell, 1963); T. O. McLoughlin, "Edmund Burke's Abridgment of English History," *Eighteenth-Century Ireland* 5 (1990): 45–59; Fuchs, *Edmund Burke*, chapter 7. See also Conniff, *Useful Cobbler*, chapter 3; Stanlis, *Edmund Burke and the Natural Law*, 196–98; and John C. Weston Jr., "Edmund Burke's View of History," *Review of Politics* 23, no. 2 (1961): 220–29, esp. 220–23.
73. See Courtney, *Montesquieu and Burke*, 46–47; Lock, *Edmund Burke*, 144; and Burke, *Correspondence*, 1:164n1.
74. See Lock, *Edmund Burke*, 164.
75. See Courtney, *Montesquieu and Burke*, especially 46–57; and Lock, *Edmund Burke*, 151.
76. Burke, *An Essay towards an Abridgment of the English History, Writings and Speeches*, 1:445.
77. See Courtney, *Montesquieu and Burke*, xiii.

Montesquieu's great goal, of course, was to make history scientific by using the inductive method of the physical sciences to find general causal patterns. The culmination of this approach was his *Spirit of the Laws* (1748). Montesquieu's theory of the *esprit général* said to animate a given historical age was of fundamental importance for both Burke and the Scots. It put particular emphasis on the relation between legal codes and nonhuman forces, especially climate, but also made room for the moral choices of individuals acting within a complex network of social, political, and religious institutions and customs.[78]

The influence of Montesquieu's approach on Burke's *English History* is clear throughout. One of the best examples of this is Burke's first chapter, "Causes of the Connection between the Romans and Britains—Caesar's two Invasions of Britain." Whereas earlier historians had attributed the invasions of Britain simply to Caesar's ambition, Burke viewed them as stemming from the interrelation of physical and moral factors, wherein Caesar's personal ambition played only a small part.[79]

In the *English History*, Burke's Montesquieuan starting point was that geography and climatic factors led to fundamentally different ways of life for northern and southern Europeans. The former were wandering, unsettled "barbarians"; the latter were geographically constrained and consequently led a more settled "pastoral," as opposed to purely hunting, life. This fact, together with their proximity to the great epicenters of ancient civilization, made them more "polished" and "cultivated." These physical factors in turn had important effects on manners. On the one hand, the numerous conflicts of northern Europe, where one empire was overthrown only to be replaced by another, were of only minimal importance, because they were merely struggles between the uncivilized, or "revolutions in empire, but none in manners." A revolution in manners, by contrast, was precisely what the Romans attempted, albeit unsuccessfully in the end, in Britain.[80]

Burke began his discussion of a specifically British history with a chapter entitled "Some Account of the ancient Inhabitants of Britain," in which he attempted to distinguish the Britons' manners and institutions prior to the Roman conquest. Britain was first inhabited by migratory Gauls, Burke argued, the best evidence for which was the "proximity of situation, and resemblance in language and manners." Burke admitted that it was hard

78. Ibid., 14–16, 22–24.
79. Ibid., 48–50.
80. Burke, *Writings and Speeches*, 1:338–39, hereafter cited parenthetically in the text.

to imagine those "extremely rude and uncultivated" times. Nevertheless, and against earlier historians, he concluded (much as Hume would) that human migrations were not the result of overpopulation, because the earth was thinly peopled in the earliest phases of history. Since human beings "subsisted chiefly by pasturage or hunting" in these times, they roamed frequently and at great distances: "It was in a great degree, from this manner of life, that mankind became scattered in the earliest times over the whole globe." Burke based this conclusion partly on "what is very commonly known of the state of North America," with its thinly scattered tribal nations occupying an enormous territory, hunting and making war on one another. Migration was thus a result of "the ancient manners and necessities" (345–47).

Britain in the time of Caesar was not much different in nature and climate from Burke's own day, but he concluded that it lacked improvement "from commerce, from riches and luxury," and consequently that "it then wore a very rough and savage appearance." The inhabitants, with the exception of one tribe that entered the island in a more "improved age" and brought with them knowledge and practice of agriculture, were engaged solely in hunting and herding. The Britons were "in their natural temper not unlike the Gauls; impatient, fiery, inconstant, ostentatious, boastful, fond of novelty; and, like all barbarians, fierce, treacherous, and cruel" (348).

Burke next moved to a discussion of the incipient civilizing process undergone by the British barbarians with the Roman invasion. Here, like later Scottish Enlightenment historians, he believed that one could accurately conjecture in the absence of direct evidence, given the universal propensities of human nature: "In all very uncultivated countries, as society is not close nor intricate, nor property very valuable, liberty subsists with few restraints. The natural equality of mankind appears, and is asserted: and therefore there are but obscure lines of any form of government. In every society of this sort, the natural connections are the same as in others, though the political ties are weak" (349). Here Burke argues, just as the Scots who were so heavily influenced by Montesquieu would later, that political ties were progressively weaker in the earlier stages of social development, when property was less well established and less valued.

Outside the family, with its rule by the powerful father, Burke believed that the Druids decided everything else during this early period. This was not surprising to Burke, for "justice was in all countries originally administered by the priesthood." This was the case because no laws could otherwise "compel men to relinquish their natural independence, had they not appeared to come down to them enforced by beings of more than human power." In a remarkable formulation that would prove tremendously important in his later political writings, Burke concluded that "the first openings of civility have been every where made by religion" (349), and ended his observations on the Druids by noting their similarity to other ancient religious orders across the globe, all of which had performed a vital civilizing function (358–59).[81]

Of the Roman emperors who succeeded Caesar, Agricola is the most important in Burke's historical narrative, for he "reconciled the Britains to the Roman government, by reconciling them to the Roman manners," and thereby "molded that fierce nation by degrees to soft and social customs." Agricola led the British into a fondness for creature comforts, while simultaneously introducing literature and the arts. "In short," Burke wrote, Agricola "subdued the Britains by civilizing them; and made them exchange a savage liberty for a polite and easy subjection." Agricola's behavior was thus "the most perfect model for those employed in the unhappy, but sometimes necessary, task of subduing a rude and free people" (368). As we shall see presently, Burke took Agricola's lesson with him when it came to giving advice for dealing with the question of African slaves in the British colony of Barbados.

In the event, however, Agricola's civilizing advances could not be maintained, as the grandeur that was Rome slowly crumbled (383–84). Following the Roman withdrawal, the people of Britain fell into anarchy, suffering at the hands of the barbarians who invaded them and falling into "disregard of religion" and "loose, disorderly manners." Historical light began to dawn on the Anglo-Saxon period only with the introduction of Christianity; "nor is there indeed any revolution so remarkable in the English story" (385, 390).

In Burke's telling of it, the Christian-led revolution in manners was a civilizing mission that had much to overcome. The manners of the Anglo-Saxons, predictably, "were such as might be expected in a rude people; fierce, and of a gross simplicity." The British barbarians were ignorant of the arts and sciences, as well as of trade and manufacture. War was their business, and hunting their pleasure (392). "But the introduction of Christianity, which under whatever form always confers such inestimable benefits on mankind, soon made a sensible change in these rude and fierce manners" (393).

---

81. These included the Jewish priesthood, the Persian Magi, the Indian Brahmins, and the Roman priesthood.

Christianity was established by, and its revolutionary effect on manners produced principally through, one institution—the monasteries. By a series of prudential actions, the monastic orders won over the Anglo-Saxon people and their rulers. At the same time, the monks were responsible for cultivating the arts and sciences; indeed, "the introduction of learning and civility into this Northern world is entirely owing to their labors." The monks kept intact the writings of antiquity and were instrumental in the pilgrimages of the age, which put the West in contact with other peoples. The seeds of knowledge discovered during these journeys were cultivated in monasteries; otherwise, Burke tells us, they would not have been cultivated at all, "for it was altogether necessary to draw certain men from the general rude and fierce society, and wholly to set a bar between them and the barbarous life of the rest of the world, in order to fit them for study, and the cultivation of arts and science" (398, 400).

The results of this process were clear.

> The Christian religion having once taken root in Kent spread itself with great rapidity throughout all the other Saxon kingdoms in England. The manners of the Saxons underwent a notable alteration by this change in their religion; their ferocity was much abated, they became more mild and sociable, and their laws began to partake of the softness of their manners, every where recommending mercy and a tenderness for Christian blood.... This, as it introduced great mildness into the tempers of the people, made them less warlike, and consequently prepared the way for their forming one body under Egbert, and for the other changes which followed. (404–5)

So it goes with Burke's *English History*, as he moves on to Alfred, the Danes, Edward the Confessor and Harold II, through William the Conqueror and the imposition of the "Norman yoke," Henry II and Becket, finishing with King John and the Magna Charta. The central intellectual force in Burke's narrative is Christianity and the Catholic Church, understood as the chief institutional shaper of manners. One vital subtext of Burke's *History* is therefore clearly a defense of civilization as he understood it, and particularly of the role of religion as the basis for it.[82] This emphasis on religion as a civilizing force, which went well beyond the effects of both geography and commerce, would crucially distinguish Burke's

---

82. See Lock, *Edmund Burke*, 155.

historical narrative from those offered by both Montesquieu and the thinkers of the Scottish Enlightenment. As we will see, it was a historiographical idiosyncrasy that would play a profound role in his later interpretation of the French Revolution.

The centrality of manners and organized Christianity in Burke's historical narrative are perhaps most powerfully evident in the juxtaposed chapters concerning the Saxons and the Normans. The former concludes Book II and the latter begins Book III, which is the final portion of the *History*. In the chapter entitled "Of the Laws and Institutions of the Saxons," Burke argued that before one could turn to the subject at hand, one had to consider the source of Saxon manners: Germany. The German Saxons were "a people without learning, without arts, without industry, solely pleased and occupied with war, neglecting agriculture, abhorring cities, and seeking their livelihood only from pasturage and hunting." As such, they were weakly united, with only a rudimentary idea of government and much love of freedom. Nevertheless, they had customs from which the ancient British constitution itself would ultimately derive. Still, while Burke ultimately agreed with Montesquieu that the ancient constitution was "invented in the woods," he concluded that for a very long time it was "a system for a rude and barbarous people, calculated to maintain them in their barbarity" (429–30).

Burke went on to discuss the evolution of the quasi-mythical legal and political institutions known as the ancient constitution in a fashion specifically calculated to stress its evolutionary nature. The development of the ancient constitution depended heavily on the manners of the time. In a remarkable passage expressing this idea, Burke concluded that static notions of constitutionalism were altogether "visionary" and unreal, as they failed to recognize that "mighty changes in manners, during so many ages, always must produce a considerable change in laws, and in the forms as well as the powers of all governments" (443). This passage is extraordinary chiefly because of Burke's explicit claim that forms of governments, and the specific powers pertaining to those governments, as well as the laws of a people, *depend on the manners* of any given age, not vice versa. As manners evolve, they produce a change in the fundamental institutions of government and the law, rather than the reverse. As we will see in later chapters, this formulation of the relationship between law and manners, under the auspices of Christianity's mission of transforming the savage and barbarian natural moral sentiments into a progressively civilized system of European manners over time, took center stage in Burke's critique of the French Revolution.

In Burke's reading, the Norman invasion of Britain was vitally important principally because it guaranteed the continuity of Christianity as a profound civilizing force on the isle, as well as introducing a new and equally profound force, feudalism. The Norman Conquest connected Britain directly to Europe from then onward. Thus it became imperative, Burke believed, to understand the status of Europe at the time of the Norman invasion (453).

After the barbarians overran the Roman Empire, and for a considerable time thereafter, all Europe was in anarchy and chaos. Animated by greed, its peoples were inept at governing and found themselves continually at war. Christianity and feudalism emerged from this chaos and transformed it, gradually, into order. In Europe, "the rudeness of the world was very favorable for the establishment of an empire of opinion." From the beginning, and most notably with Charlemagne, the papacy was also eager to expand its influence among the barbarians by allying with the territorial blandishments of more earthly powers. By 1066 the Catholic "empire of opinion," backed by force, was well established in many parts of Europe, especially France, and this ensured the importance of Christianity in shaping British manners long after the Norman invasion (454).

Although he did not develop the argument in his unfinished manuscript at any length, Burke identified "feudal discipline" as the second great factor determining the character of European manners prior to the Norman yoke. "All the kingdoms on the Continent of Europe were governed nearly in the same form; from whence arose a great similitude in the manners of their inhabitants. The feudal discipline extended itself every where, and influenced the conduct of the Courts and the manners of the people." An understanding of European feudalism would therefore "serve much to explain the whole course both of government and real property, wherever the German nations obtained a settlement" (456, 431). Along with Christianity, feudal discipline, under the aegis of the aristocracy, would propel the great evolutionary change in Anglo-Saxon manners, laws, and institutions after the Norman Conquest.

The most important aspect of feudal discipline, in Burke's view, was the oath of fealty, the pledge of loyalty given from vassal to lord. Fealty was built "upon two principles in our nature,—ambition, that makes one man desirous, at any hazard or expense, of taking the lead amongst others; and admiration, which makes others equally desirous of following him, from the mere pleasure of admiration, and a sort of secondary ambition, one of the most universal passions among men; these two principles, strong both of them in our nature, create a voluntary inequality and dependence" (431).

These two principles, ambition and admiration, are both related to the sublime.[83] Together with their "beautiful" counterpart, chivalry, these forces would enable the social arrangements of feudalism to shape and cultivate the natural moral sentiments in such a way as to create the necessary "voluntary inequality and dependence" that, together with Christianity, would underwrite and guarantee the flourishing of European civilization, a civilization that Burke believed was destined to perish with the French revolution in morals and manners.

Burke's Account *of European Empire in the New World*

It is clear that one of the reasons why Burke was so celebrated in Scotland, and why he in turn found Scottish Enlightenment historiography ripe for appropriation, synthesis, and transformation, was that both he and the Scots explicitly traced their historical lineage back to Montesquieu. Like the Scots, however, Burke aimed to push beyond Montesquieu by focusing on progressive stages of social development marked by the increased cultivation and refinement of manners in the passage from savagery to civilization. The broad conclusions of their shared approach are striking.

For example, Burke too argued that the earth was originally thinly populated but that people spread themselves over it nonetheless, because the earliest stages of social development, hunting and herding, led them to travel great distances. Like the Scottish conjectural historians, Burke maintained that Europeans became aware of this partly from their contemporaneous knowledge of North America, with its thinly scattered nations occupying an enormous territory, hunting and making war on one another. Similarly, and completely in line with Hume, Smith, Robertson, and Millar, Burke claimed that pre-Roman Britain was largely uncivilized, composed of rude-mannered hunters and herders entirely lacking in the improvements that future commercial and luxurious ages would provide. Both sides likewise agreed that in early Britain, as in all uncultivated countries, property was not very valuable, natural equality was more pervasive, and political and social ties were correspondingly weak, with increasingly abstract

---

83. See Burke, *Enquiry*, 50, 57. This is a point that has not gone unnoticed by Burke's editors, McLoughlin and Boulton (see Burke, *Writings and Speeches*, 1:431n5), or by Lock (see *Edmund Burke*, 154–55).

notions of property and complex legal, social, and political institutions developing only as societies advanced toward commerce and civilization.

But Burke's *English History* also points to what would be his fundamental and enduring difference with Scottish Enlightenment historiography, namely, his emphasis on the church and nobility as the principal forces driving the civilizing process, rather than changing modes of economic production, the position he attributed to the Scots.

The broad similarities between Burke and the Scots, rooted in their shared appreciation of Montesquieu, also helps explain Burke's immersion in Scottish Enlightenment historiography after writing the *English History*. This immersion is clearly evident in the pages of the *Annual Register*. For example, Burke held a high opinion of Hume's abilities as a historian, if not as a moral philosopher. In the *Register*'s review of Hume's *History of England*, the author, probably Burke himself, notes, "This very ingenious and elegant writer is certainly a very profound thinker.... No man perhaps has come nearer to that so requisite and so rare a quality in an historian of unprejudiced partiality."[84] As we shall see later, Burke's notion of the concept of prescription was virtually identical to Hume's.[85]

Similarly, Adam Ferguson's *Essay on the History of Civil Society* exerted an important influence on Burke's social theory. Burke is known to have held a copy of Ferguson's *Essay* in his private library, and the book was reviewed in the *Annual Register*, perhaps by Burke himself.[86] It is instructive to note that the reviewer singles out the "learned author" of the *Essay* as one who "handled this subject in the most masterly manner; the work abounds with subtle thought, ingenious sentiment, and extensive knowledge."[87] Furthermore, the *Register*'s review singles out what we, in retrospect, recognize as one of Ferguson's most important contributions to the Scottish Enlightenment, his discussion of the state of nature. The similarities between Burke's view of the state of nature and civil society and Ferguson's

---

84. Review of Hume's *History of England*, *Annual Register* (1761): 301–2.

85. For an argument that Burke and Hume shared similar views of history, see Conniff, *Useful Cobbler*, especially chapters 2 and 3. However, and more problematically, Conniff also attempts to connect Burke and Hume on issues of moral philosophy. The former position, in which Conniff situates Hume within the context of Scottish Enlightenment historiography more broadly (59–62), I find plausible; the latter I consider unsustainable for the reasons adduced above.

86. In the case of Ferguson's *Essay on Civil Society*, Copeland considers Burke's authorship "very probable" because the review for the 1767 issue parallels Burke's opinions on natural and civil society, and because of the copy of the book in Burke's private library. See "Edmund Burke and the Book Reviews in Dodsley's *Annual Register*," 467.

87. *Annual Register*'s review of Adam Ferguson's *Essay on the History of Civil Society*, 308.

will concern us later, where we will see the validity of Ronald Hamowy's contention that Burke's social theory embraces the notion of spontaneously generated social orders, while also demonstrating most clearly the "conservative and antirationalist implications of the doctrine."[88] I have already discussed Burke's close relation to Smith, and the *Register*'s later review of Smith's *Wealth of Nations* comes as little surprise.

But it is Burke's direct connection with William Robertson, the most celebrated Scottish historian of the eighteenth century, that best illustrates his broad intellectual affinity for, and deep indebtedness to, Scottish Enlightenment historiography. Burke's detailed knowledge of Robertson's work is demonstrably clear in lavish reviews in the *Annual Register* of three works by Robertson, his *History of Scotland, History of the Reign of the Emperor Charles V, with a View of the Progress of Society in Europe*, and the *History of America*. Burke almost certainly reviewed the first of these works and was possibly the reviewer of the other two.[89]

In 1777 Burke wrote to Robertson, thanking him for a copy of his *History of America*, which had appeared that year. Robertson had written a letter to Burke accompanying the book, praising him as "one of the best judges in the Kingdom of the subject on which it is written." Burke was clearly flattered by this remark, and his letter to Robertson demonstrates a strong familiarity with the Scottish historian's earlier work, as well as a deep admiration for his approach.[90]

---

88. See Ronald Hamowy, *The Scottish Enlightenment and the Theory of Spontaneous Order* (Carbondale: Southern Illinois University Press, 1987), 34.

89. As is mentioned in the editorial remarks to the letter from Burke to Robertson (Burke, *Correspondence*, 3:351n2), the long and favorable review of the *History of America* in the *Annual Register* (1777) makes the same minor criticism of the book that Burke would make to Robertson in their private correspondence. The *Register*'s review of the *History of Scotland*, written when Burke was sole editor of the venture, contains the following laudatory assessment of Robertson: "The great and just applause with which this history has been received, makes it less necessary for us to dwell upon it. Its merit is of the very first class.... He [Robertson] is admirable for the clearness with which he states all the points relative to politics and manners, that may make for the illustration of his narrative; and nobody ever introduced or made them blend with the body of the story with more propriety or grace." *Annual Register* (1759): 489–90.

90. Robertson cited in Burke, *Correspondence*, 3:350. Burke's letter to Robertson reads in part: "I am now enabled to thank you, not only for the honor you have done me, but for the great satisfaction, and the infinite Variety and compass of instruction, I have received from your incomparable Work. Every thing has been done which was so naturally to be expected from the author of the History of Scotland and the Age of Charles the fifth. I believe few Books have done more than this, towards clearing up dark points, correcting Errors, and removing prejudices" (350–51); I say more about this letter below. Burke's mention of the *Age of Charles V*, as well as the substantive content of the letter and his personal connection

The reason Burke was so approving of Robertson's approach is that it was, in many respects, obviously similar to his own in the *English History*. It is likely, however, that Robertson's praise for Burke was based on his reading of Burke's own earlier history of the New World, entitled *An Account of the European Settlements in America* (1757),[91] a work that Dugald Stewart later referred to (in a discussion of this exchange of letters) as "a very masterful sketch."[92] We know that Robertson himself spoke very highly of the *Account*.[93]

As F. P. Lock rightly notes, both Burke's and Robertson's discussions of America were informed by a belief that studying the New World's inhabitants would illuminate the shared properties of an underlying, albeit historically underdeveloped, human nature. In this sense, the *Account*, like Robertson's *History of America*, was aimed at "mapping mankind."[94] Both texts, that is, are keenly interested in the particular ways in which the stages of historical development inflected human nature so as to produce empirical variation in it. Burke's letter concerning the *History of America* in 1777, which followed upon the Scot's high praise of Burke's abilities as a historian, is thus much more than a return of courtesies. It demonstrates both men's recognition of a broadly shared approach to history.

The *Account* was a two-volume effort, published anonymously, as was frequently the case with such reference works in the eighteenth century.[95] Although they disagree about its merits, Burke scholars agree that the work was jointly produced by Edmund and Will Burke.[96] It was a work of compilation, abridgment, paraphrase, revision, and general commentary theoretically influenced by Montesquieu's *Spirit of the Laws*. Lock has

---

with Robertson, shows that he was well aware of that book's argument, even if he did not specifically review it in the *Annual Register*.

91. Edmund Burke and Will Burke, *An Account of the European Settlements in America*, 2 vols. (London: J. Dodsley, 1757; reprint, New York: Arno Press, 1972), hereafter cited parenthetically in the text by volume and page number.

92. Quoted in Lock, *Edmund Burke*, 131.

93. At one point in his *History of America*, Robertson writes: "These words I have borrowed from the anonymous Account of the European Settlements in America, published by Dodsley in 2 volumes 8 vo., a work of such merit, that I should think there is hardly any writer in the age who ought to be ashamed of acknowledging himself to be the author of it." William Roberston, *The History of America* (London, 1818), ii.437ncxvii, quoted in Fuchs, *Edmund Burke*, 108, whose own excellent piece of scholarship on this point I happily acknowledge.

94. See Lock, *Edmund Burke*, 136.

95. Burke's publisher, Dodsley, paid fifty pounds for the copyright, the receipt for which, dated 5 January 1757, was signed by Edmund Burke. See Lock, *Edmund Burke*, 125.

96. See Cone, *Age of the American Revolution*, 28–30.

argued that, since Edmund's was the superior intellect, there is some justification for attributing to him "any remark of superior insight" to be found in it; at any rate the "whole owes much to his mind."[97]

Of course, as Lock recognizes, some caution is warranted in relying on this text as an expression of Edmund Burke's views alone, for the simple fact that we can never know his precise role in the writing of it. Perhaps this is why, to an even greater extent than with the *English History*, Burke scholars have failed to address the *Account*'s arguments or to consider it an important part of Burke's corpus. We should not overstate the problem of attribution, however, for two reasons. First, James Boswell recorded in his journal that Burke had admitted to him that he had contributed to and, more important, "revised" the book.[98] Lock thus is right to say that we should treat the text as a joint, or co-authored, work. And, as with all co-authored works, we arguably do best to assume that the authors agreed in broad outline on the contents of their shared production. Second, as Lock notes, we can see the kernel of Burke's great speeches on America in the *Account*, which expresses his earliest ideas on colonial policy.[99] Indeed, perhaps the strongest reason for taking the *Account* seriously as an expression of Edmund Burke's views is precisely its consistency with his later texts and speeches about the American and French Revolutions.

Politically, the *Account* was aimed at raising awareness of the importance of maintaining well-regulated British colonies in the wake of the French and Indian Wars. Significantly, Lock notes that the viewpoint in the *Account* "is unashamedly British and expansionist. Taking for granted the continuing exploitation of the Americas for the benefit of Europe, the Burkes' chief concern is that Britain should increase its share, though with as much regard for the well-being of the natives and slaves as is consistent with the national interest."[100] This statement is accurate as far is it goes, but it raises the obvious question: just exactly how much native and slave well-being was consonant with British imperial designs?

---

97. Lock, *Edmund Burke*, 127, 130.

98. For his part, Boswell believed that "it is every where evident that [Edmund] Burke himself has contributed a great deal to it." An even stronger view of Edmund Burke's contribution is held by one of Burke's earliest biographers, James Prior. For these references, see Lock, *Edmund Burke*, 127.

99. Ibid. For important treatments of the *Account*, see Gibbons, *Edmund Burke and Ireland*, and Fuchs, *Edmund Burke*, chapter 4, as well as Lock. All three of these scholars rightly connect the Burkes' argument in the *Account* to the Scottish Enlightenment.

100. Lock, *Edmund Burke*, 131.

To answer this question, we do well to return to Burke's letter to Robertson, which makes clear that Burke was most impressed by the Scottish historian's discussion of the manners and character of the New World's savage inhabitants:

> The part which I read with the greatest pleasure is the discussion on the Manners and character of the Inhabitants of that new World. I have always thought with you, that we possess at this time very great advantages towards the knowledge of human Nature. We need no longer go to History to trace it in all its stages and periods. History from its comparative youth, is but a poor instructor. When the Egyptians called the Greeks children in Antiquities, we may well call them Children; and so we may call all these nations, which were able to trace the progress of Society only within their own Limits. But now the Great Map of Mankind is unrolled at once; and there is no state or Gradation of barbarism, and no mode of refinement which we have not at the same instant under our View. The very different Civility of Europe and of China; The barbarism of Persia and Abyssinia. The erratic manners of Tartary, and of arabia. The Savage State of North America, and of New Zealand. Indeed you have made a noble use of the advantages you have had. You have employed Philosophy to judge on Manners; and from manners you have drawn new resources for philosophy.[101]

Burke agreed with Robertson and the other Scottish Enlightenment historians that the eighteenth century possessed great advantages over earlier ages for a full understanding of human nature. Like them, Burke was excited about the present historical moment, where all the stages of human social development were accessible at once.

Indeed, Robertson's approach finds its familial predecessor in the Burkes' depiction of the "The Manners of the Americans," in Part II of their *Account*.[102] One of the reasons Robertson's *History of America* pleased Burke was no doubt its clear echo of the *Account*'s own ethnographic treatment

---

101. Burke, *Correspondence*, 3:350–51.
102. On this point, see Lock, *Edmund Burke*, 136. Of this section Lock concludes, "Given the different outlooks of Edmund and Will, the one philosophical, the other preoccupied with economic exploitation, it can confidently be ascribed to Edmund" (136).

of the Native Americans. The Burkes claim, in rather linear and universalistic terms, that "whoever considers the Americans of this day, not only studies the manners of a remote present nation, but he studies, in some measure, the antiquities of all nations" (1:167–68).

In this context, it is interesting to observe that the *Account* denies that the Native American "savages" have religion in the proper sense of that term.[103] For the Burkes, irreligion is clearly linked to the primitive economic stages of the civilizing process: "A people who live by hunting, who inhabit mean cottages, and are given to change the place of their habitation, are seldom very religious.... Though without religion, they abound in superstitions" (1:173–74). The *Account* stressed the horrific consequences of primitive savage superstition by dwelling in gruesome detail on the pagans' cruelty toward their captives (1:196–98). When the Native Americans finished torturing their victim and had finally killed him, they completed their ritual with cannibalism: "The body is then put into the kettle, and this barbarous employment is succeeded by a feast as barbarous." The scalps of the victims became the "trophies of their bravery; with these they adorn their houses." However, the particular signification of savagery was its peculiar effect on women: "The women, forgetting the human as well as the female nature, and transformed into something worse than furies, act their parts, and even outdo the men, in this scene of horror" (1:198, 201). Both of these descriptions of savagery—down to the use of the term "furies" to describe the transformation in female character—would find their precise analogue in Burke's description of Parisian ferocity in the *Reflections on the Revolution in France*, some thirty years later.[104]

The Burkes insisted that they lingered on such details in the *Account* in order to make a broader theoretical point about the civilizing effects of Christianity. Their aim was to show, in the strongest terms possible, "to what an inconceivable degree of barbarity the passions of men let loose will carry them. It will point out to us the advantages of a religion that teaches a compassion to our enemies, which is neither known nor practiced in other religions" (1:199–200).

In the Burkes' view, the ultimate source of the Native Americans' unspeakable behavior, the defining feature of the "government of the

103. Ibid., 137–38.
104. On this specific connection, see Gibbons, *Edmund Burke and Ireland*, 204–6. On the general theme, see Linda M. G. Zerilli, *Signifying Woman: Culture and Chaos in Rousseau, Burke, and Mill* (Ithaca: Cornell University Press, 1994), chapter 4, "The Furies of Hell': Woman in Burke's 'French Revolution,'" 60–94.

Americans," was their commitment to liberty and equality. "Liberty, in its fullest extent, is the darling passion of the Americans. To this they sacrifice every thing... and their education is directed in such a manner as to cherish this disposition to the utmost." For example (and absurdly), savage children were never physically punished. "Reason, they say, will guide their children when they come to the use of it; and before that time their faults cannot be very great." Consequently, "when they are grown up, they experience nothing like command, dependence, or subordination" (1:175–76). It was thus the force of Christianity, brought by the colonists to the New World, that would play the crucial role in disciplining and channeling the untamed and dangerous savage commitment to liberty and equality by shaping it in a "civilized" fashion.

This is the appropriate juncture at which to ask what Burke made of that second great non-European component of the British Empire in the New World, the slaves imported from Africa for backbreaking unremunerated labor on behalf of their white masters. As Anthony Pagden has argued, modern slavery was created by a new form of empire building, and developed initially as a means of supplying manpower for a socioeconomic unit central to the West Indies in particular, the sugar plantation.[105] What was Burke's position on slavery and the slave trade, one of the crucial components of empire in the New World? A number of scholars have insisted on Burke's deep hostility toward and early opposition to African slavery, in a fashion that would seem to support the emerging view of Burke as an anti-imperial thinker. Carl B. Cone, for example, has argued that the campaign for the abolition of the slave trade should be given honorary mention as one of Burke's great causes, and Conor Cruise O'Brien has asserted unequivocally that "Burke hated slavery."[106]

Lock, however, notes accurately that in the *Account* the Burkes accepted slavery, and made a purely economic case for treating slaves more humanely, concluding that if slaves were less brutally treated, they would be happier and more productive.[107] In fact, the *Account* defends British imperial slavery in the New World, noting that "nothing could excuse the slave trade at all, but the necessity we are under of peopling our colonies, and the consideration that the slaves we buy were in the same condition in Africa, either hereditary or taken in war" (2:128–29). In other words, the inhumanity of slavery was justified by economic considerations, an argument

---

105. See Anthony Pagden, *Peoples and Empires* (New York: Modern Library, 2003), 103.
106. Cone, *Age of the French Revolution*, 385; O'Brien, *Great Melody*, 91.
107. Lock, *Edmund Burke*, 133.

that is buttressed with the soothing reassurance that the human beings the British traded for were already enslaved anyway.

The real problem for the Burkes, then, with regard to both the Native American tribes and the African slaves in the New World was how, precisely, to achieve what they referred to as "that grand desideratum in politics, of uniting a perfect subjection to an entire content and satisfaction of the people" (1:285–86). And, as with the native savages, so too with the slaves—religion was the key to this endeavor. In this connection they pointed to the behavior of the Jesuits in the colonies of the New World as particularly laudatory and worthy of emulation. The Jesuits "bring the Indians and blacks into some knowledge of religion," which has "a good political effect; for those slaves are more faithful than ours, and, though indulged with greater liberty, are far less dangerous. I do not remember that any insurrection has been ever attempted by them; and the Indians are reduced to more of a civilized life, than they are in the colonies of any other European nation" (1:241). The *Account* singled out Jesuit policy in Paraguay, which "mollified the minds of the most savage nations; fixed the most rambling; and subdued the most averse to government," as a model for the British colonies (1:279). It was obvious to the Burkes "that human society is infinitely obliged to [the Jesuits] for adding to it three hundred thousand families in a well-regulated community, in the room of a few vagabond untaught savages" (1:285).

The British were faced with an analogous problem when it came to the management of their slaves in such places as Barbados—the difficulty of achieving the grand political desideratum of perfect subjection and perfect contentment. The *Account*'s answer to this conundrum was to follow the Jesuits' lead:

> I am far from contending in favor of an effeminate indulgence to these people. I know that they are stubborn and intractable for the most part, and that they must be ruled with the rod of iron. I would have them ruled, but not crushed with it. I would have a humanity exercised which is consistent with steadiness: And I think it clear from the whole course of history, that those nations which have behaved with the greatest humanity to their slaves, were always best served, and ran the least hazard from their rebellions. (2:127–28)

The Burkes thus concluded that a judicious use of Christianity and its formal institutions by the British slave masters in their colonies, along the lines of what was done in Paraguay with the natives and blacks—a mixture of "humanity" and the "rod of iron"—would likewise civilize Britain's African slaves, while simultaneously disciplining them to docility and humble obedience. This could be done by setting aside Sundays and other days throughout the year for the slaves to attend church and receive instruction "in the principles of religion and virtue, and especially in the humility, submission, and honesty, which become their condition." The Burkes believed that the salutary effects of Christian religious instruction would be great. The masters would behave in a more humane fashion toward their slaves, "and the slaves would of course grow more honest, tractable, and less of eye-servants" (2:129–30). That is, the slaves' transformed "manners" and newly internalized sense of propriety would ensure their obedience even when they were out of their master's sight.[108]

Burke thus concluded as far back as 1757 that Christianity had not only played the lead role in civilizing Britain but was likewise capable of civilizing the Amerindians and Africans alike, transforming them into humble, submissive, honest, and docile subjects. Like the other themes of Burke's early work discussed in this chapter, this insistence on the capacity of religion to instill social discipline, docility, and humble submission in the hearts and minds of those who should appropriately obey, and his horror at the loss of those dispositions among the masses, would prove central to his critique of the French Revolution.

---

108. The online Oxford English Dictionary defines an "eye-servant," in part, as "one who does his duty only when under the eye of his master or employer." For a fuller discussion of these themes in Burke's writings on empire, see Daniel I. O'Neill and Margaret Kohn, "A Tale of Two Indias: Burke and Mill on Empire and Slavery in the West Indies and America," *Political Theory* 34, no. 2 (2006): 192–228.

3 WOLLSTONECRAFT AND THE SCOTTISH ENLIGHTENMENT

Jane Rendall, in particular, has demonstrated that the theoretical status of women was central to Scottish Enlightenment moral philosophy and historiography, and that the Scots articulated a unique and influential understanding of women's changing role and social position over time.[1] Thinkers like John Millar, William Robertson, and Lord Kames discussed the development of the human family, and the evolving place of women within it, as a central aspect of history's four stages. These thinkers stressed the progress made by women in the growth of commercial society. As Robertson wrote in his *History of America*, "that women are indebted to the refinements of polished manners for a happy change in their state, is a point which can admit of no doubt. To despise and to degrade the female sex, is the characteristic of the savage state in every part of the globe."[2]

Lord Kames's *Sketches of the History of Man* also included a lengthy chapter entitled "The Progress of the Female Sex." Mary Catherine Moran has argued that Kames highlighted essential features of the Scots' view of women. According to Kames, men did not see women's progress in the development and improvement of their own faculties but in the increased value attached to those faculties by men. Maternal affection arose from females' supposedly innate "sensibility," an ahistorical constant in women ordained by God. Thus Kames and the Scots argued that the barbarian practice of infanticide was really proof of men's historically rooted insensibility, in combination with the low condition of women in barbarian society.[3] While it was a natural female attribute, then, sensibility only gradually became recognized and appreciated by men as they evolved through the four stages of the civilizing process.[4] As Kames put it, the "female sex have risen in a slow and steady progress, to higher and higher degrees of

---

1. See Jane Rendall, *The Origins of Modern Feminism: Women in Britain, France, and the United States, 1780–1860* (New York: Schocken Books, 1984), 7–32.
2. William Robertson, *History of America*, in *The Works of William Robertson D.D.*, 12 vols. (London, 1817), 4:103, quoted in Rendall, *Origins of Modern Feminism*, 25.
3. For Adam Smith's similar views on this subject, see Chapter 1.
4. See Mary Catherine Moran, "'The Commerce of the Sexes': Gender and the Social Sphere in Scottish Enlightenment Accounts of Civil Society," in *Paradoxes of Civil Society:*

estimation. Conversation is their talent, and a display of delicate sentiments: the gentleness of their manners and winning behavior, captivates every sensible heart. Of such refinements, savages have little conception: but when the more delicate senses are unfolded, the peculiar beauties of the female sex, internal as well as external, are brought into full light."[5]

G. J. Barker-Benfield has convincingly shown that the Scottish Enlightenment's view of women was central to the development of what he has termed the "culture of sensibility." In the eighteenth century, the term "sensibility" referred to the receptivity of the senses within the broader empirical psychological framework laid out by Newton and Locke (discussed in Chapter 1). Specifically, it was connected to the operation of the nervous system, which was understood as the material basis for consciousness. Sensibility was regarded as an inherent human capacity amenable to further development and sensitization as the nervous system responded to stimuli. Soon enough, however, sensibility became inseparably entwined with a model of innate sexual difference and "separate spheres." Women's nerves were deemed naturally more delicate and susceptible than men's; hence they had an innately greater capacity for sensibility, a greater degree of emotional connection linked to their heightened facility for affective response. To put it bluntly, men thought; women felt. In this way, Barker-Benfield argues, female subordination became naturalized on the basis of their supposedly finer sensibility.[6]

One of the most influential treatments of women in Scottish Enlightenment historiography was John Millar's "Rank and Condition of Women in Different Ages," the long opening chapter in his *Origin of the Distinction of Ranks*.[7] Moran argues that Millar's work aptly demonstrates the importance of the language of sensibility for the Scots' understanding of women. Like

---

New Perspectives on Modern German and British History, 2d ed., ed. Frank Trentmann (New York: Berghahn Books, 2003), 61–84.

5. See Henry Home (Lord Kames), *Sketches of the History of Man*, 4th ed. (1778; reprint, Bristol, 1993), 2:41, quoted in Moran, "'Commerce of the Sexes,'" 70.

6. See G. J. Barker-Benfield, *The Culture of Sensibility: Sex and Society in Eighteenth-Century Britain* (Chicago: University of Chicago Press, 1992), xvii–xviii, 3. There is an enormous literature on the subject of sensibility. I have also benefited from Janet Todd, *Sensibility: An Introduction* (New York: Methuen, 1986); Syndy McMillen Conger, ed., *Sensibility in Transformation: Creative Resistance to Sentiment from the Augustans to the Romantics* (Rutherford: Fairleigh Dickinson University Press, 1990); Stephen D. Cox, *"The Stranger Within Thee": Concepts of the Self in Late Eighteenth-Century Literature* (Pittsburgh: University of Pittsburgh Press, 1980); and John Mullan, *Sentiment and Sociability: The Language of Feeling in the Eighteenth Century* (Oxford: Clarendon Press, 1988).

7. John Millar, *The Origin of the Distinction of Ranks*, 3d ed. (London: J. Murray, 1779).

the others, Millar presented a natural and unchanging vision of womanhood as the constant against which the desires, sentiments, and historical development of men was measured. It was precisely the evolution of *men's* sexual passion over the course of the four stages that was understood as the impetus behind the progressive amelioration in women's condition.[8]

Millar maintained that in savage societies the ease of men's sexual gratification, the amount of leisure time available, and the status of women's occupations all conspired to make women's condition wretched.[9] "From the extreme insensibility, observable in the character of all savage nations," he wrote, "it is no wonder they should entertain very gross ideas concerning those female virtues which, in a polished nation, are supposed to constitute the honor and dignity of the sex."[10] With the emergence of private property and hierarchy in the herding stage, however, both leisure and the social barriers to the pursuit of unchecked sexual gratification increased, and men came to fixate on individual women in whom they developed a proprietary interest. Thereafter, men became concerned with the chastity of their women. In particular, feudal chivalry played a central role for the Scots in further improving male manners. Millar maintained that the "great respect and veneration for the ladies" at the heart of the chivalric ideal "has still a considerable influence upon our behavior towards them, and has occasioned their being treated with a degree of politeness, delicacy, and attention, that was unknown to the Greeks and Romans, and perhaps to all the nations of antiquity." This way of relating to women was a "valuable improvement" derived from "Gothic institutions and manners."[11]

Both Millar and Robertson argued that to secure their control over female chastity, men effectively transformed women into private property in the course of the civilizing process. As Robertson put it, "In countries where refinement has made some progress, women when purchased are excluded from society, shut up in sequestered apartments and kept under the vigilant guard of their masters."[12] Moran notes that neither Kames

---

8. Moran, "'Commerce of the Sexes,'" 71–72. On Millar and women, see also Paul Bowles, "John Millar, the Four-Stages Theory, and Women's Position in Society," *History of Political Economy* 16, no. 4 (1984): 619–38; and John Dwyer, "Smith, Millar and the Natural History of Love," in his *Age of the Passions: An Interpretation of Adam Smith and Scottish Enlightenment Culture* (East Lothian: Tuckwell Press, 1998), 81–100.
9. Bowles, "John Millar, the Four-Stages Theory, and Women's Position," 623.
10. Millar, *Origin of the Distinction of Ranks*, 28.
11. Ibid., 104–5.
12. Robertson, *The History of the Discovery and Settlement of America* (1777; reprint, London, 1826), 103, quoted in Moran, "'Commerce of the Sexes,'" 73.

nor Millar nor Robertson considered that women might have something to lose from a civilizing process that turned them into a form of property and left them "somewhere between the savage and the civil, between a state of nature and a state of civilization." Thus, while the Scots believed that men fully traversed the civilizing arc, women remained suspended and static, possessed of an affectionate sensibility that males increasingly came to value and that was indeed capable of combating the centrifugal tendencies of commercial society, but that nevertheless prevented them from likewise evolving and in fact reduced them to mere chattel.[13]

For the Scots, then, the relationship between the advent of commercial society and the place of women was paradoxical. On the one hand, they believed that the rich web of social relationships created by commercial society tamed, transformed, and refined the savage (male) moral personality into one identified by softer, more polished, more polite manners. This had the consequence of enabling men to value women for their allegedly natural sensibility. Yet, on the other hand, the Scots also feared that pressing commercial society too far could lead to the vice of luxury—obsession with amassing wealth and displaying material extravagance—which threatened to undermine social commitments to marriage and parenthood, fidelity and community.[14]

As John Dwyer has elegantly demonstrated, it was precisely in response to this conundrum that popular Scottish Enlightenment thinkers like James Fordyce, Dr. John Gregory, James Beattie, Hugh Blair, and Henry Mackenzie helped construct the culture of sensibility. These popular Scottish moralists, virtually forgotten today by historians of political thought, played a tremendous role in the eighteenth century. They sought to provide European men and women with a new ethical framework that could qualify them for moral action in a world undergoing rapid economic transformation that threatened to fray traditional communal ties and obliterate civic virtue. In this respect, the language of "sensibility" became increasingly important to Scottish moralists as an antidote to communal and civic decay.[15]

13. Ibid., 74.
14. On the perils of luxury in general, see Christopher J. Berry, *The Idea of Luxury: A Conceptual and Historical Investigation* (Cambridge: Cambridge University Press, 1994).
15. See John Dwyer, *Virtuous Discourse: Sensibility and Community in Late Eighteenth-Century Scotland* (Edinburgh: John Donald Publishers, 1987), 30, 52. For a highly accessible popular treatment, see James Buchan, *Crowded with Genius: The Scottish Enlightenment; Edinburgh's Moment of the Mind* (New York: HarperCollins, 2003), especially chapters 9 and 11.

Despite Adam Smith's insistence on the "manlier" virtues of self-command and self-discipline, *The Theory of Moral Sentiments*, being the most complete attempt to define the scope and characteristics of emotional interaction in the eighteenth century, provided the touchstone for later Scottish Enlightenment moralists' reliance on the concept of sensibility.[16] Whether they specifically adopted Hutcheson's notion of a moral sense, or Smith's idea that morality arose from natural moral sentiments, proved much less important than the fact that the Scots all stressed the centrality of sociability as outlined by Smith, and particularly his notion of mutual sympathy attained through group interaction, cultivation, and negotiation.[17] In fact, those who followed in Smith's wake thoroughly blurred his fine philosophical distinctions between moral sense theories, sympathy, and sensibility in their search for a language of social cohesion and harmony.

For example, in reviewing Beattie's work in 1779, the editor of the *Scots Magazine* pointed to Beattie's realization of the "happy sensibility" within the human heart that should always be encouraged, and commended its spread from one individual to another via sympathy, as Beattie himself had done. The editor noted approvingly, "Sympathy, as the means of conveying certain feeling[s] from one breast to another, might be made a powerful instrument... if the poets, and other writers of fable were careful to call forth our sensibility towards those emotions only that favor virtue, and invigorate the human mind."[18]

The basic question for the Scottish moralists was how to cultivate human sensibility in such a way as to maximize its effect as the new social and moral glue of community.[19] Their answer to this problem focused on women as the natural bearers and transmitters of sensibility. Such attributes as greater "gentleness" and "softness," connected to women's heightened affectivity or "complacency," showed female sensibility as the single most powerful force of modernity. Men needed to develop the capacity for fellow feeling if commercial society was to remain intact, and women could and should be their natural teachers in this regard. Wives could soften and soothe their husbands, who were daily buffeted by the harsh blows of a new economic world that threatened to reduce them to self-seeking atoms. Popular Scottish moralists looked to the semidivine, angelic figure

16. Dwyer, *Virtuous Discourse*, 53.
17. Ibid., 54–55.
18. *Scots Magazine*, April 1779, quoted ibid., 57.
19. Ibid.

of womanhood—a figure whose natural sensibility had been further cultivated through education and convention—as a bulwark against the erosion of community and a powerful check on aggressive and self-interested male behavior in commercial society.[20]

The Scots therefore sought to cultivate a new view of women as the catalysts and managers of sensibility within the private sphere, the familial or domestic circle. The "little society" of the family, as Scottish moralists referred to it, became the new school of virtue. Yet, as Dwyer deftly points out, while the Scots professed to treat women like "domestic angels" or "household deities," in fact they used women's supposedly heightened natural sensibility as the basis for treating them like "perpetual adolescents." Male domination was justified through the vehicle of essentialism and the concomitant logic of separate spheres. For Scottish Enlightenment thinkers, women demonstrated their heavenly status precisely by submitting to and pleasing men.[21] "Possessed of peculiar delicacy, and sensibility," Millar wrote, a woman should be content with "securing the esteem and affection of her husband, by dividing his cares, by sharing his joys, and by soothing his misfortunes." It is for these reasons that women were "trained up in the practice of all the domestic virtues."[22] Likewise, in *The Wealth of Nations*, Smith concluded of women that "every part of [women's] education" had "some useful purpose; either to improve the natural attractions of their person, or to form their mind to reserve, to modesty, to chastity, and to economy: to render them both likely to become the mistresses of a family, and to behave properly when they have become such."[23]

Dwyer extends this argument to a number of influential texts by popular Scottish moralists. Among these is James Fordyce's (1720–96) *Sermons to Young Women* (1765), a best-seller of its time, which went through four editions between June and November 1766 alone.[24] Fordyce was a moderate Presbyterian minister who received a degree from Glasgow and became a preacher in London, where he wrote a number of books on the education of youth, including the *Sermons*.[25]

20. Ibid., 118, 189, 134.
21. Ibid., 6, 96, 104–5, 137.
22. Millar, *Origin of the Distinction of Ranks*, 109, 111.
23. Adam Smith, *An Inquiry into the Nature and Causes of the Wealth of Nations*, ed. R. H. Campbell and A. S. Skinner, 2 vols. (Indianapolis: Liberty Fund, 1981), II, V.i.f.47, p. 781.
24. Dwyer, *Virtuous Discourse*, 118. On Fordyce, and to a lesser extent Dr. John Gregory, see especially chapter 6, "'A Peculiar Aptitude to Please': Complacent Women and Scottish Moralists," 117–40.
25. Ibid., 15.

Pastor Fordyce was on a mission to reestablish love in a world threatened by commercial society, but it was love of a very particular kind, predicated on what Fordyce insisted was a natural "sex in minds." In his sermon "On Female Meekness" Fordyce thus told his female pupils that, together with a delicate and gentle demeanor, they should exhibit that "timidity peculiar to your sex," along with the necessary degree of "complacence, yieldingness, and sweetness." "Manly" and "masculine" women upset the natural order of things, which had made men and women different, psychologically and morally, for good reason. He considered "requisite and natural" female qualities essential for social flourishing and regarded "meekness as the crowning grace of a woman" (he was apparently untroubled by the contradictory pronouncement that "a meek deportment is the natural and spontaneous growth of a lowly mind").[26]

Rather than "reproaching their husbands," Fordyce counseled his female readers, women ought to exhibit "a more respectful observance, and a more equal tenderness; studying their humors, overlooking their mistakes... passing by little instances of unevenness, caprice or passion, giving soft answers to hasty words, complaining as seldom as possible, and making it your daily care to relieve their anxieties." This path to an "abode of domestic bliss" was important because the "state of matrimony is necessary to the support, order, and comfort of society." And since, Fordyce acknowledged, marriage undoubtedly subjected women to "a great variety of solicitude and pain," they needed to develop "almost unconquerable attachments." "To produce these," he asked, "is it not fit they should be peculiarly sensible to the attention and regards of men?" Indeed they should; "the securing of this attention, and these regards" ought to be their "principal aim." Such were the marks of the "female angel," according to Fordyce.[27] Fordyce believed that female sensibility could best be cultivated by keeping young women at home as long as possible, thereby preparing them for spousal obedience and domestic duties, rather than allowing them to break free from the domestic into the public sphere and thus endanger their tender, developing sensibility.[28]

Mary Catherine Moran has shown that Dr. John Gregory's (1724–73) work similarly fits this patriarchal mold. Gregory was a Scottish physician, cousin of common sense philosopher Thomas Reid and good friend

---

26. James Fordyce, *Sermons to Young Women*, 2 vols., 9th ed. (London: T. Cadell and J. Dodsley, 1778), Sermon XIII, 2:221–22, 224–25, 237, 251.
27. Ibid., Sermon XIV, 2:264–65; Sermon V, 1:166–67, 191.
28. Dwyer, *Virtuous Discourse*, 122–23.

of Reid's popularizing follower, James Beattie. His most famous work, *A Father's Legacy to his Daughters* (1774) was the best-selling book on female conduct of the late eighteenth century, and he was also the author of *A Comparative View of the State and Faculties of Man with those of the Animal World* (1765). The two works were connected, as Gregory's advice to young women was articulated within the context of his particular rendering of the four-stages thesis as set forth in *A Comparative View* and can be interpreted as part of the broad Scottish response to Humean skepticism undertaken by his cousin Reid and friend Beattie. Like Beattie, Gregory's attitude toward reason was openly hostile, and he similarly regarded religion as principally nonrational, intuited through an affective moral sense that was the particular purview of women but also highly desirable for men in a potentially atomizing commercial society. In fact, Gregory argued that women had a natural attraction to religion that was actually rooted in their heightened sensibility.[29]

Gregory saw women as permanently inhabiting the intermediary position between savagery and civilization. This state of suspended animation was a result of their natural attributes. "The natural softness and sensibility of your dispositions," Gregory told his female readers, "particularly fit you for the practice of those duties where the heart is chiefly concerned." The importance of tender sensibility over good sense in women for the success of relationships between the sexes was so crucial for Gregory that he warned females to hide their intelligence if they miraculously (and unnaturally) came to possess it: "Be even cautious in displaying your good sense. It will be thought you assume a superiority over the rest of the company.—But if you happen to have any learning, keep it a profound secret, especially from the men, who generally look with a jealous and malignant eye on a woman of great parts, and a cultivated understanding."[30]

As Dwyer has shown, Hugh Blair and Henry Mackenzie held similar views of women. Blair (1718–1800) was a friend of Fordyce's educated at Edinburgh, where he later taught, and produced the enormously influential *Lectures on Rhetoric and Belles Lettres* (1783), and *Sermons* (1777–1801).[31] He was also a friend to Hume, Ferguson, Robertson, and Smith, and had an

---

29. See Mary Catherine Moran, "Between the Savage and the Civil: Dr. John Gregory's Natural History of Femininity," in *Women, Gender, and Enlightenment*, ed. Sarah Knott and Barbara Taylor (New York: Palgrave Macmillan, 2005), 8–29.

30. Dr. John Gregory, *A Father's Legacy to his Daughters*, 2d ed. (London: W. Strahan, T. Cadell, 1774), 10, 31–32.

31. See Dwyer, *Virtuous Discourse*, 15, 19–20.

idiosyncratic four-stages theory that he used to defend the historical authenticity of James MacPherson's fictitious "discovery" of the so-called Ossian poems. Like Burke and Hume, Blair also wrote on the question of taste.[32]

Blair's *Lectures on Rhetoric* defend the notion that history revealed a natural progress of knowledge, and in the *Sermons*, especially, Blair constantly extolled the private sphere as the home of that "tender sensibility" which formed the "sinews and strength of the state."[33] To amplify this trend, he encouraged the newly emerging genre of the novel, which he believed could be particularly useful "for conveying instruction, for painting human life and manners," and for cultivating sensibility.[34]

Henry Mackenzie (1745–1831) was a friend of Blair, Robertson, Smith, and Dugald Stewart. He was also the founder of the Edinburgh literary group known as the Mirror Club and the man behind the journalistic mouthpieces of the Scottish culture of sensibility, the periodicals the *Mirror* and the *Lounger*. The *Mirror* served as the principal outlet for his own work but contained efforts by numerous other popular Scottish moralists, including two essays by Beattie. Mackenzie himself is remembered for a very popular novel, *The Man of Feeling* (1771), as well as the best-known essays in the *Mirror* and *Lounger*. All of these literary efforts were calculated attempts to cultivate the sensibility of young girls by accentuating their role as keepers of the domestic hearth, as in, for example, "The Story of La Roche," a tale of religion and sensibility loosely based on the death of David Hume that was also in part an extended valorization of the virtuous, dutiful daughter.[35]

The emergence of the popular culture of sensibility had its effects even on Adam Smith and David Hume, generally recognized as the Scottish Enlightenment's two most ardent defenders of the virtues of self-command and self-discipline. In the 1759 edition of *The Theory of Moral Sentiments*, Smith had used the terms "humanity" and "sensibility" interchangeably, and he regarded them as qualities equally incapable of holding a community together. In the heavily revised 1790 edition of the text, however, Smith recast the role of sensibility, especially in Part III of that work.[36] In

---

32. See Richard B. Sher, *Church and University in the Scottish Enlightenment: The Moderate Literati of Edinburgh* (Princeton: Princeton University Press, 1985).
33. Blair, *Sermons*, quoted in Dwyer, *Virtuous Discourse*, 80, 100–101.
34. Blair, *Lectures*, quoted ibid., 141; see also 189.
35. For the Scots' view that novels (particularly Mackenzie's) were "moral preceptors," see ibid., chapter 6.
36. See ibid., "Theory and Discourse: The 6th Edition of *The Theory of Moral Sentiments*," 168–85.

the later edition he maintained that the "sense of propriety, so far from requiring us to eradicate altogether that extraordinary sensibility" that we feel for others, "is always much more offended by the defect, than it ever is by the excess of that sensibility." Smith castigated "stoical apathy" in such cases.[37] Smith, it seemed, came to soften his tone late in life, and to insist on the value of a "moderated sensibility to the misfortune of others." In fact, he went so far as to claim that "our sensibility to the feelings of others, so far from being inconsistent with the manhood of self-command, is the very principle upon which that manhood is founded." Thus he approached the end of life in the conviction that "the man of the most perfect virtue" is the one "who joins, to the most perfect command of his own original and selfish feelings, the most exquisite sensibility both to the original and sympathetic feelings of others."[38] By 1790, then, influenced by the culture of sensibility and the writings of his fellow Scots in its defense, Adam Smith was keen to show that his theory, far from being incompatible with sensibility, was built directly upon it.[39]

Of course, Smith's male paragon of virtue learned the value of sensibility from the same tutors that other Scottish moralists identified as its natural exemplars, women. In Smith's essentialist rendering, "humanity," or sensibility, was a naturally feminine virtue, whereas "generosity," predicated on Stoic self-command, was naturally male, and of greater value:

> Humanity is the virtue of a woman, generosity of a man. The fair-sex, who have commonly much more tenderness than ours, have seldom so much generosity.... Humanity consists merely in the exquisite fellow-feeling which the spectator entertains with the sentiments of the persons principally concerned, so as to grieve for their sufferings, to resent their injuries, and to rejoice at their good fortune. The most humane actions require no self-denial, no self-command, no great exertion of the sense of propriety. They consist only in doing what this exquisite sympathy would of its own accord prompt us to do.[40]

At first blush, David Hume's attitude toward women might seem more egalitarian. In his essay "Of the Rise and Progress of the Arts and Sci-

---

37. Adam Smith, *The Theory of Moral Sentiments*, ed. D. D. Raphael and A. L. Macfie (Indianapolis: Liberty Fund, 1984), III.3.14, p. 143.
38. Ibid., III.3.15, p. 143, and III.3.35, p. 152.
39. See Dwyer, *Virtuous Discourse*, 178, 182.
40. Smith, *Theory of Moral Sentiments*, IV.2.10, pp. 190–91.

ences," Hume asked, "What better school for manners, than the company of virtuous women... where the example of the female softness and modesty must communicate itself to their admirers, and where the delicacy of that sex puts every one on his guard, lest he give offense by any breach of decency"?[41] Hume pointed to the new social venues springing up around him as places where the sexes gathered together, and where men's behavior was consequently softened and reformed.

Despite his willingness to grant women access to polite society, however, Hume left no doubt about the desirability of male domination and its roots in the natural order. In the same essay we find Hume defending "gallantry" as a more desirable, because less violent, form of male domination, one that distinguishes men in commercial societies from their forebears:

> As nature has given *man* the superiority above *woman* by endowing him with greater strength both of mind and body; it is his part to alleviate that superiority, as much as possible, by the generosity of his behavior, and by a studied deference and complaisance for all her inclinations and opinions. Barbarous nations display this superiority, by reducing their females to the most abject slavery; by confining them, by beating them, by selling them, by killing them. But the male sex, among a polite people, discover their authority in a more generous, though not a less evident manner; by civility, by respect, by complaisance, and, in a word, by gallantry. In good company, you need not ask, Who is the master of the feast? The man, who sits in the lowest place, and who is always industrious in helping everyone, is certainly the person.[42]

In the last analysis, Hume shared the nearly ubiquitous late eighteenth-century view that men were naturally superior both physically and mentally, yet he saw it as a mark of their increasing civilization that they could engage in a charade of inferiority for purposes of public consumption. But it was nothing more than charade. Dwyer shows convincingly that Scottish Enlightenment arguments such as Hume's encouraged women who were docile, subservient, and complacent beings, and whose primary goal

---

41. David Hume, "Of the Rise and Progress of the Arts and Sciences," in Hume, *Political Essays*, ed. Knud Haakonssen (Cambridge: Cambridge University Press, 1998), 75.

42. Ibid., 74.

in life was to meet their husbands' wishes by superintending the domestic sphere, understood as the appropriate venue for their innate abilities.[43] Only when woman behaved accordingly should men graciously engage in the kabuki play of briefly and magnanimously switching roles with their servants. Hume's was a game that Mary Wollstonecraft would vehemently resist and deride as a farce.

Wollstonecraft on the Scottish Enlightenment Culture of Sensibility and Women's Historical Place

In 1789 an anthology of advice for young women entitled *The Female Reader* appeared, edited by a "Mr. Cresswick, Teacher of Elocution," a pseudonym of Mary Wollstonecraft.[44] A careful review of this work reveals Wollstonecraft's intimate knowledge of several of the most important works of Scottish Enlightenment moral philosophy and history. From this source we know, for example, that Wollstonecraft was well acquainted with Hugh Blair's writings, as she excerpted passages from his *Lectures on Rhetoric and Belles Lettres* and *Sermons*.[45] She also knew Henry Mackenzie's famous journalistic outlets for the culture of sensibility, the *Mirror* and *Lounger*, and was familiar with his valorization of the virtuous, dutiful daughter in "The Story of La Roche."[46]

In the pages of *The Female Reader* we find clear evidence that Wollstonecraft was also keenly aware of the Scottish Enlightenment historiographical narrative in which such defenses of the culture of sensibility were embedded. The anthology included a "Descriptive Piece" of "The Character of Mary Queen of Scots," an extract from William Robertson's *History of Scotland*.[47] Perhaps most striking of all is the final reading in the

---

43. Dwyer, *Virtuous Discourse*, especially 119, 137.

44. See *The Works of Mary Wollstonecraft*, ed. Janet Todd and Marilyn Butler, 7 vols. (New York: New York University Press, 1989) (hereafter *Works of Wollstonecraft*), 4:52; and Moira Ferguson, "The Discovery of Mary Wollstonecraft's *The Female Reader*," *Signs* 3, no. 4 (1978): 945–57.

45. See *Works of Wollstonecraft*, vol. 4, which contains excerpts from Blair's *Lectures* (p. 80) and *Sermons* (pp. 141–42). In an earlier letter to her sister Everina, dated 12 February 1787, Wollstonecraft also noted, "I am now reading some philosophical lectures, and philosophical sermons—for my own *private* improvement. I lately met with Blair's lectures on genius taste &c &c—and found them an intellectual feast." *Collected Letters of Mary Wollstonecraft*, ed. Ralph Wardle (Ithaca: Cornell University Press, 1979), 137–38.

46. See *Works of Wollstonecraft*, vol. 4. Excerpts from "La Roche," which appeared in the *Mirror*, are at 81–88; see also 93–95. For the *Lounger*, see 136.

47. Ibid., 280–81. Robertson's passage is from *The History of Scotland* (1759), II, vii.

"Narrative Pieces" section of the anthology, which is taken from "A View of the Progress of Society in Europe," the long introductory essay in Robertson's *History of the Reign of the Emperor Charles V.* Robertson's passage, entitled "The Influence of Science on the Manners of Men," clearly demonstrates Wollstonecraft's familiarity with the historical narrative at the heart of the Scottish Enlightenment.[48]

Later, in her most famous work, *A Vindication of the Rights of Woman* (1792), Wollstonecraft would directly confront the culture of sensibility in a chapter entitled "Animadversions on Some of the Writers Who Have Rendered Women Objects of Pity, Bordering on Contempt." As its title indicates, the chapter is a sustained critique of late eighteenth-century Enlightenment advice literature aimed at shaping female character, understood as a patriarchal tool of oppression. Wollstonecraft singled out two Scottish moralists for especially trenchant criticism: James Fordyce and Dr. John Gregory.[49]

Wollstonecraft noted that Fordyce's *Sermons to Young Women* had "long made a part of a young woman's library" and been taught at girls' schools, but insisted, "I should instantly dismiss them from my pupil's, if I wished to strengthen her understanding." Wollstonecraft abhorred Fordyce's "affected style" and "sentimental rant" almost as much as she abhorred his principles.[50] Almost, but not quite. Wollstonecraft argued that under

---

48. Ibid., 110–11. The long extract reads in part: "The progress of science and the cultivation of literature had considerable effect in changing the manners of European nations, and introduced that civility and refinement by which they are now distinguished.... But rude barbarians were so far from being struck with any admiration of these unknown accomplishments, that they despised them. They were not arrived at that state of society in which those faculties of the human mind that have beauty and elegance for their objects begin to unfold themselves.... The convulsions occasioned by their settlement in the empire, the frequent as well as violent revolutions in every kingdom which they established, together with the interior defects in the form of government which they introduced, banished security and leisure; prevented the growth of taste or the culture of science; and kept Europe, during several centuries, in a state of ignorance. But as soon as liberty and independence began to be felt by every part of the community, and communicated some taste of the advantages arising from commerce, from public order, and from personal security, the human mind became conscious of powers which it did not formerly perceive, and fond of occupations or pursuits of which it was formerly incapable. Towards the beginning of the twelfth century we discern the first symptoms of its awakening from that lethargy in which it had long been sunk, and observe it turning with curiosity and attention towards new objects." For the original, see William Robertson, *The Progress of Society in Europe*, ed. Felix Gilbert (Chicago: University of Chicago Press, 1972), 59–60.

49. For an excellent recent treatment that suggests the importance of the Scottish Enlightenment context, see Barbara Taylor, "Feminists Versus Gallants: Manners and Morals in Enlightenment Britain," in Knott and Taylor, *Women, Gender, and Enlightenment*, 30–52.

50. *Works of Wollstonecraft*, 5:162–63, hereafter cited parenthetically in the text.

Fordyce's teaching, "all women are to be leveled, by meekness and docility, into one character of yielding softness and gentle compliance." She wondered why girls were told they "resemble angels" when they were treated "below women," or why such meek, docile females came nearest to her contemporaries' notions of angels at all. Since "they are only like angels when they are young and beautiful," however, "it is their persons, not their virtues, that procure them this homage." Wollstonecraft rejected the title of "angel" as demeaning and condescending, seeing in Fordyce's idealized depiction of womanhood "the portrait of a house slave" (5:164–65). "Such a woman ought to be an angel," she wrote caustically, "—or she is an ass—for I discern not a trace of the human character, neither reason nor passion in this domestic drudge, whose being is absorbed in that of a tyrant's" (5:165).

Wollstonecraft similarly castigated Gregory's *A Father's Legacy to his Daughters*, which, she wrote, "had the most baneful effect on the morals and manners of the female world" (5:166). She had only contempt for Gregory's "superficial counsel" that an intelligent woman should hide the fact so as not to appear unnatural, threatening, or unattractive to men. "Let women once acquire good sense—and if it deserves the name, it will teach them; or, of what use will it be?" Wollstonecraft maintained that virtue was necessarily rooted in reason or good sense, not feigned sensibility. Why, she asked, did Gregory insist that "the whole sex should be modulated to please fools"? The problem with Gregory was that "women are always to *seem* to be this and that." "It is this system of dissimulation," she wrote, "that I despise." For Wollstonecraft, the necessity of behaving according to such socially constructed notions of femininity was psychologically damaging, for it created "the very consciousness that degrades the sex." In a remark that hinted at the scale of the democratic transformation she believed would be necessary to transform this consciousness, she warned, "till society is very differently organized" such "vestige[s] of gothic manners" as those advocated by Dr. Gregory "will not be done away by a more reasonable and affectionate mode of conduct" (5:167–69).[51]

Nor was Wollstonecraft's critique of Scottish Enlightenment moral philosophy constrained merely to its popular manifestations. For example,

51. Wollstonecraft was also well aware of the particular variant of the four-stages thesis in which Gregory situated this argument about women's appropriate place, as she knew his *Comparative View of the State and Faculties of Man with those of the Animal World* (1765). Excerpts from both works were reproduced in *The Female Reader*. For *A Comparative View of the State and Faculties of Man*, see *Works of Wollstonecraft*, 4:67, 73, 143, 145–46, 287–88, 323–24.

she was a careful reader of Adam Smith's *Theory of Moral Sentiments*. Despite her admiration for Smith's intellect, she took the great philosopher of "natural" moral sentiments to task at some length in *A Vindication of the Rights of Woman*.[52] Smith's central idea of sympathy came in for particular criticism. " 'The charm of life', says a grave philosophical reasoner, is 'sympathy'; nothing pleases us more than to observe in other men a fellow-feeling with all the emotions of our own breast." Wollstonecraft agreed, in part, but she maintained that women had to be educated by employment, broad experience, and formal schooling; only when they were men's intellectual equals would harmonious companionship based on real friendship be possible. Otherwise, men would be deprived of the pleasures of mutual sympathy, effectively isolated except during the sexual act itself (5:160).[53]

In a chapter in the *Rights of Woman* partly devoted to juxtaposing the notions of reputation versus true morality in women, Wollstonecraft again had recourse to Smith's arguments. Here she contended that if men actually allowed women to cultivate true morality, women would spend less time inventing ingenious ways to convince others of their supposed "chastity," which was a weak substitute for real virtue. In support of this argument Wollstonecraft appropriated Smith, quoting a long passage from *The Theory of Moral Sentiments* in order to establish that when virtuous behavior was cultivated, good reputation almost inevitably followed (5:203-4).[54]

In the main, however, Wollstonecraft's reading of Smith was sharply critical. She rejected his claim that the existing state of social manners, rooted in the supposedly natural moral sentiments, was a sufficient measure of moral virtue. "It is not sufficient to view ourselves as we suppose that we are viewed by others, though this has been ingeniously argued, as the foundation of our moral sentiments. Because each by-stander may have his own prejudices, beside the prejudices of his age or country"

For *A Father's Legacy to His Daughters*, see 4:68-71, 72, 75-76, 120, 325. Wollstonecraft also mentions Gregory in a footnote appearing in the preface to *The Female Reader*, 56, and two reviews she did for the *Analytical Review*, in *Works of Wollstonecraft*, 7:207 and 398. The first of these reviews also mentions Fordyce.

52. For a discussion of Wollstonecraft's criticism of Smith, see Carol Kay, "Canon, Ideology, and Gender: Mary Wollstonecraft's Critique of Adam Smith," in *New Political Science* 15 (1986): 63-76. See also Lucinda Cole, "(Anti)Feminist Sympathies: The Politics of Relationship in Smith, Wollstonecraft, and More," *English Literary History* 58, no. 1 (1991): 107-40.

53. See Smith, *Theory of Moral Sentiments*, I.i.2.1, p. 13.

54. Ibid., III.5.8, p. 167.

(5:205).[55] Wollstonecraft argued for an independent standard of morality rooted in reason and distinct from the particular social conventions that Smith defended.

Wollstonecraft attacked Smith's argument that manners were the social expression of natural moral sentiments by considering the effects of this theory on women. To Smith's essentialist claim of a natural distinction between male generosity and female humanity, she replied with what we would call today a socially constructed view of gender: "I therefore agree with the moralist who asserts, 'that women have seldom so much generosity as men'; and that their narrow affections, to which justice and humanity are often sacrificed, render the sex apparently inferior, especially, as they are commonly inspired by men; but I contend that the heart would expand as the understanding gained strength, if women were not depressed from their cradles" (5:261). In other words, women, as they were socially and culturally conditioned, did appear less generous than men, but the cause of such "narrow affections" was not nature but men's equally socially constructed and distorted ideas of what women should be. Wollstonecraft believed that this state of affairs could be expected to change only when the process of education itself, conceived in the broadest possible terms, changed.

Short of such a revolutionary change, women would remain trapped within a matrix of institutions run by men, with the consequence that they would continue to be artificially mannered and immoral "ladies" rather than virtuous, independent individuals. At best they would take on the character of the equally artificial and morally bankrupt wealthy, whom Smith had depicted negatively in a chapter of the *Moral Sentiments* entitled "Of the Origin of Ambition, and of the Distinction of Ranks."[56] In the *Rights of Woman*, Wollstonecraft quoted a full page from Smith's description of the immoral rich to drive home her point that there is no such natural category as an innate "sexual character." She argued instead that the problem of hierarchy in human relationships, regardless of its basis, was the true corruptor of human character, and corrupted both parties:

> In Dr. Smith's Theory of Moral Sentiments, I have found a general character of people of rank and fortune, that, in my opinion, might with the greatest propriety be applied to the female sex....

---

55. Wollstonecraft's footnote at the bottom of the page reads simply "Smith."
56. Ibid., I.iii.2, pp. 50–61.

> Women, commonly called Ladies, are not to be contradicted in company, are not allowed to exert any manual strength; and from them negative virtues only are expected, when any virtues are expected, patience, docility, good-humor, and flexibility; virtues incompatible with any vigorous exertion of intellect.... The same may be said of the rich; they do not sufficiently deal in general ideas, collected by impassioned thinking, or calm investigation, to acquire that strength of character on which great resolves are built.

Women's stunted character development was akin to that of the rich, and Wollstonecraft described both as "*localized*... by the rank they are placed in." This kind of artificial social hierarchy was destructive of true morality and virtue, for women and the wealthy alike (5:127).[57]

Later, as part of her reply to Scottish historiography in *An Historical and Moral View of the Origin and Progress of the French Revolution; and the Effect It Has Produced in Europe* (1794), Wollstonecraft would explicitly criticize Smith's arguments concerning commercial society as set forth in *The Wealth of Nations*. She was extremely critical of the particular form of economic inequality that was emerging in the late eighteenth century, and specifically of the consequences of the division of labor for human character and independence.

> The destructive influence of commerce, it is true, carried on by men who are eager by overgrown riches to partake of the respect paid to nobility, is felt in a variety of ways. The most pernicious, perhaps, is its producing an aristocracy of wealth, which degrades mankind, by making them only exchange savageness for tame servility, instead of acquiring the urbanity of improved reason.... The time which, a celebrated writer says, is sauntered away, in going from one part of an employment to another, is the very time that preserves the man from degenerating into a brute.... The very gait of the man, who is his own master, is so much more steady than the slouching step of the servant of a servant, that it is unnecessary to ask which proves by his actions he has the most independence of character. (6:233–34)[58]

---

57. The passage from Smith that Wollstonecraft quotes at length is found at I.iii.2.4, pp. 53–54.
58. See Smith, *Wealth of Nations*, I, I.i.7, pp. 18–19.

Smith was using the case of the "slothful and lazy" country workman as an example of why the division of labor was so beneficial for increasing productivity. But Wollstonecraft zeroed in on the human costs of the division of labor, which Smith recognized only imperfectly, namely, its tendency to thwart moral and intellectual independence and reduce human beings to servile drones. Wollstonecraft's indictment of bourgeois social climbing, which only created a new form of social hierarchy based on wealth rather than birth, clearly undermines any attempt to cast Wollstonecraft as a bourgeois ideologist.

Wollstonecraft was equally familiar with David Hume's historical work and addressed it at critical junctures in her *Vindication of the Rights of Men* and *French Revolution*. In her first *Vindication* Wollstonecraft deployed Hume's *History of England* as a historical counter to Burke, as part of her attack on Burke's celebration of the supposed wisdom of our forefathers (5:11–12).[59] As we will see in Chapter 7, in her *French Revolution* Wollstonecraft used "Hume's idea of a perfect commonwealth," found first in his *Political Discourses* (1752), at a crucial point in her narrative (6:166).[60] Wollstonecraft also included Hume's two-page celebration of the character of Queen Elizabeth I, which appeared in his *History of England under the House of Tudor* (1759), in the "Descriptive Pieces" section of *The Female Reader* (4:279–80).

As we have seen, Hume countenanced a degree of female sociability, intelligence, and assertiveness in polite circles. Wollstonecraft clearly recognized where the real power lay, however, in Hume's concept of male gallantry in such settings. In the *Rights of Woman* she quoted Hume's *Essays and Treatises on Several Subjects*, in which he compared the French and Athenian characters, to make the point that the "homage" French men paid to women was really the cynical equivalent of the mock play of the Greek saturnalia, in which female slaves were for a short time served by their male masters. Hume asserted that the French nation of men "gravely exalts those, whom nature has subjected to them, and whose inferiority and infirmities are absolutely incurable. The women, though without virtue, are their masters and sovereigns" (5:124).[61]

Wollstonecraft ridiculed this ploy, pointing out "that the men who pride themselves upon paying this arbitrary insolent respect to the sex,

59. Wollstonecraft quotes from *The History of England* (1778), vol. I, xvi, 499–500.
60. See Chapter 7.
61. The quotation from Hume is from *Essays and Treatises on Several Subjects* (1777), vol. II, "A Dialogue," 386.

with the most scrupulous exactness, are most inclined to tyrannize over, and despise, the very weakness they cherish." To the contrary, women should ask nothing more from male strangers than "that reciprocation of civility which the dictates of humanity and the politeness of civilization authorize between man and man." Otherwise, they fell right into the trap of being "exalted by their inferiority," with predictable consequences. "Confined then in cages like the feathered race, they have nothing to do but plume themselves, and stalk with mock majesty from perch to perch" (5:124–25). For Hume, "modern notions of *gallantry*" were "the natural products of courts and monarchies."[62] For Wollstonecraft, they were a form of fool's gold that led directly to women's imprisonment as prettified household slaves.

From Sensibility to Sense

There is no question that Wollstonecraft was deeply engaged with the Scottish idiom of the culture of sensibility and with the four-stages historical narrative within which it was articulated. It is also clear that by the time she wrote the *Rights of Woman*, as Anne Mellor puts it, "Wollstonecraft had come to see her society's identification of the female sex with sensibility as a prison for women."[63]

This had not always been the case. In fact, Wollstonecraft's prerevolutionary works, especially the novel *Mary, A Fiction* (1788) and the posthumously published fragment *The Cave of Fancy* (1787), were drenched in the conventional language of sensibility. The discourse of sensibility can also be found in her pedagogical works, *Thoughts on the Education of Daughters* (1787) and *Original Stories from Real Life* (1788). Even our knowledge of Wollstonecraft's familiarity with works by Hugh Blair and Henry Mackenzie, as well as with the journals the *Lounger* and the *Mirror* and their essays by Beattie and others, comes in part through the texts Wollstonecraft chose to include in an anthology for the edification of young women. It is fair to say, then, that Wollstonecraft began her writing career thoroughly ensconced in, and committed to, the culture of sensibility.[64]

---

62. Hume, "Rise and Progress of the Arts and Sciences," 72.
63. See Anne K. Mellor's introduction to Wollstonecraft's *Maria, or the Wrongs of Woman* (New York: W. W. Norton, 1994), xiii.
64. Some scholars have argued that Wollstonecraft never completely lost her affinity for the concept. For the strongest version of this argument, see Syndy McMillen Conger, *Mary*

By the time she wrote her three works in response to the French Revolution, however, Wollstonecraft's views on the discourse of sensibility had clearly undergone a radical transformation. The question is, what caused this fundamental shift in thinking? I argue in Chapter 5 that it was especially Burke's co-opting of the Scottish Enlightenment language of sensibility, synthesized with his own similar moral theory and idiosyncratic reworking of the Scots' historiographical narrative, that prompted Wollstonecraft's conversion to the viewpoint that the culture of sensibility was deeply oppressive.

In fact, scholars have stressed that Wollstonecraft's opposition to the discourse of sensibility took shape in the context of the pamphlet war touched off by the revolution controversy and Burke's *Reflections on the Revolution in France*. In this conflict, it was "a newly anti-sentimental" Wollstonecraft who squared off against Burke.[65] Burke's use of the language of sensibility was the final push Wollstonecraft needed toward the conviction that it was an insidious form of political argument whose purpose was to manipulate its audience into accepting traditional social arrangements.[66] For this reason, Wollstonecraft's "devastating critique" of "the feminization of sensibility was at the heart of her feminism."[67] Like Barker-Benfield, Mellor, Janet Todd, Stephen Cox, and others, Mary Lyndon Shanley has recognized that Wollstonecraft's argument in *A Vindication of the Rights of Woman* rooted patriarchy in the language of sensibility,[68] and Wendy Gunther-Canada has concluded that Wollstonecraft's first *Vindication*, of the rights of men, effectively "challenged the gender and class hierarchy of the *Reflections*."[69] Even Syndy Conger, who argues that Wollstonecraft never entirely gave up on the potential of the concept, recog-

---

Wollstonecraft and the Language of Sensibility (Rutherford: Fairleigh Dickinson University Press, 1994), and to a lesser extent Catherine N. Parke, "What Kind of Heroine Is Mary Wollstonecraft?" in Conger, *Sensibility in Transformation*, 103–19. For the contrary view, i.e., that as early as *Mary, A Fiction*, Wollstonecraft provided a "critique of conventional sensibility," see Gary Kelly, *Revolutionary Feminism: The Mind and Career of Mary Wollstonecraft* (London: Macmillan, 1992), 46.

65. See Janet Todd, "The Attack on Sensibility," in her *Sensibility*, 132; and Claudia L. Johnson, *Equivocal Beings: Politics, Gender, and Sentimentality in the 1790s: Wollstonecraft, Radcliffe, Burney, Austen* (Chicago: University of Chicago Press, 1995), chapter 1.

66. See Stephen Cox, "Sensibility as Argument," in Conger, *Sensibility in Transformation*, 63.

67. Barker-Benfield, *Culture of Sensibility*, 366, 2.

68. See Mary Lyndon Shanley, "Mary Wollstonecraft on Sensibility, Women's Rights, and Patriarchal Power," in *Women Writers and the Early Modern British Political Tradition*, ed. Hilda L. Smith (Cambridge: Cambridge University Press, 1998), 148–67, especially 151.

69. See Wendy Gunther-Canada, "The Politics of Sense and Sensibility: Mary Wollstonecraft and Catharine Macaulay Graham on Edmund Burke's *Reflections on the Revolution*

nizes that Burke was a "catalyst" for her attack on it in its conventional form. By the time Wollstonecraft penned the second *Vindication*, she was writing passages in which, Conger notes, "a more perfect denial of her former advocacy of sensibility hardly seems possible."[70]

The particulars of Wollstonecraft's critique of the culture of sensibility, Scottish Enlightenment historiography, and, most important, Burke's unique deployment of these ideas will concern us later. In what remains of this chapter I want to show how Wollstonecraft's disenchantment with both the discourse of sensibility and the Scottish Enlightenment historiographical narrative in which it was rooted began with the reviews she wrote between 1788 and 1792 for Joseph Johnson's periodical, the *Analytical Review*. In confronting Burke and the French Revolution, Wollstonecraft would completely reverse her position on the culture of sensibility by fully developing the critical potential of the insights she had first gleaned while reviewing various works for Johnson.

Wollstonecraft and the *Analytical Review*

In 1787 Mary Wollstonecraft journeyed to London after her dismissal as a governess for the Kingsborough family of Ireland. Upon her arrival, she became closely connected with the well-known radical publisher, Joseph Johnson. Johnson's circle included some of the most important political figures of the eighteenth century, not only leading Dissenters like Richard Price and Joseph Priestley but also Thomas Paine, John Horne Tooke, William Blake, Anna Laetitia Barbauld, Henry Fuseli, Thomas Holcroft, and Wollstonecraft's future husband, William Godwin.[71]

Although it is little remarked upon in the scholarship, some members of this circle were well versed in the ideas of the Scottish Enlightenment, and Wollstonecraft's interactions with them would clearly have given her access to those ideas. For example, her friend Richard Price was well acquainted with Adam Smith. In fact, according to Benjamin Franklin, Smith brought successive chapters of the *Wealth of Nations* for him, Price, and other *literati* to read and discuss in manuscript form while Smith was

---

in France," in Smith, *Women Writers*, 126. See also her *Rebel Writer: Mary Wollstonecraft and Enlightenment Politics* (DeKalb: Northern Illinois University Press, 2001).

70. Conger, *Wollstonecraft and the Language of Sensibility*, 97–111, 114 (quotation).

71. See Janet Todd, *Mary Wollstonecraft: A Revolutionary Life* (New York: Columbia University Press, 2000), 123–202.

working on the text in London between 1773 and 1776.[72] Similarly, Joseph Priestley, who, like Price, is often referred to as one of Wollstonecraft's mentors, was deeply influenced by the Scottish Enlightenment, having read Kames, Smith, and Millar, among others. Priestley largely adopted the Scots' four-stages thesis, with its notion of history as progressive improvement from savagery through barbarism to civilization.[73] Wollstonecraft may also have read James Burgh's *Political Disquisitions* (1774) in the course of her friendship with Burgh's widow, Hannah Harding Burgh, at Newington Green. If so, she would have seen Burgh's lengthy extracts from Adam Ferguson's *Essay on the History of Civil Society*, with its idiosyncratic version of moral development within the four-stages thesis.[74]

However, it would be difficult to overestimate the importance of Wollstonecraft's association with Joseph Johnson's journal, the *Analytical Review*, when assessing the course of her intellectual development. Wollstonecraft's work for the *Analytical* served as partial compensation for the formal education she never had, and as such her reviews provide a usually neglected resource for understanding her thinking. While we can only speculate on the substance of conversations between her friends and acquaintances for which there is often little or no hard evidence, Wollstonecraft's reviews leave solid empirical tracks. Much less guesswork is required to distinguish what she read and wrote, as opposed to what she heard and discussed. Furthermore, as the scholar who has done the most thorough work to date on these reviews argues, Wollstonecraft was fully engaged with the texts she reviewed, and in this way she developed her critical voice and laid the groundwork for her future writings.[75]

Wollstonecraft's most intense work at the journal took place between 1788 and 1792, when she frequently contributed more than thirty reviews per issue. Janet Todd has speculated that most of the *Analytical*'s staff was

---

72. See Carl B. Cone, *Torchbearer of Freedom: The Influence of Richard Price on Eighteenth-Century Thought* (Lexington: University of Kentucky Press, 1952), 59–60.

73. See David Spadafora, *The Idea of Progress in Eighteenth-Century Britain* (New Haven: Yale University Press, 1990), 241.

74. See G. J. Barker-Benfield, "Mary Wollstonecraft: Eighteenth-Century Commonwealthwoman," *Journal of the History of Ideas* 50, no. 1 (1989): 95–115. Barker-Benfield argues, "Most important, Hannah Burgh, it seems clear, introduced Wollstonecraft to her husband's ideas and his writings" (100).

75. See Mitzi Myers's articles, "Mary Wollstonecraft's Literary Reviews," in Claudia L. Johnson, ed., *The Cambridge Companion to Mary Wollstonecraft* (Cambridge: Cambridge University Press, 2002), 82–98; and "Sensibility and the 'Walk of Reason': Mary Wollstonecraft's Literary Reviews as Cultural Critique," in Conger, *Sensibility in Transformation*, 120–44.

from Scotland, where the magazine was more popular than it was in England. Scotland was also the home of its co-founder and first editor, the Edinburgh University–educated radical Thomas Christie.[76] Christie and Wollstonecraft became friends, and Christie penned a reply of his own to Burke's *Reflections*, entitled *Letters on the Revolution in France* (1791), which Wollstonecraft in turn drew on for factual material in her *Historical and Moral View of the Origin and Progress of the French Revolution*. Both writers were in France during the Terror, when Christie was arrested with other Britons. Upon his release he fled France, fearing for his life, while Wollstonecraft stayed in the country.[77]

Reviews in the *Analytical* were signed with initials that did not always correspond to those of the author, but there is a strong scholarly consensus that the pieces marked "M," "W," and "T" were written by Wollstonecraft. In addition, Janet Todd and Marilyn Butler have unearthed new evidence that connects her to particular unsigned reviews.[78] The preponderance of these reviews focus on two broad areas of interest: first, the emerging genre of the novel, especially sentimental novels aimed at a female audience, and second, history (including "natural history") and travel literature. These two areas of interest provided a rich ground for Mary Wollstonecraft to rethink her commitment to the culture of sensibility and to grapple with the arc of history within which the thinkers of the Scottish Enlightenment had situated it.

Novels

The explosion of print culture in the eighteenth century was central to the phenomenon of the Enlightenment, and the emerging genre of the

76. See Janet Todd, "Prefatory Note," *Works of Wollstonecraft*, 7:14.
77. On Wollstonecraft's connection to Christie, see Lyndall Gordon, *Vindication: A Life of Mary Wollstonecraft* (New York: HarperCollins, 2005), 137, 140–41, 198, 212; Harriet Devine Jump, *Mary Wollstonecraft: Writer* (New York: Harvester/Wheatsheaf, 1994), 26–28, 98–99; and Todd, *Mary Wollstonecraft*, 138, 198–99, 210–11, 216.
78. For the evolution of the consensus on M, W, and T, see Ralph Wardle, "Mary Wollstonecraft, Analytical Reviewer," *PMLA* 62, no. 4 (1947): 1000–1009; Derek Roper, "Mary Wollstonecraft's Reviews," *Notes and Queries* 203 (1958): 37–38; Sally N. Stewart, "Mary Wollstonecraft's Contributions to the *Analytical Review*," *Essays in Literature* 11 (1984): 187–99. Todd and Butler have sifted through the foregoing arguments, and have also produced new evidence from Wollstonecraft's personal correspondence that clearly links particular reviews to her on the basis of their internal characteristics and proximity to signed reviews. See Todd, "Prefatory Note," *Works of Wollstonecraft*, 7:14–18.

sentimental novel was critical for the development of the culture of sensibility.[79] In this context, Wollstonecraft's reviews can be seen as an attempt to reshape that discourse by resisting the model of femininity inscribed in its texts. Wollstonecraft rejected sentimental fiction's overwrought language, and its depiction of women as silly, shallow creatures of emotion, by relying on the tool of critical reason.[80]

As Saba Bahar has argued, Wollstonecraft's later, postrevolutionary work, especially her *Letters Written during a Short Residence in Sweden, Norway, and Denmark* (1796) and her unfinished novel, *Maria, or The Wrongs of Woman* (published posthumously in 1798), shows how she chose to revise aesthetic representations current in the novel, representations with which she became so familiar as a reviewer for the *Analytical*. These later texts constituted an effort to reinterpret conventional artistic representations of female suffering rooted in a language of sensibility that rendered women objects of helplessness and pity. In her travel narrative and unfinished novel, Wollstonecraft rewrote the sensibility novel's scene of women in distress according to what Bahar calls "an aesthetics of solidarity." This move elicited respect for women rather than pity, and thereby urged (male) sympathizers witnessing the spectacle of women in distress to recognize the shared sources of misery and oppression in society that created female suffering, and to join with them in changing society.[81]

Wollstonecraft laid the groundwork for this transformation in the narrative depiction of women between 1788 and 1792, when she sought an alternative model of virtuous character that separated sensibility into good and bad variants. In the former, reason instructed and commanded affect, while the latter was a form of sentimentalism, or sensualism, derived from untutored instinctive feelings.[82] She used "sensibility" in the latter sense interchangeably with "common sense" (as the popular Scottish moralists themselves had done). Wollstonecraft distinguished sensibility combined with reason from the "entirely ungoverned and emotional kind characterizing the fashionable, conventional rearing of females." Thus, in Barker-Benfield's words, "Wollstonecraft's distinction was to take 'Sense' further in her defense of woman's mind, and to be still more damning in

---

79. In general, see Roy Porter, *The Creation of the Modern World: The Untold Story of the British Enlightenment* (New York: W. W. Norton, 2000), chapters 4 and 12.
80. See Myers, "Mary Wollstonecraft's Literary Reviews," 83.
81. See Saba Bahar, *Mary Wollstonecraft's Social and Aesthetic Philosophy: 'An Eve to Please Me'* (Houndmills, UK: Palgrave, 2002).
82. See Sapiro's excellent discussion of the term in *A Vindication of Political Virtue: The Political Theory of Mary Wollstonecraft* (Chicago: University of Chicago Press, 1992), 63–72.

her analysis of the damage an exaggerated 'Sensibility' could do to women."[83] As Mitzi Myers notes, Wollstonecraft's whole career might be read as a dialectic between sense (reason) and sensibility (feeling); by putting particular emphasis on the role of critical reason, Wollstonecraft sought to distinguish "true" from "false" sensibility.[84] As we will see in subsequent chapters, Wollstonecraft came to believe that cultivating this sort of "sense" in women required nothing less than a wholesale transformation of the ideology of public and private spheres, a thoroughgoing democratization of society in its entirety, a move she saw as analogous to the civilizing process itself. It is sufficient to show here that Wollstonecraft's reviews of sentimental novels for the *Analytical* led her to jettison the conventional language of sensibility, or common sense, to which she had formerly been committed.

In her 1789 review of *The Child of Woe*, by Elizabeth Norman, for example, Wollstonecraft inveighed against the entire culture of sensibility as conveyed through novels aimed at developing female character, of which Norman's story was an example. These novels, with their "exquisite double-refined sensibility," proved "so near akin to each other, that with a few very trifling alterations, the same review would serve for almost all of them" (7:82). In such works, "dying for love is the favorite theme," weakness was "exalted into an excellence," and love, which should be made "subordinate to reason" in books meant to educate the next generation, "on the contrary is brought forward as the grand spring of action, the main business of life, and the director of the darts of death."[85]

Wollstonecraft consistently depicted such sentimental novels as ideological tools of oppression, aimed first at constructing a particular kind of female character and then at claiming that character as "natural." In 1788, in her very first review (of the novel *Edward and Harriet, or the Happy Recovery*, penned under that ubiquitous eighteenth-century pseudonym, "a Lady"), Wollstonecraft described the book as "an heterogeneous mass of folly, affectation, and improbability." The "*cant* of sensibility," she told her readers, cannot "be tried by any criterion of reason"; it was thus pointless

---

83. See Barker-Benfield, *Culture of Sensibility*, 281, 362.

84. See Myers, "Mary Wollstonecraft's Literary Reviews," 84, 94. Conger agrees in large part with this characterization, noting that Wollstonecraft's reviews "use reason—in the form of judgment—to distinguish true sensibility from false. They signal her growing suspicion that emancipating women from impossible heroic models may involve a reevaluation of the belief system of sensibility" (*Wollstonecraft and the Language of Sensibility*, 96).

85. Review of *The Exiles; or Memoirs of the Count de Cronstadt*, by Clara Reeve, in *Works of Wollstonecraft*, 7:119.

for her to attempt to review a book that she considered mere drivel (7:19). True to her word, in the three reviews that followed, Wollstonecraft provided no plot summaries whatsoever. Rather, she assessed the novels according to fine grades of distinction with respect to their greater or lesser tendency to destroy the character of the young women who were their intended audience. In *The Widow of Kent*, for example, "vice and folly are not alluringly displayed"; thus Wollstonecraft did not "absolutely condemn" it, notwithstanding the fact that sensibility was its "never failing theme." After similar observations, she concluded of *Henrietta of Gerstenfeld* that "it may appear paradoxical to assert that this story is much superior to the generality of those mis-shapen monsters, daily brought forth to poison the minds of our young females, by fostering vanity, and teaching affectation" (7:20).

If this was damning with the faintest of praise, other literary productions were even less fortunate. On *Fortescue; or, the Soldier's Reward* Wollstonecraft wrote two sentences, concluding, "this novel, only characteristic of folly and gross affectation, sinks below the general tenour of female productions. Attempts at wit, and vulgar phrases, render a farrago of nonsense very disgusting, which might otherwise be thrown aside, on account of its insipidity." *The Duke of Exeter, an Historical Romance* was "neither a romance nor a novel, but something between both"; either way, it was "intolerably stupid." *Maria Harcourt* was a "tangled skein of nonsense" (7: 121–22, 135).

Wollstonecraft was just as merciless with the female authors of sentimental novels as with the male, perhaps even more so. She could not comprehend why women would willingly take part in the construction of an imprisoning gendered identity. Some, she lamented, wrote from sheer ignorance: "Without a knowledge of life, or the human heart, why will young misses presume to write?"[86] In a review of Elizabeth Inchbald, whom Wollstonecraft considered a talented writer, she asked uncomprehendingly, "Why do all female writers, even when they display their abilities, always give a sanction to the libertine reveries of men? Why do they poison the minds of their own sex, by strengthening a male prejudice that makes women systematically weak?" (7:370).

Even Charlotte Smith, an author whom she truly admired and to whom she devoted considerable space, participated in the construction of a pernicious gendered identity for women: "Few of the numerous productions

---

86. Review of *The Fair Hibernian*, ibid., 7:191.

termed novels, claim any attention; and while we distinguish this one, we cannot help lamenting that it has the same tendency as the generality, whose preposterous sentiments our young females imbibe with such avidity."[87] In general, the best that Mary Wollstonecraft could muster by way of praise for novels, one of the chief mechanisms for transmitting the culture of sensibility to the next generation of young women, was to acknowledge the extent to which they did *not* directly poison female minds. She thus said of *The Castle of Mowbray* that "young females may peruse this book without imbibing any immoral sentiments," while *The Hermit of Snowdon* "has some little comparative merit, and contains nothing immoral" (7:134).

Only in very rare instances, as in reviewing *Julia, a Novel*, by her fellow radical and future compatriot in France during the Terror, Helen Maria Williams, did Wollstonecraft give high praise. Williams's mind, she wrote, "does not seem to be *debauched*, if we may be allowed the expression, by reading novels.... Without any acquaintance with Miss W., only from the perusal of this production, we should venture to affirm, that sound principles animate her conduct, and that the sentiments they dictate are the pillars instead of being the fanciful ornaments of her character" (7: 252). Williams, however, was a rare exception, and Wollstonecraft did not mince words when she inquired in a letter to Joseph Johnson whether he had any more "trash" for her to review that month.[88]

History

Jane Rendall took an important initial step in establishing Mary Wollstonecraft's knowledge of the Scottish Enlightenment historiographical tradition.[89] In addition to pointing out Wollstonecraft's familiarity with Smith, Hume, Robertson, Blair, and Mackenzie, Rendall demonstrates that some of the most important evidence for this connection can be found in the pages of the *Analytical Review*. For example, she cites Wollstonecraft's review of British historian John Adams's *Woman. Sketches of the*

---

87. Review of *Emmeline, the Orphan of the Castle*, by Charlotte Smith, ibid., 7:26.
88. Mary Wollstonecraft to Joseph Johnson, c. July 1788, in Wardle, *Collected Letters of Wollstonecraft*, 179.
89. See Jane Rendall, "'The grand causes which combine to carry mankind forward': Wollstonecraft, History, and Revolution," *Women's Writing* 4, no. 2 (1997): 155–72. Rendall's pathbreaking piece provides the necessary starting point for assessing Wollstonecraft's relationship to Scottish Enlightenment historiography. In what follows, I attempt to fill in the rest of the story.

History, Genius, Disposition, Accomplishments, Employments, Customs and Importance of the Fair Sex in all Parts of the World (1790). Wollstonecraft singled out the "historical part" of Adams's narrative as one that "deserves some praise" (7:291). Rendall points out that Adams drew on Robertson, Millar, and Kames, among others, for the historical part of his work.[90]

Rendall also directs us to Alexander Jardine's *Letters from Barbary, France, Spain, Portugal, etc.* (1788), which Wollstonecraft reviewed for the fourth volume of the *Analytical* in 1789. Jardine was a friend of Godwin's, and Rendall argues that he wrote precisely within the Scottish Enlightenment tradition. She notes that Wollstonecraft's review clearly illustrates how philosophical history and a historical narrative involving gender could be radicalized in what was, superficially, a mere travelogue.[91] Wollstonecraft's review of Jardine's book is favorable on the whole. Interestingly, however, what she fixes upon in Jardine's text is his rather un-Scottish view about the appropriate place of women in the civilizing process:

> The subject of female education, consequent manners, and station in society, appear to him to be of the greatest consequence in a system of civilization, or progress towards improvement. Some of his opinions will doubtless seem singular—for he exclaims against the present mode of polishing and indulging women, till they become weak and helpless beings, equally unnerved in body and mind: and hence infers, that gentleness, or rather the affectation of sickly feminine sensibility, indiscriminately wears away not only strength but identity of character. (7:109)

These remarks single out precisely that portion of Jardine's narrative that distinguished it from the likes of Kames, Millar, and Robertson—that is, Jardine's endorsement of the kind of education for women that would make them strong and independent actors in their own right and transcend the domestic sphere.[92]

---

90. See ibid., 158.
91. Ibid., 159.
92. Conversely, Wollstonecraft dismisses the "whine" of John Bennett's *Letters to a young Lady, on a Variety of useful and interesting Subjects; calculated to improve the Heart, to form the Manners, and enlighten the Understanding* (1789) as a work "interlarded with pretty periods and absurd epithets" (7:207–8). As the contemporaneous description of Bennett accompanying this review in the *Analytical* notes, he was also the "Author of Strictures on Female Education." In her earlier work, Rendall pointed out that Bennett's *Strictures on Female Education* relied on historical material taken from Millar and Robertson, among others (see *Origins of Modern Feminism*, 30–31). Wollstonecraft's review of Bennett's later work shows that, at the

For our purposes, perhaps the most fascinating and illuminating reviews Wollstonecraft wrote with respect to the Scots' historical narrative are those Rendall does not mention. These reviews pertain to works by Samuel Stanhope Smith and William Smellie, respectively.

In December 1788 Wollstonecraft reviewed Stanhope Smith's *An essay on the Causes of the Variety of Complexion and Figure in the Human Species, To Which are Added, Strictures on Lord Kaims's Discourse on the original Diversity of Mankind.* Kames's "Diversity of Men and Languages," was part of his *Sketches of the History of Man.* Samuel Stanhope Smith (1751–1819) was a Presbyterian minister who became professor of moral philosophy and eventually president of the College of New Jersey, now Princeton. Wollstonecraft's review of Stanhope Smith is one of the longest she wrote for the *Analytical*, and it repays close scrutiny.[93]

Stanhope Smith and Kames were engaged in a debate of interest to several members of the Scottish Enlightenment and to educated eighteenth-century readers in general: what, precisely, was the status of the human animal within the natural world?[94] Down to the eighteenth century, the Christian metanarrative of monogenesis had reigned supreme. It posited the original unity of the human race and attributed variations in the species to its decline from an original Edenic state. Monogenesis adhered to scriptural precedent—people had been dispersed by the Flood and by the Tower of Babel, and racial differences were a product of movement away from Eden, originating in Noah's curse on the descendants of Ham. As we know, the thinkers of the Scottish Enlightenment challenged this story by explaining variation in the species as the consequence of a maturation process from infancy to adulthood, occurring over a series of stages. But this led to the difficulty of explaining variation in skin color. Why were some people white and others black?[95]

Here the Scots disagreed among themselves. Some, like Kames and Hume, adhered to the theory of polygenesis, which held that different

---

very least, she knew Bennett's treatise on female education by name and reputation, and probably found it similarly distasteful.

93. Scott Juengel has given it just this kind of scrutiny in a fascinating essay, "Countenancing History: Mary Wollstonecraft, Samuel Stanhope Smith, and Enlightenment Racial Science," *English Literary History* 68, no. 4 (2001): 897–927.

94. See Gladys Bryson, *Man and Society: The Scottish Enquiry of the Eighteenth Century* (Princeton: Princeton University Press, 1945), 53–77.

95. See Porter, *Creation of the Modern World*, 355–57. See also Juengel, "Countenancing History," 901–10; and Silvia Sebastiani, "'Race,' Women, and Progress in the Scottish Enlightenment," in Knott and Taylor, *Women, Gender, and Enlightenment*, 75–96.

races actually represented entirely different species. Kames believed that there must have been special creations, suggested that blacks might be related to orangutans, and argued that similar great apes might yet be found in the tropics.[96] For his part, Hume understood polygenesis as the biological basis for racial inferiority, famously noting:

> I am apt to suspect the negroes, and in general all the other species of men (for there are four or five different kinds) to be naturally inferior to the whites. There scarcely ever was a civilized nation of any other complexion than white, nor even any individual eminent either in action or speculation. No ingenious manufactures amongst them, no arts, no sciences.... Such a uniform and constant difference could not happen, in so many countries and ages, if nature had not made an original distinction between these breeds of men. Not to mention our colonies, there our NEGRO slaves dispersed all over EUROPE, of whom none ever discovered any symptoms of ingenuity; though low people, without education, will start up amongst us, and distinguish themselves in every profession. In JAMAICA, indeed, they talk of one negro as a man of parts and learning; but it is likely he is admired for slender accomplishments, like a parrot, who speaks a few words plainly.[97]

Rejecting such racist arguments, Stanhope Smith set out to "establish the unity of the human species, by tracing its variety to their natural causes," namely, the influence of climate, geography, and social customs, and their impact on human anatomy.[98] Wollstonecraft sided with Stanhope Smith:

> The untutored savage and the cultivated sage are found to be men of like passions with ourselves: different external circumstances, such as the situation of the country, forms of government, religious opinions, etc. have been traced by the ablest politicians as the main causes of distinct national characters....
>
> The conclusion we would draw is apparent;—if there is a similarity of minds discernible in the whole human race, can dissimil-

---

96. See Porter, *Creation of the Modern World*, 357; and Bryson, *Man and Society*, 64–66.
97. David Hume, "Of National Characters," in *Political Essays*, 86n.
98. Stanhope Smith quoted in Juengel, "Countenancing History," 900.

itude of forms or the gradations of complexion prove that the earth is peopled by many different species of men?

The strictures annexed to this ingenious essay, make but a very inconsiderable part of the volume; but we may venture to assert, that the whole tenor of it is a masterly and philosophic answer to Lord K.'s discourse on the original diversity of mankind.

There is but one human species, then, and one human nature, and Stanhope Smith "rationally concludes that natural causes are sufficiently powerful to effect the changes observable in the human species" (7:50).

What is fascinating about Stanhope Smith's argument, and Wollstonecraft's embrace of it, is that it presented a form of radical environmentalism as a counter to the polygenetic claim. As Scott Juengel has shown, Stanhope Smith believed that environmental forces went so deep as to include skin color and physiognomy, or "countenance," itself. Stanhope Smith used this nascent eighteenth-century version of social construction to answer both Kames's and William Robertson's views about the underdeveloped, infantile, "savage" Native Americans. In a passage that Wollstonecraft quoted with praise, he claimed, "Mankind are for ever changing their habitations by conquests or by commerce. And we find them in all climates, not only able to endure the change, but so *assimilated* by time, that we cannot say with certainty whose ancestor was the native of the clime, and whose the intruding foreigner." Likewise, Wollstonecraft singled out Stanhope Smith's claim that "the impressions of education, which singly taken are scarcely discernible, ultimately produce the greatest difference between men in society" (7:52, 54). In this account, environmental circumstance largely accounts for human differentiation, biological essence basically evaporates, and "education" in the broadest possible sense becomes the crucial distinguishing marker of difference.[99] As we will see, these arguments would be the hallmarks of Mary Wollstonecraft's radical feminist and democratic argument in response to Burke and the French Revolution.

For very different reasons, it is equally valuable to consider Wollstonecraft's long review of the work of William Smellie (1740–95). Smellie was a naturalist, a member of the Antiquarian Society of Edinburgh, a printer

---

[99]. As Juengel puts it, "Animated by a strange melding of climatological evolution and democratic principles, Stanhope Smith's America stands as a corrective to radical heterogeneity and the implicit hierarchies of difference instantiated at the sight of the body" ("Countenancing History," 905).

for the University of Edinburgh, and the editor of the first edition of the *Encyclopaedia Britannica* (1768–71). He was an acquaintance of Blair's and a friend to Lords Kames and Monboddo. At Kames's urging, Smellie wrote a book, *The Philosophy of Natural History* (1790), which became quite popular, going through six American editions and being translated into German. Smellie's book contained a chapter entitled "Of the Progressive Scale or Chain of Beings in the Universe," which captured the idea of a "Great Chain of Being" in a succinct and influential fashion.[100]

Wollstonecraft reviewed Smellie's *Philosophy of Natural History* for the *Analytical* in October 1790, one of several reviews on the subject of natural history she wrote for the journal.[101] The piece is sure-footed and wide-ranging, discussing Linnaeus's taxonomic scheme as well as various works by Buffon, and contains a brief mention of Newton and Condillac, together with a reference to Pope's discussion of the great chain of being as it appears in Smellie's work.

But Wollstonecraft's review is particularly interesting because she takes issue with Smellie's conflation of instinct and reason.[102] "Mr. S. seemed aware of the difficulty attending an attempt to distinguish animals from plants; but he neither doubts nor pauses when he considers a still more complicated subject, the distinction between reason and instinct.... We cannot agree with Mr. S. that instinct is only a lesser degree of reason" (7:295). Wollstonecraft then presents her argument that there is an essential difference between reason and instinct. In a passage she quotes at length, Smellie argues that the evolutionary capacity of human architectural forms, as opposed to the static instinctive architectural patterns of animals, is evidence merely of humans' superior instincts, among which is reason itself. This is wholly incorrect for Wollstonecraft:

> If in the earlier stages of society, human architecture was extremely rude—that is inferior to the first essays of the beaver, bee, etc. it is natural to infer that reason and instinct are essentially different. The human species, considered collectively, appear to have

---

100. For Smellie, see Bryson, *Man and Society*, 62–64; and Alexander Broadie, ed., *The Scottish Enlightenment: An Anthology* (Edinburgh: Canongate Books, 1997), 803–4. For the concept of the great chain, see Arthur O. Lovejoy's much assailed but nevertheless useful *Great Chain of Being: A Study of the History of an Idea* (Cambridge: Harvard University Press, 1964).

101. See also her reviews of Riley's *A new moral System of Natural History, etc.* (7:379–83), and Buffon's *Natural History, Abridged* (7:411).

102. On this point, see Jump, *Mary Wollstonecraft*, 41.

an infancy, youth, etc.—Has any thing similar ever been observed in the brute creation? On the contrary, it is evident that the horse, dog, and sheep, and many others which it would be tedious to enumerate, transmit to their posterity *only* physical improvement; the result of their instincts seemed to be too sure for improvement, and too subtle for transmission. (7:297–98)[103]

This is an important clue to Wollstonecraft's overall stance concerning the Scottish Enlightenment. Like the Scots, she agreed that there was slow improvement in the human species' condition, which took the form of progressive "refinement" over a series of stages, analogous to the individual's maturation process. Unlike them, however, Wollstonecraft did not believe that this improvement derived from the refinement of instinctive impulses. Rather, it came from bringing reason to bear on a given field of human endeavor and benefiting from its incremental accretion over vast stretches of time. In subsequent chapters, we will see precisely how this argument played out in Wollstonecraft's analysis of the French Revolution.

Last of the multitude of Scottish Enlightenment thinkers who both positively influenced and simultaneously enraged Mary Wollstonecraft was Lord Monboddo, the eccentric jurist and intellectual rival of Lord Kames. In *A Vindication of the Rights of Woman*, Wollstonecraft, in a footnote, quoted, Monboddo's best-known work, the six-volume *Of the Origin and Progress of Language* (1773–92). A notorious contrarian, Monboddo, unlike his fellow Scots, gloried in the ancients (especially Aristotle), rejected Newton and Locke, wrote at length about the decline of civilization in the present commercialized epoch, and upheld the advantages of Sparta. While there were broad similarities between Monboddo's work and the main line of Scottish Enlightenment arguments, Monboddo emphasized, much

---

103. One cannot help but notice how Wollstonecraft's remarks predate the celebrated lines of Marx in *Capital* by more than seventy-five years. In his discussion of the labor process, Marx writes: "We are not dealing here with those first instinctive forms of labor which remain on the animal level. An immense interval of time separates the state of things in which a man brings his labor-power to market for sale as a commodity from the situation when human labor had not yet cast off its first instinctive form. We presuppose labor in a form in which it is an exclusively human characteristic. A spider conducts operations which resemble those of the weaver, and a bee would put many a human architect to shame by the construction of its honeycomb cells. But what distinguishes the worst architect from the best of bees is that the architect builds the cell in his mind before he constructs it in wax. At the end of every labor process, a result emerges which had already been conceived by the worker at the beginning, hence already existed ideally." Karl Marx, *Capital: A Critique of Political Economy*, vol. 1, trans. Ben Fowkes (New York: Vintage Books, 1977), 283–84.

like Aristotle and to a much greater extent than other Scots, the importance of humans' intellect as the distinctive capacity that separated them from other animals (although he famously classed the orangutan as one of our number), arguing that it was principally through reason that human beings constructed themselves.[104]

Thus it is not surprising that Wollstonecraft would have cited Monboddo to support her argument for the universality of human reason, her carefully drawn distinction between instinct and reason, and her identification of reason as that which distinguishes human beings from animals. "Reason," she writes, is "the simple power of improvement; or, more properly speaking, of discerning truth.... More or less may be conspicuous in one being than another; but the nature of reason must be the same in all, if it be an emanation of divinity, the tie that connects the creature with the Creator; for, can that soul be stamped with the heavenly image, that is not perfected by the exercise of its own reason?" Conversely: "'The brutes,' says Lord Monboddo, 'remain in the state in which nature has placed them, except in so far as their natural instinct is improved by the culture *we* bestow upon them'" (5:122).[105]

By way of concluding this reading of her work for the *Analytical Review*, consider Wollstonecraft's high praise for Jean-Pierre Brissot's *Travels in the United States of North America* (1791) (7:390–93). Whereas Burke would later brand Brissot as an evil Jacobin who richly deserved his fate at the guillotine, Wollstonecraft described him as "an enlightened citizen of the world, whose zeal for liberty appears to arise from the purest moral principles, and most expansive humanity." She wrote that Brissot found the key to American liberty "in their manners, or rather morals; for the Americans possess what we do not yet see the absolute necessity of acquiring, in order to settle liberty on a firm basis." In this remark we find a final clue to understanding Mary Wollstonecraft's transformation of Scottish Enlightenment moral philosophy and historiography. Wollstonecraft argued that Brissot properly juxtaposed the simple manners of the liberated, egalitarian Americans against the "artificial polish, that certain distinctions in society tend to give to the manners of the rich," in the old European world mistakenly called "civilization" (7:390–91). In subsequent chapters, we will come to understand how Wollstonecraft fully developed the deeply demo-

---

104. On Monboddo, see Spadafora, *Idea of Progress*, 317–20; and Bryson, *Man and Society*, 66–77, 95–100.

105. Wollstonecraft's footnote on Monboddo quotes his *Origin and Progress of Language* (Edinburgh, 1774), vol. I, x, p. 137; the emphasis is Wollstonecraft's.

cratic impulses evident in her early work to defend the French Revolution, even while that same Revolution executed Brissot, a man whom Wollstonecraft had befriended in Paris during the time of the Terror, and whose death she greatly lamented. For now, we return to Edmund Burke and his alternative view of deep democracy as the very embodiment of terror and the epitome of savagery itself.

4 "THE MOST IMPORTANT OF ALL REVOLUTIONS"

> Excuse me, therefore, if I have dwelt too long on the atrocious spectacle of the sixth of October 1789, or have given too much scope to the reflections which have arisen in my mind on occasion of the most important of all revolutions, which may be dated from that day, I mean a revolution in sentiments, manners, and moral opinions.
>
> — EDMUND BURKE, *REFLECTIONS ON THE REVOLUTION IN FRANCE* (1790)

One of the most remarkable aspects of Edmund Burke's interpretation of the French Revolution was the early date at which he became passionately and irrevocably opposed to it. The *Reflections* appeared in 1790, years before Louis XVI, Marie Antoinette, and the other members of the royal family were executed, before Robespierre, Marat, the Terror, and French military expansionism, the figures and events generally associated with revolutionary excess. Yet, as early as 1789, before the *Reflections* was even published, Burke's letters to his political and personal intimates provided an extraordinarily extreme assessment of the Revolution's significance. In early October of that year, for example, he wrote to his son Richard of "the portentous State of France—where the Elements which compose Human Society seem all to be dissolved, and a world of Monsters to be produced in the place of it."[1] Writing to his political ally Earl Fitzwilliam in early November, he declared that the Revolution would spell "the total political extinction of a great civilized Nation situated in the heart of this our Western System."[2] It is no surprise, then, that in the *Reflections*, written in the form of a letter to a young French correspondent, Charles-Jean-François-Depont, Burke called the Revolution a great crisis not for France alone but for all of Europe; indeed, he wrote, "the French

---

1. See *The Correspondence of Edmund Burke*, ed. Thomas W. Copeland, 10 vols. (Chicago: University of Chicago Press, 1958–78) (hereafter *Correspondence*), 6:30 (c. 10 October 1789). For an interesting Marxist reading of Burke's subsequent use of "monstrosity" as a signifier in the *Reflections*, see Mark Neocleous, "The Monstrous Multitude: Edmund Burke's Political Teratology," *Contemporary Political Theory* 3 (2004): 70–88.

2. Burke, *Correspondence*, 6:34–37 (quotation at 36) (12 November 1789).

revolution is the most astonishing that has hitherto happened in the world."[3]

Burke's assessment of the Revolution's significance lies at the rhetorical and argumentative heart of the *Reflections*, that is, the seizure of the French royal family on 6 October 1789 and its aftermath, their being "led in triumph" from Versailles to Paris. Burke cast the latter occurrence as perhaps the most horrid and shocking spectacle ever witnessed by human eyes. He compared the forced procession of the royal family to Paris to the bloodthirsty rituals of the savages of North America, described at great length in his own *Account of the European Settlements in America*. It resembled "a procession of American savages, entering into Onandaga, after some of their murders called victories, and leading into hovels hung round with scalps, their captives, overpowered with the scoffs and buffets of women as ferocious as themselves, much more than it resembled the triumphal pomp of a civilized martial nation."[4]

While the dismembered heads of the royal guards, borne on pikes, announced this procession, "the royal captives who followed in the train were slowly moved along, amidst the horrid yells, and shrilling screams, and frantic dances, and infamous contumelies, and all the unutterable abominations of the furies of hell, in the abused shape of the vilest of women."[5] As we have seen, in the *Account* Burke had described in gruesome detail the Native Americans' cruelty toward their captives, including their use of their victims' scalps as "trophies of their bravery" to "adorn their houses." In that earlier narrative, no less than in the *Reflections*, the particular signification of savagery was seen most clearly in its peculiar effect on the nature of women. In the *Account* as in the *Reflections*, women forgot both their human and their tender female nature, and, "transformed into something worse than furies, act their parts, and even outdo the men, in this scene of horror." For Burke, the transformation of civilized French women into savages akin to the American tribes signified in microcosm the horrors wrought by the Revolution and its principles.[6]

---

3. *The Writings and Speeches of Edmund Burke*, ed. Paul Langford, 8 vols. to date (Oxford: Clarendon Press, 1981–) (hereafter *Writings and Speeches*), 8:60. I have also relied on the older Bohn's British Classics edition, *The Works of the Right Honourable Edmund Burke*, 8 vols. (London: Bell & Daldy, 1872) (hereafter *Works of Burke*).

4. Burke, *Writings and Speeches*, 8:117. On the connection between this passage and the *Account*, see Luke Gibbons, *Edmund Burke and Ireland: Aesthetics, Politics, and the Colonial Sublime* (Cambridge: Cambridge University Press, 2003), 183–85, 204–7.

5. Burke, *Writings and Speeches*, 8:122.

6. Edmund Burke and Will Burke, *An Account of the European Settlements in America*, 2 vols. (London: J. Dodsley, 1757; reprint, New York: Arno Press, 1972), 1:201, 198. The

Beneath such remarks, I argue, lurked the ultimate Burkean nightmare vision: the emergence of political democracy reinforced by deliberate policies of social and cultural democratization. My argument here and in Chapter 6 is that Edmund Burke equated "savagery" with democracy and understood the process of deep democratization—encompassing the private as well as the public sphere—as the literal death of Western civilization. As the epigraph that opens this chapter suggests, Burke's identification of "the most important of all revolutions" as the one in "sentiments, manners, and moral opinions" was crucial to his understanding of the process of democratization. Moreover, Burke's conclusion that democracy was a total way of life, one predicated on the radical transformation of natural moral sentiments, was built upon his unique synthesis of Scottish Enlightenment arguments and the positions set forth some thirty years earlier in his *Philosophical Enquiry*, *English History*, and *Account of the European Settlements in America*.

In a series of deeply insightful articles, John Pocock has convincingly, if partially, shown the importance of Scottish Enlightenment historiography for Burke's understanding of the French Revolution. Pocock has also demonstrated that Burke did not simply rely on the Scots' arguments as given in making sense of the Revolution; in fact, he modified their four-stages thesis in crucial ways.[7] Burke believed that the Scots offered a

---

transformation of women's natural character always served as one of the leading signifiers of civilization's descent into savagery in Burke's writings on the French Revolution. For example, in a letter he wrote to the bishop of Saint-Pol-de-Léon in September 1792, Burke explicitly contrasted the behavior of English and French women. English women gave succor to the French aristocrats, who barely escaped the "Fangs of Cannibals" to find their way to Britain's shores. Their behavior exhibited "Sentiments of a tender Nature" and "the piety congenial to their Sex." Burke found himself touched by such behavior, "especially when I am obliged to compare it with the atrocious actions of those furies of Hell in whom the Systems taught in public markets and at corners of Streets to the Lowest of the people, and the Habits by every artifice introduced by the modern Philosophy have extinguished in France all the softness of the Sex, and even defaced and destroyed the frame and constitution of human nature itself." *Correspondence*, 7:208–9. The best general discussion of this theme in Burke's work is Linda M. G. Zerilli, *Signifying Woman: Culture and Chaos in Rousseau, Burke, and Mill* (Ithaca: Cornell University Press, 1994).

7. For Pocock's view of Burke, see especially "The Political Economy of Burke's Analysis of the French Revolution," in his *Virtue, Commerce, and History: Essays on Political Thought and History, Chiefly in the Eighteenth Century* (Cambridge: Cambridge University Press, 1985), 193–212; his introduction to Burke's *Reflections on the Revolution in France* (Indianapolis: Hackett, 1987), vii–lvi; and his "Edmund Burke and the Redefinition of Enthusiasm: the Context as Counter-Revolution," in *The French Revolution and the Creation of Modern Political Culture*, vol. 3, ed. François Furet and Mona Ozouf (Oxford: Pergamon Press, 1989), 19–43. In a similar vein, see also Richard Bourke, "Edmund Burke and Enlightenment Sociability: Justice, Honour, and the Principles of Government," *History of Political Thought* 21, no. 4 (2000): 632–56.

materialist historical narrative in which changing modes of economic production underpinned the progressive development of natural moral sentiments and their expression in increasingly polished manners. As we saw in Chapter 2, Burke countered this argument with an idealist inversion of the Scots' thesis. He insisted that modes of economic production were necessarily embedded in a rich soil of natural moral sentiment that was nurtured by two institutions, the nobility and the church.[8] As Burke put it in the *Reflections:* "Nothing is more certain, than that our manners, our civilization, and all the good things which are connected with manners, and with civilization, have, in this European world of ours, depended for ages upon two principles; and were indeed the result of both combined; I mean the spirit of a gentleman, and the spirit of religion."[9] In short, Burke turned the Scots on their heads while retaining their central discursive terms. To invert Marx's view of Hegel, one might say that Burke sought to recover the mystical kernel within the rational shell of the Scottish Enlightenment historical thesis.

This is precisely why Burke could refer to the revolution in morals and manners that ultimately transformed civilization back into savagery as the most important revolution of all. A people like the French could survive the destruction of their commercial and economic production, "the gods" of the Scottish Enlightenment "oeconomical politicians," while leaving civilization intact, so long as civilization's chief institutional guarantors, the nobility and the church, remained in place. But if these two pillars should be "trodden down under the hoofs of a swinish multitude" (in that famous turn of phrase), the results would be catastrophic. In that event, the soil of natural moral sentiment that provided the basis for civilization's progress would erode, the economic superstructure would collapse, and the civilized people of polite, commercial society would regress to the more primitive stages of the civilizing process, becoming "gross, stupid, ferocious, and at the same time, poor and sordid barbarians."[10]

Very few scholars, Pocock included, have recognized that Burke's insistence on the centrality of the church and nobility to the civilizing process goes all the way back to his *English History* and *Account of the European Settlements in America*. Moreover, Burke scholars in the Cambridge School mold, in particular, have refrained from asking a fundamental question about

---

8. See Pocock's introduction to Burke's *Reflections*, xxxii–xxxiii; his "Political Economy of Burke's Analysis," 197–99; and his "Burke and the Redefinition of Enthusiasm," 31.

9. Burke, *Writings and Speeches*, 8:129–30.

10. Ibid., 8:130–31.

Burke that emerges from this fact. Specifically, what did he believe was so special about the "spirit of a gentleman" and the "spirit of a religion"?

To answer this question, one must recognize the links between Burke's historical analysis of the French Revolution and the arguments he articulated in *A Philosophical Enquiry into the Origin of our Ideas of the Sublime and Beautiful*,[11] and his other early writings on epistemology and moral philosophy. I submit that if we want to know why Burke saw the French Revolution as the end of Western civilization, we must focus our attention at the intersection of Burke's moral/aesthetic categories and his transformation of Scottish Enlightenment historiography in the wake of his *English History* and *Account of the European Settlements in America*. I contend that these interpretive streams come together in Burke's view of the importance of the nobility and the church, and the consequences of their demise. Let us begin, then, with the main argument of Burke's *Enquiry*, and subsequently consider how that argument intersected with his idiosyncratic appropriation of Scottish Enlightenment moral theory and historiography in both the *Reflections* and its famous addendum, *An Appeal from the New to the Old Whigs* (1791), which is subtitled *In Consequence of Some Late Discussions in Parliament, Relative to the Reflections on the French Revolution*.

Burke on the Sublime and the Beautiful: Fear and "Love"

As James T. Boulton notes in his invaluable introduction to the text, Burke's *Enquiry* proceeds from the general to the specific. It begins with a discussion of the psychological factors that govern human experience generally, moves to an investigation of particular objects of aesthetic response and the intrinsic qualities that Burke believed led one to experience a given object as either sublime or beautiful, and concludes with a discourse on the efficient causes of the experiences of sublimity and beauty.[12] Put another way, Burke starts with a general theory of human response, fixes the location of the sublime and beautiful with respect to it, and assesses their specific modus operandi, all with the goal of moving closer to a precise theory of the passions.

Within this framework, Burke claims that human passions generally fit

---

11. Edmund Burke, *A Philosophical Enquiry into the Origin of our Ideas of the Sublime and Beautiful*, 2d ed., ed. James T. Boulton (1759; Notre Dame: University of Notre Dame Press, 1968), hereafter cited parenthetically in the text.

12. Boulton, "Introduction," xxxix–lxxxi.

into one of two categories, depending on whether their source is pain or pleasure. As we know, for Burke, as for his friend Adam Smith, these categories related to survival and reproduction, or what Burke called "self-preservation" and "society." In Burke's account, the passions pursuant to self-preservation turned "on *pain* and *danger*," hence they were "the most powerful of all the passions." These contrasted with the weaker social passions, which included "the society of the *sexes*, which answers the purposes of propagation" (38, 40). Let us consider briefly how Burke's theory of the sublime and beautiful fits into this schema.

In his famous study of the sublime, Samuel Monk notes that the foundation of Burke's particular theory of sublimity is terror.[13] Burke insists, "Whatever is fitted in any sort to excite the ideas of pain, and danger," or otherwise "operates in a manner analogous to terror, is a source of the *sublime*; that is, it is productive of the strongest emotion which the mind is capable of feeling." Why is the sublime more affective than the beautiful? Because it is connected with pain: "I say the strongest emotion, because I am satisfied the ideas of pain are much more powerful than those which enter on the part of pleasure." Torment is more affective than pleasure and, by logical extension, death is more affective than pain; indeed, Burke calls death the "king of terrors" (39–40). The passions of self-preservation are simply painful when their causes immediately affect us. However, Burke informs his readers, this is not always true. These causes "are delightful when we have an idea of pain and danger, without being actually in such circumstances." This "delight," or mitigated terror associated with pain and danger viewed from a safe distance, is the experience of sublimity. "Whatever excites this delight," Burke writes, "I call *sublime*" (51).

The social passions linked to beauty stem from two sources, or "societies." The first is the society of sex, which concerns that kind of love that "contains a mixture of lust; its object is the beauty of women." Nature draws men to women in general, but they are "attached" to particular individuals of the female sex by their beauty. The second society is that

---

13. See Samuel H. Monk, *The Sublime: A Study of Critical Theories in Eighteenth-Century England* (New York: Modern Language Association of America, 1935), 87. I have benefited particularly from Vanessa L. Ryan, "The Physiological Sublime: Burke's Critique of Reason," *Journal of the History of Ideas* 62, no. 2 (2001): 265–79; and Terry Eagleton, "Aesthetics and Politics in Edmund Burke," *History Workshop Journal* 28 (1989): 53–62. See also Frances Ferguson, *Solitude and the Sublime: Romanticism and the Aesthetics of Individuation* (London: Routledge, 1992), chapter 2, "The Sublime of Edmund Burke, or the Bathos of Experience," 37–54; and Andrew Ashfield and Peter de Bolla, eds., *The Sublime: A Reader in Eighteenth-Century Aesthetic Theory* (Cambridge: Cambridge University Press, 1996).

shared with other human beings and animals, which produces a form of love unmixed with sexual desire. Under this second kind of love, in a phrase of underappreciated importance for his political theory, Burke lists sympathy, imitation, and ambition, the three "principal links" in the "great chain of society" (51, 42, 44).

Having placed sublimity and beauty within the broader context of his theory of the passions, Burke proceeds in Parts II and III of the *Enquiry* to an extended discussion of the intrinsic qualities that make an object either sublime or beautiful. In each case he offers examples to strengthen his argument that the sublime and beautiful are "ideas of a very different nature, one being founded on pain, the other on pleasure"; thus there is "an eternal distinction between them" (124).

Part II of the *Enquiry* is Burke's fullest account of the sources of the sublime, i.e., those conditions, characteristics, or attributes of an object that combine to produce the most powerful emotion of which the human mind is capable. There are two central concepts at work here. The first, as we have seen, is terror, "the common stock" and "ruling principle" of everything sublime, the lesser effects of which are "admiration, reverence and respect" (64, 57–58).

The second concept is contained in the section entitled "Power," which was added to the second edition of the *Enquiry*. Burke clearly links sublimity with power: "I know of nothing sublime which is not some modification of power." Furthermore, power is invariably connected to pain, and thus to terror, for "pain is always inflicted by a power in some way superior, because we never submit to pain willingly." Indeed, our first reaction before a man or animal of prodigious strength is terror at the prospect that such enormous power might be used for "rapine and destruction."[14] Burke drives home the point that "power derives all its sublimity from the terror with which it is generally accompanied" by considering the few cases in which it is possible to strip a sublime being of its strength, or its capacity for raping and pillaging. The result? "When you do this, you spoil it of every thing sublime, and it immediately becomes contemptible," since "contempt" is the natural response to "a strength that is subservient and innoxious." Why is this the case? For Burke, the answer is simple: "nothing can act agreeably to us, that does not act in conformity to our will; but to act agreeably to our will, it must be subject to us; and therefore can never be the cause of a grand and commanding conception" (64–66).

14. On this point, see Ryan, "Physiological Sublime," 274.

Burke illustrates this point in a stunning example of the difference between dogs and wolves. Dogs possess strength, speed, and other qualities "we" find convenient and pleasurable. In fact, he claims, they are the "most social, affectionate, and amiable animals of the whole brute creation." Yet, Burke informs us, "love approaches much nearer to contempt than is commonly imagined; and accordingly, though we caress dogs, we borrow from them an appellation of the most despicable kind, when we employ terms of reproach; and this appellation is the common mark of the last vileness and contempt in every language" (66–67). As we shall see, this argument and others like it, which equate love, beauty, weakness, subservience, and contempt in an indissoluble chain, would incur Mary Wollstonecraft's wrath.

Power is also key to understanding the (male) personification and most obvious political ramifications of the Burkean sublime. "The power which arises from institutions in kings and commanders, has the same connection with terror." Thus, for example, "sovereigns are frequently addressed with the title of *dread majesty*," and the young in particular "are commonly struck with an awe which takes away the free use of their faculties" when they face "men in power." In an argument analogous to the one he made in the *Note-Book*, Burke caps his discussion of the relation between sublimity, power, and terror with his description of God the Father. To the imagination, God's power is "by far the most striking"; "to be struck with his power, it is only necessary that we should open our eyes." However, when we do, we are virtually overwhelmed by a combination of terror and awe in the presence of omnipotence, and "we shrink into the minuteness of our own nature, and are, in a manner, annihilated before him." Consequently, we can never "wholly remove the terror that naturally arises from a force which nothing can withstand. If we rejoice, we rejoice with trembling... we cannot but shudder at a power which can confer benefits of such mighty importance" (67–68).[15]

In Part III of the *Enquiry* Burke explains his theory of beauty, that quality in human beings that causes love. As Burke has already informed his readers, love may be mixed with lust, but the two feelings are really distinguishable. We can love others, and we can love inanimate objects, without desiring them sexually, as "we" desire women. Now, beauty requires "no assistance from our reasoning"; in fact, "even the will is unconcerned" in the perception of beauty. Rather, "the appearance of beauty as effectu-

---

15. On this example, see ibid., 273–74.

ally causes some degree of love in us, as the application of ice or fire produces the ideas of heat or cold" (92).

As men personify sublimity, so women personify Burkean beauty. This is not to say that beauty and perfection are synonymous terms—quite the contrary. Beauty, "where it is highest in the female sex, almost always carries with it an idea of weakness and imperfection. Women are very sensible of this; for which reason, they learn to lisp, to totter in their walk, to counterfeit weakness, and even sickness. In all this, they are guided by nature. Beauty in distress is much the most affecting beauty.... Who ever said, we *ought* to love a fine woman, or even any of these beautiful animals, which please us?" (110).

As with things sublime, the irresistible (if imperfect) objects of beauty share their own particular set of characteristics. Beautiful objects are small and smooth. This is true of leaves, slopes of earth, streams, birds, beasts, "in fine women, smooth skins; and in several sorts of ornamental furniture, smooth and polished surfaces" (113–14). Beautiful bodies show gradual deviation. This is most obviously true of beautiful birds and, of course, women:

> Observe that part of a beautiful woman where she is perhaps most beautiful, about the neck and breasts; the smoothness; the softness; the easy and insensible swell; the variety of the surface, which is never for the smallest space the same; the deceitful maze, through which the unsteady eye slides giddily, without knowing where to fix, or whither it is carried. Is not this a demonstration of that change of surface continual and yet hardly perceptible at any point which forms one of the great constituents of beauty? (115)

Returning from his giddy reverie on female cleavage, Burke notes that strength is anathema to beauty. "An appearance of *delicacy*, and even of fragility, is almost essential to it." This is true of trees, dogs, horses, and, of course, women. "The beauty of women is considerably owing to their weakness, or delicacy, and is even enhanced by their timidity, a quality of mind analogous to it." Interestingly enough, to be beautiful, these weak and timid female bodies, with their smooth and swelling breasts, also should be fair and mild in color, like "weak whites," and never "dusky or muddy" (116–17). Burke concludes his extraordinary explication of the beautiful with a brief discussion relating specific senses to the broad characteristics of the beautiful he has sketched. Thus we find, for example, that what makes objects beautiful to the touch is "the slightness of the resistance they make" (120).

Burke ends Part III of the *Enquiry* by comparing directly the sublime and beautiful, and it is worth reiterating his gendered conclusions on this score. There appears to him a "remarkable contrast" between them. "There is a wide difference between admiration and love. The sublime, which is the cause of the former, always dwells on great objects, and terrible; the latter on small ones, and pleasing"; thus "we submit to what we admire, but we love what submits to us" (124, 113). As a result, in human relationships, "those virtues which cause admiration, and are of the sublimer kind, produce terror rather than love." Fortitude, justice, wisdom, and so on are the virtues of men; they do not make men "amiable." When we draw this comparison of the sublime and the beautiful down to "our first and most natural feelings," the implications are perfectly clear to Burke: "The authority of a father" in fact "hinders us from having that entire love for him that we have for our mothers, where the parental authority is almost melted down into the mother's fondness and indulgence" (110–11). This gendered reading of the principles of sublimity and beauty had profound implications for Burke's interpretation of the French Revolution, as we shall see presently. It also infuriated Mary Wollstonecraft, and thus played an important part in the creation of modern feminism, as well as of modern conservatism.

"Habitual Social Discipline": The Sublime and Beautiful Past

Burke's entire interpretation of the European civilizing process hinged on the appropriate deployment of the principles of the sublime and the beautiful through the institutions of the nobility and the church. In order to understand how, let us unpack Burke's "aesthetic" understanding of these two institutions.

The Nobility

As we know from our reading of the *English History*, Burke saw "feudal discipline" as one of the two great factors determining the character of the European civilizing process.[16] To recap, Burke had argued that Euro-

---

16. Burke, *Writings and Speeches*, 1:456, hereafter cited parenthetically in the text.

pean feudalism had ensured a shared system of manners among its adherents. Burke focused particularly on the relationship of "voluntary inequality and dependence" at the heart of the oath of fealty between lord and vassal. In the *English History*, Burke argued that fealty was built "upon two principles in our nature,—ambition, that makes one man desirous, at any hazard or expense, of taking the lead amongst others; and admiration, which makes others equally desirous of following him, from the mere pleasure of admiration, and a sort of secondary ambition, one of the most universal passions among men; these two principles, strong both of them in our nature, create a voluntary inequality and dependence" (1:431). Again we see that ambition and admiration, two principal motors of human conduct, are intimately connected to the sublime. And, like everything partaking of sublimity, the oath of fealty was ultimately rooted in terror transmuted into "delight"—or, in this case, acquiescence born of admiration in the face of superior power fueled by ambition.

But, while ambition and admiration provided the *masculine* bases for fealty, or voluntary servitude on the part of the masses, there was also a second, *feminine*, dimension to fealty, and it is this that Burke particularly stresses in the *Reflections*. Burke paid special attention to the feudal ethos of chivalry, which, he claimed, separated early modern Europe from all other societies. Burke insisted that chivalry "has given its character to modern Europe. It is this which has distinguished it under all its forms of government, and distinguished it to its advantage from the states of Asia." In Burke's view, "the old feudal and chivalrous spirit of *Fealty*" provided a mechanism for the peaceful production and reproduction of political, social, and gender inequality "without confounding ranks." Chivalric manners enabled the nobility to flourish free from fear, which in turn freed everyone from tyranny; thus all were "subdued by manners" (8:127, 129). To quote a well-known passage from the *Reflections*, chivalry was the "decent drapery of life" that provided "all the pleasing illusions, which made power gentle, and obedience liberal, which harmonized the different shades of life, and which, by a bland assimilation, incorporated into politics the sentiments which beautify and soften private society" (8:128).

In other words, chivalry played a crucial role in cementing voluntary inequality and dependence by beautifying the hierarchically structured body politic, thereby engaging the natural moral sentiment of attachment and deference of the common people for their superiors. It encouraged their fealty precisely by "embodying" beauty in such lovable chivalric icons as Marie Antoinette, who functioned as a national symbol of beauty. "There ought to be a system of manners in every nation which a well-formed mind would be disposed to relish. To make us love our country, our country ought to be lovely" (8:129). At the same time, however, chivalry also obliged sovereigns to submit to a code of manners ("the soft collar of social esteem") that mitigated the violence generally associated with their power (8:127).

Absent chivalry, there would be nothing to soften the harsh, sublime realities of political power, a power that rested on the ruling class's ability to produce terror in its subjects, such terror always providing the key to sublimity. Take away the chivalric code, and you would destroy natural social hierarchies, with dire consequences. Without the gloss of beautiful social manners, even the execution of the powerful might hold no special meaning; indeed, it might be seen as no more significant than the murder of a peasant, a patent absurdity for Burke: "On this scheme of things, a king is but a man; a queen is but a woman; a woman is but an animal; and an animal not of the highest order. All homage paid to the sex in general as such, and without distinct views, is to be regarded as romance and folly. Regicide, and parricide, and sacrilege, are but fictions of superstition, corrupting jurisprudence by destroying its simplicity. The murder of a king, or a queen, or a bishop, or a father, are only common homicide" (8:128).

Burke elaborated his view of the need for voluntary inequality and dependence, the sine qua non of a civilized polis, in *An Appeal from the New to the Old Whigs* (1791). Central to his argument in the *Appeal* is the notion that for "a people," properly understood, to exist, the masses must "be in that state of habitual social discipline, in which the wiser, the more expert, and the more opulent conduct, and by conducting enlighten and protect, the weaker, the less knowing, and the less provided with the goods of fortune. When the multitude are not under this discipline, they can scarcely be said to be in civil society."[17]

This is not mere rhetoric. Burke is quite clear that the "natural aristocracy" rested on the requisite level of "habitual social discipline" that fealty helped to provide. "When great multitudes act together, under that discipline of nature, I recognize the PEOPLE." Without such discipline, "the people" ceased to exist, and right social relations dissolved into anarchy. "When you disturb this harmony; when you break up this beautiful order, this array of truth and nature, as well as of habit and prejudice; when you separate the common sort of men from their proper chieftains, so as to

---

17. *Works of Burke*, 3:82, 85.

form them into an adverse army, I no longer know that venerable object called the People in such a disbanded race of deserters and vagabonds."[18]

The fundamental nature of this claim for understanding Burke's political theory cannot be overstated,[19] and it is profoundly consistent with his earlier work. Recall that in the *Account of the European Settlements in America* the Burkes had argued that the defining feature of the "government" of the Americans, understood in the broadest sense of that term, and the ultimate source of their "savagery," was their commitment to unfettered liberty and undue equality. Such liberty was the "darling passion" of savages, who fostered it by refusing to punish their children when educating them. Consequently, they failed to inculcate in the next generation the vital qualities of command, dependence, and subordination.[20]

Even Uday Mehta, the strongest advocate of the view that Burke was an anti-imperialist defender of cultural pluralism and difference, maintains that Burke's views on empire, including his views on India, were "integral to his broader political thinking," including his thinking about the French Revolution.[21] Mehta is right to argue that the central importance of social order as a requirement for individual liberty unifies Burke's writings, and to point out that Burke clearly specifies the conditions required for freedom. Mehta also acknowledges that these always include a "natural aristocracy" with a prescriptive claim to political authority, and a "spirit of religion" as a necessary prerequisite for bridling the spirit of liberty. Burke saw India and the American colonies as just such "well-ordered realities," and this enabled him simultaneously to defend the claims of the colonial settlers in the Americas and the native peoples of the Indian subcontinent.[22]

Mehta's view is accurate as far as it goes, but it does not go nearly far enough. In fact, Burke's concept of order suggests a very different interpretation of Burke's relation to the imperial project, particularly in the New World, one that is entirely consistent with his understanding of the French Revolution. Burke's commitment to "well-ordered" societies

18. Ibid., 3:85, 87.
19. On this theme, see especially John MacCunn, "What Is a People?" in his *Political Philosophy of Burke* (London: Edward Arnold, 1913), 50–67. See also Frans De Bruyn, "Edmund Burke's Natural Aristocrat: The 'Man of Taste' as a Political Ideal," *Eighteenth-Century Life* 11, no. 2 (1987): 41–60; and Donald Winch, *Riches and Poverty: An Intellectual History of Political Economy in Britain, 1750–1834* (Cambridge: Cambridge University Press, 1996), 180.
20. See Chapter 2.
21. See Uday Singh Mehta, *Liberalism and Empire: A Study in Nineteenth-Century British Liberal Thought* (Chicago: University of Chicago Press, 1999), 138–44, 166, 173, 179–82 (quoted at 153).
22. Ibid., 174, 162, 180–81 (quoted at 174).

governed by an elite standing atop a hierarchical system of ranks, aided by the putatively civilizing power of religion, was precisely what led him to defend the expansion of Britain's white brethren into the "savage" expanses of North America, to defend slavery as a means of "civilizing" the Africans, *and* to decry the French Revolution—which represented the breakdown of such order—as a reversion to savagery. Ultimately, it is the commitment to social hierarchy and order, and not a fondness for cultural pluralism and difference, that explains Burke's position on all of these issues.[23]

Moreover, by examining the sources of Burke's central concept of habitual social discipline, we can see how and why he believed that such hierarchy was entirely natural. Burke's view coincides with that of Adam Ferguson and his friends and associates in the Scottish Enlightenment, for whom civil society was, paradoxically, both natural as well as artificial. "The state of civil society, which necessarily generates this aristocracy," Burke agrees, "is a state of nature; and much more truly so than a savage and incoherent mode of life." This is because, in words that could have been taken from Ferguson himself, "art is man's nature." Thus some men

---

23. Indeed, the kinder, gentler Burke that emerges from Mehta's reading (which shows Burke arguing for the equivalence of British and Indian culture) is a fiction. Burke in fact saw a deeper theoretical divide, one that placed the Native Americans and African slaves firmly beyond the pale of civilization. Ironically, Mehta himself unwittingly alerts us to this when he quotes from one of Burke's famous speeches against imperial excess in India: "This multitude of men [Indians] does not consist of an abject and barbarous populace; much less of gangs of savages like the Guaranies and the Chiquitos, who wander on the waste borders of the Amazons, or the Plate" (Burke's speech on Fox's India bill, quoted ibid., 186). This remark clearly expresses an underlying theoretical consistency that enables Burke to treat Indian civilization as Britain's equal precisely by contrasting it to an alien world of savagery and barbarism ripe for imperial conquest. Similar theoretical strategies in the hands of others would impose a catastrophic fate on the groups in question by justifying their subjugation or obliteration. Luke Gibbons characterizes his own book, *Edmund Burke and Ireland*, as a study that "can be seen as complementing Mehta's focus on India by integrating Burke's aesthetics and his Irish background more fully into [Burke's] searching critiques of colonialism" (xii). I believe that Gibbons's argument, though a good deal more nuanced than Mehta's, is nevertheless susceptible to the same sort of criticism. For a similar, if briefer, difficulty, see James Conniff, *The Useful Cobbler: Edmund Burke and the Politics of Progress* (Albany: State University of New York Press, 1994), 133–35. A somewhat different version of the same general argument is made in Michel Fuchs, *Edmund Burke, Ireland, and the Fashioning of the Self* (Oxford: Voltaire Foundation, 1996). Fuchs concludes his often insightful reading of the *Account* by asserting that it shows Burke "suffocating beneath an accumulation of contradictions, political, historical, and personal" (110–11), in its failure, for example, to consistently condemn slavery and the slave trade. Where Fuchs sees contradiction, I see a deeper consistency, but not one that leads to the sorts of interpretive conclusions simultaneously endorsed by Mehta, Gibbons, and others. For a further articulation of these themes, see Daniel I. O'Neill and Margaret Kohn, "A Tale of Two Indias: Burke and Mill on Empire and Slavery in the West Indies and America," *Political Theory* 34, no. 2 (2006): 192–228.

"form in nature, as she operates in the common modification of society, the leading, guiding, and governing part." They are "the soul to the body, without which the man does not exist."[24]

The European "natural aristocracy" was born simultaneously of artifice and nature, the product of feudal fealty and the habitual social discipline it helped to infuse into the social fabric. The natural aristocracy was "an essential integrant part of any large body rightly constituted"; without it, Burke concluded, "there is no nation." The natural aristocracy derived principally from being "bred in a place of estimation" and needed to stand on "elevated ground." In order to emerge, it also required such additional equipage as the leisure to read, reflect, and converse with others from various walks of life, the chance to hold high military command, the opportunity to act as lawyers, judges, and professors, and to circulate among wealthy traders, as well as the opportunity to consistently appear before the public eye.[25] As scholars have pointed out, with rare exceptions it was in fact the *hereditary* male nobility who formed the natural aristocracy, because in the eighteenth century they were among the very few who could meet Burke's rather steep set of criteria.[26]

Women's capacity to embody the principle of beauty and be loved by the masses helped their aristocratic men govern smoothly. Along with the sublime (male) sources of fealty, chivalry thus acted as a powerful force, helping to ensure that the masses remained in a state of habitual social discipline. The nobility's contribution to the production of social harmony through fealty, or voluntary inequality and dependence, was what led Burke to regard that institution as one of two centrally responsible for the civilizing process in Europe.

Burke saw clearly that the destruction of the nobility was one of the French Revolution's central goals. By abolishing all vestiges of feudal privilege on the night of 4 August and seizing power in the National Assembly, the makers of the Revolution had destroyed chivalry, usurped the legitimate representative function of the natural aristocracy, and acted in the name of "a people." They did so on the pretense of the "pretended *rights of man*"; but, Burke insisted, these "cannot be the rights of the people. For to be a people, and to have these rights, are things incompatible. The one

---

24. *Works of Burke*, 3:86–87. For a discussion of Ferguson's claim, in *An Essay on the History of Civil Society*, that "art itself is natural to man," see Chapter 1 of this volume. For Burke's connection to Ferguson, see Chapter 2.
25. *Works of Burke*, 3:85–86.
26. See especially De Bruyn, "Edmund Burke's Natural Aristocrat."

supposes the presence, the other the absence, of a state of civil society."[27] With the breakdown of habitual social discipline and "civil"—that is to say, civilized—society, France was rapidly becoming instead "the tyranny of a licentious, ferocious, and savage multitude, without laws, manners, or morals, and which, so far from respecting the general sense of mankind, insolently endeavors to alter all the principles and opinions, which have hitherto guided and contained the world, and to force them into a conformity to their vows and actions."[28] In Burke's reading, the French had defied nature, ignored common sense as their proper guide, and declared war on natural hierarchy by declaring war on the nobility. The result was sure to be savagery.

The Church

The second great pillar in Burke's account of European civilization, the second institution that had made for habitual social discipline in the masses, was an established church, which inculcated the "spirit of religion." As with the nobility, Burke defends the spirit of religion on three interrelated bases: first, from the perspective of his epistemology of sense and feeling; second, on the basis of his narrative of history; and, third, through a defense of its "aesthetic" institutional function.

With regard to the first of these, Burke argues that, unlike the French, the British "feel inwardly, that religion is the basis of civil society, and the source of all good," and "that man is by his constitution a religious animal; that atheism is against, not only our reason but our instincts; and that it cannot prevail long." If, however, the British, in a fit of "drunken delirium" and riot after downing that heady potion drawn from the French "alembic of hell," should strip off Christianity like so much useless clothing, the second great source of European civilization would be irretrievably lost. Burke therefore takes pains to discuss the established church, the leading British prejudice that, together with his friend James Beattie, he believed stemmed from the "early received, and uniformly continued sense of mankind," or common sense.[29]

Second, in an argument that goes back to the *English History*, Burke contended that, everywhere in Europe, Christianity had historically pro-

27. *Works of Burke*, 3:95.
28. Ibid., 3:14.
29. Burke, *Writings and Speeches*, 8:141–43, hereafter cited parenthetically in the text.

vided the impetus for the civilizing process. Burke believed that Christianity, and especially the monasteries, had changed the rude and fierce manners of the early Britons, which transformed their laws and character, a trend that continued after the Norman Conquest. Along with feudalism and chivalry, this made the Christian religion one of the two civilizing forces in Europe. However, as Burke tells Depont in the *Reflections*, "your assembly set to sale the lands of the monastic orders," thus making the "spoil of the church" the "only resource of all their operations in finance; the vital principle of all their politics; the sole security for the existence of their power" (8:200, 171). The nationalization of church lands in France, which ruined the church financially in order to back the issuance of paper money (the *assignats*), thereby destroyed the second institution responsible for civilizing Europe.

But how, exactly, did Christianity shape the civilizing process? The third defense of religion that Burke offers in the *Reflections*, and undoubtedly the most important, answers this question. It pertains to the "aesthetic" institutional function of an organized church. Burke begins with a broad generalization about human social arrangements. "Society requires," he writes, that "the inclinations of men should frequently be thwarted, their will controlled, and their passions brought into subjection. This can only be done *by a power out of themselves;* and not, in the exercise of its function, subject to that will and to those passions which it is its office to bridle and subdue" (8:111). This external power, of course, is government, specifically, the institutions of the state. The question is how such power becomes perceived as legitimate, and this is where Burke sees the greatest role of the church.

An established church gave the state the appearance of legitimacy; it "consecrated the commonwealth" and its natural leaders, the aristocracy. Burke contends that this act could only be the effect of sublimity. It was therefore the unique role of the church to ensure political legitimacy by "infusing" the state with "such sublime principles" as exerted a "wholesome awe upon free citizens; because, in order to secure their freedom, they must enjoy some determinant portion of power" (8:143).[30]

In the *Enquiry*, as we have seen, Burke had argued that power, terror, and pain were inextricably linked; thus we fear our fathers and call the king "dread majesty." At the pinnacle of power and terror is God, whose

---

30. Here I am very much in agreement with Winch, *Riches and Poverty*, 186.

power is so great that it virtually overwhelms and annihilates us, freezing us into terrified submission, leaving us trembling in fear and stupefaction. The church's ability to legitimize the state in an act of sublime consecration is thus ultimately due to its connection with God the Father—the ultimate patriarchal power and therefore the ultimate terror. It is as the steward of his power on earth that an established church derives its consecrating function; by serving as a surrogate for an omnipotent God on earth, the church links secular with divine power and intention.

Burke insists that the need for citizens to approach the state with fear and awe is particularly important in the case of popularly elected governments.[31] This is because in such governments the share of responsibility that falls to any individual actor is necessarily small, and the reins of public opinion, necessarily weak. Consequently, he concludes, "a perfect democracy is therefore the most shameless thing in the world. As it is the most shameless, it is also the most fearless" (8:144). Quite simply, the masses pose a greater threat of tyrannizing over their legitimate representatives from the natural aristocracy when the sublime influence of the church is absent. Consecration ensures that the people, in making their nominations for political office, "will not appoint to the exercise of authority, as to a pitiful job, but as to an holy function." In the wake of this sublime act, both the nominating and the taking of office are powers "which any man may well tremble to give or to receive." Without the church, the people would soon forget the wisdom of their forefathers, destroy their inheritance, and come to believe that they were free to change the state as frequently as their fancy dictated, crumbling in only a few generations, like disconnected monads, into the "dust and powder of individuality," to be dispersed by the winds (8:145–46).

It was thus to defend an ongoing civilizing process that the state had been consecrated through a sublime religious establishment that helped ensure habitual social discipline among the masses. It did so principally by filling them with fearful reverence in the presence of the state's representatives, understood as extensions of God's will and his plan for the family of man on earth. The would-be reformer ought therefore to approach the

---

31. My reading of this portion of Burke's argument, in its emphasis on the connection between sublimity and consecration, shares a great deal in common with William Corlett's acutely attuned rendering of these passages in *Community Without Unity: A Politics of Derridian Extravagance* (Durham: Duke University Press, 1989), 131–35. I agree wholeheartedly with Corlett's formulation of a "Positive/Negative Fear Distinction" in Burke, and his assertion that democracy most assuredly constitutes the negative side of that dichotomy.

defects and corruptions of the state as he or she would the sublime and terrifying head of any family, or "little platoon" (8:97), the most basic building block of Burkean society. He should, in Burke's words, "approach to the faults of the state as to the wounds of a father, with pious awe and trembling solicitude" (8:146).

It is ultimately the church's consecration of the state that makes the Burkean polis a partnership in science and art, that mystical conservative communion between the living, the dead, and the yet to be born, the memorable "great primaeval contract of eternal society" (8:147). In this way the church made the state an ongoing moral project. According to Burke, the English considered the fusion of church and state essential; it was "the foundation of their whole constitution." In fact, church and state were "ideas inseparable in their minds" (8:149).

Under normal circumstances, therefore, in addition to teaching the masses the just measure of fear required for their discipline and obedience to a system of social ranks, the church also educated the nobility. As in the *English History*, Burke argued in the *Reflections* that the monastic monopoly on education remained intact in England, and that learning was appropriately transmitted through the church to the nobility. "Our education is in a manner wholly in the hands of ecclesiastics, and in all stages from infancy to manhood.... By this connection we conceive that we attach our gentlemen to the church; and we liberalize the church by an intercourse with the leading characters of the country" (8:149–50). Burke argued that the English had clung so tenaciously to the old ecclesiastical educational institutions that very little about them had changed since the fourteenth or fifteenth century. Here we see clearly Burke's commitment to the intertwined and mutually reinforcing relation of the church and the nobility.

In Burke's view, then, civilization was a historical achievement that required a balanced institutional alchemy of the sublime and the beautiful. Burkean politics necessitated the judicious use of both carrot and stick to keep the masses in that state of habitual social discipline vital for a people, as opposed to a simple gaggle of aimless individuals, to emerge and develop in a civilized fashion. The nobility dangled the carrot of beauty, enabling the nonviolent reproduction of fealty, or voluntary inequality and servitude, by engaging the affections of the masses for their superiors. The church wielded the stick of sublimity via awe, fear, and the threat of divine eternal retribution, thereby ensuring that God's representatives, drawn from the natural aristocracy, would be obeyed by the common folk.

Natural Moral Sentiments and the Fear of Contagion

By 1790 Burke had already begun to fear the spread of the French Revolution and thus the destruction of Western civilization. By obliterating its two institutional pillars, the Revolution threatened to send Europe reeling into savagery. He noted in the *Reflections*, as he had in the *English History*, that the British had always adopted their system of manners from the French. Quoting Virgil, Burke called the French *gentis incunabula nostrae*—the cradle of the English people. Thus, he tells the Frenchman Depont, "France has always more or less influenced manners in England; and when your fountain is choked up and polluted, the stream will not run long, or not run clear with us, or perhaps with any nation. This gives all Europe, in my opinion, but too close and connected a concern in what is done in France." From the beginning, then, Burke thought of the French Revolution as "a plague," and urged that "the most severe quarantine ought to be established against it" (8:131, 140).

Burke then posed an important rhetorical question to his readers: why does he "feel" so differently from Richard Price and other radicals who wished to see the Revolution's principles spread across the channel. "Because it is *natural* I should" (8:131). Burke's extended response to this query is built entirely on the philosophical presuppositions of his early work.[32] Expanding on the reasons for his "natural" opposition to the destruction of the French monarchy, Burke insists it is "because we are so made as to be affected at such spectacles" in a particular fashion: "In those natural feelings we learn great lessons; because in events like these our passions instruct our reason.... *We are alarmed into reflection*; our minds (as it has long since been observed) are purified by terror and pity; our weak unthinking pride is humbled, under the dispensations of a mysterious wisdom" (8:131–32, emphasis added). Here Burke relies on the categories of the *Enquiry* to reiterate his long-standing argument that civilization, predicated upon ranks, is ultimately rooted in natural feelings, and the parenthetical insertion in this passage is clearly self-referential. Indeed, Burke identifies the very title of his magnum opus as an effect of the sublime.

Years after writing his treatise on the sublime and the beautiful, and after his immersion in Smith's *Theory of Moral Sentiments* and Beattie's com-

---

32. For the standard discussion of the language of "nature" in the *Reflections*, one that foregrounds the importance of the *Enquiry* to an understanding of the text, see James T. Boulton, *The Language of Politics in the Age of Wilkes and Burke* (London: Routledge and Kegan Paul, 1963), chapter 7.

mon sense philosophy, Burke's fundamental understanding of the basis of morality had not changed: "Nature" calls in "the aid of her unerring and powerful instincts, to fortify the fallible and feeble contrivances of our reason" (8:84) in accordance with God's mysterious wisdom, thereby providing the common ground for the shared sympathetic responses codified in the social morality of manners. Burke saw events in France as a revolt against the natural moral order and the social hierarchies built upon it.[33] In words suffused with the assumptions of Scottish moral sense philosophy and his own *Enquiry*, Burke declared that the revolutionaries "are so taken up with their theories about the rights of man, that they have totally forgotten his nature. Without opening one new avenue to the understanding, they have succeeded in stopping up those that lead to the heart. They have perverted in themselves, and in those that attend to them, all the well-placed sympathies of the human breast" (8:115).

These remarks precede the "apostrophe," or celebration of Marie Antoinette, the most famous passage in the *Reflections* and thus in all Burke's writings. It is vital for our understanding of Burke's exclamation to recognize the extent to which it is an attack on the perversion of natural morals and attendant social manners of the revolutionaries, which promised civilization's collapse, an argument structured around the epistemology of sense and feeling that Burke derived from the Scottish Enlightenment and his own early philosophical work.

"*Influenced by the inborn feelings of my nature*," Burke exclaims, "the exalted rank of the persons suffering, and particularly the sex, the beauty, and the amiable qualities of the descendant of so many kings and emperors... *adds not a little to my sensibility on that most melancholy occasion.*" It is Marie Antoinette's beauty in particular that affects Burke at the prerational level, which activates his common sense or natural sensibility as he ponders the momentous events of 6 October 1789. In his most famous passage we thus find him arguing, in a fashion consistent with everything he ever wrote on the topic, for the legitimacy of inborn instincts and natural sensibility as the appropriate measure of our response to moral phenomena. He claims that, "as a man," it was natural for Louis XVI to feel similarly; moreover, "as a prince, it became him to feel for the strange and frightful transformation of his civilized subjects" (8:125, emphasis added).

33. On this point, see De Bruyn, "Edmund Burke's Natural Aristocrat"; and two works by Rodney W. Kilcup, "Reason and the Basis of Morality in Burke," *Journal of the History of Philosophy* 17, no. 3 (1979): 271–84, and "Burke's Historicism," *Journal of Modern History* 49 (September 1977): 394–410.

Marie Antoinette thus figures in Burke's work as the sentient embodiment of European civilization, the culmination, as it were, of a process that led from rude savagery and barbarism to the polish and refinement of hierarchical, civilized, commercial society. In describing her as he did, Burke sought to play on the sensibility of his readers, encouraging them to come to her defense and thereby to the defense of the old order. Burke's famous apostrophe represents in condensed form the paean to female beauty he had penned in the *Enquiry*, a depiction of beauty that was meant to irresistibly attach the natural moral sentiments of the masses to her, thus ensuring that the broader institution of the nobility, which she literally "embodied," remained loved and worthy of their voluntary servitude. This is why Burke paints such an extraordinary picture of Marie, drawn from his mind's eye, as she looked when still the young dauphiness, when he saw her on his only trip to France, in 1773. "Surely," he wrote, "never lighted on this orb, which she hardly seemed to touch, a more delightful vision. I saw her just above the horizon, decorating and cheering the elevated sphere she just began to move in,—glittering like the morning-star, full of life, and splendor, and joy" (8:126).

The hardheaded point of this most romantic of Burkean images is that the French Revolution had destroyed this beautiful creature, together with the institutions that had made her possible in the first instance, and this served as a marker of its broader threat. Marie was on the brink of destruction, and so was civilization itself. Swords no longer leapt from scabbards, chivalry was dead, and European civilization was on the verge of extinction.

As we know, the thinkers of the Scottish Enlightenment had celebrated chivalry for its treatment of women in supposedly progressive ways that differentiated and privileged Europe's civilized system of manners from that of barbarians and savages.[34] For Burke, however, chivalry was even more important than that, for it helped to guarantee fealty and habitual social discipline. What Burke truly lamented in the eclipse of chivalric manners was the loss of "that generous loyalty to rank and sex, that proud submission, that dignified obedience, that subordination of the heart, which kept alive, even in servitude itself, the spirit of an exalted freedom." Burke mourned the loss of the "sensibility of principle" that inspired voluntary

---

34. On this theme, see Pocock's introduction to Burke's *Reflections*, xxxii–xxxiii; his "Political Economy of Burke's Analysis," 197–98; and his "Burke and the Redefinition of Enthusiasm," 31–32.

acquiescence to hierarchy, through which "vice itself lost half its evil, by losing all its grossness" (8:127).[35]

We see what is "naturally" supposed to happen under the chivalric system of manners when Marie Antoinette, the very apotheosis of beauty, is attacked. In the *Reflections*, Burke brings the argument of the *Enquiry* to bear on his assertion that, in the absence of a perversion of our moral sentiments, God has so constituted human beings as to make them feel pity for the French royal family. Burke had argued in the *Enquiry* that sympathy might in fact turn on pain, thus connecting it with self-preservation and making it a source of the sublime; or it might turn on pleasure, connecting it with society and beauty. He drew a rather controversial conclusion from this analysis, that "we have a degree of delight, and that no small one, in the real misfortunes and pains of others," because "terror is a passion which always produces delight when it does not press too close." This conclusion follows strictly from Burke's premises. It is easy to see how the pleasant experiences of others make for fellow feeling, but Burke must explain, in a fashion consistent with his initial assumptions, how human sympathy is possible in the face of "wretchedness, misery, and death itself." The answer is simple: "As our Creator has designed we should be united by the bond of sympathy, he has strengthened that bond by a proportionable delight; and there most where our sympathy is most wanted, in the distresses of others." This delight, however, is not "unmixed" but is "blended with no small uneasiness." The delight we take in scenes of misery keeps us from shunning them, while the pain we feel prompts us to relieve ourselves by relieving those who suffer.[36]

---

35. On this point, consider Burke's reply to his sometime friend and intellectual foil, Philip Francis, who informed Burke that in his opinion everything he had written about the queen in this passage was "pure foppery." In a wounded response that presaged the end of their friendship, Burke implored Francis: "Is it absurd in me, to think that the Chivalrous Spirit which dictated a veneration for Women of condition and of Beauty, without any consideration whatsoever of enjoying them, was the great Source of those manners which have been the Pride and ornament of Europe for so many ages? . . . I tell you again that the recollection of the manner in which I saw the Queen of France in the year 1774 [actually 1773] and the contrast between that brilliancy, Splendor, and beauty, with the prostrate Homage of a Nation to her, compared with the abominable Scene of 1789 which I was describing did draw Tears from me and wetted my Paper. These Tears came again into my Eyes almost as often as I looked at the description. They may again. You do not believe this fact, or that these are my real feelings, but that the whole is affected, or as you express it, 'downright Foppery'. My friend, I tell you it is truth—and that it is true, and will be true, when you and I are no more, and will exist as long as men—with their Natural feelings exist." See Burke, *Correspondence*, 6:88–92 (20 February 1790), quoted at 90–91. For Francis's letter, see 85–87.

36. Burke, *Enquiry*, 44–46.

To watch royalty suffer is thus to experience terror at a distance, by definition the "delightful" experience of the sublime that Burke describes in the *Enquiry*. Delight keeps us from turning away from the horrid sight of the royal family's plight, while the pain we naturally feel when confronted with it prompts us to relieve ourselves by relieving them. We pity the assailed Bourbon monarchs, feel compelled to act accordingly, and thus to intervene and prevent further harm to them.

At least we do so if we are the British, and are not in the midst of a perverse revolution that "shock[s] the moral sentiments of all virtuous and sober minds" (8:173). Burke took great pains to contrast the situation on the two sides of the channel in this respect:

> In England we have not been completely emboweled of our natural entrails; we still feel within us, and we cherish and cultivate, those inbred sentiments which are the faithful guardians, the active monitors of our duty, the true supporters of all liberal and manly morals.... We preserve the whole of our feelings still native and entire, unsophisticated by pedantry and infidelity. We have real hearts of flesh and blood beating in our bosoms. We fear God; we look up with awe to kings, with affection to parliaments; with duty to magistrates; with reverence to priests; and with respect to nobility. Why? Because when such ideas are brought before our minds, it is *natural* to be so affected; because all other feelings are false and spurious, and tend to corrupt our minds, to vitiate our primary morals, to render us unfit for rational liberty. (8:137–38)

As Burke had argued in the *Enquiry*, fear of God is entirely natural, as are the secondary effects of the sublime associated with kings, magistrates, priests, and (male) nobility (awe, duty, reverence, and respect). The common feature is the underlying sense of terror felt at the prospect of power being used to inflict pain. Simultaneously, however, Burke believed that the instinctive social passions built chiefly upon sympathetic fellow feeling were capable of softening and beautifying the harsh realities of this power, thereby producing a system of manners that enabled European civilization to flourish.

These normal conditions still prevailed in England, which had not undergone a perverse revolution led by the mad converts of Rousseau, Voltaire, and Helvetius. The English had not yet been philosophized into "savages"; they had not "lost the generosity and dignity of thinking of the fourteenth century," and they knew that "no discoveries are to be made, in morality"; thus they did not act in "defiance of the process of nature" (8:137, 218).

Such a viewpoint enables us to grasp more fully one of those quintessential Burkean concepts, "prejudice." Burke maintained that the British were "generally men of untaught feelings" who not only cherished their prejudices but "the longer they have lasted, and the more generally they have prevailed, the more we cherish them." To understand what Burke meant by prejudice, it is essential to recognize its connection to Scottish Enlightenment arguments. Burke argued that the British were afraid to rely on any individual's reason, both because it was small and because individuals would do better to avail themselves of the accumulated wisdom of the ages. He notes in this regard that "many of our men of speculation" attempt to "discover the latent wisdom" that prevails in prejudices, because "they think it more wise to continue the prejudice, with the reason involved, than to cast away the coat of prejudice" (8:138). "Our men of speculation" probably refers directly to the philosophers of the Scottish Enlightenment

For Burke as for those thinkers, manners were the embodiment of the code of social morality, the crystallization and manifestation of instinctive human nature. Taken together, the nobility and church, along with the specific beliefs they transmitted, were what Burke meant by the collective term "prejudice." Prejudices, then, can be understood in Burke's lexicon as the concrete expression of the prevailing network of morals and manners in a given society; as such, they expressed a form of reason, even if they seemed irrational. Why? Because the reason and wisdom they reflected was God's, implanted in the species, largely incomprehensible through the individual's rational faculties but affectively intuited and expressed in the totality of human social relations.

Thus Burke agreed with Adam Ferguson, Adam Smith, and the other Scottish defenders of the concept of spontaneously generated social orders, that large-scale institutions and human social interactions were so intricate as to fall beyond an individual's or group's capacity for rational design. As Burke put it, in a sentence that could have been written by Adam Ferguson himself: "The nature of man is intricate; the objects of society are of the greatest possible complexity." Consequently, "the science of constructing a commonwealth" should not "be taught *a priori*," because "the real effects of moral causes are not always immediate." Instead, that which begins ill may turn out well, and vice versa. Similarly, "in states there are often some obscure and almost latent causes, things which appear at first view of little moment, on which a very great part of its prosperity or adversity may most essentially depend" (8:111–12).

It seems that Burke had learned well the law of unintended consequences from his Scottish Enlightenment friends. For them, too, the science of government, as a crucial part of the science of man, should not proceed *a priori* but inductively and empirically, with full awareness of the human animal's limited rational capacity. As Ferguson had argued, no government, and no constitution (at least no good one) could result from a plan; such things were complex networks of social machinery derived from innumerable, unplanned individual actions accreting over long stretches of time. Burke, following the Scots, contended that prejudices, or the received matrix of social manners and their institutional vehicles of transmission, should govern our behavior. For both Burke and the Scots, recourse to such prejudices was all to the good because "through just prejudice, [man's] duty becomes a part of his nature" (8:138).

In the *English History* Burke had argued that the civilizing force of manners provided the basis for Britain's ancient constitution, which evolved slowly as a result of changes in manners, producing important changes in law and governments over time. Similarly, the complex sociopolitical system of European civilization and its underlying system of manners had to be treated with reverential awe, as an "*entailed inheritance* derived to us from our forefathers, and to be transmitted to our posterity." At bottom this is because such institutions were the "happy product of following nature, which is wisdom without reflection, and above it" (8:83).[37]

We find a similar connection in the vaunted Burkean defense of "prescription," or Burke's preference for titles or rights established by long, uninterrupted use and possession from time immemorial. In the *Reflections* Burke railed against the confiscation of property carried out by the French National Assembly as an act that "openly reprobate[d] the doctrine of prescription," which had sanctified earlier expressions of might and, "through long usage, mellow[ed] into legality governments that were violent in their commencement" (8:200, 213).[38]

---

37. See Chapter 2.
38. In a letter he wrote later to Captain Thomas Mercer, who was fighting in France, Burke expanded on the concept, claiming that "*prescription*... gives right and title. It is possible that many estates about you were originally obtained by arms, that is, by violence... but it is *old violence;* and that which might be wrong in the beginning, is consecrated by time, and becomes lawful." See letter of 26 February 1790, *Correspondence,* 6:95.

Burke's notion of prescription has received interesting treatment from scholars,[39] but the similarity between his understanding of the concept and that of the Scots, most notably Hume, has generally gone unnoticed.[40] Of course, for Burke, unlike Hume, inherited constitutional forms were the products of a progressive theory of social manners understood as the empirical embodiment of natural morality, itself slowly progressing over time. For Burke, prescription was rooted in prejudice, and prejudice was rooted in nature.

This is not to say that changes in the constitution could not theoretically occur—as conservative readers of Burke have always been especially fond of insisting. But any such alterations had to be slow and incremental, as if conducted under the gaze of those fearsome patriarchs, the "canonized forefathers" of yesteryear, themselves ultimately suffused with the power attendant upon all sublimity, ensuring that any changes, no matter how small, would be "tempered with an awful gravity." Thus Burke tells Depont that the British "have chosen our nature rather than our speculations, our breasts rather than our inventions, for the great conservatories and magazines of our rights and privileges" (8:85).

The French, however, had foolishly proceeded in the opposite direction. They had cast off religion and encouraged "a ferocious dissoluteness in manners" (8:88). France might have retained all its old hierarchical orders and had an "obedient people, taught to seek and to recognize the happiness that is to be found by virtue in all conditions; in which consists the true moral equality of mankind." Instead, the masses were taken in by a "monstrous fiction," an idea that inspired false and vain expectations that served "only to aggravate and embitter that real inequality, which it never can remove." The French thus taught their king, the father of their nation, to "tremble" in the face of the "delusive plausibilities, of moral politicians." "This was unnatural," Burke writes; therefore, "the rest is in order" (8:87–89).[41] In truth, for Burke, the rest was complete disorder.

---

39. See J. G. A. Pocock, "Burke and the Ancient Constitution: A Problem in the History of Ideas," *Historical Journal* 3, no. 2 (1960): 125–43, which considers Burke in the British common law tradition; and Paul Lucas, "On Edmund Burke's Doctrine of Prescription; or, An Appeal from the New to the Old Lawyers," *Historical Journal* 11, no. 1 (1968): 35–63.

40. Hume wrote, "Time and custom give authority to all forms of government, and all successions of princes; and that power, which at first was founded only on injustice and violence, becomes in time legal and obligatory." *A Treatise of Human Nature*, ed. L. A. Selby-Bigge (Oxford: Clarendon Press, 1896), III.ii.10, p. 566.

41. Burke tells his readers elsewhere that the French "seem in everything to have strayed out of the high road of nature" (8:103).

Burke on Democratic Savagery:
The Democratization of the Public Sphere

In the aftermath of the destruction of civilization's two principal institutional conduits, what was the nature of the savagery that ensued, according to Burke? What was the "monstrous fiction" at the heart of the French Revolution, before which its king trembled? What did the death of Western civilization look like? The short answer is that the collapse of civilization meant the rise of a shameless political, social, and cultural democracy that undermined the innate moral sentiments of the masses and transformed them from disciplined and docile subjects into fearless participatory citizens. Once the institutions of church and nobility were thrown off, discipline and obedience broke down, and Burke watched in horror as the savage democratic swine ran amok.

Given the "materials" of which the French National Assembly was composed, the results of revolutionary folly were "inevitable" and "necessary," "planted in the nature of things." The French method of proceeding was directly opposite to that of the British House of Commons, an institution filled with "every thing illustrious in rank, in descent, in hereditary and acquired opulence, in cultivated talents, in military, civil, naval, and political distinction, that the country can afford" (8:91, 94–95). Burke's assessment of this "material" has been conveniently ignored by many scholars, from the older natural law school to the architects of the new scholarly orthodoxy on Burke and empire, with misleading interpretive consequences when it comes to assessing Burke's animating political passions.

The foremost of Burke's antipathies was what he regarded as the French revolutionaries' attempts to establish a "despotic democracy" based on popular sovereignty and broad public participation, one opposed to "reciprocal control" and thus anathema to all of "the principles of the British constitution." If democracy was adopted as a legitimate form of government, it would mean that "the house of lords is, at one stroke, bastardized and corrupted in blood. That house is no representative of the people," in either form or semblance (8:184, 107). Burke asked incredulously, "Is it then a truth so universally acknowledged, that a pure democracy is the only tolerable form into which human society can be thrown, that a man is not permitted to hesitate about its merits, without the suspicion of being a friend to tyranny, that is, of being a foe to mankind?" (8:173–74; see also 132).

Burke did much more than hesitate when it came to democracy. As Don Herzog has recently made clear in his extraordinary book on the rise of conservatism,[42] Burke's profound contempt for the impertinent lower orders and their new-fangled public agency is one of the most striking features of his writings on the French Revolution. To take only one example, Burke argues in the *Reflections* that "the occupation of an hair-dresser, or of a working tallow-chandler, cannot be a matter of honor to any person—to say nothing of a number of other more servile employments. Such descriptions of men ought not to suffer oppression from the state; but the state suffers oppression, if such as they, either individually or collectively, are permitted to rule. In this you think you are combating prejudice, but you are at war with nature" (8:100–101).[43]

Burke warns the French that their egalitarianism is "like a palsy" that "has attacked the foundation of life itself." But "those who attempt to level," he says, "never equalize. In all societies, consisting of various descriptions of citizens, some description must be uppermost. The levellers therefore only change and pervert the natural order of things." Burke scoffs at "the artificers and clowns, and money-jobbers, usurers, and Jews" enfranchised by democratic politics, and at the absurd notion that such people could be the "fellows" or even the "masters" of the old nobility (8:100). Elsewhere he objects that no political scheme underwritten by "shameless women of the lowest condition, by keepers of hotels, taverns, and brothels, by pert apprentices, by clerks, shop-boys, hair-dressers, fiddlers, and dancers on the stage" could possibly culminate in a social and political world that was anything other than "both disgraceful and destructive" (8:297).

Two years after the *Reflections* appeared, Burke wrote a letter to his friend and fellow MP, William Weddell, in which he clearly articulated his fear that the French disease of leveling, that monstrous fiction which had mutated into a plague incapable of being quarantined, would spread to Britain. Burke argued that Charles James Fox and his "New Whig" compatriots, themselves aristocrats, were unwittingly furthering their own demise by supporting the Revolution. Burke insisted again that the French revolutionaries' goal was the destruction of the natural aristocracy in its entirety through the obliteration of the natural moral sentiments on which inequality was built, and their subsequent replacement by the unwashed democratic masses. He tells Weddell that if honor exists it must be sought in

42. Don Herzog, *Poisoning the Minds of the Lower Orders* (Princeton: Princeton University Press, 1998).
43. Herzog's chapter, "The Trouble with Hairdressers" (ibid., 455–504), is particularly edifying.

men the best born, and the best bred, and in those possessed of rank which raises them in their own esteem, and in the Esteem of others, and possessed of hereditary settlement in the same place, which secures with an hereditary wealth, an hereditary inspection.—That these should all be Scoundrels; and that the Virtue, honor, and public Spirit of a Nation should be only found in its Attorneys, Pettyfoggers, Stewards of Manors, discarded officers of Police, shop boys, Clerks of Counting houses, and rustics from the Plough, is a paradox, not of false ingenuity, but of Envy and Malignity. It is an error not of the head but of the heart. The whole man is turned upside down before such an inversion of all Natural Sentiment, and all natural reason, can take place.[44]

As Linda Zerilli has argued, however, and as we have already seen in Burke's description of the October Days, the political consequences of the French Revolution's affront to the natural order of things were perhaps played out most clearly and dramatically for Burke in the spectacle of political women acting in the revolutionary public sphere.[45] Burke writes that the assembly was overseen by "women lost to shame, who, according to their insolent fancies, direct, control, applaud, explode . . . and sometimes mix and take their seats amongst [the men]; domineering over them with a strange mixture of servile petulance and proud presumptuous authority." Such female political agency was to make a "farce of deliberation," to transform the "sacred institute" of a representative national assembly into a "profane burlesque" and an "abominable perversion," one that had completely lost the guidance of its natural leaders and utterly abandoned its consecrated nature. By such abominable acts as enabling fearless women to participate in politics, the assembly had become a product of the devil himself (8:119).

Of course, Burke could never bring himself to believe that the Revolution's democratizing impulse was rooted in genuine popular discontent with the Old Regime in France. Rather, he consistently interpreted the French Revolution as a dark, insidious plot foisted on the masses by a small cabal of *philosophes* and their political allies. As early as 1790, years before the Terror, Burke had maintained that the academies were acting as "seminaries" for the "polluted nonsense" of the *philosophes*. Politicians

44. See Burke, *Correspondence*, 7:50–63 (31 January 1792), quoted at 62.
45. See Zerilli, "The 'Furies of Hell': Woman in Burke's 'French Revolution,'" in Zerilli, *Signifying Woman*, 60–94.

who imbibed such ideas in coffee houses were in turn backed by nothing more than "the terror of the bayonet, and the lamp-post, and the torch to their houses" (8:118).

In such passages, which grew increasingly frequent and shrill after the *Reflections*, Burke described what he was seeing not as the erasure of the principle of sublimity with the breakdown of established religion, but rather its transmogrification and terrifying deployment in the service of the revolutionaries, who were creating a world shorn of the softening principles of beauty and voluntary fealty to the nobility. "In the groves of *their* academy, at the end of every vista, you see nothing but the gallows. Nothing is left which engages the affections on the part of the commonwealth ... our institutions can never be embodied, if I may use the expression, in persons; so as to create in us love, veneration, admiration, or attachment" (8:128–29).

It has long been a favorite argument of Burkeans generally, whether "conservative" or "liberal," that what Burke objected to about the French Revolution was its recourse to political violence and terror in the service of radical change, rather than gradual reform from within the parameters of the Old Regime, which, they argue, he might have welcomed, or at least tolerated. Leaving aside the claim sometimes made by such scholars that the French Revolution was "totalitarian," a uniquely twentieth-century phenomenon that has no meaning in the eighteenth century, it is worth noting that from the beginning Burke's adversaries, whether Philip Francis, Thomas Paine, or Mary Wollstonecraft, always attacked him for what they perceived as his sympathy for Marie Antoinette and the corrupt French Catholic Church at the expense of the masses who suffered under Bourbon absolutism. In their own ways, all of these critics contended that for the vast majority of French people, the *ancien régime* was far more terrifying than the French Revolution, and that Burke's "beautiful" nobility, far from softening the harsh blows of life under the Old Regime, was an institution centrally implicated in administering them.[46]

Regardless of which of these arguments one finds more compelling, it is abundantly clear from all of Burke's writings on the topic that he regarded

---

46. For Philip Francis's side of the exchange of letters regarding Burke's *Reflections*, see Burke, *Correspondence*, 6:85–87 and 150–55 (letters dated 19 February 1789 and 3–4 November 1790). For Paine, see *The Rights of Man*, ed. Gregory Claeys (Indianapolis: Hackett, 1992). For Wollstonecraft, see Chapters 5 and 7 of this volume. For the conservative claim that Burke was resisting "totalitarianism," see Peter Stanlis, *Edmund Burke and the Natural Law* (Ann Arbor: University of Michigan Press, 1958), 247–48; for the liberal version, see

the French Revolution as a kind of democratic revolution from above. As for the people themselves, he consistently deprived them of any intellectual or political agency in the revolutionary drama. They were mere dupes of the *philosophes*, whose absurd theories were backed by the sublimity of power, terror, and fear. Burke clearly believed that once the yoke of habitual social discipline, that admixture of fear and love, was rashly thrown off, the ignorant masses would lose their bearings completely and drift in a dangerously aimless way. "As to the people at large, when once these miserable sheep have broken the fold, and have got themselves loose, not from the restraint, but from the protection of all the principles of natural authority, and legitimate subordination, they became the natural prey of imposters." For Burke, France in the 1790s was increasingly under the dominion of such democratic charlatans, who "pretend[ed] to have made discoveries in the *terra australis* of morality."[47]

Whether one agrees or disagrees with Burke as to the driving force behind the French Revolution—an intellectual cabal leading the ignorant masses away from their objective interests or authentic popular discontent—this is an old, ideologically freighted debate that need not concern us. The question we might fruitfully pursue concerns Burke's interpretation of the nature and meaning of the discoveries that these philosophic imposters claimed to have made in the new land of uncharted morality, and how they came to play such a major role in his thinking about the significance of the French Revolution. At the heart of this assessment, I argue, lay the revolutionaries' attempt, as Burke saw it, to support the shift toward political democratization with radical social and cultural democratization. I also want to make clear that Burke understood these twin aspects of democratization as necessarily intertwined and mutually reinforcing, and that he believed that the evil genius of the Revolution's leaders lay in their attempt to foster democracy as a total way of life. By looking carefully at Burke's post-*Reflections* writings, we can see the extraordinary extent to which he believed that deep democracy was the realization of the nightmare of savagery; as we will see presently, it was Mary Wollstonecraft's dream of civilization.

Conor Cruise O'Brien, *The Great Melody: A Thematic Biography of Edmund Burke* (Chicago: University of Chicago Press, 1992), 596, 608.

47. Burke, *A Letter to a Member of the National Assembly* (1791), in *Writings and Speeches*, 8:300, 305.

5 | VINDICATING A REVOLUTION IN MORALS AND MANNERS

Mary Wollstonecraft's *A Vindication of the Rights of Men* was the first published reply to Burke's *Reflections on the Revolution in France*. She wrote it hastily. Burke's work appeared on the first of November 1790, and her answer, initially anonymous, was in print by the end of the month. In December a second edition, bearing her name on the title page, appeared.[1] In this chapter I argue that we can best understand Wollstonecraft's direct contribution to the Revolution controversy as a critique of Burke's moral theory and the historical narrative used to defend it, seen through the lens of her own critical engagement with Scottish Enlightenment moral philosophy and historiography. In response to Burke's deployment of the language of instinctive "common sense" feelings, or "sensibility," as a means of naturalizing the historical development of political, social, and gender hierarchies, Wollstonecraft argued that these forms of inequality were not only pernicious but socially constructed. Her chief claim was that morals were virtues learned only through the exercise of reason, and that hierarchies of all sorts had created an artificial system of manners over the course of European history that worked to stunt the development of virtue, and thus of civilization. Wollstonecraft asserted that all such hierarchies had to be replaced by new relationships constructed on the basis of democratic equality, and she believed that this was the great potential of the French Revolution.

Wollstonecraft's first *Vindication* zeroes in on the core of Burke's argument, showing that his vision of history depends on a particular understanding of the role played by the nobility and church. By linking historical analysis of these two institutions with a sharp critique of Burkean moral theory, Mary Wollstonecraft emerges as Edmund Burke's most powerful critic. Moreover, as I show in the second half of this chapter, her critique of Burke also acted as a springboard for the foundational work of modern feminism, *A Vindication of the Rights of Woman* (1792). Feminism's most

---

1. All quotations of Wollstonecraft are from *The Works of Mary Wollstonecraft*, ed. Janet Todd and Marilyn Butler, 7 vols. (New York: New York University Press, 1989), hereafter cited as *Works of Wollstonecraft*.

famous early work can thus be read as part of an extended reply to the founding father of modern conservatism, occasioned by the French Revolution and forged by a radical egalitarian who had appropriated and utterly transformed the Scottish Enlightenment discourses of moral philosophy and historiography.[2]

False Sensibility and Faulty Historiography: Wollstonecraft's Reply to Burke

Identifying Burke as a Theorist of "Common Sense," or "Sensibility"

In the short "advertisement" affixed to *A Vindication of the Rights of Men*, Wollstonecraft writes that in reading Burke's *Reflections* she soon became indignant at "the sophistical arguments, that every moment crossed me, in the questionable shape of natural feelings and common sense." The importance of this remark for understanding Wollstonecraft's overall political theory is difficult to overestimate. From the outset, she categorized

---

2. In Chapter 7 I extend this argument to Wollstonecraft's lesser-known but tremendously important *Historical and Moral View of the Origin and Progress of the French Revolution*. In interpreting the *Vindications*, what follows is particularly indebted to Virginia Sapiro, *A Vindication of Political Virtue: The Political Theory of Mary Wollstonecraft* (Chicago: University of Chicago Press, 1992), and Barbara Taylor, *Mary Wollstonecraft and the Feminist Imagination* (Cambridge: Cambridge University Press, 2003). I have also benefited from Gary Kelly, *Revolutionary Feminism: The Mind and Career of Mary Wollstonecraft* (London: Macmillan, 1992), and Wendy Gunther-Canada's, *Rebel Writer: Mary Wollstonecraft and Enlightenment Politics* (DeKalb: Northern Illinois University Press, 2001). None of these scholars, however, has read the *Vindications* against the backdrop of the Scottish Enlightenment language of politics, as I am doing here. For other important, but distinctively different, arguments dealing specifically with Wollstonecraft's first *Vindication*, see David Bromwich, "Wollstonecraft as a Critic of Burke," *Political Theory* 23, no. 4 (1995): 617–34; James Conniff, "Edmund Burke and His Critics: The Case of Mary Wollstonecraft," *Journal of the History of Ideas* 60, no. 2 (1999): 299–318; and Mitzi Myers, "Politics from the Outside: Mary Wollstonecraft's First *Vindication*," *Studies in Eighteenth-Century Culture* 6 (1977): 113–32. Steven Blakemore, in *Intertextual War: Edmund Burke and the French Revolution in the Writings of Mary Wollstonecraft, Thomas Paine, and James Mackintosh* (Madison: Fairleigh Dickinson University Press, 1997), claims that Wollstonecraft's argument "reinforces traditional sexual stereotypes" by "suggesting the superiority of the 'masculine.'" In Blakemore's view, Wollstonecraft "subverts" her own position "by accepting the denigration of character traits traditionally associated with femininity and hence implicitly endorses the suggested superiority of traditional masculinity" (81); thus Wollstonecraft ultimately "resembles Burke" (80; chapter 3 is entitled "Reflected Resemblances"). The interpretation that follows is decidedly different from Blakemore's.

Burke specifically and accurately as a theorist of common sense, or sensibility. That is, she read Burke as defending a discourse that Scottish Enlightenment thinkers were central to articulating, and one that she had come to find particularly pernicious as a result of her work for Joseph Johnson's *Analytical Review*. Reading Burke's *Reflections* fully convinced Wollstonecraft of the dangers of the culture of sensibility and the ease with which its essentialist assumptions could be placed in the service of a profoundly conservative politics. Above all else, then, Wollstonecraft identified Burke's commitment to the culture of sensibility as the linchpin of his position, the vehicle through which he "leveled many ingenious arguments in a very specious garb."[3] Sensibility was the fundamental Burkean idea she was most concerned to address.[4]

Of course, Wollstonecraft's use of the phrase "specious garb" was itself a play on Burke's "decent drapery of life," or the system of manners drawn from chivalry that had made power seem gentle, and obedience easy, by beautifying the body politic. For Burke the old system of manners had worked by softening the sublime realities of political power, underwritten by the natural aristocracy's connection to the church, and the church's consequent ability to induce terror in the masses. Wollstonecraft aimed to pull away this beautiful curtain, to get at Burke's unadorned moral presuppositions, or, as she told him, "to show you to yourself, stripped of the gorgeous drapery in which you have enwrapped your tyrannic principles," by "attacking the foundations of your opinions."[5]

From the beginning, then, Wollstonecraft's reply to Burke marked out a wide terrain that called for an extraordinarily complex reply to both the

---

3. *Works of Wollstonecraft*, 5:5.

4. On this theme, see Janet Todd's chapter "The Attack on Sensibility," in her *Sensibility: An Introduction*, (New York: Methuen, 1986), 129–46; Mary Lyndon Shanley, "Mary Wollstonecraft on Sensibility, Women's Rights, and Patriarchal Power," in *Women Writers and the Early Modern British Political Tradition*, ed. Hilda L. Smith (Cambridge: Cambridge University Press, 1998), 148–67; Wendy Gunther-Canada, "The Politics of Sense and Sensibility: Mary Wollstonecraft and Catharine Macaulay Graham on Edmund Burke's *Reflections on the Revolution in France*," in Smith, *Women Writers*, 126–47; Stephen Cox, "Sensibility as Argument," in *Sensibility in Transformation: Creative Resistance to Sentiment from the Augustans to the Romantics*, ed. Syndy McMillen Conger (Rutherford: Fairleigh Dickinson University Press, 1990), 63–82; G. J. Barker-Benfield, *The Culture of Sensibility: Sex and Society in Eighteenth-Century Britain* (Chicago: University of Chicago Press, 1992), especially 366, 2; Kelly, *Revolutionary Feminism*, 23–54; and Claudia L. Johnson, *Equivocal Beings: Politics, Gender, and Sentimentality in the 1790s: Wollstonecraft, Radcliffe, Burney, Austen* (Chicago: University of Chicago Press, 1995), chapter 1.

5. *Works of Wollstonecraft*, 5:37, 9.

Reflections and the *Philosophical Enquiry into the Origin of our Ideas of the Sublime and Beautiful*.[6] She started by rejecting Burke's rhetoric as "the equivocal idiom of politeness," and offered instead her own definition of the *Enquiry*'s central categories, identifying "truth, in morals," as "the essence of the sublime" and "simplicity" as "the only criterion of the beautiful."[7]

For Wollstonecraft the "truly sublime" individual was one who could use reasoned principles to govern the "inferior springs" of affect in order to earn respect. Burke's *Enquiry* had insisted, to the contrary, "that respect chills love" (5:8–9). This is right on point. Burke had claimed that we submit to and respect only what "we" (males) admire, but "love" only what submits to us. He also maintained, however, that love was much closer to contempt than most people imagined. Thus, men love weak women, but it is for this very reason that they cannot respect them.[8] Wollstonecraft regarded such conclusions as derived from the "*manie*," or mental illness, of sensibility (5:8), a disease that had driven Burke mad. This is an ironic play on the politics of the time, of course, as Burke was often accused of trying to make a power grab in the wake of George III's fits of mental illness.[9] Wollstonecraft caustically claimed that sensibility had driven Burke madder than the king, and concluded "that all your pretty flights arise from your pampered sensibility." Alas, Burke's *Reflections* "foster every emotion till the fumes, mounting to your brain, dispel the sober suggestions of reason" (5:19).

Wollstonecraft had hit upon Burke's most basic argument: that instinctive moral sentiments and feelings buttressed hierarchies of all sorts, thereby justifying them by linking them to nature:

> I perceive, from the whole tenor of your Reflections, that you have a moral antipathy to reason; but, if there is any thing like argument, or first principles, in your wild declamation, behold the result:—that we are to reverence the rust of antiquity, and term

---

6. For a very interesting discussion, see Ronald Paulson's chapter "Burke, Paine, and Wollstonecraft: The Sublime and the Beautiful," in his *Representations of Revolution, 1789–1820* (New Haven: Yale University Press, 1983), 57–87.

7. *Works of Wollstonecraft*, 5:7, hereafter cited parenthetically in the text.

8. See Edmund Burke, *A Philosophical Enquiry into the Origin of our Ideas of the Sublime and Beautiful*, ed. James T. Boulton (Notre Dame: University of Notre Dame Press, 1968), 66–67, and Chapter 4 of this volume.

9. On this theme, see Robert Kaufman, "The Madness of George III, by Mary Wollstonecraft," *Studies in Romanticism* 37, no. 1 (1998): 17–25.

the unnatural customs, which ignorance and mistaken self-interest have consolidated, the sage fruit of experience: nay, that, if we do discover some errors, our *feelings* should lead us to excuse, with blind love, or unprincipled filial affection, the venerable vestiges of ancient days.

As these remarks indicate, Wollstonecraft also saw a practical political payoff in Burke's interpretation of the relation between moral philosophy and social theory. Depicting struggle as unnatural and useless reified the old order and ensured that human beings would "remain for ever in frozen inactivity" (5:10). Burke had analogized family and polity and believed that humble obedience on the part of inferiors in both realms was both natural and necessary. Wollstonecraft rejected this argument as trading on blindness, ignorance, and immorality in the name of upholding a self-interested status quo.

Wollstonecraft also unmistakably couched her critique of the Burkean notion of prescription in a unique transformative interpretation of the Scottish Enlightenment discourse on the relationship between morals, manners, and civilization: "The civilization which has taken place in Europe has been very partial, and, like every custom that an arbitrary point of honor has established, refines the manners at the expense of the morals, by making sentiments and opinions current in conversation that have no root in the heart, or weight in the cooler resolves of the mind.... The man has been changed into an artificial monster by the station in which he was born" (5:10).

As we will see, this was Mary Wollstonecraft's most important argument in response to Burke, as well as her most basic revision of the Scottish Enlightenment historical thesis. In her view, the antidemocratic European civilizing process was incomplete, having cultivated manners at the expense of morals. We were left with a system of social manners that went against human reason and was incapable of tutoring initial affect and transforming mere sentiment into true morality. Wollstonecraft derided chivalric manners, lauded by Burke and the Scots, as a system predicated on "artificial feelings" that were produced and reproduced through political, economic, and sexual hierarchies that precluded the development of reason, and thus of moral and civic virtue, producing instead a society of "artificial monster[s]" (5:29, 10). Burke had sought to naturalize this system by playing on the culture of sensibility; Wollstonecraft countered that real civilization could only be achieved by extending democratic equality into every sphere of human interaction, because "true happiness" could "only be enjoyed by equals" (5:10–11).[10]

Deconstructing Burkean Moral Theory

Wollstonecraft accused Burke of trading on artificial feelings derived from chivalry and naturalized through the language of sensibility in an attempt

---

10. This broad conclusion is in fundamental agreement with Taylor and Sapiro, although it is arrived at by a very different approach from either of theirs. For Sapiro's view, see especially "Wollstonecraft, Feminism, and Democracy: 'Being Bastilled,'" in *Feminist Interpretations of Mary Wollstonecraft*, ed. Maria J. Falco (University Park: Pennsylvania State University Press, 1996), 33–45. See also Laura Brace, "'Not Empire, but Equality': Mary Wollstonecraft, the Marriage State, and the Sexual Contract," *Journal of Political Philosophy* 8, no. 4 (2000): 433–55. My argument is in tension with readings of Wollstonecraft's work as ideology. These interpretations view Wollstonecraft as a bourgeois liberal principally interested in extending the rights of men to women in the public sphere for the purposes of enabling capitalism to flourish, or as one whose work essentially performed that function irrespective of her intentions. See, for example, Zillah R. Eisenstein, *The Radical Future of Liberal Feminism* (New York: Longman, 1981), 89–112; Mary Poovey, *The Proper Lady and the Woman Writer: Ideology as Style in the Works of Mary Wollstonecraft, Mary Shelley, and Jane Austen* (Chicago: University of Chicago Press, 1985); Tom Furniss, *Edmund Burke's Aesthetic Ideology: Language, Gender, and Political Economy in Revolution* (Cambridge: Cambridge University Press, 1993), especially 191, and his "Gender in Revolution: Edmund Burke and Mary Wollstonecraft," in *Revolution in Writing: British Literary Responses to the French Revolution*, ed. Kelvin Everest (Milton Keynes: Open University Press, 1991), 65–100; Isaac Kramnick, *Republicanism and Bourgeois Radicalism: Political Ideology in Late Eighteenth-Century England and America* (Ithaca: Cornell University Press, 1990); and Timothy J. Reiss, "Revolution in Bounds: Wollstonecraft, Women, and Reason," in *Gender and Theory: Dialogues on Feminist Criticism*, ed. Linda Kauffman (New York: Basil Blackwell, 1989), 11–50. For the difficulties with this position, see Taylor, *Mary Wollstonecraft*, 166–75, and below. For various other readings of Wollstonecraft that put her in some version of the "liberal feminist" camp, see Daniel Engster, "Mary Wollstonecraft's Nurturing Liberalism: Between an Ethic of Justice and Care," *American Political Science Review* 95, no. 3 (2001): 577–88; Gal Gerson, "Liberal Feminism: Individuality and Oppositions in Wollstonecraft and Mill," *Political Studies* 50, no. 4 (2002): 794–810; Ewa Badowska, "The Anorexic Body of Liberal Feminism: Mary Wollstonecraft's *A Vindication of the Rights of Woman*," in *Mary Wollstonecraft and the Critics, 1788–2001*, ed. Harriet Devine Jump, 2 vols. (New York: Routledge, 2003), 2:320–40. The counterthesis, i.e., that Wollstonecraft ought to be understood as a classical republican, as put forward by G. J. Barker-Benfield, "Mary Wollstonecraft: Eighteenth-Century Commonwealthwoman," *Journal of the History of Ideas* 50, no. 1 (1989): 95–115, is also problematic. Pressed too forcefully, such a move turns Wollstonecraft into a backward-looking thinker by situating her within a republican tradition that systematically excluded women from citizenship. This, in turn, could lead one to draw what I think is a misleading conclusion, namely, that Wollstonecraft actually believed in the concept of "republican motherhood" and was a de facto supporter of a separate spheres rationale, as in Joan B. Landes, *Women and the Public Sphere in the Age of the French Revolution* (Ithaca: Cornell University Press, 1988). For the difficulties with this view, see Taylor, *Mary Wollstonecraft*, 212, 223 and associated notes.

to engage the sympathy of his audience in defense of the Old Regime. She pointed to a specific passage from the *Reflections* to illustrate her contempt for this duplicity: Burke's description of the "leading in triumph" of the French royal family from Versailles to Paris in the aftermath of the events of 6 October 1789. For Burke, as we have seen, this march signified the French devolution from civilization to savagery, a regression embodied most tellingly in the transformation of women into "the furies of hell," yelling, screaming, and dancing in the procession's lead. As such, it becomes the starting point for his unique blending and transformation of the Scottish Enlightenment's philosophical and historical presuppositions into a charge that the revolutionaries were destroying civilization for the sake of democratic savagery. Wollstonecraft quotes this passage directly, chiding Burke: "Probably you mean women who gained a livelihood by selling vegetables or fish, who never had had any advantages of education" (5:30).

In beginning her response to the passage in this way, she demystifies and denaturalizes Burke's depiction of these figures and so attempts to undermine the response that Burke intended to provoke. Throughout the *Reflections*, she tells Burke, and specifically in this passage about the forced march to Paris,

> you frequently advert to a sentimental jargon, which has long been current in conversation, and even in books of morals, though it never received the *regal* stamp of reason. A kind of mysterious instinct is *supposed* to reside in the soul, that instantaneously discerns truth, without the tedious labor of ratiocination. This instinct, for I know not what other name to give it, has been termed *common sense*, and more frequently *sensibility;* and, by a kind of *indefeasible* right, it has been *supposed*, for rights of this kind are not easily proved, to reign paramount over other faculties of the mind, and to be an authority from which there is no appeal. (5:30)

Wollstonecraft accurately read Burke's *Reflections* as part of the culture of sensibility, which hinged on the validity of instinctive, as opposed to rational, responses to moral phenomena.[11] Nowhere, she points out, was

---

11. Stunningly, the dean of the natural law school of Burke interpretation, Peter Stanlis, excerpts and directly quotes portions of this passage—namely, "a kind of mysterious instinct is *supposed* to reside in the soul, that instantaneously discerns truth, without the tedious labor of ratiocination. This instinct... [is] an authority from which there is no appeal" (the emphasis is Wollstonecraft's)—in order to demonstrate what he takes to be *Wollstonecraft's*

Burke's commitment to this discourse more evident than in his celebration of Marie Antoinette, the opening salvo in his attack on the egalitarian morals and manners of the rebellious French. In the *Reflections*, we recall, Burke had argued that it was the exalted rank of the persons suffering—their sex, beauty, and lineage—that naturally activated his sensibility. This was an assertion that hearkened back to the *Enquiry*, and to the closely woven tradition of Smith and Beattie, and it summoned forth Burke's own attempt to engage the "natural" sensibility of his readers, thereby encouraging them to defend the old order by defending its embodiment in Marie Antoinette.[12] Burke asserted that it was entirely natural that he should feel differently from Price, and defended this point by relying on the *Enquiry's* central categories of sublimity and beauty, contending that the passions necessarily instructed weak human reason and instinctively summoned forth sympathetic fellow feeling in all rightly constituted minds, prompting them to relieve their uneasiness by ending the suffering of the afflicted French royal family.

Wollstonecraft mocked this argument. Burke's "natural" sympathy was conspicuously selective, she pointed out, reserved for the likes of the brilliantly arrayed Marie Antoinette, whose rank supposedly mitigated her vice. "Misery, to reach your heart, I perceive, must have its cap and bells; your tears are reserved, very *naturally* concerning your character... for the downfall of queens, whose rank alters the nature of folly, and throws a graceful veil over vices that degrade humanity." Burke showed no concern whatsoever for single working mothers with hungry babies, whose "vulgar sorrows" could not move him to commiserate with them; the best they could do was to "extort an alms" (5:15–16).

Wollstonecraft parodied Burke's notion of a supposedly instinctive, universal common sense: "This subtle magnetic fluid, that runs round the

---

supposed commitment to the doctrines of instinctive feeling and common sense. Stanlis brackets the passage with the following gloss: "She regarded the cultivation of knowledge as an impediment to moral and political truth, and 'natural' instinct as an infallible guide.... On this theory Burke, with his great learning and skepticism toward infallible private instincts, was hopelessly corrupt." Stanlis, *Edmund Burke and the Natural Law* (Ann Arbor: University of Michigan Press, 1958), 142. This is an extraordinary misrepresentation of Wollstonecraft's argument, which proceeds by taking what she obviously meant as a criticism of Burke (and an accurate one at that) and presenting it as a description of her own position. The result diminishes our understanding of both thinkers considerably.

12. See Chapter 4. Wollstonecraft leaves open the slim possibility that Burke is not a true believer in sensibility and common sense but is cynically manipulating its popularity in an attempt to garner support for the *ancien régime*. Either way, she found his reliance on the discourse reprehensible.

whole circle of society, is not subject to any known rule.... It dips, we know not why, granting it to be an infallible instinct, and, though supposed always to point to truth, it pole-star, the point is always shifting, and seldom stands due north" (5:30–31). This remark emphasizes the problem, never satisfactorily resolved by contemporary conservatives, that moral intuitionism is supposed to yield universal truths, yet every attempt to establish such truths empirically dissolves when confronted with the dizzying array of culturally and historically relative beliefs and practices.

Against this view, Wollstonecraft maintained that while initial affective responses, or the "feelings of the heart," were indeed "sacred," they were adamantly not to be confused with virtue, which was "an acquisition of the individual, and not the blind impulse of unerring instinct." In her view the achievement of virtue required the "cultivation of reason," or what she called the "tedious labor of ratiocination." It was the ability to reason, after all, that distinguished human beings from animals. She contrasted this "arduous task" with the simplistic process described by "men of lively fancy" like Burke, who, "finding it easier to follow the impulse of passion, endeavor to persuade themselves and others that it is most *natural*.... But if virtue is to be acquired by experience, or taught by example, reason, perfected by reflection, must be the director of the whole host of passions" (5:30–32).

Wollstonecraft's critique of moral intuitionism was not based on the supposedly unalloyed optimism of some fictitious, monolithic "Enlightenment project." In fact she demonstrated a keen awareness of human frailty and of the obvious limits of reason. But she believed that this was not the whole story. Anyone who had studied the "slow progress of civilization" could see that virtue would be promoted by the greater exercise of our critical reasoning capacities. Wollstonecraft's argument, *contra* the Scots and Burke, was simply that such virtue as human beings were capable of achieving in public and private life would be more likely if they were guided by such capacities, and did not cherish their prejudices, as Burke said, simply "because they were prejudices." Reason, she told Burke, was the "foundation of virtue," and its exercise produced "that 'primary morality,' which you term 'untaught feelings'" (5:33).

Part of the problem with Burke's *Reflections*, then, was that it was not reflective enough. In Wollstonecraft's view, Burke had relied on intuition and affect and had never taken the time to cultivate reason or develop real moral principles. She asked him pointedly, for example, what he meant by relying on such ploys as "inbred sentiments," and countered that "the appetites are the only perfect inbred powers that I can discern" (5:32). She warned her readers, however, that they should refrain from confusing such "mechanical instinctive sensations" as appetite "with emotions that reason deepens, and justly terms the feelings of *humanity*," the latter a term that "discriminates the active exertions of virtue from the vague declamations of sensibility" (5:53). Instinct had to be distinguished from morality, which was the result of rationally developing affective responses. Morality was learned, and it led humans toward humanity. The unthinking recourse to common sense, or sensibility, by contrast, actually mutilated the innate materials of feeling, and codified their defects in oppressive codes of social manners.

Wollstonecraft used this argument to turn the Scottish Enlightenment historical thesis back onto Burke. If one denied that reason was capable of improving human behavior over time, by progressively expanding and refining the social affections and passions, then Burke himself had to answer why the "first rude horde" was not the most moral people of all (5:32). Furthermore, if moral sentiments were not *acquired*, whence the ability to criticize any social practices based on them? These questions lead us to a consideration of Wollstonecraft's broader critique of Burke's view of history and the institutions of the church and nobility as they related to the civilizing process.

Challenging Burke's View of Church, Nobility, and the Civilizing Process

"In the infancy of society," Wollstonecraft argued, social interaction was determined by "the lawless power of an ambitious individual," or weak princes were compelled to acquiesce to all the demands of "licentious barbarous insurgents" (5:11). That is, during the early stages of society, power came to rest in the hands of a single individual or small group, under whose leadership other barbarians could be resisted. To make this argument, Wollstonecraft relied on David Hume's depiction of Edward III (1327–77) in his *History of England*.

With this remarkable move, Wollstonecraft used the Scottish Enlightenment historical thesis to undermine Burke's own reliance on that thesis, by arguing that he had glorified the ignorance of the past and undercut the notion of historical progress. It was in this same vein that she considered the reign of another Plantagenet king, Richard II (1377–99), Edward's successor. In her reading, Richard was no more than a weak, ambitious king who could not control the nobility but needed their financial backing to wage his wars of self-aggrandizement. She asks Burke pointedly if such events formed the "venerable pillars of our constitution" (5:11).[13]

In the *Reflections* Burke had argued that the English had not lost the generosity and dignity of the fourteenth century. Wollstonecraft turned the tables on Burke, asking him incredulously where this was to be found. "The boasted virtues of that century," she wrote, all smack of "headstrong barbarism." The British constitution was in fact "settled in the dark days of ignorance." Wollstonecraft thus recast Burke's revered civilization as a remnant of anachronistic barbarism, a time when minds "were shackled by the grossest prejudices and most immoral superstition," which had bequeathed to the present age a set of institutions predicated on a system of artificial manners and immoral hierarchies. Wollstonecraft maintained that the founders of modern Britain had in fact cobbled together a mess that scarcely deserved the name constitution (5:12–13). Moreover, she provided her readers with a sustained critique of the two social institutions Burke saw as chiefly responsible for perpetuating this "natural" system of manners, the church and the nobility.

In the *Reflections*, Burke had drawn on the *Enquiry* to argue that people naturally feared God's unfathomable power.[14] This proved wholly unacceptable to Mary Wollstonecraft, who claimed: "I FEAR God! I bend with awful reverence when I enquire on what my fear is built.—I fear that sublime power, whose motive for creating me must have been wise and good; and I submit to the moral laws which my reason deduces from this view of my dependence on him.—It is not his power that I fear—it is not to an arbitrary will, but to unerring *reason* I submit" (5:34).

In answer to Burke, Wollstonecraft conducted her own enquiry, and in response to the Burkean notions of power and terror as the ruling principles of the sublime, and fear of God as their most obvious example, she granted that she, too, feared God. However, in a brilliant manipulation of Burke's aesthetic and moral categories, she bent them to her own radical, democratic purposes. She told Burke at the outset that since both the sublime and the beautiful depended on truth, one appropriately submitted, or "feared," only God's "unerring *reason*" and omniscience, not some

---

13. For a discussion of Wollstonecraft's use of Hume in her response to Burke, see Gordon Spence, "Mary Wollstonecraft's Theodicy and Theory of Progress," *Enlightenment and Dissent* 14 (1995): 105–27.

14. Edmund Burke, *The Writings and Speeches of Edmund Burke*, ed. Paul Langford, 8 vols. to date (Oxford: Oxford University Press, 1981–), 8:137–38, hereafter *Writings and Speeches*.

irresistible irrational power. Burke had argued for accepting the prevailing order as an outgrowth of natural moral sentiments, codified in social manners. Wollstonecraft transmuted this into an argument on behalf of critical reason and individual self-respect: "This fear of God makes me reverence myself.... I do not trouble myself, therefore, to enquire whether this is the fear the *people* of England feel:—and, if it be *natural* to include all the modifications which you have annexed—it is not" (5:34).[15]

In particular, Wollstonecraft tells Burke that if he had even a measure of enlightened self-respect, he would not have argued that the Anglican Church in Britain was formed under the auspices of religious piety. She turned again to history and argued that relations between church and state in the British constitution were established "as Europe was emerging out of barbarism" (5:34). While Wollstonecraft agreed with the broad Scottish Enlightenment claim that at times private interest had the unintended consequence of promoting the public good, she adamantly disagreed with Burke's view of the church as a morally beneficent institution. Having undermined his notion of the ultimate in patriarchal sublimity, God the Father, she turned next to God's institutional representation on *terra firma*.

For Burke, the church legitimized political power by connecting it with the supreme terror and ultimate power, God, through an act of sublime consecration. Consequently, the state awed the citizenry, which was especially necessary in the case of democratically elected governments, as the masses would otherwise shamelessly and fearlessly threaten to tyrannize their legitimate representatives from the natural aristocracy. As well as awing the masses by teaching them fear of the state and respect for rank, Burke also believed that the church beneficially controlled the education of the nobility. This demonstrated the tight connection between the twin institutional vehicles of civilization responsible for the infusion of the sublime and beautiful elements of social morality. Burke even went so far as to argue that these English institutions sprang "from the simplicity of

---

15. For the most thorough discussion of Wollstonecraft as a religious thinker, see Taylor, "For the Love of God," chapter 3 of her *Mary Wollstonecraft*. Taylor makes clear the increasingly leveling, egalitarian implications of Wollstonecraft's idiosyncratic and changing religious commitments. Here, however, I am stressing (as Taylor does not) Wollstonecraft's specific criticism of religious *institutions* in historical perspective. For other views on Wollstonecraft and religion, see Daniel Robinson, "Theodicy Versus Feminist Strategy in Mary Wollstonecraft's Fiction," *Eighteenth-Century Fiction* 9, no. 2 (1997): 183–202; Mary Wilson Carpenter, "Sibylline Apocalyptics: Mary Wollstonecraft's *Vindication of the Rights of Woman* and Job's Mother's Womb," *Literature and History* 12, no. 2 (1986): 215–28; and Eileen M. Hunt, "The Family as Cave, Platoon, and Prison: The Three Stages of Wollstonecraft's Philosophy of the Family," *Review of Politics* 64, no. 1 (2002): 81–119.

our national character, and from a sort of native plainness and directness of understanding" rooted in common sense.[16]

Wollstonecraft quoted this last passage, replying that she lacked "that respect for the whole body [of the clergy], which, you say, characterizes our nation" and warned her readers, "now we are stumbling on *inbred* feelings and secret lights again." Wollstonecraft denied the universal validity of such "lights." She attacked the institutional function of the church, telling Burke—an Irish transplant to English soil—that when the English did not know what to do with *their* children, they turned them into clergymen. For this reason churchmen were frequently far from the stainless purveyors of morality that supposedly consecrated the Burkean state. In another play on Burke's words, she wrote: "'Such sublime principles are *not constantly* infused into persons of exalted birth'"; they do "sometimes think of 'the paltry pelf of the moment.'" Burke's majestic "consecration *for ever*; a word, that from lips of flesh is big with a mighty nothing, has not purged the *sacred temple* from all the impurities of fraud, violence, injustice, and tyranny. Human passions still lurk in her *sanctum sanctorum*; and, without the profane exertions of reason, vain would be her ceremonial ablutions; morality would still stand aloof from this national religion, this ideal consecration of a state" (5:35). As an institution, the established church was thoroughly corrupt and immoral, incapable of consecrating anything.

Wollstonecraft turned next to the question of the nobility and to a "curious paragraph" (5:35) from Burke—the passage in which he describes the appropriate way to nominate and elect officials to political office in a state that has been duly consecrated by an established church, that is, as a "holy function."[17] Wollstonecraft put the issue to Burke directly: "The only way in which the people interfere in government, religious or civil, is in electing representatives. And, Sir, let me ask you, with manly plainness—are these *holy* nominations? Where is the booth of religion?" Certainly Burke's extraordinary comments could not be meant as a description of the electoral process of late eighteenth-century British politics. Where, Wollstonecraft demanded to know, amid the well-financed "drunken riot" and buying of votes did one find Burke's pristine world of moral virtue? The process was

---

16. See Burke, *Writings and Speeches*, 8:141, and Chapter 4 of this volume. Recall that Burke had informed his French correspondent, Depont, that in England the education of "our" young nobility and gentlemen was "wholly in the hands of ecclesiastics" (149).

17. See ibid., 8:145. Wollstonecraft affixed the passage to her text. See *Works of Wollstonecraft*, 5:36n15.

corrupt, the elected representatives were corrupt, and the supposedly holy institution that conferred the sublime consecration was itself incurably corrupt (5:36).

Along the same lines, Wollstonecraft rejected Burke's claim that placing the education of the nobility in the hands of the clergy was a boon to both institutions that strengthened respect for religion. All the clergy learned from their noble charges was to offer "servility to superiors, and tyranny to inferiors." And, since "among unequals there can be no society," she asked Burke, "is it not natural for them to become courtly parasites, and intriguing dependents on great patrons, or the treasury?" (5:39). Wollstonecraft agreed that there was indeed a mutually reinforcing connection between the church and the nobility, the sublime, and the beautiful, but it was a vicious connection that stunted the civilizing process, because it was founded on, and perpetuated, inequality.

With respect to the church and the nobility, Wollstonecraft concluded that Burke had whitewashed British history, by "affix[ing] a meaning to laws that chance, or, to speak more philosophically, the interested views of men, settled, not dreaming of your ingenious elucidations." In the Middle Ages, rapacious priests were one of the few groups who exercised their God-given reason. They had done so in a wholly self-interested fashion, to secure vast amounts of property by manipulating the instruments of divine terror for the purpose of extorting the flock's worldly possessions in return for absolution of their sins (5:39). Wollstonecraft argued that the same was true of Burke's cherished natural aristocracy, who held the reins of political power in eighteen-century Britain. While the House of Commons might be a bastion of hereditary wealth and rank, Burke's claim "that it contains every thing respectable in talents" was "very problematical." For Wollstonecraft, the messy reality of greed and ignorance evinced by the British historical record held equally true for France. Therefore, in establishing a new constitution, the French revolutionaries needed to appeal to a higher source than the *"imagined* virtues of their forefathers" (5:41–42).

The Birth of Modern Feminism

In *A Vindication of the Rights of Men*, Wollstonecraft brought her critique of Burke's moral theory and historical imagination to bear on the place of women within the European civilizing process. In doing so, she connected the particular plight of women within the Old Regime to the broader problems of moral intuitionism and essentialism, and their associated social, economic, and political hierarchies. That is to say, Wollstonecraft's analysis of the problems women faced was of a piece with her broader criticism of Burke's moral theory and historical narrative, and it was this analysis that served as a conceptual and theoretical bridge for her treatise on women, which followed two short years later.

Once again Burke's *Enquiry* provided Wollstonecraft with a way into the argument that men had essentialized women's nature. She excoriated the behavior of the "fair ladies" in the New World who attended whippings and invented new tortures for their slaves, yet managed to shed tears only after they "exercise[d] their tender feelings by the perusal of the last imported novel." She asked Burke where the "infallibility of sensibility" was to be found in such radically inverted and abominable behavior. In one fell swoop Wollstonecraft placed significant blame for such moral perversity at the feet of the culture of sensibility, and in particular indicted its most effective vehicle of transmission, the sentimental novel. She had reviewed dozens of such novels for the *Analytical*, and she loathed them for their depiction of morally deformed female characters as something to be upheld and emulated. She thus explicitly linked Burke's *Enquiry* to the propagation and popularization of the discourse of sensibility. In her reading, Burke's argument was no more than an elaborate attempt to show that "beautiful weakness [was] interwoven into a woman's frame," that the "chief business of her life" was "to inspire love," and that "Nature ha[d] made an eternal distinction" between men and women. The result was one kind of slavery in the New World, and women's very different, but nevertheless very real, enslavement at the hands of men in the Old:

> These ladies may have read your Enquiry concerning the origin of our ideas of the Sublime and Beautiful, and, convinced by your arguments, may have labored to be pretty, by counterfeiting weakness. You may have convinced them that *littleness* and *weakness* are the very essence of beauty; and that the Supreme Being, in giving women beauty in the most supereminent degree, seemed to command them, by the powerful voice of Nature, not to cultivate the moral virtues that might chance to excite respect, and interfere with the pleasing sensations they were created to inspire. (5:45–46)[18]

---

18. For Wollstonecraft's opposition to slavery, and her analogy between women and slaves, see Moira Ferguson, *Colonialism and Gender Relations from Mary Wollstonecraft to Jamaica Kincaid* (New York: Columbia University Press, 1993).

Here Wollstonecraft carried Burke's argument about beauty to its logical conclusion. If women believed, as Burke said, "that to be loved, women's high end and great distinction! they should 'learn to lisp, to totter in their walk, and nick-name God's creatures,'" then they would, in fact, "turn all their attention to their persons, systematically neglecting morals to secure beauty." Of course, Wollstonecraft recognized that Burke would no doubt attempt to "exculpate" himself "by turning the charge on Nature, who made our idea of beauty independent of reason." Burke would claim "that Nature, by making women *little, smooth, delicate, fair* creatures, never designed that they should exercise their reason to acquire the virtues that produce opposite, if not contradictory, feelings." If women used reason to develop virtue, Wollstonecraft claimed, then they might actually become respected and admired, or sublime, and Burke would never stand for this, as it might "disturb the soft intimacy of love" by running together the two fundamental principles of his social theory that were meant to remain permanently separated by nature. Wollstonecraft maintained that arguments like Burke's effectively made "any attempt to civilize the heart" according to rational principles "a mere philosophic dream" (5:45–46). This extraordinary denial of an allegedly innate female character, written more than two hundred years ago in response to the founding father of modern conservatism, might well be reckoned as one of the most significant moments in modern feminism.

In *A Vindication of the Rights of Men*, however, Wollstonecraft was just as concerned to expose the consequences that a "libertine" Burkean view of woman had for *both* sexes. In the process she demonstrated that, from its inception, feminism was concerned with the *necessary* interconnections between men and women, and between the public and the private spheres, and insisted that democratic equality must extend to both sexes and both spheres, for the benefit of both. In one of the clearest examples of this argument, one that expressed directly her understanding of the relationship between false notions of female beauty and male citizenship, she informed Burke that "the character of a master of a family, a husband, and a father, forms the citizen imperceptibly... but, from the lax morals and depraved affections of the libertine, what results?—a finical man of taste, who is only anxious to secure his own private gratifications, and to maintain his rank in society" (5:23). Burke's cultural ideal, the "natural" aristocrat and man of taste who could settle moral issues through his natural, inborn moral intuition, Wollstonecraft turned completely on its head.

For her, this man was a misogynist who had essentialized specious notions of female beauty and destroyed his capacity for virtuous citizenship, while simultaneously doing everything within his power to procure property and place.

Of course, she told Burke, the same system of manners was particularly injurious to the development of moral virtue in women. Young girls frequently married to procure social rank through the only route open to them. They then played the coquette, and whiled away their time in marriages lacking in respect and therefore devoid of love. Women could not be respectable because men prevented them from becoming so, and instead systematically transformed them into "weak beings" (5:23). As such, they might be the recipients of Burkean "love," treated as affectionate pets, but they were really the objects of contempt. Burke and the other architects of the culture of sensibility had consistently denied women the capacity to reason, and thus prevented them from pursuing civic and moral virtue in public or private life, ensuring their perpetual subservience. This system turned women into "vain inconsiderate dolls" rather than the "prudent mothers and useful members of society" they were capable of being (5:25). It perniciously undercut females' capacity for rational democratic citizenship, reducing them to the childlike objects preferred by men like Burke.

Defending the French Revolution

In the concluding pages of the *Rights of Men*, Wollstonecraft not only brought together her critique of Burke's theory of morals and manners, and of the social hierarchies that perpetuated it, she also blended this critique with a democratic defense of the French Revolution. Since "inequality of rank must ever impede the growth of virtue," it was only by beginning with individual liberty, and protecting it with a slate of rights conducive to equality, that artificial manners and ranks could be demolished, and real advances in the civilizing process begun. Wollstonecraft argued that these democratic wheels could not be set in motion by those with a vested interest in the perpetuation of that old world, be they nobles or churchmen. The abolition of titles that served as the "corner-stone of despotism" would have to be done by men who lacked them (5:46–47). The true terror and power of the Old Regime was largely masked by the meretricious drapery of chivalric manners, a system codified in titles, ranks, and ceremonies, personified in kings and queens, and guaranteed by the unequal distribution of property. The only response to such a system was to act as the French revolutionaries had and confiscate church lands. Burke, of course, had seen the seizure of church lands as one of the signal evils of the Revolution. For Wollstonecraft, needless to say, Burke's appeals to sensibility and beauty, and to the long duration of ill-gotten property, could not alter the justice of this act. About prescription she asked: "Can there be an opinion more subversive of morality, than that time sanctifies crimes, and silences the blood that calls out for retribution, if not for vengeance?" Injustice could never claim prescription, she argued, or else slaveholders could make the same arguments in their defense, as could defenders of the caste system in India (5:49–51).

At the same time, while Burke could lament the downfall of a church and nobility underwritten by old violence, Wollstonecraft believed that he remained unmoved by the plight of the intergenerational victims of that violence, the poor. Wollstonecraft rejected Burke's argument that the poor should be content with the "consolation" of "eternal justice," and that whoever deprived them of that consolation effectively "deadens their industry." Burke's advocacy of "natural" inequality, which the poor were to accept, and his use of the Christian notion that true happiness cannot be found on earth, drew forth Wollstonecraft's ire: "This is contemptible hard-hearted sophistry, in the specious form of humility, and submission to the will of Heaven.—It is, Sir, *possible* to render the poor happier in this world without depriving them of the consolation which you gratuitously grant them in the next" (5:55). But Burke, with his "rhetorical flourishes and infantine sensibility," had inverted the scales of moral outrage. The poor were broken in body and spirit, their intellects undeveloped, in little better condition than their animals, which they tyrannized over when not aping the other vices of the rich. She asked Burke directly—what where the outrages of 6 October 1789, "when the gorgeous robes were torn off the idol human weakness had set up," compared to such misery? "Man preys on man; and you mourn for the idle tapestry that decorated a gothic pile, and the dronish bell that summoned the fat priest to prayer. You mourn for the empty pageant of a name" (5:58).

So much for Edmund Burke's vaunted purveyors of civilization, the church and nobility. Wollstonecraft concluded her reply with a reference to the passage in which Burke called France the cradle of English civilization and the spring of England's system of morals and manners. For Burke, this meant that when the French fountain was polluted, the English stream would soon follow, which gave Europe a deep stake in preserving the Old Regime in France.[19] Wollstonecraft's final remarks to Burke respond in exactly the fashion that would have filled her adversary with the greatest dread, by calling for a democratic revolution in morals and manners in the private sphere to reinforce a formally democratizing public sphere. Such a thoroughgoing revolution would emancipate the English from the remnants of the *ancien régime*, just as the French revolutionaries were beginning to emancipate themselves: "our manners, you tell us, are drawn from the French.... If they were, it is time we broke loose from dependence—Time that Englishmen drew water from their own springs; for, if manners are not a painted substituted for morals, we have only to cultivate our reason, and we shall not feel the want of an arbitrary model" (5:60). In *A Vindication of the Rights of Woman*, Mary Wollstonecraft would systematize the parameters of this democratic revolution specifically with respect to women, in the context of simultaneously challenging the French revolutionaries themselves to be true to the principles for which she believed they stood.

The French Revolution and the "Revolution in Female Manners"

Mary Wollstonecraft's feminism, and thus modern feminism itself, emerged from the French Revolution controversy, her engagement with Burke and the Scottish Enlightenment, and the theoretical commitment to radical egalitarianism that grew out of that process. Far from arguing merely for an extension to women of the rights men enjoyed in the public sphere, Wollstonecraft's call for a "revolution in female manners" demanded no less than the radical transformation of political, economic, social, and gender relations. Only then could true civilization be realized (5:114).[20]

---

19. Burke, *Writings and Speeches*, 8:131.
20. On the importance of this phrase in Wollstonecraft's work, see Anne K. Mellor, "A REVOLUTION in Female Manners," chapter 2 of her *Romanticism and Gender* (London: Routledge, 1993), 31–39; Gary Kelly, "'A Revolution in Female Manners,'" chapter 5 of his *Revolutionary Feminism*, 107–39; and Mitzi Myers, "Reform or Ruin: 'A Revolution in Female Manners,'" *Studies in Eighteenth-Century Culture* 11 (1982): 199–216. In general, see Miriam Brody's introduction to *A Vindication of the Rights of Woman* (New York: Penguin, 1992), 1–70, especially 37–57.

Framing the Question of Women's Subordination

A Vindication of the Rights of Woman considered the place of women within the European civilizing process from a perspective informed by, but simultaneously deeply critical of, the Scottish Enlightenment. In Wollstonecraft's dedication to the French revolutionary Talleyrand, she notes that "manners and morals" have often been "confounded." Whereas manners ought to reflect the moral base on which they rest, "when various causes have produced factitious and corrupt manners, which are very early caught, morality becomes an empty name" (5:66). Burke and the Scots had conflated morals and manners; Wollstonecraft aimed to uncouple them, and to place both on a more secure footing.

In her most famous work, then, Wollstonecraft modified Scottish Enlightenment assumptions about historical progress along the lines sketched in her earlier response to Burke. Again she argued that, when surveying the globe, one either had to admit to extraordinary natural differences between people or conclude "that the civilization which has hitherto taken place in the world has been very partial." Like the Scots and Burke, Wollstonecraft was comparing stages of civilization. Very much unlike them, however, her panoramic assessment of the manners of women in polished European society was extremely negative. In fact, "the conduct and manners of women" actually "prove that their minds are not in a healthy state," because "strength and usefulness are sacrificed to beauty." Thus women's "understanding" had been blunted, with the consequence that "civilized" women of her own time wanted merely to "inspire love, when they ought to cherish a nobler ambition, and by their abilities and virtues exact respect" (5:73).

In the second *Vindication*, Wollstonecraft thus built upon her earlier critique of Burke to indict a culture that proved itself barbaric by unduly naturalizing an "exquisite sensibility, and sweet docility of manners" for women, while simultaneously blocking the means of rational self-development that would enable them to achieve moral and civic virtue. Burke's ideal women were like Marie Antoinette—the cultural embodiments of the old hierarchical system of manners. Such women spent their youth developing the social skills men valued; "meanwhile strength of body and mind are sacrificed to libertine notions of beauty," and females ultimately devoted themselves to getting ahead in "the only way women can rise in the world," that is, through marriage. "And this desire making mere animals of them, when they marry they act as such children must be expected to act:—they dress; they paint, and nickname God's creatures." In this way, Wollstonecraft argued, the "constitution of civil society," not nature, turned women into "insignificant objects of desire" (5:75–76).

Given this system of social production, it was little wonder that most women were incapable of playing greater roles in the social compact. At the same time, Wollstonecraft underlined her earlier point that men like Burke merely pretended to idolize such weak women; their notion of love was in fact much closer to contempt. Wollstonecraft then exposed the logical consequence of this corrupt system of artificial manners: trapped as they were in this hierarchical, male-dominated world, women sought to exercise power in the only way they could, by recourse to "cunning, the natural opponent of strength, which leads them to play off those contemptible infantine airs that undermine esteem even whilst they excite desire" (5:77). This is a central point for Wollstonecraft, and a powerful illustration of the extent of corruption in social relations. Women and men were both debased by this system of manners, and neither sex could achieve true moral virtue until it was overthrown and the sexes were placed on a more equal footing.

The Causes and Consequences of Women's Oppression

Early on in the *Rights of Woman*, Wollstonecraft set out some basic principles generally consonant with the strain of British radical thought that took its lead from a particular reading of Locke, combined with some standard notions derived from the French Enlightenment. Among these ideas, as we have already seen, was the notion that what distinguished humans from the rest of animal creation was their capacity for reason. Wollstonecraft measured human perfection by the degree to which reason informed individual conduct, law, social institutions, and individual beliefs. Only when it informed them to a great degree would virtuous conduct be possible as a general rule and prescription and prejudice cease to be the prime movers of social life (5:81–82).

Of course, none of these arguments was unique to Wollstonecraft, but she brought them to bear on Scottish Enlightenment moral theory and historical inquiry to develop a new and powerful theoretical perspective. Wollstonecraft used the basic tool of critical reason, much maligned by some postmodern feminists as a tool of oppression, to extraordinary democratic effect[21] against the defenders of the *ancien régime*, Edmund Burke, and, ultimately, the thinkers of the Scottish Enlightenment themselves.

History and Hierarchy: "Partial Civilization" and "Female Manners"

As she had in *A Vindication of the Rights of Men*, Wollstonecraft cast her narrative in the historical idiom of the Scottish Enlightenment. "In the infancy of society, when men were just emerging out of barbarism, chiefs and priests, touching the most powerful springs of savage conduct, hope and fear, must have had unbounded sway." Subsequently, "clashing interests" and "ambitious struggles" were "the origin of monarchical and priestly power, and the dawn of civilization." "As wars, agriculture, commerce, and literature, expand the mind," however, "despots are compelled, to make covert corruption hold fast the power which was formerly snatched by open force" (5:87).

The broad process Wollstonecraft depicts here is obviously derived from her reading of the Scots: in the infancy of society savages clung together, seeking protection from a small group of strongmen. The chiefs and priests exploited the savage emotions of hope and fear, and thereby held power in the early stages of the civilizing process. Following Hume, Wollstonecraft argued that internecine struggles among these ruling factions led to monarchy, nobility, and a powerful church, producing a system of ranks underwritten by feudal land tenure. Gradually, however, the people obtained some measure of power, a process akin to the solidification of king, lord, and commons in *The History of England*. First war, then agriculture, commerce, and literature, progressively expanded the mind, hemming in the power of kings, nobles, and church.

As in her first *Vindication*, however, and in a departure from Burke and the Scots, Wollstonecraft argued that "the civilization of the bulk of the people of Europe is very partial." The freedom they had enjoyed in an earlier age had been transformed into "splendid slavery" for the majority, and the "wretchedness" that resulted from "hereditary honors, riches, and monarchy" was so great that "men of lively sensibility," like Burke, had "almost uttered blasphemy in order to justify the dispensations of providence" (5:82).

---

21. On this theme, see Frances Ferguson, "Wollstonecraft Our Contemporary," in Kauffman, *Gender and Theory*, 51–62.

Nevertheless, although Wollstonecraft rejected the notion that social inequality was a natural expression of God's will, the myth of the noble savage cut no ice with her. Together with the Scots, she held that only societies developing toward civilization could lead to human improvement and provide the context for the development of natural human sociability. It is for this reason that Wollstonecraft rejected Rousseau's argument in *A Discourse on the Origin of Inequality*, both because it was based on the assumption that human beings were solitary by nature and because she read Rousseau as arguing that a state of nature was preferable to civilization. For Wollstonecraft, it was both impossible and undesirable to go back to what she would later call "Rousseau's golden age of stupidity" (6: 288). She argued that Rousseau did not distinguish which evils "were the consequence of civilization" and which were "the vestiges of barbarism" (5:84). The progressive nature of the civilizing process notwithstanding, Wollstonecraft regarded the corrupt manners of the era as the latter, which she believed were very strong indeed.

As both Virginia Sapiro and Barbara Taylor have forcefully argued, Wollstonecraft saw the oppression of women as a particular instance of a more general problem, widespread social inequality.[22] Thus in the *Rights of Woman* Wollstonecraft expanded her critique of Burke's two principal civilizing institutions, the church and the nobility, to encompass every profession and institution based on inequality. She insisted that "every profession, in which great subordination of rank constitutes its power, is highly injurious to morality." In a memorable phrase, she derided all forms of inequality as different shades of the "pestiferous purple," or that which "renders the progress of civilization a curse" (5:86–87).

As in the first *Vindication*, this was particularly true of organized religion. Wollstonecraft reiterated her claim that churches were built on inequality and, as such, institutions that retarded the development of reason, virtue, and civilization: "The blind submission imposed at college to forms of belief serves as a novitiate to the curate, who must obsequiously respect the opinion of his rector or patron, if he mean to rise in his profession" (5:86).

It is Wollstonecraft's critique of the military, however, that other great training ground of the nobility, that stands out as one of the most arresting arguments of *A Vindication of the Rights of Woman*.

22. See Sapiro, *Vindication of Political Virtue*, chapters 3 and 4; and Taylor, *Mary Wollstonecraft*, especially chapter 5, to which the following discussion is indebted.

> A standing army... is incompatible with freedom; because subordination and rigor are the very sinews of military discipline; and despotism is necessary to give vigor to enterprises that one will directs. A spirit inspired by romantic notions of honor, a kind of morality founded on the fashion of the age, can only be felt by a few officers, whilst the main body must be moved by command, like the waves of the sea; for the strong wind of authority pushes the crowd of subalterns forward, they scarcely know or care why, with headlong fury. (5:86)

Wollstonecraft contended that an elaborate code of chivalric manners animated the conduct of military leaders, but even these manners did not extend to the masses of men under their command, who were guided simply by power and blindly subordinated to authority. "Every corps is a chain of despots" filled with those "submitting and tyrannizing without exercising their reason." As such, they also became "dead weights of vice and folly on the community." The townspeople were surrounded by a group of "idle superficial young men, whose only occupation is gallantry, and whose polished manners render vice more dangerous, by concealing its deformity under gay ornamental drapery." Civilian neighbors aped the "polished manners" of the noble army officers, and thus the morality of the townspeople near military bases was ruined (5:86).

While opposition to a standing army was a common feature of republican arguments in the eighteenth century, the uniquely feminist move that Wollstonecraft made in this analysis was her analogy between military men and women. In many ways, she argued, the social construction of both groups was similar, especially in the case of officers and the ladies of polite society. Both were distinguished by their artificial manners and their corrupted sense of morals, the direct results of their education or lack thereof. Like women, soldiers went into the world bereft of knowledge and reasoned principles, with predictably similar consequences. "Where is then the sexual difference, when the education has been the same? All the difference that I can discern, arises from the superior advantage of liberty, which enables [soldiers] to see more of life.... And as for any depth of understanding, I will venture to affirm, that it is as rarely to be found in the army as amongst women; and the cause, I maintain, is the same" (5:92–93).

Like ladies, officers were especially attentive to their persons, fond of dancing, crowded rooms, adventure, and ridicule. Wollstonecraft wondered why women should be castigated for being fond of soldiers' scarlet coats, when after all soldiers loved to dress up as well. In short, the "great misfortune" for both women and soldiers was that they "both acquire manners before morals, and a knowledge of life before they have, from reflection, any acquaintance with the grand ideal outline of human nature. The consequence is natural; satisfied with common nature, they become a prey to prejudices, and taking all their opinions on credit, they blindly submit to authority." The signal difference between soldiers and women was that all men retained their rank with respect to the sexes; every man was still considered superior to any woman. Apart from that, they were birds of a feather. (5:93).

The antidote to this poison for both sexes was social equality, which Wollstonecraft saw as the only means to the "perfection of man in the establishment of true civilization" (5:87). To effect the democratic cure, however, Wollstonecraft argued that one must first know the disease thoroughly; and it manifested itself nowhere more clearly than in the case of "ladies."

Creating and Perpetuating "Ladies"

In one important way, Wollstonecraft's position in the second *Vindication* is in close agreement with Burke's *Enquiry*. Like Burke, Wollstonecraft maintained that male authority, whether in public or in private, had always been underwritten by physical power. She believed that the *"divine right of husbands"* was predicated, as Burke would have it, on unequal power relations between sublime, powerful, and terrifying men and beautiful, weak women, or, as Wollstonecraft put it, on man's willingness "to exert his strength to subjugate his companion, and his invention to show that she ought to have her neck bent under the yoke, because the whole creation was only created for his convenience or pleasure" (5:110, 95).

However, while Wollstonecraft agreed that men often complained justly about women's character, unlike Burke she believed that female character was the "effect of ignorance!" Since the system of manners was not built on rational morality, women's behavior was marked by "cunning," the recourse of the servile. From the beginning of their lives, women were taught that cunning, together with "*outward* obedience, and a scrupulous attention to a puerile kind of propriety," would garner them male company, "and should they be beautiful, every thing else is needless, for, at least, twenty years of their lives" (5:88). So, in order to exert some measure of influence over men, women gave up the path of reason and morals to pursue that of manners. They strove to become the "ladies" of Burke's *Enquiry*, in order to use youth's beauty to make men "love" them.

As we have seen, Wollstonecraft compared these ladies with the rich, as described by Adam Smith in *The Theory of Moral Sentiments*, and argued that the social ideal for each of these groups, while different, proved that they both had "acquired all the follies and vices of civilization, and missed the useful fruit." With respect to women, this meant that "their senses are inflamed, and their understandings neglected, consequently they become the prey of their senses, delicately termed sensibility, and are blown about by every momentary gust of feeling. Civilized women are, therefore, so weakened by false refinement, that, respecting morals, their condition is much below what it would be were they left in a state nearer to nature" (5:129–30). Wollstonecraft clearly linked the effects of the civilizing process to a highly artificial system of female manners that had been naturalized and reified by men, and subsequently internalized by women, under the guise of the culture of sensibility.

Unlike Burke and the Scots, however, Wollstonecraft was emphatic that this female character was a product of patriarchal power and male domination of all the relevant institutions of self-development, both public and private. Women were allowed to pursue only those endeavors that would land them a man, such as reading sentimental novels and becoming dilettantes in music and poetry. Through such means their character was "formed in the mold of folly"; "overstretched sensibility" weakened female minds "and prevent[ed] intellect from attaining that sovereignty which it ought to attain to render a rational creature useful to others" (5:130).

As discussed earlier, in the second *Vindication* Wollstonecraft focused on one of the chief tools used to reproduce the patriarchal system of female manners, educational advice books for young girls. Echoing the arguments she had made in her reviews for the *Analytical*, Wollstonecraft came to view these books, which Scottish Enlightenment thinkers like Fordyce and Gregory played such an important role in articulating, as ideological tools of oppression: "All the writers who have written on the subject of female education and manners from Rousseau to Dr. Gregory, have contributed to render women more artificial, weak characters, than they would otherwise have been; and, consequently, more useless members of society... my objection extends to the whole purport of those books, which tend, in my opinion, to degrade one half of the human species, and render women pleasing at the expense of every solid virtue" (5:91). Wollstonecraft's aim in taking up these works was not to conduct a thorough review of the advice literature on female manners, but rather to hold up some representative samples of the culture of sensibility for purposes of "attacking the boasted prerogative of man," or the "iron scepter of tyranny, the original sin of tyrants," which was "all power built on prejudices, however hoary" (5:170).

That Wollstonecraft based her alternative vision of womanhood in the second *Vindication* on what we, in retrospect, would refer to as the concept of social construction is perhaps most evident in a chapter entitled "Observations on the State of Degradation to which Woman is Reduced by Various Causes." Here she turned directly to the sources of women's subordination and the system of manners governing female character. And, as in her reply to Burke, Wollstonecraft left no doubt where the notion that men and women were natural opposites ultimately rested. The claim that men were capable of reasoning and thinking, and women only of feeling, "has ever been the language of men" (5:122): "Ignorance is a frail base for virtue! Yet, that it is the condition for which woman was organized, has been insisted upon by the writers who have most vehemently argued in favor of the superiority of man; a superiority not in degree, but essence; though, to soften the argument, they have labored to prove, with chivalrous generosity, that the sexes ought not to be compared; man was made to reason, woman to feel." On men's "sensual error" of denying women's ability to reason "has the false system of female manners been reared, which robs the whole sex of its dignity" (5:132, 122).

Wollstonecraft countered such Scottish and Burkean arguments with the Lockean notion that the ability to generalize ideas through the use of reason was fundamental to human beings. While people's ability to reason varied, Wollstonecraft argued that "the nature of reason must be the same in all, if it be an emanation of divinity, the tie that connects the creature with the Creator; for, can that soul be stamped with the heavenly image, that is not perfected by the exercise of its own reason?" Yet "every thing conspires to render the cultivation of the understanding more difficult in the female than the male world" (5:122–23). Not only had men essentialized women's nature, they had simultaneously created the institutions and social forces that prevented women from developing their reason, generalizing their ideas, and cultivating a virtuous character. Wollstonecraft refused to accept this naturalization of female character, and insisted instead on the contingency of a history dominated by men. This most fundamental of criticisms found its way explicitly back to Burke when she asked,

"Why are we to love prejudices, merely because they are prejudices?" (5:182).[23] Her insistence that social inequality was the historical product of contingent power relations branched out in many directions, "for many are the forms that aristocracy assumes" (5:131).

The key to the ideology of natural inequality, of course, was sensibility. Wollstonecraft had set about dismantling that idea in her reply to Burke, and she expanded that critique by dismissing the definition of sensibility offered by that great explicator of eighteenth-century words, Samuel Johnson: "And what is sensibility?" she asked. "'Quickness of sensation; quickness of perception; delicacy.' Thus is it defined by Dr. Johnson; and the definition gives me no other idea than that of the most exquisitely polished instinct.... I may be allowed to infer that reason is absolutely necessary to enable a woman to perform any duty properly, and I must again repeat, that sensibility is not reason" (5:132–33). "Numberless are the arguments," she concluded, "supposed to be deduced from nature, that men have used morally and physically, to degrade the sex." But the causes that "universally act upon the morals and manners of the whole sex" to degrade women "all spring from want of understanding" (5:137, 145).

Wollstonecraft's argument, she said, "branches into various ramifications.—Birth, riches, and every extrinsic advantage that exalt a man above his fellows, without any mental exertion, sink him in reality below them." This egalitarian, deeply democratic attack on the hydra-headed problem of inequality was the background against which Wollstonecraft called for a "revolution in female manners." But she also believed that the civilizing process was slow, and that the intellectual conclusions that one should derive from it frequently arrived late. "Man, accustomed to bow down to power in his savage state, can seldom divest himself of this barbarous prejudice, even when civilization determines how much superior mental is to bodily strength." Ultimately, however, she asked if it was not absurd for men to "expect virtue from a slave, from a being whom the constitution of civil society has rendered weak, if not vicious" (5:113–16).

The "Revolution in Female Manners"

Clearly, for Wollstonecraft, a revolution in female manners required nothing short of a thorough reconstruction of political, economic, social, and gender relations on an egalitarian basis. It would also require a broad claim

---

23. Wollstonecraft's own footnote to this passage—"Vide Mr. Burke"—leaves no doubt as to its intended target.

for women's rights in all of these areas, aimed simultaneously at extending the "rights of man" to women in the public sphere and overturning the rights men exercised *over* women in the private sphere. As Carole Pateman has stressed, and as Wollstonecraft's arguments resoundingly confirm, since the first articulation of rights doctrines in the early modern period, feminists like Wollstonecraft have always been concerned with their two-dimensional character. In Pateman's formulation, the first dimension of rights consists of the well-known civil and political liberties that uphold the freedom of citizens, while the second dimension includes the rights that men enjoy by virtue of their sex. These are the patriarchal rights that men exercise over women to deny women's freedom. Historically, then, feminists have both demanded *and* criticized and rejected the "rights of man."[24] Bearing this argument in mind, I want to flesh out the specific contours of Wollstonecraft's "revolution in female manners" in terms of the rights claims she thought it would require and the deeply democratic difference that she believed those claims would make by working on both dimensions of the rights of man simultaneously.

Of course, Wollstonecraft argued for extending to women the basic package of civil and political rights guaranteed to men in the French revolutionaries' *Declaration of the Rights of Man*, thereby universalizing the first dimension of rights by making them applicable to women in their capacity as actors in the public sphere. In the preface to her second *Vindication*, dedicated to Talleyrand, who was actively involved as a legislator in the French Assembly, she even went so far as to compare the revolutionaries to "tyrants of all denomination," from kings to fathers, when they

---

24. Carole Pateman, "The Rights of Man and Early Feminism," *Swiss Yearbook of Political Science* (1994): 19–31, especially 21. See also Pateman, "Democracy, Freedom, and Special Rights," in *Social Justice: From Hume to Walzer*, ed. David Boucher and Paul Kelly (New York: Routledge, 1998), 215–31; Pateman, "Women's Writing, Women's Standing: Theory and Politics in the Early Modern Period," in Smith, *Women Writers*, 363–82, especially 369; and Pateman, *The Sexual Contract* (Stanford: Stanford University Press, 1988). For the reasons why Wollstonecraft should be considered a feminist (which some regard as an anachronistic term in the absence of a social movement), see also Karen Offen, "Was Mary Wollstonecraft a Feminist? A Contextual Re-Reading of *A Vindication of the Rights of Woman*, 1792–1992," in *Quilting a New Canon: Stitching Women's Words*, ed. Uma Parameswaran (Toronto: Sister Vision, 1996), 3–24. Like Pateman and Offen, I conclude that it is Wollstonecraft's concern with substantive themes shared by later thinkers to whom we apply the term in an uncontroversial fashion that justifies calling her a feminist, even in the absence of a social movement capable of realizing those shared ends prior to the nineteenth century. Indeed, Wollstonecraft played a vital role in articulating many of the themes that provided the theoretical underpinning of those later movements, as their leaders self-consciously acknowledged.

"*force[ed]* all women, by denying them civil and political rights, to remain immured in their families, groping in the dark" of domestic isolation. "Who made man the exclusive judge," she asked, "if woman partake with him the gift of reason?" (5:67). Wollstonecraft thus used the universal theoretical potential of the discourse of rights to push the revolutionaries to accept the radical upshot of their purported commitments. If they failed to do so, they were hypocrites. For her, a woman "must not, if she discharge her civil duties, want, individually, the protection of civil laws." So, too, she insisted that women "ought to have representatives, instead of being arbitrarily governed without having any direct share allowed them in the deliberations of government" (5:216–17).

Simultaneously, however, Wollstonecraft initiated an attack on the second dimension of the rights of man, that which upheld male power, by arguing for a thorough overhaul of the legal system, especially the common law of coverture. As William Blackstone famously depicted it, coverture meant that marriage made the husband and wife "one person in law," where "the very being or legal existence of the woman is suspended during the marriage" or (what amounts to the same thing), "at least is incorporated and consolidated into that of the husband," under whose "cover" she existed entirely.[25] Throughout the eighteenth century and well into the nineteenth, the common law of coverture effectively ensured that married English women, like African slaves, were civilly dead. Wollstonecraft's response was that the "laws respecting woman...make an absurd unit of a man and his wife; and then, by the easy transition of only considering him as responsible, she is reduced to a mere cypher" (5:215). Coverture legally codified the Burkean notion that women must necessarily submit to sublime male power, and that male will thereby subsumes, or covers, female will. The practical consequence was a code of law in which violence against women within the confines of the family, such as marital rape and domestic beatings, were not simply rendered invisible; for legal purposes they were assumed to be in accord with wives' actual wishes in the first instance.

Thus, in order to understand Wollstonecraft's position concerning the "rights of man," we must recognize the mutually reinforcing and two-pronged quality of her arguments. For example, a logical extrapolation from Wollstonecraft's position concerning the first dimension of men's

---

25. See Blackstone, *Commentaries on the Laws of England* (1765), Book I, xv, cited in *Works of Wollstonecraft*, 5:215.

rights is that by gaining civil and political equality in public, women would eventually be able to elect representatives that kept them from being arbitrarily governed by men in private. So, too, her demand that the common law of coverture be abolished was aimed at truly guaranteeing women's life and liberty (fundamental features of the first dimension of the rights of man) by protecting their persons in private. Extending the logic of the first dimension of rights into the private sphere, where the second dimension had previously remained untouched, thereby *enabled* meaningful political participation by women in public. Only when the threats to life and liberty posed by men's rights in private were eliminated did Wollstonecraft believe that political efficacy in public became a real possibility for women.

This is the context in which to understand certain aspects of Wollstonecraft's argument in the *Rights of Woman* that have been unduly narrowed by some scholars, such as the entire chapter she devotes to a discussion of eighteenth-century associational psychology, entitled "The Effect Which an Early Association of Ideas Has Upon the Character" (5:185–90).[26] In this discussion, which immediately follows her condemnation of the female conduct books, Wollstonecraft asked whether it is at all surprising that women, who were educated according to the dictates of writers like Fordyce and Gregory, seemed to suffer from "a defect of nature." She thought this was a particularly likely mistake when one considered the "determinate effect an early association of ideas has on the character," combined with women's "subordinate state in society." Women could never "recover their lost ground" in relation to men; was it any wonder, then, that they "neglect[ed] their understandings, and turn[ed] all their attention to their persons?" (5:185).

Wollstonecraft maintained that one important aspect of patriarchal rights was men's control of the process of character formation in women, beginning at a very early age. By strictly limiting the range of female experiences, men strictly limited the range of ideas that women could entertain. In an argument that echoed her review of William Smellie's

26. But see Virginia Sapiro's piece, "A Woman's Struggle for a Language of Enlightenment and Virtue: Mary Wollstonecraft and Enlightenment 'Feminism,'" in *Perspectives on Feminist Political Thought in European History: From the Middle Ages to the Present*, ed. Tjitske Akkerman and Siep Stuurman (New York: Routledge, 1998), 122–35, especially 126–28; and Taylor's *Mary Wollstonecraft*, 86–89. For a discussion of the political importance of associational psychology, see Roy Porter, *The Creation of the Modern World: The Untold Story of the British Enlightenment* (New York: W. W. Norton, 2000).

work for the *Analytical*, Wollstonecraft melded the tools of associational psychology into a radically egalitarian argument for thoroughly reconstructing female character from the earliest stage of life. She claimed that it was essential to initiate the revolution in female manners at birth because of the extraordinary influence of early experiences on the formation of human character, via the "associations" that those experiences necessarily summoned forth. "So ductile is the understanding, and yet so stubborn, that the associations which depend on adventitious circumstances, during the period that the body takes to arrive at maturity, can seldom be disentangled by reason. One idea calls up another, its old associate, and memory, faithful to the first impressions, particularly when the intellectual powers are not employed to cool our sensations, retraces them with mechanical exactness" (5:186).

Moreover, such "habitual slavery, to first impressions" proved to have "a more baneful effect on the female than the male character," since "business" and other "employments of the understanding" worked to "break associations that do violence to reason" in men. Females, however, were made women when they were still children (by copying the manners of their mothers), and as women were taught to act like children. Unlike men, they had no public sphere employment that could enable them to undo a pernicious chain of associations. Through a "cruel association of ideas," women were "only taught to observe behavior, and acquire manners rather than morals": "Every thing that they see or hear serves to fix impressions, call forth emotions, and associate ideas, that give a sexual character to the mind" (5:186–187).

If this process of social construction was to be fundamentally altered, the first links of the associational chain had to be broken. To combat the second dimension of the rights of man and reconstruct female character, women had to be educated very differently. Wollstonecraft therefore defended a first-dimension right to publicly subsidized national coeducational institutions. Educating boys and girls together from a very early age would counteract the pernicious effects of the prevailing system of female character formation by giving girls access to the same broad range of early experiences as boys, thus producing a more complex and richer association of ideas, and a very different female character. She believed that this was the appropriate approach, especially since "public education, of every denomination, should be directed to form citizens" (5:233–34).[27]

27. For the general argument, see chapter 12, "On National Education," 5:229–50.

A right to publicly subsidized coeducational institutions was not, however, sufficient to counter patriarchal rights. Given her Lockean epistemology of associational psychology, Wollstonecraft viewed character formation as a function of varied experience and therefore comprehended "education" in the broadest sense possible, because "employment of the thoughts shapes the character both generally and individually." But "the thoughts of women ever hover round their persons," with the result that "false notions of female excellence," by "calling the attention continually to the body, cramp the activity of the mind" (5:144–45). Drawing this analysis to its logical conclusion, Wollstonecraft contended that it was "of great importance to observe that the character of every man is, in some degree, formed by his profession" (5:87). Her goal was not so much better schooling for young girls as it was a thorough democratic overhaul of the process of women's social construction, writ large.

Now, while Wollstonecraft argued that women, like men, must be "active citizens," it is undoubtedly true that she saw the role of many women as one of managing their families and educating the children who would in turn become the next generation of citizens. As Pateman has convincingly argued, Wollstonecraft focused on women's "specific capacities, talents, needs and concerns," and argued that in many instances the expression of their citizenship would be functionally differentiated from that of men; that is, it would be equal, but different. Wollstonecraft was in fact one of the very first thinkers to attempt to navigate a course between the Charybdis of sameness and the Scylla of difference, a dilemma that has confronted feminists ever since.[28]

To this end, Wollstonecraft also made overtures in the direction of something like a right to a guaranteed basic income for all women, including married women whose unpaid and invisible labor in the home would thus be recognized as vital to the state's flourishing. In contemporary human rights parlance, we might view Wollstonecraft's argument as analogous to current feminists' second-generation rights claims that women's unpaid work in private must be accounted for as a means of achieving their financial independence from men, and therefore as central to undermining patriarchal rights, or the second dimension of the rights of man. Wollstonecraft declared that a married woman "must not be dependent

---

28. In fact, Pateman has christened the difficulty of attempting to reconcile female equality and difference "Wollstonecraft's Dilemma"; see Pateman, "The Patriarchal Welfare State," in her *Disorder of Women: Democracy, Feminism, and Political Theory* (Stanford: Stanford University Press, 1989), 196–97.

on her husband's bounty for her subsistence during his life, or support after his death," because it was "vain to expect virtue from women till they are, in some degree, independent of men." This was true for married as well as single women. As long as married women were "absolutely dependent on their husbands they will be cunning, mean, and selfish," and would be neither good wives nor good mothers (5: 216–17, 211–12).

As we have seen, however, Wollstonecraft's feminism was embedded in a much broader range of egalitarian commitments, and she contended that all "unnatural distinctions established in society" must be abolished. Fundamental among these "unnatural" types of inequality was property distribution. In one of many passages that undermine the reading of Wollstonecraft as a bourgeois liberal, she wrote, "From the respect paid to property flow, as from a poisoned fountain, most of the evils and vices which render this world such a dreary scene to the contemplative mind." Indeed, it was "in the most polished society that noisome reptiles and venomous serpents lurk under the rank herbage," and where "one class presses on another," with all "aiming to procure respect on account of their property" (5:211). Needless to say, this was a radical counterargument to Burke and the Scottish Enlightenment.

It was in the context of arguing for greater economic equality, and against the class tensions produced by commercial society, that Wollstonecraft pointed to the particular hardships faced by women, and provided novel solutions to ameliorate those difficulties. "There must be more equality established in society, or morality will never gain ground," she argued. "Virtuous equality" would never be realized so long as "one half of mankind be chained to its bottom by fate" (5:211).

Women therefore had to have another first-dimension right, that of full and equal access to those public occupations that had previously been the sole province of men. They might "be physicians as well as nurses," said Wollstonecraft, "study politics," or pursue "business of various kinds," assuming "they were educated in a more orderly manner, which might save many from common and legal prostitution." She asked plaintively, "Is not that government then very defective, and very unmindful of the happiness of one half of its members, that does not provide for honest, independent women, by encouraging them to fulfill respectable stations?" (5:218–19).

Again, this is a claim concerning the first dimension of the rights of man—a government guarantee of equal access to employment—that is understood simultaneously to have profound implications for destroying the second dimension of those rights. If women had the ability to study and practice medicine, business, or politics, Wollstonecraft argued that many might resist selling their bodies on the streets, or the "legal prostitution" of marriage, wherein they were subjected to the common law of coverture, and existed "merely to gratify the appetite of man, or to be the upper servant, who provides his meals and takes care of his linen" (5:109, 218). Wollstonecraft conceptualized equal employment opportunities as a pathway to financial independence that could free women from the patriarchal rights that their husbands had to their bodies in the form of unmitigated sexual access and unremunerated labor. Put differently, employment in the public sphere might enable women to resist the sublime male power that left them submissive and terrified at the prospect of rapine and destruction being visited upon them if they resisted.

Similarly, Wollstonecraft insisted that women had a right to financial assistance from the fathers of their children, regardless of whether those children were born in wedlock. She did this specifically with reference to an argument made by Adam Smith in *The Theory of Moral Sentiments*. Smith had pointed to the care of infant children as proof of civilization's progress and refinement of manners over the four stages of historical development. Whereas barbarians left their children on rocks in the open air to die if they could not care for them, Smith wrote, the civilized members of commercial societies, infused with sensibility, would never dream of committing such an atrocity.[29] For Wollstonecraft, writing as a woman, the tale was not such a simple one of linear moral progress:

> Contrasting the humanity of the present age with the barbarism of antiquity, great stress has been laid on the savage custom of exposing the children whom their parents could not maintain; whilst the man of sensibility, who thus, perhaps, complains, by his promiscuous amours produces a most destructive barrenness and contagious flagitiousness of manners. Surely nature never intended that women, by satisfying an appetite, should frustrate the very purpose for which it was implanted? I have before observed, that men ought to maintain the women whom they have seduced; this would be one means of reforming female manners, and stopping

---

29. See Adam Smith, *The Theory of Moral Sentiments*, ed. D. D. Raphael and A. L. Macfie (Indianapolis: Liberty Fund, 1984), V.2.13–2.16, pp. 209–11, and Chapter 1 of this volume.

an abuse that has an equally fatal effect on population and morals. (5:209)

The practice Wollstonecraft discusses is clearly the abortion of pregnancies that the mother would have otherwise wanted to come to term. Regardless of one's position on this issue, what is remarkable is Wollstonecraft's analysis of the root cause of the problem: the behavior of men of sensibility who blithely impregnated women, only to disavow any responsibility for their actions. Her answer to this problem was for men to take financial responsibility for the children they fathered, rather than casting female behavior as a vestige of savagery or barbarism in order to uphold their own power and irresponsibility.

This brings us to Wollstonecraft's views on the relations between parents and children. Here, she argued, women needed to develop their rational faculties and enlarge their understandings, or else *they* would be tyrants, domineering over their children, who would unfailingly learn to be tyrannical in turn. "To be a good mother—a woman must have sense, and that independence of mind which few women possess who are taught to depend entirely on their husbands" (5:222–23). Similarly, in discussing children's duty to their parents, Wollstonecraft argued, probably with Burke in mind, that there was a tendency "to make prescription always take place of reason, and to place every duty on an arbitrary foundation. The rights of kings are deduced in a direct line from the King of kings; and that of parents from our first parent" (5:224). In this way Wollstonecraft rejected, at least implicitly, a view of patriarchy that went back to Sir Robert Filmer, and which she believed was far from dead, at least when it came to justifying parental tyranny over their children.

In his *Account of the European Settlements in America*, Burke had argued that liberty and equality were the true signifiers of savagery. This absurd set of commitments could be seen specifically in savages' unwillingness to physically punish their children, and in their belief that reason would guide those children eventually, before which time their faults could not be great enough to require corporal punishment. The upshot of such faulty parenting, for Burke, was that savage children, since they never experienced anything like command, dependence, or subordination, rejected these things as adults, with dire consequences.[30]

30. See Edmund Burke and Will Burke, *An Account of the European Settlements in America*, 2 vols. (London: J. Dodsley, 1757; reprint, New York: Arno Press, 1972), 1:175–76, and Chapter 2 of this volume.

Conversely, Wollstonecraft argued that the only basis for filial obedience was the faithful discharge of parental duties. For her, the parent-child relationship was really one of "reciprocal duty" based on reason. If parents fulfilled their duties, they had strong claims to the allegiance and obedience of their children; if they did not, they had none. Wollstonecraft specifically lamented the "blind obedience" and "slavish bondage to parents" demanded of young girls, which merely fitted them for their later fate in marriage: "thus taught slavishly to submit to their parents, they are prepared for the slavery of marriage" (5:224, 226).

Such arguments demonstrate the very great extent to which Wollstonecraft linked the democratization of the public sphere with the democratization of the private; she was firmly convinced that "public affections, as well as public virtues, must ever grow out of the private character" (5:234). As with Burke's little platoons, so with Wollstonecraft, the family was a deeply political institution: "A man has been termed a microcosm; and every family might also be called a state"; therefore, since "public virtue is only an aggregate of private," when morality is "polluted in the national reservoir," it "sends off streams of vice to corrupt the constituent parts of the body politic" (5:264, 249). Just like Burke, Wollstonecraft argued that the tenor of politics in the public sphere would be heavily conditioned by the tenor of private sphere interactions within the family. Unlike him, however, she contended that women must have their characters prepared for the duties of democratic citizenship. "Public spirit must be nurtured by private virtue." The "preposterous distinctions of rank" in fact did just the opposite, thereby stunting the civilizing process and rendering "civilization a curse, by dividing the world between voluptuous tyrants, and cunning envious dependents" (5:210, 215). Unlike Rousseau, Wollstonecraft's feminist insight enabled her to broaden her theoretical commitment to democracy to encompass the family among the institutions and social practices predicated on power and inequality, and in dire need of egalitarian overhaul.

In the last analysis, then, Mary Wollstonecraft's *Vindication of the Rights of Woman* called the French revolutionaries to task on a number of fronts. Her argument was that their failure to apply the democratizing logic of rights to both the public *and* private spheres would effectively uphold the second dimension of the rights of man while simultaneously locking women out of the first. Such a failure, she insisted, would show that men would always, "in some shape, act like a tyrant, and tyranny, in whatever part of society it rears its brazen front, will ever undermine morality." Male tyranny hindered the progress of democracy and therefore of civilization itself by denying "JUSTICE for one half of the human race" (5:68–69).

At the most basic level, Wollstonecraft believed that extending the first dimension of the rights of man to women in private directly undermined the second dimension of patriarchal rights. At the same time, the undermining of patriarchal rights via that extension also made for the real fulfillment of democratic citizenship rights and meaningful political participation in public, thereby enabling the first dimension of rights to flourish. In Wollstonecraft's work, rights were a kind of wedge, a means to a broader end, and that end was thoroughgoing democracy. Rights that may appear purely first-dimensional (the right to equal education, the right of equal access to employment in the public sphere) Wollstonecraft understood as having vital second-dimension effects. She saw the experiences that they provided as enabling a reconstruction of female character in ways that helped women resist the naturalization of their inequality, while also opening the door to financial resources that freed them from male power. In this sense, the category of a purely first-dimensional rights claim simply did not exist for Wollstonecraft. In turn, she saw the resistance to the patriarchal rights of man as necessarily extending into the public sphere, and transforming it.

Mary Wollstonecraft thus defended the French Revolution as a potentially radical emancipatory event capable of transforming both the public and private spheres and ushering in true egalitarian civilization. As we will see, Wollstonecraft's belief that the French Revolution spelled the dawn of a democratic civilization would be sorely tested in the years 1792–94, but she never abandoned it. Meanwhile, Edmund Burke, too, saw the impetus toward deep democracy as at the heart of the revolutionary experiment. For him, however, that vision was a horrifying nightmare that drew from his pen some of the most profound lamentations in the history of Western political thought. It is to Burke's vision of Wollstonecraft's deepest desire — the full democratization of life — that we now turn.

6 | BURKE ON DEMOCRACY AS THE DEATH OF WESTERN CIVILIZATION

> These are choice speculations, with which the Author [Lord Auckland] amuses himself, and tries to divert us, in the blackest hours of the dismay, defeat and calamity of all civilized nations. They have but one fault, that they are directly contrary to the common sense and common feeling of mankind. If I had but one hour to live, I would employ it in decrying this wretched system, and die with my pen in my hand...
>
> — EDMUND BURKE, *Letters on a Regicide Peace* (1795)

> I hope and supplicate, that all provident and virtuous Wives and Mothers of families, will employ all the just influence they possess over their Husbands and Children, to save themselves and their families from the ruin that the Mesdames de Staals and the Mesdames Rolands, and the Mesdames de Sillery, and the Mrs. Helena Maria Williams, and the Mrs. Woolstencrofts &c &c &c &c and all that Clan of desperate, Wicked, and mischievously ingenious Women, who have brought, or are likely to bring Ruin and shame upon all those that listen to them. You ought to make their very names odious to your Children. The Sex has much influence. Let the honest and prudent save us from the Evils with which we are menaced by the daring, the restless, and the unprincipled.
>
> — EDMUND BURKE TO MRS. JOHN CREWE (1795)

Burke claimed never to have read Wollstonecraft's reply to him, despite its having been sent directly to his home.[1] Nevertheless, it is clear from his letter to Mrs. John Crewe, quoted above, that he counted Wollstonecraft as one of a new brand of politically active women who were ingenious and evil supporters of the French Revolution, and whose very names ought to

---

1. The epigraphs to this chapter are taken from, respectively, Edmund Burke, *The Writings and Speeches of Edmund Burke*, ed. Paul Langford, 8 vols. to date (Oxford: Clarendon Press, 1981–) (hereafter *Writings and Speeches*), 9:58, and *The Correspondence of Edmund Burke*, ed. Thomas W. Copeland, 10 vols. (Chicago: University of Chicago Press, 1958–78) (hereafter *Correspondence*), 8:304. For Burke's denial that he ever read Wollstonecraft's *Vindication of the Rights of Men*, see Burke, *Correspondence*, 6:214.

be made the objects of hatred to future generations. For Burke, Wollstonecraft was a British Jacobin bent on joining the French revolutionaries in their democratic project of destroying Western civilization. We have already seen how Burke framed the Revolution in a unique melding of Scottish Enlightenment moral philosophy and historiography with the leading themes of his earlier work. I concluded Chapter 4 by suggesting that Burke saw the French Revolution as a process in which newly emerging political democracy was being bolstered by intentional policies of social, cultural, and sexual democratization. Having already considered Burke's remarks on public sphere democracy, I turn in this chapter to the latter portion of that claim. My focus here is on what Burke wrote after the *Reflections on the Revolution in France*, which elaborates his view of the French Revolution as a catastrophe that would turn natural human feelings, and the various hierarchical relations derived from them, on their head. In some of the most extraordinary prose in the history of Western political thought, Burke decried what he saw as the revolutionaries' systematic attempt to break down natural authority relations within the family, to foster adultery, sexual promiscuity, and divorce, to establish the legal equality of nontraditional families and their offspring, to precipitate an explosion in popular entertainment of all sorts, and to use the new power of the press to shape and control public opinion to spread their egalitarian message. Burke explicitly connected this egalitarian cultural revolution in morals and manners with the advent of political democracy, and he depicted this process as the wholesale collapse of civilization into savagery. He steadfastly maintained that the French were introducing a new system of democratic manners precisely to accommodate and support their new scheme of democratic politics, based on the theory that democracy in the public sphere required equality in the private sphere. As we will see, Burke would fight to the bitter end of his life against the rise of this new world.

The Agents of Revolution

It is perhaps best to begin this exploration by isolating Burke's thinking about the social agents responsible for the French Revolution. Pocock rightly points out that the *philosophes*, or "men of letters," who were so prominent in the *Reflections on the Revolution in France* remained the driving force of the mammoth *Letters on a Regicide Peace* (1795–97) as well. The speculators in public debt who played such an important role in the

Reflections, however, were displaced in Burke's later writings by the "politicians" as the second revolutionary force. These were the bureaucrats, clerks, and technicians of national power who came to the *philosophes* for guidance in making their theoretical project concrete.[2] Let us consider each of these groups in turn.

Regarding the "cannibal philosophers of France," Burke nearly exhausted his voluminous vocabulary and finally took literary refuge in the satanic and scatological. When acting in concert, he maintained, "a more dreadful calamity cannot arise out of Hell to scourge mankind." The philosophers were like "the principle of Evil himself, incorporeal, pure, unmixed, dephlegmated, defecated evil."[3]

In Burke's rendering, the philosophers had one principal focus with respect to the Old Regime, which was "the utter extirpation of religion" from France, and ideally from Europe and the entire world. All considerations of French empire were secondary to this. "Their temporal ambition was wholly subservient to their proselytizing spirit in which they were not exceeded by Mahomet himself." Indeed, Burke regarded the philosophers as representing a kind of atheistic Islam, engaging in an unholy form of jihad, which they pursued with "fanatical fury."[4]

In a reformulation of the eighteenth-century bogeyman of religious enthusiasm,[5] Burke argued that those "who have made but superficial studies in the Natural History of the human mind," by which he probably meant David Hume, have regarded "religious opinions as the only cause of enthusiastic zeal, and sectarian propagation." This was a big mistake, according to Burke, because "there is no doctrine whatever, on which men can warm, that is not capable of the very same effect." Man's "social nature" actually "impels him to propagate his principles," whatever they may be.[6] Thus atheism could be just as fanatical as any form of religion. It was crucial to recognize, Burke argued, that if fanatical atheistic enthusiasm

---

2. See J. G. A. Pocock, "The "Political Economy of Burke's Analysis of the French Revolution," in Pocock, *Virtue, Commerce, and History: Essays on Political Thought and History, Chiefly in the Eighteenth Century* (Cambridge: Cambridge University Press, 1985), 205–6; and his introduction to Burke's *Reflections on the Revolution in France* (Indianapolis: Hackett, 1987), xxxvii.

3. Burke, *Writings and Speeches*, 9:174, 176.

4. Ibid., 9:278.

5. On this theme, see Pocock's "Edmund Burke and the Redefinition of Enthusiasm: The Context as Counter-Revolution," in *The French Revolution and the Creation of Modern Political Culture*, vol. 3, ed. François Furet and Mona Ozouf (Oxford: Pergamon Press, 1989), 19–43.

6. Burke, *Writings and Speeches*, 9:278.

was left out of the equation, "we omit the principal feature in the French Revolution."[7]

This view would loom increasingly large in Burke's reading of the Revolution in the final years of his life. Burke's concern for the eclipse of organized religion in the West was of a piece with everything he ever wrote, from the earliest point in his career. He never wavered in his notion that Christianity was one of the two central forces propelling the European civilizing process, guaranteeing the sublime consecration of the state, enabling habitual social discipline such that the "people" could exist and flourish under the guidance of the natural aristocracy. Burke believed that the *philosophes* understood just how much the European Old Regime owed to Christianity, which is precisely why they concluded that its hierarchical institutions and ideas had to be destroyed before democratization could proceed.

As early as 1791 Burke described the French Revolution as a unique war, "unprecedented in the annals of Europe"; and he encouraged the church to see that it would usher in a state of affairs that was "absolutely new." He pled with the archbishop of Nisibis and the pope's nuncio not to attempt peaceful relations with the new French regime, because its goal was nothing short of eliminating the religious "Empire of Opinion." We know that the church's control and transmission of this empire (indeed, even the phrase itself) went back to Burke's argument in the *An Abridgment of the English History* and was central to that work's analysis of the emergence of European civilization. The church's survival was thus part and parcel of the political survival of the Old Regime: "Foolish it would be, foolish below all degrees in the Scale of Folly, for Princes to suffer the Empire of Opinion to be Abolished in the World, Armies will but ill supply it, Opinion sooner or later will give or take away all its efficacy from that power. When opinion fails Armies will turn upon their Keepers, Domestic Troops will become seditious; Foreign Troops will show themselves mercenary." Burke concluded that if Louis XVI had "carefully cultivated the Policy of Opinion," even if "he had possessed no Troops, he might now [still] be a king."[8]

In Burke's view, the perpetuation of religion's sublime monopoly on the empire of opinion far transcended the internal divisions within Christianity itself, as the revolutionaries well recognized:

7. Ibid., 9:279.
8. Burke to the archbishop of Nisibis, with copy to the pope's nuncio, 14 December 1791, Burke, *Correspondence*, 6:458–59.

> As the grand prejudice, and that which holds all the other prejudices together, the first, last, and middle Object of their Hostility, is Religion. With that they are at inexpiable war. They make no distinction of Sects. A Christian, as such, is to them an Enemy. What then is left to a real Christian, (Christian as a believer and as a Statesman) but to make a league between all the grand divisions of that name, to protect and to cherish them all; and by no means to proscribe in any manner, more or less, any member of our common party. The divisions which formerly prevailed in the Church, with all their overdone Zeal, only purified and ventilated, our common faith; because there was no common Enemy arrayed and embattled to take advantage of their dissensions: But now nothing but inevitable ruin will be the consequence of our Quarrels.... Depend upon it, they must all be supported; or they must all fall in the crash of a common Ruin.[9]

When one comprehended the scale of the Jacobin attack on Christianity, the petty sectarian squabbles between Catholics and Protestants that so troubled the eighteenth century appeared trifling and absurd. The real enemy was revolutionary secularism.

Burke's concern to unify Catholics and Protestants in a holy war against the atheists can be seen in a letter of May 1795 to his friend and Irish MP Sir Hercules Langrishe. Burke expressed his fear that the oppression of Irish Catholics might turn them on the Protestant ascendancy, until they "become what are called *Franco-Jacobins*, and reject the whole together." "The worst of the matter," he told Langrishe, is that "you are partly leading, partly driving, into Jacobinism that description of your people whose religious principles—church polity, and habitual discipline—might make them an invincible dyke against that inundation."[10] Burke hoped that the Catholics, trained to hierarchy and discipline, might join the Protestants in fighting off the atheists, but he feared that discriminatory policies toward Catholics were actually driving them into the hands of the devil himself.

Burke argued that to the second force driving the Revolution, the "politicians," the issue of religion was entirely secondary. While they were disbelievers, they gave it little thought. The politicians soon found that they

---

9. See Burke to William Smith, 29 January 1795, ibid., 8:130. For Burke's bountiful expression of similar sentiments, see his letters to Fitzwilliam of 10 February 1795 and his correspondence with Rev. Hussey in the same year, ibid., 8:144–48, 142–43, 199–205, 245–50.

10. Burke to Sir Hercules Langrishe, 26 May 1795, ibid., 8:255.

could not do without the philosophers, however, because they came to understand that the destruction of religion, together with the confiscation and liquidation of church property, would be the principal means of financing their wars of territorial aggrandizement. Of the two types of revolutionaries, then, "the philosophers were the active internal agitators, and supplied the spirit and principles: the second gave the practical direction."[11]

Burke's vision of the French Revolution was not, at base, one of the petit bourgeoisie seizing the property of the landed nobility and church in order to throw off the economic yoke of feudalism and usher in the new capitalist order. While it was certainly true that the property of those old orders was seized, property confiscation was secondary for Burke. It was a bribe held out to the masses to win their complicity. The philosophers and politicians acted in consort to win the people over by holding out material enticements. For Burke, property was important chiefly because it materially nourished the two institutions of church and nobility that had cultivated and protected the old system of morals and manners. The French revolutionaries were primarily interested in confiscating that property for the purpose of eradicating the two civilizing institutions it fed.

As Pocock argues, Burke's reading of the Revolution was one in which an alliance of intellectuals and the technocrats of state power became intoxicated with the new enthusiasm of social engineering. Burke believed that the Revolutionaries were intent on destroying the manners that had constituted Old Regime civilization, in order to impose their own purposes upon it. Whereas for other eighteenth-century thinkers, like Hume or Gibbon, religious enthusiasm was merely a religious psychopathology, what Burke dreaded was a new form of enthusiastic zeal embodied in the alliance between intelligentsia and bureaucrats, one divorced from the old social constraints of the natural aristocracy.[12] Burke maintained that this combination of "philosophers and politicians," acting in consort, had produced a "silent revolution in the moral world [which] preceded the political, and prepared it."[13] As Pocock argues, Burke saw the specter haunting Europe not as Marx's capitalist bourgeoisie replacing feudalism but rather as an "ideologized mass" animated by this unholy alliance. Burke's story was of an eschaton to history played out according to Smith and the historiog-

11. Burke, *Writings and Speeches*, 9:280.
12. See Pocock's introduction to Burke's *Reflections*, xxxvii–xxxviii; and Pocock, "Burke and the Redefinition of Enthusiasm," 32–34.
13. Burke, *Writings and Speeches*, 9:291. See Pocock, "Political Economy of Burke's Analysis," 207.

raphy of the Scottish Enlightenment, rather than Marx; it was the end of "a history of manners and revolutions in manners."[14]

As Pocock notes, this distinction can be seen in the following passage (among others):

> We have not considered as we ought the dreadful energy of a State, in which the property has nothing to do with the Government... and where nothing rules but the mind[s] of desperate men. The condition of a commonwealth not governed by its property was a combination of things, which the learned and ingenious speculator Harrington, who has tossed about society into all forms, never could imagine to be possible. We have seen it; the world has felt it; and if the world will shut their eyes to this state of things, they will feel it more.[15]

The twentieth century certainly taught thinking people the dangers of grand political scheming and massive social engineering. It is nevertheless curious that, together with the natural law school and others, Pocock seems keen to credit Burke's analysis as clairvoyant and prophetic in its isolation of the "theory of totalitarianism" at the heart of the French Revolution.[16] This is the second place where I make a fundamental break with Pocock's often brilliant analysis of Burke's work.[17] It is my contention, against Pocock and others, that what Burke feared about the French Revolution was not its theoretical resonance with a later century's Nazis, Red Guards, or Khmer Rouge. To the contrary, what Burke saw as the substantive content of the ideal in the heads of the desperate social engineers driving the French Revolution was deep democracy—that is, democracy in the public sphere reinforced by democracy in the private sphere. Such

---

14. Pocock's introduction to Burke's *Reflections*, xxxviii; and Pocock, "Burke and the Redefinition of Enthusiasm," 34.

15. Burke, *Writings and Speeches*, 9:289. See Pocock, "Political Economy of Burke's Analysis," 208.

16. Pocock writes, "We may protest that France in 1797 was in full retreat from Jacobinism; but the emergence of the Nazis, the Red Guards, and the Khmer Rouge in our time suggests that Burke's last work [the *Letters on a Regicide Peace*] was the *1984* of its generation. He had discovered the theory of totalitarianism and was enlarging it into prophecy" ("Introduction," xxxvii). See also Pocock's "Burke and the Redefinition of Enthusiasm," 32–34. For other examples of the argument that what Burke objected to about the French Revolution was its "totalitarian" character, see Chapter 4 of this volume, n. 46.

17. The other such break, as I argued in Chapter 4, is in my insistence on the centrality of Burke's aesthetic to his political theory.

was the particular political character of the revolutionaries' new-fangled secular, "atheistic" enthusiasm. It was precisely the *substantive democratic content* of the grand scheme that the revolutionaries proposed to institute in place of the Old Regime, not simply the fact of social engineering itself, let alone totalitarian social engineering, that Burke viewed as the end of Western civilization. The "savagery" Burke feared was not totalitarianism; it was democracy.

The Democratic Death of the Little Platoon

In 1791 Burke wrote two pieces that were a direct comment on and elaboration of his argument in the *Reflections*. The first of these was the *Appeal from the New to the Old Whigs*, a portion of the argument of which we have already considered. The title of that work comes from Burke's method of responding to his erstwhile "new" Whig allies, led by Charles James Fox, who ardently defended the French Revolution, a stance that led Burke to break tearfully with them on the floor of the House of Commons. Burke "appeals" to evidence from the speeches and writings of an earlier generation of "old" Whigs to demonstrate that his view of the French Revolution as entirely antithetical to the British constitution and the Glorious Revolution of 1688 (and implicitly discordant with the American Revolution) was accurate on its own, fully consonant with true Whig principles, and demonstrative of his political consistency. In the *Appeal*, Burke argued that the *Reflections* was aimed partly at convincing the public that British support for the French Revolution would pose the gravest of all threats, that is, "the utter overthrow of...the whole system of its manners, in favor of the new constitution, and of the modern usages, of the French nation."[18]

Far from an approximate emulation of the British constitution, Burke maintained, "what was done in France was a wild attempt to methodize anarchy; to perpetuate and fix disorder." It was a "foul, impious, monstrous thing, wholly out of the course of moral nature," and it went "far beyond any example that can be found in the civilized European world of our age." Burke professed utter disbelief at Fox's admiration of the Revolution, and he contrasted the *ancien régime*'s civilized system of morals and manners with the "licentious, ferocious, and savage multitude, without

---

18. *The Works of the Right Honourable Edmund Burke* (London: Bell & Daldy, 1872) (hereafter *Works of Burke*), 3:7.

laws, manners, or morals and which, so far from respecting the general sense of mankind, insolently endeavors to alter all the principles and opinions, which have hitherto guided and contained the world, and to force them into a conformity to their views and actions."[19] Destroying the old system of manners, together with the institutions that had cultivated and developed it, constituted an attack on human nature and civilization. It was a radical form of political revision that aimed at thoroughly reconstructing social, cultural, and political institutions after first violently ripping out the innate moral sense found in all human beings. How did this attack proceed?

As I have argued, we fundamentally misunderstand Burke if we think he believed that just because universal moral, sexual, social, and political obligations could not be *rationally* affirmed, they could not be affirmed at all. Nothing could be further from Burke's position. In the *Appeal*, in a fashion wholly consistent with the epistemology of sense and feeling at the root of his moral theory, Burke argued that while we can never hope to rationally comprehend our obligations and duties, we nevertheless know them and are bound by them, irrespective of our will, because they *feel natural*.

Burke's position goes far beyond what is usually meant by the phrase "tacit consent," insofar as that term conveys the idea that individuals have obligations quite apart from any expressed conveyance of their will. Burke's argument is that will and duty have little if anything to do with each other. The key to his notion of obligation is contained in a series of passages from the *Appeal* that further develop the argument first expressed in the *Reflections*, that the state was a moral essence, a "covenant" of a very particular kind. Anyone who considered "civil society" should remember "that if we owe to it any duty, it is not subject to our will. Duties are not voluntary. Duty and will are even contradictory terms."[20]

Burke reminded his readers that God, the sublime and "awful Author of our being," defined our existential place in the temporal order of things. Consequently, we have obligations whose "duties are all compulsive." As an example, Burke cited marriage, in which "the duties are not matters of choice. They are dictated by the nature of the situation." Yet from these "instincts" and "physical causes, unknown to us, perhaps unknowable, arise moral duties, which, as we are able perfectly to comprehend, we are

---

19. Ibid., 8–9, 14.
20. Ibid., 76, 78.

bound indispensably to perform." Husbands and wives, parents and children ("without their actual consent") are knit together in particular natural relationships, duty bound, "because the presumed consent of every rational creature is in unison with the predisposed order of things."[21]

None of these arguments was new. The primacy of nature and instinct as the basis of all moral relations and social and political obligations, the insistence on the strict limits of reason, the inability to rationally ascertain God's will, but the ability to know it and the necessity of acting upon it, all go back to Burke's earliest work. In the *Appeal*, Burke argues that it is from these natural "physical relations" within the family that the "social ties and ligaments" that bind us in particular ways to our country first emerge.[22] This echoes his famous argument in the *Reflections* about the "little platoon" of the family, which functions as the seed of public affections, including love of country and ultimately of mankind itself.[23] Of course, the phrase "little platoon," and Burke's subsequent insistence on the centrality of the family as the cornerstone of Western civilization, have been favorite conservative leitmotifs ever since.

What has been ignored in most interpretations of Burke, however, is his description of the *character* of the relationship that obtains between the polity and the family, and the transformation of that relationship during the French Revolution.[24] This is curious, since Burke insists that it is these supposedly natural familial relationships that train the masses to politics and ensure that any remotely "democratic commonwealth" yielded the appropriately deferential modes of citizenship guaranteed by "habitual social discipline" for a people to emerge, governed by the natural aristocracy.[25] Appropriately conditioned, political subjects know that "the votes of a majority of the people, whatever their infamous flatterers may teach in order to corrupt their minds," could not alter the moral and political

21. Ibid., 79–80.
22. Ibid., 80.
23. Burke, *Writings and Speeches*, 8:97–98.
24. I draw here on my article "Burke on Democracy as the Death of Western Civilization," *Polity* 36, no.2 (2004): 201–25. For an exception to the general disregard of the family in Burke's work, see Eileen Hunt Botting, *Family Feuds: Wollstonecraft, Burke, and Rousseau on the Transformation of the Family* (Albany: State University of New York Press, 2006). However, that book's argument and conclusions are very different from my own with respect to both Burke and Wollstonecraft. For an interesting reading of Burke's position on the broader institutions of what we refer to today as "civil society," see also Richard Boyd, *Uncivil Society: The Perils of Pluralism and the Making of Modern Liberalism* (Lanham, Md.: Lexington Books, 2004), 153–75.
25. *Works of Burke*, 3:78, 85. See Chapter 4.

world any more than they could "alter the physical essence of things."[26] Improperly trained within the initial confines of the family, however, the unruly masses posed a tremendous threat to Western civilization, as we will see presently.

Burke began to delineate the consequences of the revolutionaries' approach to the civilizing process in general, and to familial relations in particular, in his second defense of the *Reflections*, known as *A Letter to a Member of the National Assembly* (1791). He subtitled the piece *in Answer to Some Objections to his Book on French Affairs* and addressed it to François-Louis-Thibault de Menonville, who had been a member of the Estates General. Menonville admired Burke's work, and had specifically asked him to clarify certain ideas expressed in the *Reflections* that seemed to him unduly extreme. In the *Letter*, Burke described instead, in astonishing terms, the consequences that he believed could be expected when a people threw off the yoke of habitual social discipline, that admixture of fear and love, of the sublime and the beautiful, by destroying the church and nobility, and chose instead for their guides philosophic imposters, who "pretend[ed] to have made discoveries in the *terra australis* of morality."[27] In visiting this land of untried, untrue, unnatural morality with Burke, we go upstream, into the horrifying democratic heart of conservative darkness.

Burke had concluded in the *Appeal* that only "the moral sentiments" of the revolutionaries could possibly "put some check on their savage theories." But, he cautioned, the moral sentiments will not survive a system "which has for its basis the destruction of all prejudices, and the making the mind proof against all dread of consequences flowing from the pretended truths that are taught by their philosophy. In this school the moral sentiments must grow weaker and weaker each day."[28]

In the *Letter to a Member*, Burke singled out Rousseau in particular as the mastermind behind the social and cultural policies of these "bold experimenters" in the brave new world of untried morality. "His blood they transfuse into their minds and into their manners. Him they study; him they meditate." While "Rousseau is their canon of holy writ," Burke insisted, "Rousseau is a moralist, or he is nothing."[29] The revolutionaries turned to

---

26. Ibid, 3:76–77.
27. Burke, *Writings and Speeches*, 8:305.
28. *Works of Burke*, 3:108.
29. Burke, *Writings and Speeches*, 8:312–13. For an excellent discussion of Burke's critique of Rousseau, see Frans De Bruyn, "Edmund Burke's Natural Aristocrat: The 'Man of Taste' as a Political Ideal," *Eighteenth-Century Life* 11, no. 2 (1987): 41–60. See also David R.

Rousseau because their goal was to find convenient substitutes for all of the principles that had formerly regulated human will and action. "They find dispositions in the mind, of such force and quality, as may fit men, far better than the old morality, for the purposes of such a state as theirs." According to Burke, that old morality was centered on humility, the basis of the Christian system and the foundation of all virtue. In its place the revolutionaries erected a moral philosophy based on intellectual hubris, or vanity, the worst of vices because it perverted all other human qualities. Rousseau, the "insane *Socrates* of the National Assembly," was vanity incarnate, a man brazen enough to make a mad public confession of his mad private faults.[30]

Burke's assault on Rousseau was extremely personal, but its purpose was entirely related to his overarching critique of the French Revolution. His point was precisely that Rousseau's life was an object lesson drawn from his works, one that demonstrated how intellectual vanity could be turned upon our natural moral sense, thus intentionally "reversing the train of our natural feelings." Under the instruction of his writings and with the lessons of his life in hand, the revolutionaries therefore "attempted in France a regeneration of the moral constitution of man."[31]

They chose Rousseau as the means of revolutionizing love itself, that most basic of natural moral sentiments, thereby determining anew who and what should be loved, and how love should be expressed. This was the very core of their revolution in morals and manners. In the *Letter*, Burke

---

Cameron, *The Social Thought of Rousseau and Burke: A Comparative Study* (London: Weidenfeld and Nicolson, 1973); and Annie M. Osborn, *Rousseau and Burke: A Study of the Idea of Liberty in Eighteenth-Century Political Thought* (London: Oxford University Press, 1940).

30. Burke, *Writings and Speeches*, 8:313–14.

31. Ibid., 8:315. In this vein, see also Burke's letter of 1 June 1791 to Claude-François de Rivarol, a royalist and agent for the émigré French nobles at Brussels, in which Burke writes, "I have observed that the Philosophers in order to insinuate their polluted Atheism into young minds, systematically flatter all their passions natural and unnatural. They explode or render odious or contemptible that class of virtues which restrain the appetite. These are at least nine out of ten of the virtues. In the place of all these they substitute a virtue which they call humanity or benevolence. By these means, their morality has no idea in it of restraint, or indeed of a distinct settled principle of any kind. When their disciples are thus left free and guided only by present feeling, they are no longer to be depended on for good or evil. The men who to day snatch the worst criminals from justice, will murder the most innocent persons to morrow" (*Correspondence*, 6:270). As in the *Letter*, we see the revolutionaries infusing the ethics of vanity into the rising generation, flattering them by playing to their unbridled appetites and sapping them of their capacity for moral restraint and Christian humility. Abstract benevolence or humanity replaces natural moral obligation. The species is loved universally but detested individually; fixed principles evaporate, and moral anarchy and chaos ensue.

tells his French correspondent that "love has so general and powerful an influence" on "that part of life which decides the character for ever" that the very "mode and the principles on which it engages the sympathy, and strikes the imagination, become of the utmost importance to the morals and manners of every society. *Your rulers were well aware of this; and in their system of changing your manners to accommodate them to their politics, they found nothing so convenient as Rousseau.*"[32]

The nature of the unheard-of shift that the revolutionaries proposed was from understanding love as a natural moral sentiment that yielded unquestioned acquiescence to relations of hierarchy and subordination, to understanding love as a relation of democratic equality based on free choice. In this way, after destroying the nobility and the church, the revolutionaries aimed their policies of social and cultural democratization first and foremost at the family. Burke maintained this was done with the clear intention of democratizing manners to accommodate them to democratic politics, and thereby to make public and private equality mutually reinforcing. Let us consider this remarkable argument in a bit more detail.[33]

Burke tells Menonville that the revolutionaries had begun by poisoning the minds of children against the natural authority of their parents: "Your masters reject the duties of this vulgar relation, as contrary to liberty; as not founded in the social compact; and not binding according to the rights of men; because the relation is not, of course, the result of *free election*; never so on the side of the children, not always on the part of the parents."[34] This deliberately "savage, and hard-hearted" democratic lesson was part of "their scheme of educating the rising generation, [infusing in them] the principles which they intend to instil, and the sympathies which they wish to form in the mind, at the season in which it is the most susceptible" (8:311–12). To this end the revolutionaries employed tutors (as Rousseau himself was) to brainwash the next generation of children with the mantra of equality.

---

32. Burke, *Writings and Speeches*, 8:317 (emphasis added).

33. My argument in what follows intersects in part with the work of Seamus F. Deane. See his "Burke and the French Philosophes," *Studies in Burke and His Time* 10, no. 2 (1968–69): 1113–37. Deane also suggests (following John A. Lester Jr.'s Ph.D. dissertation, "An Analysis of the Conservative Thought of Edmund Burke," Harvard University, 1942) that Burke's views on these matters evinced the "possible strong influence" of his reading of James Beattie (1136). On this latter point, see also Deane's *The French Revolution and the Enlightenment in England, 1789–1832* (Cambridge: Harvard University Press, 1988), especially 17–18.

34. Burke, *Writings and Speeches*, 8:315–16, hereafter cited parenthetically in the text.

At the same time, these tutors, once inside noble homes, were in a position to further destroy the family by desecrating the sanctity of marriage, specifically by sleeping with the wives and daughters of the nobility. They "betray the most awful family trusts, and vitiate their female pupils. They teach the people, that the debauchers of virgins, almost in the arms of their parents, may be safe inmates in their house, and even fit guardians of the honor of those husbands who succeed legally to the office which the young literators had pre-occupied, without asking leave of law or conscience. Thus they dispose of all the family relations of parents and children, husbands and wives" (8:316).

Once this is achieved, "there is but one step to a frightful corruption":

> The rulers in the National Assembly are in good hopes that the females of the first families in France may become an easy prey to dancing-masters, fiddlers, pattern-drawers, friseurs, and valets de chambre, and other active citizens of that description, who having the entry into your houses, and being half-domesticated by their situation, may be blended with you by regular and irregular relations. By a law, they have made these people your equals. By adopting the sentiments of Rousseau, they have made them your rivals. In this manner, these great legislators complete their plan of levelling, and establish their rights of men on a sure foundation. (8:317)

In these passages Burke described the ultimate horror—that the nobility would be completely eradicated through the intermixture of blood, via sexual conquest, of its wives and daughters with the beasts of the lower orders. The debauching of virgins, and the illicit couplings of humble tutors of philosophy and their ilk with women of the nobility, would pave the way for similar unions with the unwashed. Under the aegis of Rousseau's revolutionizing of love, these people would "blend" themselves with the nobility, thus truly leveling the *ancien régime* and establishing in the flesh the democratic equality promised by the rights of man. They would literally breed the ancient order out of existence. In using Rousseau as a means of perverting morality, the French were attempting to democratize the "little platoon" of the family, the basic building block of political society, by doing away with its claims to rest on natural hierarchical relations of authority and submission.

As we saw in Chapter 4, a particular understanding of the family was at the heart of both the *Enquiry* and *Reflections*. In the *Enquiry* Burke had argued that in the private sphere of the family, men "loved" their women with an admixture of lust, which is equivalent to saying that women had to *submit*, one way or the other. Women simply could not be objects of love unless they proved agreeable to men, yet they could not prove agreeable unless they submitted to male will. Men, after all, "loved" only where they found submission. To be sure, this was very different from saying that men respected women. In fact, they *could not* respect them, precisely because women lacked the sublime attributes that would merit respect. Instead, for Burke, women were (literally) much closer to dogs. Men loved dogs very much; of course, they also held them in the utmost contempt—a feeling that Burke insisted was very close to love—because of their servile nature. Indeed, there is no greater term of reproach in the Burkean lexicon than that of the highly lovable and utterly contemptible "dog," a term that is, strictly speaking, matched perhaps only by "woman."

Burke is unmistakably clear and forthright in his assertion that within the family the sublime authority of the father is underwritten, as by definition all things sublime are, by his power and the consequent terror that the father will use his power to inflict pain. The Burkean private sphere was a world of natural hierarchy and subordination based ultimately on the male head of household's ability to instill terror in his wife and children via the omnipresent threat of physical force. If one prefers to use the contemporary language for such matters, Burke is crystal clear that patriarchal power within the private sphere is always *ultimately guaranteed* by the threat of domestic violence, or what Burke called "rapine and destruction."

As we have seen, Burke's argument in defense of patriarchal rights loomed large in the *Reflections on the Revolution in France*. What the powerful father taught within the family was servile submission to men in power, and it was precisely this kind of submission that was required for political flourishing at the macrocosmic level. Submission to power ensured that would-be reformers "approach to the faults of the state as to the wounds of a father, with pious awe and trembling solicitude." Similarly, the submission (to the point of invisibility) of women in the public sphere was learned through acquiescence to male power in the private. In this respect, the Burkean public and private spheres are mutually reinforcing, and Burke's denial of the universal rights of man to women in public went hand in hand with a spirited defense of the universal patriarchal rights of man in private.

Rather than accept the patriarchal family as the bedrock of Western civilization, the French revolutionaries acted like unruly, patricidal children, using their untamed freedom to play the part of democratic witch doctors. They acted like "children of their country who are prompt rashly to hack that aged parent in pieces, and put him in the kettle of magicians, in hopes that by their poisonous weeds, and wild incantations, they may regenerate the paternal constitution, and renovate their father's life" (8:146). For Burke, the result of the breakdown of the family, that critical first school of submission, was the very essence of savagery:

> They endeavor to subvert those principles of domestic trust and fidelity, which form the discipline of social life. They propagate principles by which every servant may think it, if not his duty, at least his privilege, to betray his master. By these principles, every considerable father of a family loses the sanctuary of his house.... They destroy all the tranquility and security of domestic life; turning the asylum of the house into a gloomy prison, where the father of the family must drag out a miserable existence, endangered in proportion to the apparent means of his safety; where he is worse than solitary in a crowd of domestics, and more apprehensive from his servants and inmates, than from the hired bloodthirsty mob without doors, who are ready to pull him to the lantern. (8:319)

Here we have Burkean horror encapsulated: natural ranks within the family are intentionally undermined, familial hierarchy and discipline break down, mirroring and reinforcing the similar democratic breakdowns occurring outside the father's window. In the end, the patriarch is deprived even of the security and sanctuary of his home. Far from being the fearsome, powerful, and sublime source of unquestioned authority, the father now lives in fear himself from his wife, children, and servants—all those who should appropriately obey but no longer will, either within doors or without.

By 1793 Burke had concluded that such policies had "estranged" the masses "from every civil, moral, and social, or even natural and instinctive sentiment, habit, and practice, and have rendered them systematically savages" (8:462–63).[35] And, like the savages families Burke wrote about in *An*

---

35. A similar formulation can be seen in a 1791 letter to Earl Fitzwilliam, wherein Burke referred to what was happening in France as a "Grand Revolution in Human affairs" and accused his erstwhile New Whig allies of going in for "French Levelling and confusion, by

Account of the European Settlements in America, these, too, valued liberty and equality above all else, and discipline and obedience not at all.

This conclusion is further supported by a reading of the *Letters on a Regicide Peace*. Burke began the first of these letters in 1795, after reading a copy of Lord Auckland's *Some Remarks on the Apparent Circumstances of the War in the Fourth Week of October 1795*, a pamphlet whose author envisioned peace with the revolutionaries and acceptance of the status quo in France. By the time he took up his pen, the French royal family had been executed, the Revolution had passed through the Terror, French armies held sway over most of Europe, and Burke's greatest hope for the future, his son Richard, had died suddenly and unexpectedly. Burke wrote like a man with nothing left to lose.

In the *Regicide Peace*, Burke famously declared that "manners are of more importance than laws" because they either "barbarize or refine us, by a constant, steady, uniform, insensible operation, like that of the air we breathe in." The French revolutionaries were aware of this, which is why they used various mechanisms, including the law itself, to create "a system of manners, the most licentious, prostitute, and abandoned that ever has been known, and at the same time the most coarse, rude, savage, and ferocious." In fact, Burke argued, not a single thing in the Revolution, from phrases and gestures down to the fashion of hats and shoes, was left to accident. Everything was the result of design, part of a scheme aimed at perverting the natural moral sentiments (9:242).

The revolutionaries' approach to marital relations was one of the most egregious instances of their evil intent. Christianity, by confining marriage to heterosexual couples and rendering it "indissoluble," had done more toward advancing the "civilization of the world" than any other institution. However, the French assembly, that "Synagogue of Anti-Christ," took the opposite approach. "By a strange, uncalled for declaration, they pronounced, that marriage was no better than a common, civil contract."

---

which no house is safe from its Servants, and no Officer from his Soldiers, and no State or constitution from conspiracy and insurrection. I will not enter into the baseness and depravity of the System they adopt; but one thing I will remark, that its great Object is... totally to root out that thing called an *Aristocrat* or Nobleman and Gentleman. This they do not profess; but in France they profess it and do it; and the party here spare no pains to magnify all that is done there, and to propagate its principles... which can have no other Effect than to root out all principle from the Minds of the Common people, and to put a dagger into the hands of every Rustic to plunge into the heart of his Landlord." Fox and his allies were intent on spreading what was essentially a French egalitarian disease, aimed at eradicating the natural aristocracy (*Correspondence*, 6:450–51).

In a typical ploy, the revolutionaries put their sentiments in the mouths of "characters" who paraded before them as if on stage.[36] One such was "in the figure of a prostitute, whom they called by the affected name of 'a mother without being a wife.'" This "creature" then proceeded to call for a repeal of the legal penalties all "civilized" states had placed upon bastards. Shortly thereafter, "in consequence of the principles laid down, and the manners authorized," bastards were put on the same legal footing as children from intact marriages (9:243–44).

Amplifying upon this abomination, succeeding assemblies established "a kind of profligate equity," giving women the same license to divorce at their pleasure as men, so long as either party gave a month's notice. The absurd justification for this action was more astonishing still to Burke: "women had been too long under the tyranny of parents and of husbands." Under such policies, Burke insisted, marriage would fall into "so degraded a state of concubinage" that even London pimps would not rent out one of their charges for so short a period as the typical French marriage lasted. Burke had scanned the Parisian newspapers for the results of such a drastic policy, he said, and the evidence shocked him. In "civilized nations," the papers did not carry a list of divorces as part of their regular pronouncements; in France, however, such statistics held the place of honor. And, in the first three months of 1793, the number of divorces in Paris was nearly a third of the total number of marriages in that city, "a thing unexampled, I believe, among mankind." Burke inquired after the same statistics in Britain and claimed that all the divorces in all its courts over a hundred years amounted to little more than one-fifth of those in Paris over a three-month period. He checked the divorce rates in Paris for several months, he told his readers, until he grew tired, but the proportions remained the same (9:244–45).

The liberalization of divorce law was one of the key features of the new democratic system of manners. While permitted in some countries, divorces that removed women from the "guardianship and protection" of men had been discouraged in all. The French "Legislators of vice and crime" were well aware of this history, and they sought the mutual reinforcement of laws and manners for the purpose of completely destroying marriage as an institution enabling social cohesion (9:244). "Their law of divorce, like all their laws, had not for its object the relief of domestic uneasiness, but the

---

36. For an interesting reading of Burke's political theory that looks at his use of theatrical metaphors, see Paul Hindson and Tim Gray, *Burke's Dramatic Theory of Politics* (Aldershot, England: Avebury, 1988).

total corruption of all morals, the total disconnection of social life" (9: 245) In his *Letter to a Noble Lord*, Burke described "the whole revolutionary system" as "the very reverse, and the reverse fundamentally, of all the laws, on which civil life has hitherto been upheld in all the governments of the world" (9:172). According to Burke, the egalitarian transformation of marriage law was an unmitigated disaster, and it consequences were an inevitable descent into savagery.

> It appears as if the contract that renovates the world was under no law at all. From this we may take our estimate of the havoc that has been made through all the relations of life. With the Jacobins of France, vague intercourse is without reproach; marriage is reduced to the vilest concubinage; children are encouraged to cut the throats of their parents; mothers are taught that tenderness is no part of their character; and to demonstrate their attachment to their party, that they ought to make no scruple to rake with their bloody hands in the bowels of those who came from their own. (9:245)

Divorce, casual sex, parricide, infanticide: such were the effects of liberal divorce law, and in particular of allowing wives to divorce their husbands and normalizing single parenthood.

Burke mocked the notion of accepting such a thing into the family embrace of civilized Europe by imagining the absurdity of a visit from the regicide ambassadors to Britain: "What a rattling of a thousand coaches of Duchesses, Countesses and Ladys Marys, choking the way and overturning each other in a struggle, who should be first to pay her court to the *Citoyenne*, the spouse of the twenty-first husband, he the husband of the thirty-first wife, and to hail her in the rank of honorable matrons before the four days duration of marriage is expired!" (9:113).

Social and Cultural Democratization

At the same time that they were revolutionizing divorce law and the family, and with the same aim of rooting out the innate moral sentiments, the Jacobins also instituted a whole series of measures designed to "relax [the] morals" of French citizens, in an attempt to democratize the private sphere. These policies were by no means accidental, Burke insisted.

> They were made an affair of state.... [The revolutionaries] have all along avowed them as part of their policy; and whilst they corrupt young minds through pleasure, they form them to crimes. Every idea of corporal gratification is carried to the highest excess, and wooed with all the elegance, that belongs to the senses. All elegance of mind and manners is banished. A theatrical, bombastic, windy phraseology of heroic virtue, blended and mingled up with a worse dissoluteness, and joined to a murderous and savage ferocity, forms the tone and idiom of their language and their manners. (9:246, 114)

To cultivate these new democratic manners aimed at poisoning minds, especially those of the young and impressionable, all kinds of shows and exhibitions calculated to inflame and vitiate the imagination and pervert the moral sense were contrived. "In their culture it is a rule always to graft virtues on vices. They think every thing unworthy of the name of public virtue, unless it indicates violence on the private. All their new institutions, (and with them every thing is new) strike at the root of our social nature" (9:243). In Paris alone, Burke assured his readers, there were no less than nineteen or twenty theaters, and all crowded every night. He also pointed to the (at least) fourfold increase in opera houses, theaters, and public shows of every kind, as well as increases in brothels and gaming houses (9:114, 246). In fact, Burke claimed to have it on "good authority, that under the scaffold of judicial murder, and the gaping planks that poured down blood on the spectators, the space was hired out for a show of dancing dogs." While indulging in all manner of sex, liquor, gambling, and popular theater and music, ordinary people could be seen proclaiming their heroic virtue in the coarsest of language, parading it in their plays, and commemorating it in operas and all sorts of public spectacles (9:246–47).

One of the most interesting aspects of this wholesale democratization, according to Burke's later writings, was the explosion of eighteenth-century print culture.[37] As we will see in the following chapter, Wollstonecraft would also stress the importance of the rise of mass print culture for the success of the Revolution; for her, of course, it was an event to be celebrated, whereas for Burke it was a complete disaster. In Burke's analysis, the revolutionaries' deployment of the newly emerging techniques of

---

37. In general, see Roy Porter, *The Creation of the Modern World: The Untold Story of the British Enlightenment* (New York: W. W. Norton, 2000), chapter 4.

mass media to shape the public's views and wrest the empire of opinion from the monopolistic grasp of organized religion had special importance in the democratizing process. "Above all," he argued, the revolutionaries controlled "the press, of which they had in a manner, entire possession," and which "made a kind of electric communication everywhere." This instant communication was vital, because, it became increasingly apparent to Burke, "the press, in reality, has made every Government, in its spirit, almost democratic" (9:292).

The most in-depth discussion of the importance Burke attached to the press is found in the unauthorized version of the first two *Letters on a Regicide Peace*, published by John Owen. Burke had employed Owen to print portions of the first two letters for Burke's personal use, but Owen decided to publish them. The pirated and authorized versions of the work are very similar, but we find some passages in Owen's publication that are unavailable in the other. These passages stress the necessity of controlling public opinion for carrying out (or preventing) a successful revolution in morals, manners, and civilization, because opinion was "the very ground and pillar of Government, and the main spring" and "rudder" of human action. It is

> the great primary object of speculative and doctrinal philosophy to regulate opinion. It is the great object of political philosophy to promote that which is found, and to extirpate what is mischievous, and which directly tends to render men bad citizens in the community, and mischievous neighbors out of it. Opinions are of infinite consequence. They make the manners—in fact, they make the laws: they make the Legislator. They are, therefore, of all things, those to which provident Government ought to look most to in their beginnings. After a time they may look to them in vain. When, therefore, I am told that a war is a war of opinions, I am told that it is the most important of all wars. (9:295)

In Burke's narrative of history, the church and nobility had been the two institutions central to controlling the "empire of opinion," and thus to shaping the natural moral sentiments of the masses into civilized codes of manners. Near the end of his life, Burke became increasingly convinced that capturing the new medium of popular print journalism was likewise central to this endeavor, a fact of which the makers of the Revolution were all too well aware.

This strand of Burke's argument wends its way through his correspondence, where, as early as 1792, we find him focusing on the Jacobins' use of the press to manipulate the moral sentiments, destroying those that are natural and substituting an artificial, democratic system of morals and manners in their place. In a letter to the bishop of Saint-Pol-de-Léon, written a week after the September massacres of 1792, Burke focused on the work of a "corps of Newspaper writers in the Interest of the Cannibal Faction." These writers were well aware that the "prompt undeformed feelings of men" would not bear a direct narrative of such acts as the massacre of unarmed men, innocent women and children, and priests in their churches. So they waited a day or two and then began palliating, apologizing, and then eventually praising as heroism the disgusting acts that would otherwise appall human nature.[38]

Similarly, in a letter to Lord Fitzwilliam, we find a discussion of the connections between the British radicals and their Jacobin counterparts, with special emphasis on the radicals' control of newspapers and their attempts to manipulate moral sentiments through them. Burke warned Fitzwilliam of the British Jacobins' power, which was derived from their "almost complete possession of the newspapers," used as means to their egalitarian end, "which is so odious to the natural and unsuborned feelings of mankind." Indeed, all of their newspaper writing tended "to corrupt the principles and the Sentiments of the people."[39] Burke wrote to his son Richard that there was much to fear from the newly undisciplined vox populi, and he warned continually against the "Newspapers of Hell," which were "doing their Business diligently—and do all they can to stir up the Mob."[40]

Burke argued that revolutionary institutions tended to make the common people "beasts of prey, furious and savage" (9:246). In fact, the revolutionaries' reversion to savagery was so complete, Burke insisted from across the English Channel, that they had literally become cannibals: "To all this let us join the practice of *cannibalism*. . . . By cannibalism, I mean their devouring, as a nutriment of their ferocity, some parts of the bodies of those they have murdered; their drinking the blood of their victims, and forcing the victims themselves to drink the blood of their kindred slaughtered before their eyes" (9:245). For Burke, the revolutionaries'

---

38. Burke to bishop of Saint-Pol-de-Léon, 13 September 1792, in Burke, *Correspondence*, 7:210.
39. Burke to Lord Fitzwilliam, 5 October 1792, ibid., 7:229.
40. Burke to Richard Burke, c. 1 October 1792, ibid., 7:225.

supposed cannibalism was convincing proof that the French had made a complete break with Western civilization via a social and cultural revolution made with the unmistakable purpose of solidifying their formally democratic politics: *"The whole body of this new scheme of manners in support of the new scheme of politics, I consider as a strong and decisive proof of determined ambition and systematic hostility."* The revolutionaries had violently torn France "from every one of the ideas and usages, religious, legal, moral, or social, of this civilized world," and had "made a schism with the whole universe; and that schism extended to almost everything great and small" (9:249, emphasis added).

Burke's Final Crusade

After writing the *Reflections on the Revolution in France*, and while simultaneously mapping the contours of the equalitarian disaster confronting him, Burke simultaneously engaged in what might best be described as a one-man cultural crusade on behalf of Western civilization.[41] He believed that the mutually reinforcing nature of democratization necessitated an all-out, total, and, as befitted the enemy, savage war. "The new school of murder and barbarism, set up in Paris, having destroyed (so far as in it

---

41. There is a burgeoning scholarly interest in Burke as a theorist of international relations, and my argument here intersects in important ways with that of Jennifer M. Welsh, *Edmund Burke and International Relations: The Commonwealth of Europe and the Crusade Against the French Revolution* (New York: St. Martin's Press, 1995). I have also benefited from the work of Vilho Harle, "Burke the International Theorist—or the War of the Sons of Light and the Sons of Darkness," in *European Values in International Relations*, ed. Vilho Harle (New York: Pinter Publishers, 1990), 58–79. See also R. J. Vincent, "Edmund Burke and the Theory of International Relations," *Review of International Studies* 10 (1984): 205–18; two essays by Richard Boucher, "The Character of the History of the Philosophy of International Relations and the Case of Edmund Burke," *Review of International Studies* 17 (1991): 127–48, and "Edmund Burke and Historical Reason in International Relations," in Boucher's *Political Theories of International Relations: From Thucydides to the Present* (Oxford: Oxford University Press, 1998), 308–29; David Armitage, "Edmund Burke and Reason of State," *Journal of the History of Ideas* 61, no. 4 (2000): 617–34; and two essays by Richard Bourke, "Liberty, Authority, and Trust in Burke's Idea of Empire," *Journal of the History of Ideas* 61, no. 3 (2000): 453–71, and "Sovereignty, Opinion, and Revolution in Edmund Burke," *History of European Ideas* 25 (1999): 99–120. Burke's writings on international relations have recently been anthologized in *Empire and Community: Edmund Burke's Writings and Speeches on International Relations*, ed. David Fidler and Jennifer M. Welsh (Boulder, Colo.: Westview Press, 1999), and in David Bromwich, ed., *Edmund Burke: On Empire, Liberty, and Reform* (New Haven: Yale University Press, 2000).

lies) all the other manners and principles which have hitherto civilized Europe, will destroy also the mode of civilized war, which, more than any thing else, has distinguished the Christian world" (8:320).

If the *Reflections* struck readers like Wollstonecraft as histrionic, that text proved mild in comparison with what came after, a mammoth outpouring of prose depicting the French Revolution in truly apocalyptic, eschatological terms. Burke literally believed that he was witnessing the death of Western civilization, and it was an event of biblical proportions, akin to the end of times. To Earl Fitzwilliam, in late November 1793, Burke wrote, "The Abyss of Hell itself seems to yawn before me. I must act, think, and feel according to the exigencies of this tremendous season."[42] And so he did.

In the *Letter to a Noble Lord* (1796), that stunning, vitriolic retort to the duke of Bedford's opposition to a pension for Burke's parliamentary service, Burke maintained that the French Revolution was unprecedented and that its unique character resided in its complete destruction and replacement of all civilized morality: "Before this of France, the annals of all time have not furnished an instance of a *complete* revolution. That revolution seems to have extended even to the constitution of the mind of man.... The moral scheme of France furnishes the only pattern ever known, which they who admire will *instantly* resemble." This total revolution provided the basis for the most just war ever, in order to save Britain from what Burke referred to, echoing the *Reflections*, as a disease or plague. He described the Revolution's democratic principles as a "dreadful pestilence which beginning in France, threatens to lay waste the whole moral, and in a great degree the whole physical world, having done both in the focus of its most intense malignity" (9:147, 168).

In letter after private letter, Burke described the fight against the French Revolution and the rise of democratic savagery as a battle against evil itself. In three separate missives in 1795 he depicted the Revolution as the "Grand and dreadful Evil of our time," "the grand Evil of our time," and a "great Crisis for good or Evil."[43] As befitted a man looking down from the lip of hell into the bottomless void, Burke painted the French Revolution in Manichean terms, not as a clash of civilizations but as an unprecedented battle to the death between the forces of civilization and savagery, light and darkness.[44] In 1793 he described it to Sir Gilbert Elliot as "*a*

42. Burke to Lord Fitzwilliam, 29 November 1793, Burke, *Correspondence*, 7:496.
43. Burke to William Smith, 29 January 1795; Burke to Reverend Thomas Hussey, 4 and before 10 February 1795, ibid., 8:132, 136, and 143, respectively.
44. On this theme, see especially Harle, "Burke the International Theorist."

Civil War; but on a far larger Scale, and on far more important objects, than civil wars have generally extended themselves to, or comprehended."[45] Similarly, in a 1794 letter to Captain Woodford, Burke insisted, "I cannot persuade myself, that any examples or any reasonings drawn from other Wars and other politics are at all applicable to it—and I truly and sincerely think, that all other wars and all other politics have been the games of Children in comparison to it."[46]

In this Manichean world of good and evil, light and darkness, hierarchical civilization and democratic savagery, Burke lumped together everything he opposed in the term Jacobinism. His use of the term was not demarcated by party; as such, it was not meant to sort out particular actors within the drama of the French Revolution, who were themselves temporally circumscribed and flanked by friends and enemies. Burke had no interest in such narrow distinctions. Rather, "Jacobinism" functioned in his later work as a catch-all term for the principles of all those who opposed the Old Regime, be they French, British, Irish, or anything else. This viewpoint is perhaps best encapsulated in a letter Burke sent to the comte de Mercy-Argenteau, wherein he explained that those opposing the Revolution were really "at war with a principle" on behalf of the "Cause of Humanity itself." "It is not the Cause of Nation as against nation," he wrote, but rather "the cause of mankind against those who have projected the subversion of that order of things under which our part of the world has so long flourished, and indeed been in a progressive State of improvement, the Limits of which, if it had not been thus rudely stopped, it would not have been easy for the imagination to fix. If I conceive rightly of the Spirit of the present combination it is not at War with France but with Jacobinism."[47]

But what, precisely, was the spirit of Jacobinism? The best and most extended answer to this question Burke ever provided is found in a letter he wrote to William Smith, an Irish MP. Burke posed to Smith that very question, and he answered for him that Jacobinism was the attempt

> to eradicate prejudice out of the minds of men, for the purpose of putting all power and authority into the hands of the persons capable of occasionally enlightening the minds of the people. For this purpose the Jacobins have resolved to destroy the whole

---

45. Burke to Sir Gilbert Elliot, 22 September 1793, Burke, *Correspondence*, 7:432.
46. Burke to Captain Woodford, 13 January 1794, ibid., 7:521–22.
47. Burke to comte de Mercy-Argenteau, c. 6 August 1793, ibid., 7:387.

frame and fabric of the old Societies of the world, and to regenerate them after their fashion: To obtain an army for this purpose, they every where engage the poor by holding out to them as a bribe, the spoils of the Rich. This I take to be a fair description of the principles and leading maxims of the enlightened of our day, who are commonly called Jacobins.[48]

Jacobinism was the attempt to root out "prejudice"—that matrix of manners built on the bedrock of natural hierarchy, reinforced and cultivated by the church and nobility and firmly implanted in all rightly constituted individuals and societies. As ever, the French Revolution was a democratic coup from above inspired by the *philosophes*, with Rousseau in the theoretical lead; it was an unholy, unnatural experiment in social engineering made for the purposes of demolishing the sublime paternal constitution of the nation and implanting absurd notions of radical egalitarianism into the minds of the duped masses, who were bribed with the property of the rich.

Similarly, in his *Preface to Brissot's Address to his Constituents* (1794), Burke considered the work of a man whose writings Wollstonecraft had lauded in the *Analytical* and whose death she would later mourn. In doing so, Burke insisted that the Jacobins had attained their power by extirpating "every principle of religion, morality, loyalty, fidelity, and honor" from the minds of their countrymen, and substituted in their stead an entirely new and unnatural scheme against which there should be "no neutrality." No middle ground, no equivocation, no compromise with Jacobinism was possible. "They who are not actively, and with decision and energy, against Jacobinism, are its partisans. They who do not dread it, love it.... Such is the nature of Jacobinism, such is the nature of man, that this system must be regarded either with enthusiastic admiration, or with the highest degree of detestation, resentment, and horror." And the essence of this system, as Burke emphasized by quoting Camille Desmoulins, was "*to disorganize Europe; perhaps to purge it of its tyrants by the eruption of the volcanic principles of equality*" (8:502, 519–20).

In this context, Burke's last writings can be seen as a furious effort to drum up opposition to the savage onslaught of equality, a phenomenon he depicted in his letter to the duke of Bedford as "the death dance of Democratic Revolution" (9:152). Burke wrote against the possibility of such an abomination at a fevered pace virtually until the day he died in 1797,

---

48. Burke to William Smith, 29 January 1795, ibid., 8:129–30.

coming about as close as possible to keeping his promise of perishing pen in hand. His post-*Reflections* writings stand as an extraordinary last testament to the founding father of modern conservatism's wholesale antipathy to the spread of deep democracy.

In *Thoughts on French Affairs* (1791), for example, which started as an internal memorandum meant to influence official London, Burke argued that the French Revolution was a "Declaration of a *new species* of Government, on new principles." For this reason, events in France could not be compared to other political revolutions: "*It is a Revolution of doctrine and theoretic dogma*. It has a much greater resemblance to those changes which have been made upon religious grounds, in which a spirit of proselytism makes an essential part" (8:340–41). The closest analogue to the French Revolution in the Western experience was the Protestant Reformation, whose "effect was *to introduce other interests into all countries, than those which arose from their locality and natural circumstances*" (8:341). The principles of the Reformation, such as the appropriate relation between faith and works, were meant to apply universally, not simply locally, and the spread of those ideas had culminated in full-scale civil war within the civilized European community. So it was with the French Revolution, whose dogma was the principle of unmitigated majority rule. Burke expanded this argument in *Remarks on the Policy of the Allies* (1793), which was also originally meant to sway political decision makers in Britain. There he argued that the French Revolution posed such a threat to Western civilization because it was "a system founded on the supposed *Rights of the Man, and the absolute equality of the human race*" (8:459).

By 1793, when Burke drew up his *Remarks on the Policy of the Allies*, Louis XVI had been executed and the French Convention had declared war on Britain and Holland. All Europe was indeed becoming engulfed in a civil war precipitated by the French Revolution. Before Britain could proceed, Burke believed that the one thing necessary was to answer the question, "whom [do] we consider *as the people of France?*" (8:457). His answer was unequivocal. The "moral" France was "separated from the geographical." The nobility and the church, the two orders responsible for guaranteeing the civilizing process, were the moral France, cleft from their homeland, living itinerant, displaced lives across Europe (8:465).

Consequently, the British invasion had to be led by these French émigrés, the only group capable of re-civilizing their countrymen. France had been "jacobinized" for four full years, and the "ferocious savages" could not "cohere together for any purpose of civilized society, if left as now they are." Thus, Burke informed British policymakers, "there must be a means not only of breaking their strength within themselves, but of *civilizing* them; and these two things must go together, before we can possibly treat with them, not only as a nation, but with any division of them." The nobility and clergy were "an immense body of physicians and magistrates of the mind," preserved "from the contagion of the horrid practices, sentiments, and language of the Jacobins." Together they formed a "corps of instruments of civilization" capable of "re-establishing order in France, and for thus securing its civilization to Europe" (8:468–69).

This line of argument reached its apex in the *Letters on a Regicide Peace*, in which Burke noted that the revolutionaries had usurped the simple name "France" and that Lord Auckland, in his ridiculous pamphlet envisioning potential peace with them, had stupidly followed their lead. For Burke, of course, this was wholly inapt, and the problems it raised were not matters of semantic nicety. Auckland assumed that "we were in a common political war with an old recognized member of the commonwealth of Christian Europe" (9:50). Nothing could have been further from the truth. As such, France no longer existed. In Burke's theoretical lexicon, the French had ceased entirely to be "a people," since the masses were no longer in a state of habitual social discipline governed by a natural aristocracy, the necessary prerequisite for making them one.

It was against this backdrop that Burke believed British policymakers should reject conclusions like Auckland's that the French Revolution, which a peace would consolidate, ought not to give Britons cause for alarm. Burke saw no assurances "against the moral terrors of this successful empire of barbarism" that "threatened to demolish a system of civilization under which his Country enjoys a prosperity unparalleled in the history of Man" (9:61). To the contrary, the revolutionaries had already destroyed law, religion, institutions of all sorts. Burke had never "heard of any country, whether in Europe or Asia, or even in Africa on this side of Mount Atlas," proceeding in such a fashion. The French had systematically destroyed in their own country all the cultural, social, legal, and religious institutions that connected them harmoniously to Christian Europe (9:240).

Rather than peace with the regicides, Burke argued for a return to first principles in the tricky waters of international relations, by recourse to what one might call the irrational sources of cultural binding. In international relations, Burke noted, nations were apt to rely too heavily on formalities. It would be a grave mistake, however, to lay undue weight on written treaties and compacts, or even on self-interest, as the guarantor of international obligations: "Men are not tied to one another by papers and seals. They are led to associate by resemblances, by conformities, by sympathies. It is with nations as with individuals. Nothing is so strong a tie of amity between nation and nation as correspondence in laws, customs, manners, and habits of life. They have more than the force of treaties in themselves. They are obligations written in the heart." In these lines, which echo the notion of sympathy in the *Enquiry*, as well as in his friend Adam Smith's *Theory of Moral Sentiments*, Burke advanced fellow feeling, the cornerstone of innate morality embedded in evolving social manners, as the cement of international as well as interpersonal relations. Sympathetic fellow feeling produced a kind of "conformity and analogy" between nations, in which "peace is more of peace, and war is less of war." The reasons for this had to be sought in Europe's shared religion, laws, and manners (9:247–48).

In an argument that went all the way back to the *English History*, Burke also maintained in the *Letters on a Regicide Peace* that a shared European "system of manners" effectively "softened, blended, and harmonized" Europe's citizens. Burke consistently referred to this "*aggregate* of nations" as "a Commonwealth" whose ties were rooted in Christianity, feudalism, chivalry, and a broadly shared legal inheritance (9:248). Within this commonwealth there was a "law of civil vicinity," or "a *Law of Neighborhood*," which could be used (and should have been used from the start) to stem the tide of the French Revolution. "The vicinage of Europe had not only a right, but an indispensable duty, and an exigent interest, to denunciate this new work before it had produced the danger we have so sorely felt, and which we shall long feel" (9:250–52).[49]

In fact, while the closest Western comparison to the French Revolution was the Reformation, Burke believed it resembled still more closely the radical attacks on the West made from the outside, like those by Genghis Khan, or Muhammad and Islam (9:289).[50] In this sense, what it required

---

49. In a letter to William Windham, c. 2 February 1795, Burke wrote that there ought to have been in Britain a parliamentary resolution declaring "that no part of Europe, and least of all this part of it is safe whilst any power, under any Name exists in France, professing the principles, and executing the Views, and actuated by the policy, which has made the predominant Faction there so mischievous to Religion, Laws, manners, Commerce and the common Liberty and independence of all Nations and all Governments." Ibid., 8:134.

50. For Burke's comparison with the Mongol Empire and Genghis Khan, see also his 1795 letter to an unknown correspondent, ibid., 8:363.

was not so much an ordinary war but something akin to a cultural crusade.[51] The French Revolution was thus far worse than a simple change in government: "It is a destruction and decomposition of the whole society" (9:253). It could only be assumed that such a violent breach with the civilized community of Europe was made to force mankind to adopt their new democratic system, or to live in permanent hostility with the most powerful community ever known (9:249).

Finally, Burke responded to potential criticisms of such a crusade by recourse to his aesthetic category of the sublime. In a debate aimed at convincing Parliament of the need for a holy war against France, Burke returned to his early aesthetic arguments in considering the case of Algiers, which had been raised by his former friend and political ally, Charles James Fox. Fox had drawn a distinction between maintaining peaceful relations with a country and approval of that country's political system, and had put forth the case of Algiers, where the British maintained a consulate despite Algiers's involvement in piracy. For Fox, the circumstances were directly analogous; even if one disapproved of the French system, there was no more need for war with France than there was for war with Algiers.

Burke maintained that even if one could compare the moral turpitude of Algiers and France, which he categorically denied, this would still miss the point. There was little threat of "corruption" or "contagion" from Algiers. This was a point that those who directly analogized the two cases seemed totally oblivious to, so Burke attempted to enlighten them with the following striking example:

> I can contemplate, without dread, a royal or a national tiger on the borders of Pegu. I can look at him, with an easy curiosity, as prisoner within bars in the menagerie of the Tower. But, if by Habeas Corpus, or otherwise, he was to come into the Lobby of the House of Commons whilst your door was open, any of you would be more stout than wise, who would not gladly make your escape out of the back windows. I certainly should dread more from a wild cat in my bed-chamber, than from all the lions that roar in the deserts behind Algiers. But in this parallel it is the cat that is at a distance, and the lions and tigers that are in our ante-

---

51. Here, I think Welsh's depiction of Burke as a "crusader," in part II of *Edmund Burke and International Relations*, is exactly right.

chambers and our lobbies. Algiers is not near; Algiers is not powerful; Algiers is not our neighbor; Algiers is not infectious.... When I find Algiers transferred to Calais, I will tell you what I think of that point. (9:259)[52]

The diseased tiger of revolutionary France, carrying in its veins the lethal democratic contagion fatal to civilization itself, was, figuratively, in British foyers and lobbies. Its proximity and power were sources of unmitigated terror, sublimity transmogrified and transcendent, lacking the necessary distance required to temper and transform fear into "delight." For Burke there was nothing delightful about the infectious French disease of democracy—it was simply terrifying. Just as surely as the Rousseauan politicians of this fearsome system were at the bar of its assembly destroying the church and nobility, relaxing divorce laws, and disseminating the leveling spectacle of popular entertainment, so its tutors were literally in the bedrooms of the French nobility, attempting to synthesize theory and practice by diluting and democratizing the aristocracy's bloodlines through an interbreeding of the orders.

Darkness

In 1797 the armies of the French Revolution were overrunning Europe, and the prospects of a "regicide peace" looked greater than ever. Burke was mired in debt, bereft alike of party and Parliament (he left the House of Commons in 1794), and emotionally shattered by the loss of his son and potential successor. At the end of his life Burke became convinced that the French Jacobins, together with their conspiratorial English allies, would crown their revolution by vanquishing both his adopted land and his beloved Ireland. Though financially ruined, heartsick, and fearful at the prospect that European civilization would be eclipsed, Burke did not go gently.

Burke ultimately invoked the legend of John Žižka against his revolutionary tormentors. According to legend, Žižka, a Bohemian Hussite general in the early 1400s, commanded that after his death his body should be flayed, his flesh thrown to the birds and beasts of prey, and his skin made

---

52. For a fascinating discussion of this example, see Ronald Paulson, *Representations of Revolution, 1789–1820* (New Haven: Yale University Press, 1983), 67.

into a drum with which to frighten his enemies. Burke asked of the democratic French and British Jacobins, "Why will they not let me remain in obscurity and inaction? Are they apprehensive, that if an atom of me remains, the sect has something to fear? Must I be annihilated, left, like old *John Zisca's*, my skin might be made into a drum, to animate Europe to eternal battle, against a tyranny that threatens to overwhelm all Europe, and all the human race?" Like so much else in Burke, this was no mere rhetorical flourish. He literally came to believe that the "Jacobins" would pursue him beyond the grave (9:147).[53]

Accordingly, just before Edmund Burke died in July 1797, he requested that the exact whereabouts of his remains on his Beaconsfield estate in Buckinghamshire remain a secret, to keep them from being disinterred and desecrated after the democratic revolutionaries conquered Britain.[54] We might profitably read this last act as thoroughly consistent with the founding father of modern conservatism's everlasting hostility to deep democracy, understood as the death of Western civilization and the triumph of savagery.

As we will see, Mary Wollstonecraft, too, melded and transformed the Scottish Enlightenment narrative of history as the development from savagery to civilization in her reading of the French Revolution. But she did so in terms that precisely inverted Burke's analysis. Wollstonecraft saw the Revolution as the first step in the development of real civilization. But she also believed that the corrupt European system of manners and artificial hierarchies, which had stunted reason and poisoned moral and civic virtue, destined the French Revolution to massive bloodshed.

---

53. The legend is described at 147n1, as cited in F. G. Heymann, *John Žižka and the Hussite Revolution* (Princeton: Princeton University Press, 1955), 442.

54. See Isaac Kramnick, *The Rage of Edmund Burke: Portrait of an Ambivalent Conservative* (New York: Basic Books, 1977), 189, including note; and Elizabeth Lambert, *Edmund Burke of Beaconsfield* (Newark: University of Delaware Press, 2003), 168.

7 | WOLLSTONECRAFT ON DEMOCRACY AS THE BIRTH OF WESTERN CIVILIZATION

In this final chapter, I take up Mary Wollstonecraft's least-read work, her history of the French Revolution. My argument is that Wollstonecraft's text can be interpreted as the third installment of a response to Burke's narrative of the Revolution as the death of Western civilization and its devolution into democratic savagery. While starting with many of the same theoretical presuppositions as the historians of the Scottish Enlightenment whom she had read in such depth, Wollstonecraft transformed the Scots' language of politics into a democratic defense of the Revolution, thereby powerfully challenging Burke's depiction of the event. Wollstonecraft denied the central claim of the Scottish four-stages historical thesis, that the "polished" state of European manners necessarily indicated a higher stage of moral and social development among its inhabitants. Rather, in *An Historical and Moral View of the Origin and Progress of the French Revolution; and the Effect It Has Produced in Europe* (1794), Wollstonecraft rewrote the entire history of manners from the basis of a theoretical belief in the social construction of character and a political commitment to equality.[1]

Wollstonecraft appropriated the Scots' underlying notion of a civilizing process and adapted it to her own theoretical and practical ends. She

---

1. The first discussion connecting Wollstonecraft's *An Historical and Moral View of the Origin and Progress of the French Revolution; and the Effect It Has Produced in Europe* (1794) to Scottish Enlightenment historiography is Jane Rendall's incisive "'The grand causes which combine to carry mankind forward': Wollstonecraft, History, and Revolution," *Women's Writing* 4, no. 2 (1997): 155–72. On Wollstonecraft's historical narrative and the Scots, see also Anna Neill, "Civilization and the Rights of Woman: Liberty and Captivity in the Work of Mary Wollstonecraft," *Women's Writing* 8, no. 1: 99–119, reprinted in *Mary Wollstonecraft and the Critics, 1788–2001*, ed. Harriet Devine Jump, 2 vols. (New York: Routledge, 2003), 2:418–35. However, Neill's essay problematically assumes that Wollstonecraft's texts mimic the Scots' approach and conclusions; therefore it asserts that, as with the Scots, Wollstonecraft's arguments "necessarily link female emancipation to a particular mode of subsistence in which a gendered division of labor is clearly laid out" (419; see also 427). Such a move situates Wollstonecraft far too close to the Scots' arguments and misses the radical democratic upshot of her critical appropriation and fundamental revision of Scottish Enlightenment ideas. For example, as I argued in Chapter 5, Wollstonecraft steadfastly *opposed* a gendered division of labor, one of the many instances in which her revolutionizing of the Scots' arguments led her to drastically different conclusions from theirs. For a useful general overview

sought to explain revolutionary violence as a predictable consequence of moral underdevelopment, while simultaneously defending the French Revolution itself as a great step forward in the evolution of civilization—indeed, as an event that marked the beginnings of real civilization based on equality.

The third and final installment of Wollstonecraft's interpretation of the foundational event of political modernity thus continued the work of the two *Vindications*. In these texts she had effectively rejected the Scottish Enlightenment's consensus on the relationship between morals and manners. In the first *Vindication*, she had argued against Burke and the Scots that manners were not the empirical crystallization of natural moral sentiments intuited by "common sense," or sensibility. Rather, like morals themselves, manners were socially constructed modes of social interaction. As such, manners *ought* to be based on morals, but right morals in turn had to be based on the application of critical reason, which she saw as the defining capacity of human nature. Wollstonecraft argued, however, that the prevailing system of manners in Europe was an artificial and pernicious code of social interaction developed in a hierarchical institutional context that lacked a rational basis. European manners therefore served to perpetuate existing political, economic, and gender inequalities, which precluded the development of reason and thus true morality. In the second *Vindication*, which she referred to as a treatise "on female rights and manners," Wollstonecraft focused specifically on the effects of the Old Regime's hierarchical system of manners on women in particular, and she called for a democratic "revolution in female manners."[2] Part of Wollstonecraft's purpose in writing the second *Vindication* was to challenge the French to make good on the theoretical commitment to equality that she believed was at the heart of the Revolution, and to extend its emancipatory democratic potential to women in both public and private. As events unfolded, however, the Revolution itself came in need of defense. In order to provide it, Wollstonecraft effectively rewrote the Scots' entire narrative of the civilizing process.

---

of some important themes in the text, albeit one that does not situate it within the context of the Scottish Enlightenment, see Tom Furniss, "Mary Wollstonecraft's French Revolution," in *The Cambridge Companion to Mary Wollstonecraft*, ed. Claudia L. Johnson (Cambridge: Cambridge University Press, 2002), 59–81.

2. *The Works of Mary Wollstonecraft*, ed. Janet Todd and Marilyn Butler, 7 vols. (New York: New York University Press, 1989) (hereafter *Works of Wollstonecraft*), 5:73, 114, 251.

Letter on the Present Character of the French Nation: A Contrapuntal Prologue

In December 1792 Wollstonecraft left London and Joseph Johnson's *Analytical Review* for Paris, where she lived until 1795. These were the bloodiest years of the Revolution within France itself. In his memoir of her life, Wollstonecraft's future husband, William Godwin, related that during the summer of 1793 she saw the streets of Paris literally running with blood from the guillotine. When she proclaimed her deep dismay, a bystander who feared for her life warned Wollstonecraft that it would be safer to hide such discontent, lest she suffer the same fate.[3]

Soon thereafter, Wollstonecraft's political friends and allies among the Girondins, including the man Burke would describe as a quintessential Jacobin, Brissot (whose book on his travels in America Wollstonecraft had lauded in the pages of the *Analytical*), were being purged in the Terror. Wollstonecraft, pregnant at the time, collapsed in grief at the news of Brissot's execution, and by all accounts she was spared arrest herself only by registering as the wife of her lover, the American Gilbert Imlay, at the American embassy in Paris. It seems that Wollstonecraft's name might actually have been mistakenly listed in Parisian papers among those believed imprisoned during the Terror.[4] Thus, while Burke visited France only once, in 1773, and described subsequent events from a safe distance across the English Channel, Wollstonecraft interpreted the unfolding of the French Revolution from a much closer and more perilous position.

Wollstonecraft put forward her initial impressions shortly after her arrival in Paris, in the brief *Letter on the Present Character of the French Nation*,[5] dated two weeks after the French Convention had unanimously declared war against Great Britain on 1 February 1793. The piece was initially intended as an introduction to a series of letters on the subject of French character, but the introductory essay was the only part of that project Wollstonecraft would finish. Despite its brevity, however, the *Letter* is extremely important, because it sets forth basic themes that would play

---

3. William Godwin, *Memoirs of the Author of A Vindication of the Rights of Woman*, ed. Pamela Clemit and Gina Luria Walker (Toronto: Broadview Literary Texts, 2001), 89.
4. See Ralph Wardle, *Mary Wollstonecraft: A Critical Biography* (Lawrence: University of Kansas Press, 1951), 194–95.
5. *Works of Wollstonecraft*, 6:443–46, hereafter cited parenthetically in the text (all citations are to volume 6).

an important role in the history of the Revolution that she would undertake shortly thereafter.

In the *Letter*, Wollstonecraft described the theoretical problem as one of "investigating the modification of the passion[s]" so as "to trace to their source the causes which have combined to render this nation the most polished, in a physical sense, and probably the most superficial in the world" (444). From the outset of her stay in France, Wollstonecraft sought to explain a paradox that required her to rewrite the history of the relationship between morals, manners, and civilization in a fashion consonant with her argument in the *Vindications*. Like Burke and the Scots, Wollstonecraft agreed that the passions were modified over time in civil society, that they became progressively more "polished." But she concluded that this polished refinement really undermined true morality, making the French nation similar in character to the socially constructed vision of "ladies," the rich, and the military that she had dissected in *A Vindication of the Rights of Woman*.

This view of the French seems to have come from Wollstonecraft's first impressions in Paris, when she declared that the whole mode of life in France tended to make the people "frivolous" and exhibit "vanity" (443). On the surface, this portion of her analysis seems similar to Burke's. As we know, Burke singled out vanity as the key to the new French system of morality under the revolutionaries, who applied the principles of Rousseau (vanity incarnate) and the *philosophes* to undermine the natural moral sentiments and the social hierarchies they supported. But Wollstonecraft's reading of French character inverted Burke's. Burke assumed that vanity was an artificial vice connected to the sin of intellectual hubris, an egalitarian error that prevented people from accepting their place in the natural order of things. Wollstonecraft looked instead at the social conditions that gave rise to French vanity and superficiality.

Wollstonecraft emphasized that this diseased condition was not peculiar to the French. "Vanity" was not some essential biological or cultural trait of the French alone, any more than it was an ideological tool of the *philosophes*. Rather, it was a human characteristic that emerged from particular historically derived relationships at specific moments in the civilizing process: "Remember that it is not the morals of a particular people that I would decry; for are we not all of the same stock? But I wish calmly to consider the stage of civilization in which I find the French," in order to "giv[e] a sketch of their character" and unravel "the circumstances which have produced its identity" (444). If we want to understand the path of the

Revolution, Wollstonecraft is telling us, we have to ask the right questions. What stage in the civilizing process had the French reached? Within that process, what causal factors had formed French character, and what were the consequences of that character?

Wollstonecraft's initial impressions of France depart radically from the standard caricature of facile Enlightenment optimism about the French Revolution and its consequences. On the one hand, Wollstonecraft wished she could simply believe that real liberty and equality were emerging out of the "chaos of vice and follies, prejudices and virtues, rudely jumbled together" that she saw around her. But if the "aristocracy of birth" was leveled "only to make room for that of riches," she feared "that the morals of the people will not be much improved by the change, or the government rendered less venal." Such remarks show again the extent to which Wollstonecraft was troubled by the consequences of commercial society. "Little is to be expected," she wrote, "from the narrow principle of commerce which seems every where to be shoving aside *the point of honor* of the *noblesse*" (444–45).

In other words, far from joining Scottish Enlightenment thinkers in a defense of commercial society, Wollstonecraft wondered aloud about the synthesis of wealth and virtue that the Scots had attempted to achieve; perhaps "polished" manners could not coexist with real moral virtue. The *ancien régime* might fall, only to be replaced by new forms of inequality similarly injurious to the development of public and private virtue. "Every thing whispers to me," she wrote, "that names, not principles are changed... the turn of the tide has left the dregs of the old system to corrupt the new" (446).[6]

The optimism of Wollstonecraft's first two *Vindications* was clearly tempered by the experience of visiting France in the midst of the Revolution's bloodiest phase. She confessed to her readers, "Before I came to France, I cherished, you know, an opinion, that strong virtues might exist with the polished manners produced by the progress of civilization," but this "golden age" was fading before "the attentive eye of observation." Not only had her "theory of a more perfect state" been thrown into question, she said; she even openly wondered if evil was not the "grand mobile" of human action after all (444–45).

6. These remarks on the dangers of economic inequality are at odds with interpretations of Wollstonecraft that label her a "bourgeois ideologist," or simple apologist for capitalism. On Wollstonecraft's pessimism about commercial society in the *Letter*, and at points in the *French Revolution*, see Gordon Spence, "Mary Wollstonecraft's Theodicy and Theory of Progress," *Enlightenment and Dissent* 14 (1995): 105–27.

While Wollstonecraft's proposed series of letters on French character never materialized, her brief introduction to the project gives us an interesting insight into the factors she considered most important in analyzing the Revolution's path. The *Letter* also serves as a contrapuntal prologue to her *Historical and Moral View of the Origin and Progress of the French Revolution*, a book written about events in 1789 from the perspective of 1793. It functions as counterpoint because, despite her horror at the violence, and unlike Wordsworth, Coleridge, Mackintosh, and many other British radicals, Wollstonecraft never stopped defending the French Revolution, even after the Terror. She did not condone revolutionary violence, however, but sought to explain it.

This is a distinction we would do well to remember, as many have simply asserted that those who supported the Revolution at the time, and those who defend it today, were (or are) defenders of the Terror. This has been perhaps the favorite arrow in conservative quivers from Burke onward, and it has taken many a radical casualty. Yet Wollstonecraft's largely forgotten *French Revolution* offers a powerful rebuke to this argument. To put it simply, Wollstonecraft never accepted that the passion for democratic equality, which she and Burke agreed was the theoretical principle at the heart of the Revolution, had *caused* the Terror. Instead, she accused Burke, and by extension his disciples, of propagating a grand version of the *post hoc ergo propter hoc* fallacy: whoever supported the principles of 1789 ipso facto supported 1793, because terror is ever the teleological terminus of all revolution. Wollstonecraft not only rejected this argument, she reversed it, explaining the Terror as the predictable consequence of the injustice and inequality on which the *ancien régime* was built. In her view, more democracy, not a return to corrupt morals created by pernicious hierarchies, was the only solution to the problem of revolutionary violence and the only pathway to true civilization.

Wollstonecraft's Historical Presuppositions

In the preface to her *French Revolution*, Wollstonecraft urged her readers to contemplate the Revolution with the "cool eye of observation" (6)[7] in order to judge it properly, and to "guard against the erroneous inferences

---

7. For a useful reading that stresses the importance of this phrase, see Harriet Devine Jump, "'The cool eye of observation': Mary Wollstonecraft and the French Revolution," in *Revolution in Writing: British Literary Responses to the French Revolution*, ed. Kelvin Everest (Milton Keynes: Open University Press, 1991), 101–19.

of sensibility." If they did, they would see that the Revolution was really "the natural consequence of intellectual improvement, gradually proceeding to perfection in the advancement of communities, from a state of barbarism to that of polished society." Moreover, she announced her intent to show that "the folly, selfishness, madness, treachery, and more fatal mock patriotism" that marred the Revolution were ultimately "the common result of depraved manners." A poisoned system of social interaction was the inevitable result of a system of social construction built upon inequality, the necessary "concomitant of that servility and voluptuousness which for so long a space of time has embruted the higher orders of this celebrated nation" (6–7). From the beginning, then, while Wollstonecraft deployed the Scottish Enlightenment historical narrative of a civilizing process, she also rejected its assumption that moral sentiments naturally progressed as well, and she set about the task of transforming the four-stages thesis for her own democratic purposes.

"Men in a savage state," Wollstonecraft argued, lacked "intellectual amusements, or even fields or vineyards to employ them," and relied instead "for subsistence on the casual supply of the chase." They "seem continually to have made war, one with another, or nation with nation" (146). Given "the social disposition of man," however, "in proportion as he becomes civilized," narrow self-love expands outward to embrace increasingly broad circles of humanity, a change explained in part by the bonds of "sympathy." Like the Scots, Wollstonecraft believed that this occurred with the movement from loose savage societies, where hunting and war predominated, into settled agricultural societies (223, 146).

Wollstonecraft also saw agricultural settlements as stepping-stones to the development of the arts and commerce, and to the increasing importance of private property, together with the complex legal means that assured its security. Much as Hume had argued in his essay "Of the Rise and Progress of the Arts and Sciences," Wollstonecraft contended that "whilst [the arts] were in their infancy [man's] restless temper, and savage manners, still kept alive his passion for war and plunder; and we shall find, if we look back to the first improvement of man, that as his ferocity wore away, the right of property grew sacred" (147).

Wollstonecraft also agreed with the Scots that the degree of civilization achieved by the Greeks and Romans was "partial" at best. The majority of people in the ancient world were oppressed, women were "merely household, breeding animals," and the entire social edifice was built on the degrading institution of slavery. She too held that even the relative degree of civilization achieved in the ancient world was undone by the barbarian invasions of the Roman Empire (109–10).[8] Thereafter, the "prowess or abilities of the leaders of barbarians gave them likewise an ascendancy in their respective dynasties," which "produced the distinctions of men, from which the great inequality of conditions has originated" (147). Like Adam Smith and John Millar, Wollstonecraft sought to fix the origin of the distinction of ranks. She found its beginnings in the early stages of the civilizing process, when barbarian leaders used their military skill to exert social dominance.

Throughout the early portion of the long millennium following the sack of Rome, Wollstonecraft argued, there was little development beyond the "savage state" owing to lack of "philosophical principles"; consequently manners became "ferocious." The masses "were, strictly speaking, slaves; bound by feudal tenures, and still more oppressive ecclesiastical restraints; the lord of the domain leading them to slaughter, like flocks of sheep; and the ghostly father drawing the bread out of their mouths by the idlest impositions" (113). With such remarks Wollstonecraft reinforced her rejection of the civilizing function that Burke had ascribed to the bulwarks of the *ancien régime*, the church and the nobility. As in the *Vindication of the Rights of Men*, she indicted the medieval church as a sublime instrument of terror that tricked the people by threatening them with divine punishment. Far from furthering their civilization, the church fostered fearful acquiescence to their worldly lot. In Wollstonecraft's view, religion was often synonymous with barbarism itself in medieval times, and Burke's twin pillars of civilization were in fact institutions of oppression. Like Robertson, Millar, and Kames, but very much unlike Burke, Wollstonecraft treated the medieval Catholic Church as a major obstacle to human progress.[9]

For Wollstonecraft as for the Scots, however, the Christian millennium was not one of total darkness, and "the state of society" was simultaneously "slowly meliorating itself till the seventeenth century" (113). The three moments she isolated within this evolution were the advent of the Crusades, chivalry, and the Protestant Reformation. Just as Robertson had traced an emerging Europe from the nadir of the eleventh century in *A View of the Progress of Society*, a work with which we know she was familiar, Wollstonecraft viewed the civilizing process as likewise evolving from this

---

8. On this point, see Rendall, "Wollstonecraft, History, and Revolution," 162.
9. See ibid., 163.

era. Like Robertson, she singled out the Crusades as an important turning point and encompassed the Reformation within the history of manners (23, 113).[10] Concerning chivalry, she contended, "the spirit of chivalry, assuming a new character during the reign of the gallant Francis the first, began to meliorate the ferocity of the ancient gauls and franks. The point *d'honnneur* being settled, the character of a *gentleman*, held ever since so dear in France, was gradually formed; and this kind of bastard morality, frequently the only substitute for all the ties that nature has rendered sacred, kept those men within bounds, who obeyed no other law" (23–24).

Wollstonecraft described a multifaceted and complex historical process. The Crusades undermined the worst brutalities of feudalism by freeing many vassals; the Protestant Reformation reformed the clergy, and this in turn altered opinions and began to reform manners. Likewise, feudalism begot chivalry, which itself evolved over the centuries. She pointed to the reign of Francis I (1515–47) as particularly significant in chivalry's development. As the chief rival of Charles V, Francis was also an important figure for Robertson, for whom both kings were transitional figures in the move from barbarism to polite manners with the emergence of court culture and the European system of nation-states.[11]

As Pocock argues, and as we saw in Chapter 3, Scottish Enlightenment thinkers focused on the rise of the chivalric ethos as a crucial moment in the shift from barbarism to polite society. For them, chivalry tempered brute warrior courage for the knightly class, and encouraged a sense of responsibility to others through the development of a higher stage of social morality, reflected in more polished manners. It was especially in gender relations that the Scots believed manners were chiefly refined, and we have seen the particular emphasis they placed on chivalry in improving the social condition of women. For the Scottish historians the rise of chivalry was thus a "revolution in manners" within the feudal world, one in which barbarian warriors began to acquire more humane codes of conduct, toward both those who were weaker and each other. This in turn, according to the Scots, helped promote the circulation of material goods and the skills required to produce them.[12]

---

10. For Robertson's view, see especially J. G. A. Pocock, *Barbarism and Religion*, vol. 2, *Narratives of Civil Government* (Cambridge: Cambridge University Press, 1999), 279–80, 291–99.

11. Ibid., 289–91.

12. See three essays by J. G. A. Pocock: his introduction to Burke's *Reflections on the Revolution in France* (Indianapolis: Hackett, 1987), xxxii–xxxiii; "The Political Economy of Burke's

For Wollstonecraft, however, chivalry was far more equivocal, and its system of manners was marked by multiple and ambivalent consequences. On the one hand, she agreed with the Scots (and Burke) that in Europe chivalry had softened and improved the ferocious manners of the ancient Gauls and Franks, especially by creating and shaping "the character of a gentleman" and the concept of honor. On the other hand, she insisted that chivalric manners reflected at best an artificial or "bastard" kind of morality devoid of a rational basis. As she had argued in both *Vindications*, true morality and virtuous conduct could be produced only when reason instructed and shaped instinctive feelings. Wollstonecraft therefore regarded the chivalric system of manners as a temporary substitute for morality that played an incrementally useful role at a narrowly defined period within the civilizing process. It prevented the worst excesses of savagery and barbarism, but it was not based on the progressive refinement of natural moral sentiments.

To the contrary, Wollstonecraft contended that European manners, understood as modes of social interaction codified in "partial" laws, were ultimately immoral because they were irrational, and she believed that clinging to the old system of manners would undermine the civilizing process. European manners were not Burke's decent drapery of civil life, nor were they the outgrowth of natural moral sentiments embodied in social mores and laws, appropriately perpetuated by the church and nobility. They were outmoded relics of an irrational past, and as such it would have been "a kind of sacrilege not to strip them of their gothic vests" (110–11).

The legacy of the increasingly artificial and complex system of European manners had extremely negative consequences, even as feudalism waned. "What has hitherto been the political perfection of the world?" she asked. "In the two most celebrated nations [England and France] it has only been a polish of manners, an extension of that family love, which is rather the effect of sympathy and selfish passions, than reasonable humanity. And in what has ended their so much extolled patriotism? In vain

---

Analysis of the French Revolution," in his *Virtue, Commerce, and History: Essays on Political Thought and History, Chiefly in the Eighteenth Century* (Cambridge: Cambridge University Press, 1985), 198; and "Edmund Burke and the Redefinition of Enthusiasm: The Context as Counter-Revolution," in *The French Revolution and the Creation of Modern Political Culture*, vol. 3, ed. François Furet and Mona Ozouf (Oxford: Pergamon Press, 1989), 31. On these themes, see also Silvia Sebastiani, "'Race,' Women, and Progress in the Scottish Enlightenment," in *Women, Gender, and Enlightenment*, ed. Sarah Knott and Barbara Taylor (New York: Palgrave Macmillan, 2005), 75–96.

glory and barbarity—every page of history proclaims.... Why?—because it was factitious virtue" (21).

Wollstonecraft's argument was not without nuance. Though she was troubled by many of the consequences wrought by commercial society, she echoed Hume and his fellow Scots that it was wrongheaded to argue blindly "against the luxury introduced with the arts and sciences; when it is obviously the cultivation of these alone, emphatically termed the arts of peace, that can turn the sword into a ploughshare" (23). Like William Robertson and the others, Wollstonecraft stressed the importance of scientific and intellectual progress made in the context of the "friction of arts and commerce," progress she believed would bring peace and "a gradual softening of manners" (16) by allowing reason, rather than blind passion, to inform social, economic, and political questions.[13]

Like Burke, Wollstonecraft understood the importance of the print medium and its spread. She saw the printing press as a key technological advance that undermined the ancient argument about the cyclical nature of commonwealths. Because printing disseminated knowledge through all social ranks, she believed that there could be no return to barbarism or savagery, the rudimentary forms of social development (109). With the technological means to transmit intellectual progress, Wollstonecraft thought, it was finally possible to develop rational moral virtue and ultimately revolutionize the old system of manners.

All the same, she also believed that "the remains of superstition, and the unnatural distinction of privileged classes, which had their origin in barbarous folly," persisted well into the early modern period. These things went largely unchallenged until the seventeenth century, she wrote, when several English writers, most notably Locke, brought reason to bear on moral and political philosophy for the first time (16–17). The tardiness of this development, though, meant that the social institutions and mores of her day constituted "a rude mass, which time alone has consolidated and rendered venerable" (21). In fact, it had "demanded ages of improving reason and experience in moral philosophy, to clear away the rubbish, and exhibit the first principles of social order" (15–16). If there was a

---

13. For the similarity between Wollstonecraft's position and Robertson's, see Rendall, "Wollstonecraft, History, and Revolution," 163. On Wollstonecraft's "ambivalent" and "divided" view of commerce, and the ways in which such a view simultaneously connects her to and distinguishes her from the thinkers of the Scottish Enlightenment, see Chris Jones, "Mary Wollstonecraft's *Vindications* and Their Political Tradition," in Johnson, *Cambridge Companion to Mary Wollstonecraft*, 51–54.

complement to this view in the Scottish Enlightenment, it was that of John Millar, the Foxite "New Whig," who himself challenged Burke's view of the Revolution and stressed the modernity of English liberty against Burke's defense of the ancient constitution.[14] But Wollstonecraft's remarks clearly pushed much further than anything advocated by Millar. Like Thomas Paine's, hers was a response to Burke's preference for the world of the dead over that of the living. She too insisted that it was the prerogative of the current generation to wholly remake the present with the materials at hand, rather than defer to an inheritance both irrational and oppressive.

Wollstonecraft remained optimistic. She believed that in her lifetime reason could finally be brought to bear on the outdated code of irrational manners, reforming them in a direction that was more egalitarian and humane. She thought that such changes were beginning to dissolve the vestigial untamed passions that ruled "when the hordes of European savages began to form their governments," a time in which ignorance and "narrowness of mind naturally produce[d] ferociousness of temper" (23). "What nobleman," she asked, "even in the states where they have the power of life and death, after giving an elegant entertainment, would now attract the detestation of his company, by ordering a domestic to be thrown into a pond to fatten the fish"? She multiplied such examples to show that the progress of reason demanded that practices once openly public had at least to be hidden in the late eighteenth century. "Formerly kings and great men openly despised the justice they violated; but, at present, when a degree of reason, at least, regulates governments, men find it necessary to put a gloss of morality on their actions, though it may not be their spring.... An affectation of humanity is the affectation of the day; and men almost always affect to possess the virtue, or quality, that is rising into estimation" (111–12).

Wollstonecraft's argument was complex. She clearly denied the Scottish and Burkean naturalization of historically progressive social, economic, and political institutions. Civil society was not a beneficent spontaneous order achieved over centuries of incremental, unplanned human conduct. But the development of the arts and sciences in commercial society, together with the technological means of their transmission, meant that intellectual progress could finally be used to carry out a democratic revolution. In this virtuous circle, theoretical advances in moral and political philosophy could reshape both public and private spheres on the basis of equality, and

---

14. See Rendall, "Wollstonecraft, History, and Revolution," 164.

such equality would enable the development of critical reason, thereby enabling further intellectual progress. Wollstonecraft relied on one of the Scots' favorite developmental images to symbolize this new history of manners, describing European society as moving from the savagery and barbarism of its infant state, defined by force and violence, through adolescence, to full maturity. In this light, Wollstonecraft believed that an "irrational" code of hierarchical manners was an anachronism that would be utterly transformed, together with its supporting institutions, in civil society's growth to democratic maturity (21–22). The same developmental process was also in play, in various stages, throughout Europe, a fact that could be seen through comparative analysis.

A Comparative Assessment of Contemporary European "Civilization"

Wollstonecraft's interpretation of both the inevitability of the French Revolution and its specific course fit within her overarching view of history. As with the thinkers of the Scottish Enlightenment, this entailed the comparative analysis of nations relative to their particular phase of development in the civilizing process, understood as a universal historical dynamic. Wollstonecraft engaged in such comparison at length in her *French Revolution*.

In Wollstonecraft's view, Britain stood out as the European nation freest, in a relative sense, from tyranny. "With respect to the improvement of society, since the destruction of the Roman Empire, England seems to have led the way, rendering certain obstinate prejudices almost null, by a gradual change of opinion" (70). Compared to their European kin, therefore, the English "were the only free people in existence" (113). And, like the Scots, she saw the development of commercial society as playing an important role in the expansion of political liberty in Britain.

But while Wollstonecraft thought the British constitutional system "ingenious in theory," this very fact helped to explain its stagnation in the wake of intellectual progress. Because the British thought their system "the most perfect the human mind was capable of conceiving," they mistakenly believed "that they actually possessed an extensive liberty, and the best of all possible governments," instead of pressing on with reforms that would "secure the[ir] real possession." Wollstonecraft saw this as problematic, because in her view political liberty had no specific basis beyond the Magna Charta, at least until the Habeas Corpus Act of 1679 and the

Glorious Revolution of 1688 (113–14). Furthermore, the Glorious Revolution actually produced just enough liberty that "political questions were no longer discussed in England on a broad scale," a fact that "stops the progress of civilization, and leads the people to imagine, that their ancestors have done every thing possible to secure the happiness of society, and meliorate the condition of man, because they have done much" (17–18). This limited praise is the most Wollstonecraft ever afforded Burke's canonized forefathers.

In contrast, however, the rest of Europe was far less developed. Among those places where Wollstonecraft argued that political liberty was simply nonexistent were Venice, Genoa, Switzerland, Holland, Sweden, Italy, Spain, Portugal, and Germany. Like many Enlightenment thinkers, however, Wollstonecraft singled out Russia, where Catherine continued the expansionist policies and ruthless Westernization of Peter the Great, as particularly retrograde and despotic. The result was an unmitigated disaster that confounded entirely the separate stages of the civilizing process. Russia had "arrived at that stage of civilization" where Catherine the Great "vainly endeavored, indeed, to make the sweet flowers of liberty grow under the poisonous shade of despotism." Hers was a "hasty attempt to alter the manners of a people" that instead "produced the worst effect on their morals" (114–15). True liberty in social interaction had to be preceded by equality, because only equality was conducive to the development of reason and morality. Absent such cultivation, liberty would devolve into pure private license, lacking in a moral foundation and useless in a despotism that drained it of any larger civic purpose.

For Wollstonecraft, intellectual progress in continental Europe lagged for two reasons that were fundamental to the British Enlightenment's philosophical and political critique of the *ancien régime:* resistance to empiricism and the continued influence of priests and nobles on society at large.[15] The "men who studied were content to see nature through the medium of books, without making any actual experiments themselves"; and the chief writers were priests and "literary sycophants of courts," who continued to "confound the understanding of unlettered men" (115).

Slowly, however, "the benefits of civil liberty began to be better understood: and in the same proportion we find the chains of despotism becoming lighter" (115). In Italy, the arts began to be cultivated again under the

---

15. On this theme, see Roy Porter, *The Creation of the Modern World: The Untold Story of the British Enlightenment* (New York: W. W. Norton, 2000).

patronization of the Medicis in Florence (1434–1737). Yet it was chiefly with the advances in science, especially by Newton, that "analytical truths, including political, which at first were viewed only as splendid theories, begin to pervade every part of Europe." This was noticeable in Germany, where new theories found their way into seminaries, colleges, and courts. Provincial German courts patronized writers and even protected intellectuals who held unpopular religious and political opinions. At these courts, as the amusements of the day yielded "to the pleasures of colloquial disquisition on subjects of taste and morals, the ferocity of northern despotism began imperceptibl[y] to wear away, and the conditions of its slaves to become more tolerable." Such "rational modes of instruction in useful knowledge," in fact, "promise to render the Germans, in the course of half a century, the most enlightened people in Europe. Whilst their simplicity of manners, and honesty of heart are in a great degree preserved, even as they grow more refined, by the situation of their country; which prevents that inundation of riches by commercial sources, that destroys the morals of a nation before its reason arrives at maturity" (116).

Of all the European nations of the late eighteenth century, the Germans had the best chance of becoming culturally and morally refined, not by becoming still more commercialized but rather by preserving "simplicity of manners," while becoming more intellectually advanced and thus developing their morals. Like Voltaire, however, Wollstonecraft also seemed convinced, somewhat naïvely, that Frederick the Great of Prussia, the famous pseudo-enlightened monarch of the period, had played a positive role in this transitional process (116–17).

Yet, in Wollstonecraft's assessment of the contemporary landscape, it is the post-Lockean, non-European land of America that stood out as the true home of civilized liberty:

> America fortunately found herself in a situation very different from all the rest of the world; for she had it in her power to lay the first stones of her government, when reason was venturing to canvass prejudice. Availing herself of the degree of civilization of the world, she has not retained those customs, which were only the expedients of barbarism; or thought that constitutions formed by chance, and continually patched up, were superior to the plans of reason, at liberty to profit by experience. (20)

America was truly the "new world," where the Anglo-Americans rejected the whole notion of spontaneously generated social orders and combined the best "principles of their ancestors" with the intellectual progress available in the highest stages of the civilizing process, leaving behind the vestiges of barbarism that continued to poison the old world. It must be said that, in this ode to America, Wollstonecraft conveniently ignored African slavery in the New World, which she had elsewhere so eloquently condemned. This is surely a major blind spot. Nevertheless, Wollstonecraft maintained that all European eyes "were watchfully fixed on the practical success of this experiment in political science." To them, the "Anglo-Americans appeared to be another race of beings, men formed to enjoy the advantages of society, and not merely to benefit those who governed." Interestingly, Wollstonecraft argues that when the French came to the aid of the colonists in their "noble struggle against the tyrannical and inhuman ambition of the British court, it imparted to them that stimulus, which alone was wanting to give wings to freedom" (115, 20; see also 62).

But what were the conditions in France itself that created the climate for its own revolution? Wollstonecraft insisted that it was imperative to understand the particular stage of French manners and civilization if one wanted to understand both the timing and the trajectory of the French Revolution, and she analyzed the Revolution in the context of her theory of the civilizing process.

Articulating a "Moral View" of the French Revolution

Historical Background

If intellectual progress was slowly beginning to transform the world of early modern European manners and institutions by grounding them on rational morals, this posed a difficulty for one who sought to defend the French Revolution as a significant advance in the civilizing process. Wollstonecraft was aware of the problem, and she encapsulated it within her particular historical presuppositions:

> If, from the progress of reason, we be authorized to infer, that all governments will be meliorated, and the happiness of man placed on the solid basis, gradually prepared by the improvement of political science: if the degrading distinctions of rank born in barbarism, and nourished by chivalry, be really becoming in the estimation of all sensible people so contemptible, that... in the course of fifty

years... if the complexion of manners in Europe be completely changed from what it was half a century ago, and the liberty of its citizens tolerably secured: if every day extending freedom be more firmly established in consequence of the general dissemination of truth and knowledge: it then seems injudicious for statesmen to force the adoption of any opinion, by aiming at the speedy destruction of obstinate prejudices; because these premature reforms, instead of promoting, destroy the comfort of those unfortunate beings, who are under their dominion, affording at the same time to despotism the strongest arguments to urge in opposition to the theory of reason. Besides, the objects intended to be forwarded are probably retarded, whilst the tumult of internal commotion and civil discord leads to the most dreadful consequence—the immolating of human victims. (45–46)

These words were written during the Terror, a time when the most dreadful consequences of the Revolution were indeed unfolding in Paris. They provoke a crucial question: what constituted a "moral view" of the French Revolution for Mary Wollstonecraft? We might regard her text as a response to this query articulated in the language of her revised history of manners. Indeed, we should see the term "moral view" itself as having a double meaning, referring both to a historical narrative and also to a normative assessment of the Revolution itself. To achieve these inseparable ends, Wollstonecraft applied her historical thesis specifically to the French case.

She began with chivalry, which helped to soften the behavior of the Guise family, as well as that of Henry IV (1553–1610). During the time of Richelieu, however, intrigue, dissimulation, and "finesse" were the rule of the day. Richelieu was followed by Mazarin ("dissimulation personified"), and the way was gradually paved for Louis XIV (1638–1715). In Wollstonecraft's words, the Sun King "accelerated the perfection of that species of civilization, which consists in the refining of the senses at the expense of the heart." During that period, as chivalry further polished manners and "politeness took [the] place of humanity," feudal tournaments and feasts were succeeded by a fondness for the theater (24).

With respect to the French literature of the 1600s, everything except work by Molière "reflected the manners of the court, and thus perverted the forming taste." While Molière wrote for all humankind, the "task of imitating the drapery of manners" was left to inferior talents such as Corneille and Racine. Wollstonecraft considered Racine, not Molière, the father of the French stage. This was important because French national character was formed in part by the French affection for public entertainment, particularly the theater. "Their national character is, perhaps, more formed by their theatrical amusements, than is generally imagined: they are in reality the schools of vanity" (24–25).

As in her *Letter on the Present Character of the French Nation*, Wollstonecraft's *French Revolution* isolated vanity as the defining French national characteristic, one particularly prominent among the nobility. It was a trait whose origins were to be found in the development of the artificial chivalric code of manners that became particularly exaggerated in the seventeenth century. As such, it yielded "cold declamatory exstasies," cynical sentiments that while "spouted from the lips come oftener from the head than the heart." While the intellect could bring reason to bear on untutored natural affect to produce moral virtue, it was also capable of papering over a cold moral vacuum, dressed up in the drapery of false sensibility. Even Louis XIV's wars were "theatrical exhibitions" (25–26).

The regency that followed the Sun King's death, led by the duc d'Orléans, was no better. "In the character of the regent we may trace all the vices and graces of false refinement; forming the taste by destroying the heart." The duke "pitied the distresses of the people, when before his eyes; and as quickly forgot these yearnings of heart in his sensual stye." Things got no better when Louis XV came of age. Together with his mistresses and nobles, he went about "corrupting the morals whilst breaking the spirit of the nation" (27–28).

Having provided this historical backdrop, Wollstonecraft turned to the reign of Louis XVI and Marie Antoinette. Like Burke, Wollstonecraft focused not on the king but on his bride. Indeed, one can read Wollstonecraft's indictment of Marie Antoinette as a measured response to Burke's celebration of her as the personification of the *ancien régime*. For both writers Marie was a living archetype, a cultural touchstone. For Burke she was the glittering apotheosis of the old system of natural manners; for Wollstonecraft she epitomized a morally bankrupt world.

It was at the end of Louis XV's reign, "during this general depravation of manners," that Marie arrived in Paris. "In such a voluptuous atmosphere," Wollstonecraft asked rhetorically, "how could she escape contagion?" (29). Wollstonecraft went on to paint a picture of Marie Antoinette every bit as memorable as Burke's, although it remains virtually unknown to historians of political thought. The "unfortunate queen of France" had a very fine person; and her lovely face, sparkling with vivacity, hid the want of intelligence. Her complexion was dazzlingly clear; and, when she was pleased, her manners were bewitching; for she happily mingled the most insinuating voluptuous softness and affability, with an air of grandeur, bordering on pride, that rendered the contrast more striking.... Lost then in the most luxurious pleasures, or managing court intrigues, the queen became a profound dissembler; and her heart hardened by sensual enjoyment to such a degree, that when her family and favorites stood on the brink of ruin, her little portion of mind was employed only to preserve herself from danger.... A court is the best school in the world for actors; it was very natural for her to become a complete actress, and an adept in all the arts of coquetry that debauch the mind, whilst they render the person alluring. (72–74)

Wollstonecraft agreed with Burke: Marie Antoinette represented the high water mark of *ancien régime* manners, a system that to her mind was the very soul of artificiality and moral poison. For Marie and her kind, the superficial pretense of morality was everything. As a result, her "opening faculties were poisoned in the bud." Just as she had contended in the *Rights of Woman*, Wollstonecraft argued here that "it is certain, that education, and the atmosphere of manners in which a character is formed, change the natural laws of humanity" (73, 72).

Yet some of the French nobility and churchmen in Paris in the post-feudal world eventually grew bored with courtly intrigue, and turned instead to the literary and philosophical talents who had migrated to the capital (225). Here Wollstonecraft also agreed with Burke: the *philosophes* had helped light the fuse for the French Revolution. In her view, they used the force of critical reason to mold noble manners anew, and reformed nobles thus developed a taste for democratic leveling. Chief among the philosophical talents she mentions in this connection are Voltaire, Rousseau, and the physiocrats.

These writers "greatly contributed to produce that revolution in opinion, which, perhaps alone can overturn the empire of tyranny." Rational public opinion, that great changer of manners, was basic to Wollstonecraft's understanding of the Revolution, and her insistence on its importance reinforces the emphasis she placed on the printing press as the key technological advance. "In France," she wrote, "new opinions fly from mouth to mouth, with an electrical velocity, unknown in England" (19). Here too Wollstonecraft agreed with Burke in part, but again to a very different end. For her, too, public opinion was central to the democratic revolution. Its "electrical velocity," which Burke had noted with alarm, was vital for obliterating the Old Regime's empire of opinion and replacing it with a new one based on the principle of equality.

Understanding the Path of Revolution

As we have seen throughout this book, Wollstonecraft believed that some human passions were inborn. She also put tremendous weight on the capacity for critical reason, which she believed was the distinctive component of human nature. Wollstonecraft argued, moreover, that when appropriately cultivated, critical reason was capable of assessing, tutoring, taming, or even sublimating our initial affective urges, as required for the development of moral and civic virtue. She was thus convinced of some affective hardwiring in human beings, but she also thought that reason was a *potentially* dominant and guiding component of human nature that could bring the passions to heel.

At the same time, as we have seen, Wollstonecraft held that developing the capacity for critical reason required a broader world of egalitarian political, social, economic, and gender relationships that did not inculcate unreflective obedience to hierarchy and power. The only way critical reason could tame the natural passions (most especially the negative ones) was to be developed, and it could never be developed sufficiently within hierarchical institutions whose whole purpose was the perpetuation of the status quo. Still worse, Wollstonecraft argued, by requiring unthinking obedience to authority, these hierarchical institutions actually cultivated a whole host of negative passions that were artificial rather than innate.

Having applied these theoretical presuppositions in historical context, Wollstonecraft concluded that the French had reached that stage of history at which government was compelled to tend to the welfare of its citizens or be dissolved. "Society seems to have arrived at that point of civilization, when it becomes necessary for governments to meliorate its condition, or a dissolution of their power and authority will be the consequence of a wilful disregard of the intimations of the times" (146). Unfortunately, she argued, the "degeneracy of the higher orders" was such that they continued to domineer over the weak and check all efforts at reform (46). The nobles obstinately "determined to subvert every thing, sooner than resign their privileges; and this tenacity will not appear astonishing, if we call to mind, that they considered the people as beasts of burden, and trod them under foot with the mud. This is not a figure of rhetoric; but a melancholy truth!" (75).

In making her case for the causes of the French Revolution, Wollstonecraft attempted to persuade her readers not to abandon the Revolution because of its violence. The Terror was a predictable, if lamentable, outcome of a social order defined by "inequality of conditions," most obviously in wealth. "The rich have for ages tyrannized over the poor, teaching them how to act when possessed of power, and now must feel the consequence. People are rendered ferocious by misery; and misanthropy is ever the offspring of discontent." "How, in fact," Wollstonecraft wondered, "can we expect to see men live together like brothers, when we see only master and servant in society?" (46). Revolutionary violence proved eminently comprehensible, albeit tragic, when one understood how a world wracked by such inequality had malformed French character, both creating and accentuating a whole host of negative passions. "The character of the French," she argued, which "had been so depraved by the inveterate despotism of ages," was what "generated all the succeeding follies and crimes" (123).

Wollstonecraft's historical narrative covered only the events of 1789: the convocation of the Estates General; its transfiguration into the National Assembly; the taking of the Bastille; the abolition of feudalism on the night of 4 August; the *Declaration of the Rights of Man and the Citizen;* and the October Days. But she interpreted each of these milestones from the perspective of the Terror, and "philosophically"—that is, from within the framework of her broad historical thesis concerning manners and their relationship to moral development.

This becomes clear in Wollstonecraft's reading of these events. With respect to the calling of the Estates General, she asserted that the French quickly got ahead of themselves in their zeal to overturn the Old Regime, without guarding against the consequences of precipitous political innovation. "The strongest conviction of reason cannot quickly change a habit of body; much less the manners that have been gradually produced by certain modes of thinking and acting" (53). The old system of manners could not be altered overnight, and the attempt to bring about such a rapid revolution in manners risked simply exchanging one set of outrages for another.

Wollstonecraft was likewise ambivalent about the Estates General transforming itself into a National Assembly. While it represented the will of the nation and presaged the broader transformation of European politics, she remained circumspect about the potential of the French to achieve this transition peacefully. In fact, Wollstonecraft's chapter on the National Assembly ends with a tearful lament for the violence done against the king, nobles, and clergy by the revolutionaries, and for the internal ferment in France (49, 85). She also treated the taking of the Bastille cautiously. On the one hand, those "disgusted with the vices and artificial manners produced by the great inequality of conditions in France" rightly hailed its destruction. On the other, this act undoubtedly augured violence (106).

In turning to the formal abolition of feudalism on 4 August, Wollstonecraft maintained that while a great deal had been gained in this act, selfish ambition was still too much in the air. The nobles and the clergy, who had been against the merging of the orders into a National Assembly and the doubling of the Third Estate, began conspiring against the loss of their special privileges, a measure that played into the hands of the radicals in the Assembly. "This disposition to intrigue, and want of sincerity, so generally remarked in the French character," in turn "laid the foundation of universal distrust" (143). Predictably, then, many of the revolutionaries were motivated by ambition, selfishness, insincerity, and vanity. These individual qualities, absolutely essential for success in the old hierarchical world, proved fatal to a rational moral assessment of France's political and social needs.

Wollstonecraft's text thus presents us with a multifaceted interpretation of the Revolution, one in which political action occurs within a historical process that creates the parameters of moral agency. She argued that the past contained both progressive and retrograde elements in tension with each other. In this struggle, the weight of the "irrational" past, in which the French character had developed under extraordinary conditions of inequality, undermined the environment necessary for the development of morality. The First and Second Estates held all the political power, systematically precluding the equality necessary for the development of moral character. Thus the "morals of the whole nation were destroyed by the manners formed by the government" (123). The violence of the Revolution therefore had to be understood as a consequence of long-standing tendencies in the French national character. Wollstonecraft insisted that it was "necessary for us to attend closely to these considerations" in attempting to form a "just opinion" of the French Revolution, "because, from a superficial view of things of this nature, we frequently attribute to the passions, or innate turpitude of man, what was merely the effect of moral depravity" (145–46).

Interestingly, Wollstonecraft claims that the specific contours of the French character mirrored those of the "lady," that personification of superficiality she had deconstructed in the *Vindications*. Like the behavior of such a factitious creature, the conduct of the revolutionaries was marked by sudden transitions between extremes. A "variety of causes have so effeminated reason, that the French may be considered as a nation of women; and made feeble, probably, by the same combination of circumstances, as has rendered these insignificant" (121). The arbitrary, selfish, and vapid Marie Antoinette was the embodiment of these socially constructed traits, and her personal characteristics effectively permeated the French national character.

Wollstonecraft extended this argument in an effort to explain the seeming contradictions of revolutionary violence, maintaining that while it might have appeared strange for a people who often left the theater before a play reached its *denouement* to have produced "monsters" capable of the worst atrocities, it was actually entirely predictable: "we ought to recollect, that the sex, called the tender, commit the most flagrant acts of barbarity when irritated.—So weak is the tenderness produced merely by sympathy, or polished manners, compared with the humanity of a cultivated understanding. Alas!—It is morals, not feelings, which distinguish men from the beasts of prey!" (125–26).

Unlike Burke, Wollstonecraft maintained that innate affective dispositions were not, in and of themselves, reliable moral guides; at best they provided the raw material for morality that could develop only when properly tutored by reason. The narrow effects of sympathy, which were limited only to those nearest us, like "sophisticated" manners, those pale substitutes for rational morals, proved unable consistently to produce humane behavior. Rather, they created a nation of people capable simultaneously of leaving a play before the bloodshed and butchering one another at the guillotine like barbarians. Now, this argument clearly *does* echo Wollstonecraft's depiction of slaveholders' wives who impassively invented new tortures for their African chattel, only to turn around and shed crocodile tears at the latest imported novel of sensibility.[16]

The problem with the French Revolution, then, was that "from implicitly obeying their sovereigns," as women were forced to do, "the French

---

16. See Chapter 5.

became suddenly all sovereigns," and therefore predictably ran from "out of one extreme into another" (47). It was little wonder, according to Wollstonecraft, that the people came to be led by radicals who "began to look for a degree of freedom in their government, incompatible with the present state of their manners; and of which they had no perfect idea" (158).

> It too frequently happens, that men run from one extreme to another, and that despair adopts the most violent measures. The French people had long been groaning under the lash of a thousand oppressions; they were the hewers of wood, and drawers of water, for the chosen few. It was, therefore, to be apprehended, after they had once thrown off the yoke, which had imprinted on their character the hateful scars of servitude, that they would expect the most unbridled freedom, detesting all wholesome restraints, as reins they were not now bound to obey. (136)

Thus inequality spawned both the "depravity of the higher class, and the ignorance of the lower respecting practical political science" (142), and made it predictable that the leaders of the French Revolution would attempt to outstrip the slow progress of reason, with its incremental effects on transforming the old system of manners. "From the commencement of the revolution, the misery of France has originated from the folly or art of men, who have spurred the people on too fast; tearing up prejudices by the root, which they should have permitted to die gradually away" (159).

The deformation of French character under the *ancien régime*, like the deformation of female character, best explained the Revolution's excesses. When "the lower class" eventually "became free, the most daring innovators became the greatest favorites with the public." Like demagogues, these "designing knaves" had "conceived the plan of rising to eminence by accumulating the foibles of the multitude, who, loosened from all restraint, were easily caught by the insidious arts of the most contemptible anarchists." Indeed, "the nobility, whose order would probably lose most by the revolution," in fact "made the most popular motions, to gain favor with the people; tickling the spirit they could not tame." Wollstonecraft finds this unsurprising, because "the despotism of the former government of France having formed the most voluptuous, artificial character, in the highest orders of society, [made] it less extraordinary to find the leading patriots men without principles or political knowledge" (142, 145, 136).

Institutional Democracy and the Civilizing Process

Wollstonecraft supported the theoretical ideals she saw at the core of the Revolution wholeheartedly, particularly what she saw as its ultimate goal of radical egalitarianism. She believed, however, that these theoretically just principles faced a serious problem of immediate practical implementation in the inauspicious historical circumstances created by the *ancien régime* itself. She therefore argued that, in practice, the French revolutionaries should have been very wary of attempting large-scale social and political transformations in the short term, precisely because such changes would necessarily occur in a historical context where reason had been insufficiently developed to tame the innate passions, and where a whole range of artificial, negative passions had been created.

Wollstonecraft's text promoted the *theoretical* idea of gradual revolution, one whose specific political and social measures remain ever sensitive to the limits imposed by the present stage of civilization, its system of manners, and the moral base those manners reflected. "The revolutions of states ought to be gradual; for during violent or material changes it is not so much the wisdom of measures, as the popularity they acquire by being adapted to the foibles of the great body of the community, which gives them success" (166).

Accordingly, Wollstonecraft argued for a limited monarchy as a necessary transitional institution that would satisfy ordinary people. Just "as savages are naturally pleased with glass and beads," so too "crowns are a necessary bauble to please the multitude," and this would be true "as long as the manners of barbarians remained" (164).

Similarly, the issue of a limited executive branch veto in the hands of the king is a highly instructive instance of the link between Wollstonecraft's historical understanding, her theoretical ideals, and her practical political proposals. On the one hand, she rejected the notion of an *absolute* executive veto as absurd: "The wisdom of giving to the executive part of a government an absolute *veto*" in fact "seems to be giving a power to one man to counteract the will of a whole people—an absurdity too gross to merit refutation." A conditional, transitional veto in the hands of the executive, however, would "prevent an overwhelming aristocracy from concentrating all authority in themselves" (164).

Wollstonecraft's position was that an executive with limited veto power should be accepted as a necessary evil in the transition to democratic self-government. But she went on to argue that in "the progressive influence of knowledge on manners," in which the world was moving from "childish ignorance" to the wisdom of adulthood, this temporary solution should, and would, cease: "for, as they grow wiser, the people will look for the solid advantages of society; and watching with sufficient vigilance their own interest, the *veto* of the executive branch of the government would become perfectly useless; though in the hands of an unprincipled, bold chief magistrate, it might prove a dangerous instrument" (164).

Wollstonecraft approached the question of a unicameral versus a bicameral legislature in a similar fashion. For her it was a truism that the "will of the people being supreme, it is not only the duty of their representatives to respect it, but their political existence ought to depend on their acting conformably to the will of their constituents. Their voice, in enlightened countries, is always the voice of reason." In the "infancy of society," nonetheless, while "the science of political liberty" was slowly advancing, it was also necessary that "equal care" be taken "not to produce the miseries of anarchy by encouraging licentious freedom" (210).

Under such circumstances as prevailed in France, Wollstonecraft argued, it would be wise to introduce legislative bicameralism, in the form of an upper house, or senate, to check the evils of demagoguery and faction that could dominate a single assembly. "Until the principles of governments become simplified, and a knowledge of them be disseminated, it is to be feared, that popular assemblies will often be influenced by the fascinating charms of eloquence: and as it is possible for a man to be eloquent without being either wise or virtuous, it is but a common precaution of prudence in the framers of a constitution, to provide some check to the evil." Thus, in the current "state of reason," the same sort of solution, or check, should apply in France. "The obvious preventative is a second chamber, or senate," to prevent the deleterious consequences of "faction" (164–65). Still, Wollstonecraft argued that the upper house, like the executive veto, should be understood only as a necessary temporary mechanism on the road to democratic self-government in the form of unicameralism.

Until the progress of reason modified manners to the extent required for simple, unchecked, popular sovereignty and unicameral legislative supremacy, Wollstonecraft regarded such measures as only prudent. In fact, she argued, no people required such checks more than the French, who, although devoid of "experience in political science," nevertheless "seem to have fixed on a system proper only for a people in the highest stage of civilization" (165, 161–62).

Wollstonecraft distilled this problem in Scottish Enlightenment terms by reference to David Hume's fanciful arguments concerning the "perfect commonwealth," a representative democracy whose features included a widely extended franchise, annual elections, and unpaid representatives who were to do their constituents' bidding:[17]

> Thus it happened in France, that Hume's idea of a perfect commonwealth, the adoption of which would be eligible only when civilization has arrived at a much greater degree of perfection, and knowledge is more generally diffused than at the present period, was nevertheless chosen as the model of their new government, with a few exceptions, by the constituent assembly: which choice doubtless proceeded from the members not having had an opportunity to acquire a knowledge of practical liberty. (166)

The inevitable consequences of attempting to institute a much more democratic government in the all too imperfect present, according to Wollstonecraft, were chaos and bloodshed. Therefore, while the bloody path of the Revolution was in no way forgivable, it was entirely foreseeable once the First and Second Estates resisted the initial moderate reforms urged by the Third.

Wollstonecraft likewise believed that the immediate prospects for European monarchies would be equally violent. "Every nation, deprived by the progress of its civilization of strength of character, in changing its government from absolute despotism to enlightened freedom, will, most probably, be plunged into anarchy, and have to struggle with various species of tyranny before it is able to consolidate its liberty" (213). She concluded that the transition from the passionate ignorance of adolescent barbarism to the rational enlightenment of maturity would clearly be a rough one. As long as "despotism and superstition exist," it was a sad fact that "the convulsions, which the regeneration of man occasions, will always bring forward the vices they have engendered, to devour their parents" (126). Wollstonecraft knew that the conditions that lead a people to make a revolution in the first place virtually guarantee that no revolution will be bloodless.

---

17. For mention of this passage, see Rendall, "Wollstonecraft, History, and Revolution," 166. For Hume's "Idea of a Perfect Commonwealth," see his *Political Essays*, ed. Knud Haakonssen (Cambridge: Cambridge University Press, 1998), 221–33.

Wollstonecraft believed that all unicameral democratic plans would be "ever considered as utopian by all men who had not traced the progress of reason, or calculated the degree of perfectibility the human faculties are capable of attaining." And she herself argued that while such a "political plan" was the long-term goal, it was also "the most improper for the degenerate society of France" (162). Wollstonecraft nevertheless urged her readers to rededicate their efforts to slowing transforming their governments, on the basis of rational advances in the "science of government," to unicameralism, or "a polity more simple—which promises more equal freedom, and general happiness to mankind" (167). She concluded that it was the attempt to implement this "sublime" theoretical ideal in unfavorable historical circumstances that "afforded an opportunity to superficial politicians, to condemn it as absurd and chimerical, because it has not been attended with immediate success" (166). Yet one would be mistaken in "attributing that imperfection to the theory [the revolutionaries] adopted, which was applicable only to the folly of their practice" (219).

Wollstonecraft's Hope

In the end, however, Mary Wollstonecraft wanted far more democracy than someone like David Hume, let alone Edmund Burke, could imagine or desire. In fact, she understood democratization as synonymous with the civilizing process itself, and argued that anything less than mutually reinforcing equality in both the public and the private spheres was a vestige of barbarism, a form of tyranny that undermined the capacity for human perfectibility by preventing people from developing their full range of capacities and talents. Wollstonecraft believed that such hierarchical social and political arrangements had made "the great bulk of people" in fact "worse than savages" (221).

Against this backdrop, she argued that the *Declaration of the Rights of Man and the Citizen*, with its basic guarantee of equal rights, was both an expression of popular will and a simplified set of political truths expressing in concrete form the rational wisdom of political philosophers as it had developed historically. Wollstonecraft's defense of the *Declaration* rested on the idea that, in publicly adopting this list of individual rights as fundamental law, the French were codifying the tools necessary for democratization. They were simplifying their modes of social and political interaction, or manners, by basing them on the rational moral maxim of equality. A basic list of individual rights was thus a theoretical wedge that served as a necessary starting point in the process of developing a virtuous citizenry capable of fully democratic self-government. At no earlier period had "the scanty diffusion of knowledge permitted the body of the people to participate in the discussion of political science." But, in her own time, she believed that intellectual progress was "emancipating mankind, by making government a science, instead of a craft, and civilizing the grand mass, by exercising their understandings about the most important objects of inquiry." The most important of these concerns, of course, was the hydra-headed problem of inequality. And Wollstonecraft believed that the first "end of government, ought to be, to destroy this inequality by protecting the weak." In this way, she argued, the National Assembly "established beyond a possibility of obliteration, the great principles of liberty and equality" (17–18, 220). In the last analysis, the prospect of such a future led Wollstonecraft to conclude that from the "chaotic mass" of the French Revolution, "a fairer government is rising than has ever shed the sweets of social life on the world," precisely because it "promise[d] more equal freedom, and general happiness to mankind" than any other political experiment to date (47, 167).

Wollstonecraft's belief that democracy and true civilization were inseparable thus never wavered, even during the Terror. She always believed that "to consult the public mind in a perfect state of civilization, will not only be necessary, but it will be productive of the happiest consequences, generating a government emanating from the sense of the nation, for which alone it can legally exist." In theory, of course, because the "progress of reason" was gradual, it was ideal for any nation to "advance the simplification of its political system" toward democracy "in a manner best adapted to the state of improvement of the understanding of the nation." In practice, however, the "sudden change which had happened in France, from the most fettering tyranny to an unbridled liberty," made it "morally impossible" for this to be done in an incremental, peaceful fashion. Far from celebrating the violence she saw all around her, however, Wollstonecraft considered it "a deplorable reflection, that such evils must follow every revolution" (212–13):

> The late arrangement of things seems to have been the common effect of an absolute government, a domineering priesthood, and a great inequality of fortune; and whilst it completely destroyed the most important end of society, the comfort and independence of the people, it generated the most shameful depravity and

weakness of intellect; so that we have seen the French engaged in a business the most sacred to mankind, giving, by their enthusiasm, splendid examples of their fortitude at one moment, and at another, by their want of firmness and deficiency of judgment, affording the most glaring and fatal proofs, of the just estimate, which all nations have formed of their character. (231)

Nonetheless, and despite the consequences wrought by a French character socially constructed by inequality, Mary Wollstonecraft persisted in her democratic insistence that "all the advantages of civilization cannot be felt, unless it pervades the whole mass" and succeeds in "humanizing every description" of human beings; this alone was "the true perfection of man" (220). And, Wollstonecraft insisted, if her readers would contemplate the French Revolution "coolly and impartially" with a "philosophical eye," they would agree that it was bringing such a world into being. This was true in spite of the "excrementious humors exuding" from "a state diseased" (235).

Unfortunately, Mary Wollstonecraft herself would not live to witness the vicissitudes of her democratic dream, or even to develop a "moral view" of the French Revolution in its entirety. She died from complications associated with childbirth in 1797, the same year her great adversary Edmund Burke died. And, until the end, the first modern feminist maintained a view of history that was precisely the opposite of Burke's. Hers was an argument that necessarily linked the progress of civilization with the deepening of democracy, and that accounted for the violence of the French Revolution as a destructive consequence of the unnatural inequalities of the past. In its thoroughgoing commitment to both public- and private-sphere equality, Wollstonecraft's final work occasioned by the French Revolution was thus a profound extension of the argument at the heart of her first two *Vindications*.

CONCLUSION

The broad question at the heart of this book was how two of the canonical figures of modern conservatism and feminism interpreted the foundational event of political modernity, the French Revolution. I conclude that we misunderstand Burke if we see his writings as a cautious antidote to the type of grandiose political scheming that sometimes leads to violence, whether articulated in the language of natural law or any other. So, too, we misunderstand Wollstonecraft if we think of her writings merely as an attempt to extend the public rights enjoyed by men to women, and thus as inaugurating a project whose goals have been largely achieved in the West. If, instead, we see these thinkers as standing at the headwaters of two respective traditions sprung from the Revolution controversy, then we can recognize that modern conservatism and feminism began in a fundamental disagreement about democracy, understood by both sides as a thoroughgoing phenomenon that encompassed a mutually reinforcing relationship between the public and the private spheres. If Burke's and Wollstonecraft's works are ideological touchstones, then conservatism was born in an anguished cry against democracy understood as the literal end of Western civilization, while feminism was born in a cautious yet optimistic embrace of democracy understood as the dawn of a civilization worthy of the name.

This conclusion is open to a simple objection: if Burke and Wollstonecraft believed that radical egalitarianism was the theoretical impetus behind the French Revolution, they were simply wrong. After all, even at the most basic level we can see that Wollstonecraft's plea to Talleyrand and his male compatriots fell on deaf ears, as women did not win the suffrage in France until more than 150 years after she took the revolutionaries to task for their patriarchal hypocrisy. From this perspective, Wollstonecraft had far less to hope for from the French Revolution, and Burke far less to fear. But this criticism misses the point. The question we began with was one of theoretical imagination, not so much what the French

Revolution actually would achieve, or in fact did achieve, but rather what it was perceived to represent or *signify*.

Such acts of theoretical imagination matter, because present-day political theory and practice are at least in part structured and influenced by past political thinking, and the canon of the history of political thought may be seen as a series of tributaries whose texts and ideas sometimes still feed into the stream of the present. This is why the study of past thinkers and texts is one essential method for approaching the questions that animate us today. Historically informed political theory can help us to reframe contemporary debates by rethinking our intellectual inheritance from the perspective of a past liberated from its ill-fitting molds. One famous practitioner of contextualism, rightly troubled by the charge of antiquarianism, responds that it is only through its critical examination that we can keep the past from bewitching the present.[1] Allow me to give three specific examples of what might be done in this connection from my broad conclusions about the two canonical figures considered in this book, Edmund Burke and Mary Wollstonecraft.

First, an important strand of the contemporary debate concerning human rights has focused on rights specific to women. According to one side of this debate, the very notion of "women's human rights" is redundant and simply cannot be defended as a logical extrapolation from the original human rights document, the *Declaration of the Rights of Man and the Citizen*. Critics claim that once these rights have transcended their exclusionary past and been universally applied to women in the public sphere, the idea that human rights law should be somehow differentially attuned to the particular problems faced by women, especially as these frequently occur in the private sphere at the hands of nonstate actors, appears as a kind of incoherent special pleading that betrays ignorance of liberalism's history.

Now, I think that this way of framing the issue fundamentally misrepresents what is at stake in the claim that "women's rights are human rights," but it does so in ways that only become clear in historical perspective. If my arguments about Wollstonecraft and the genesis of modern feminism are right, then contemporary feminist claims are not a betrayal of the supposedly fixed logic of liberalism. Insisting that women's rights are human rights, whatever one thinks of the claim, is not a betrayal of the "liberal

---

1. See Quentin Skinner, *Liberty Before Liberalism* (Cambridge: Cambridge University Press, 1998), 116–17. These points are also indebted to James Tully's excellent formulation in "Political Philosophy as a Critical Activity," *Political Theory* 30, no. 4 (2002): 533–55.

feminist" Mary Wollstonecraft. Instead, current feminist arguments about the connection between women's rights and human rights are really about the requirements for deep democracy. In this light, they are clearly of a piece with the most important early feminist's theoretical project, a project that saw civilization and deep democracy as synonymous.[2] By revisiting Wollstonecraft's arguments in their historical context, we might say that those who wish to deny women's human rights in the present by recourse to historical tradition will find no comfort there. The "liberal feminist" Wollstonecraft never existed; she is quite simply a figment of our contemporary imagination.

Now to the second example. In the past quarter-century or so, a range of conservative public intellectuals involved in America's so-called culture wars have been very important in shaping public policy debates. A number of these thinkers have explicitly invoked Burke's texts in their arguments. Like many present-day conservatives, Burke certainly dreaded the radical social and cultural transformations he saw taking place around him, and he condemned those changes for perverting and destroying human beings' supposed natural moral sense, thereby rendering them incapable of distinguishing good from evil. Like today's conservatives, Burke decried the breakdown of natural authority relations within the family, along with the rise in adultery and sexual promiscuity, the skyrocketing divorce rate, the demise of the intact two-parent family, the legal equality of nontraditional families, the extraordinary increase in crass popular entertainment of all sorts, and the mass media. This is not to say, necessarily, that underlying the concerns of contemporary American conservatives is a Burkean antipathy toward democracy and a concomitant longing for a hierarchically structured world governed by a natural aristocracy. But it is important to insist at the very least that *Burke* was crystal clear regarding the tight linkages between leveling sociocultural practices on the one hand, and formal politics on the other, as well as the connection these relationships bore to the civilizing process. And what Burke meant by the *end* of civilization was the *beginning* of democracy.

I suspect that almost all American conservatives would reject Burke's antipathy to formal democratic equality in the shape of universal suffrage and the like. At the same time, it is evident that many of them share

---

2. For a contemporary theoretical argument that links a robust defense of individual rights with the deepening of democracy in the current, globalized context in a way we can assume Wollstonecraft would have approved of, see Michael Goodhart, *Democracy as Human Rights: Freedom and Equality in the Age of Globalization* (New York: Routledge, 2005).

Burke's revulsion at social and cultural leveling. As thinkers as different as Marx, Rousseau, and Wollstonecraft have long argued, however, one cannot so easily cleave the formal public requirements of democratic equality from the character of our multiple private relationships. The founding father of modern conservatism would himself agree with such a claim, as it was precisely the demon of deep democracy that he saw at the core of the French Revolution. In any event, the "conservative democratic" Burke, no less than the liberal feminist Mary Wollstonecraft, is a historical nonentity.

Third and finally, it is worth noting a striking irony that a careful historical reconstruction of the Burke-Wollstonecraft debate presents to theoretically minded participants in the increasingly violent international politics of the early twenty-first century. Today, citizens of the "civilized democratic" West are frequently told by our leaders that we face an enemy "other" usually described as "savage" or "barbarian" in its hostility to our values and way of life. This enemy's "barbaric" culture is often exemplified by the way it treats its women—abusing them in private and barring them from full citizenship in civic life. The antidote to this "savagery" and "barbarism," we are told, especially by conservatives of various stripes, is the spread of freedom and equality in public and private—in short, the spread of democracy.

The irony in all of this is palpable. The founding father of modern conservatism himself was also chiefly concerned with the collapse of civilization into barbarism and savagery. For Burke, however, democratization was not the solution to these problems but the problem itself. Of course, an eager "paleo-conservative" would probably respond that the urge to democratize the other was not the brainchild of the intellectual heirs of Burke but rather the neoconservative infidels who betrayed the true faith. Unfortunately, that overworked and frequently casuistic distinction ignores the historical record with regard to Burke, and thus misunderstands the relationship between a militaristic foreign policy and the rise of conservatism. As I have attempted to show, and as much as any "neoconservative" would ever hope, Edmund Burke sought a cultural crusade against the savage and barbarian forces within Europe that were spreading in such a way as to threaten the very existence of Western civilization. Indeed, he envisioned a total war against the purveyors of those principles, and he spent the last years of his life feverishly expending his enormous talent and energy in seeking to drum up support for it on exactly those terms. "Paleo-conservatives," therefore, can find no refuge in the hypothetically chastened foreign policy of their forebear, which is after all no more than a theoretical mirage. Rather, Burke sought an all-out war against the first "savages" and "barbarians" to haunt the conservative imagination—democrats, among whose profound absurdities was not *denying* women equality in their private and public relationships but rather *endorsing* it. Mary Wollstonecraft was not a victim of savagery, in Burke's account, because she was denied equality; to the contrary, she was a savage herself precisely because she fought so tirelessly for it. I believe that the genealogical relationship that conservatism and feminism's theoretical forebears saw between savagery, civilization, and democracy ought to lead us to reflect a bit more deeply on contemporary attempts to reverse its polarity rhetorically. If substantively true, such a change would indeed be a theoretical paradigm shift of the first order, if not an entirely unprecedented one.

This is my way of answering the "so what?" question that is inevitably asked by those outside the narrow specialization of the history of political thought. In the end, my hope is that this interpretation of Burke's and Wollstonecraft's texts in historical context will inspire readers to reexamine for themselves the intellectual traditions that we have inherited, and reassess the contemporary uses we make of them.

BIBLIOGRAPHY

Armitage, David. "Edmund Burke and Reason of State." *Journal of the History of Ideas* 61, no. 4 (2000): 617–34.
Ashcraft, Richard. *Revolutionary Politics and Locke's "Two Treatises of Government."* Princeton: Princeton University Press, 1986.
Ashfield, Andrew, and Peter de Bolla, eds. *The Sublime: A Reader in Eighteenth-Century Aesthetic Theory.* Cambridge: Cambridge University Press, 1996.
Badowska, Ewa. "The Anorexic Body of Liberal Feminism: Mary Wollstonecraft's *A Vindication of the Rights of Woman*." In *Mary Wollstonecraft and the Critics, 1788–2001*, ed. Harriet Devine Jump, 2 vols., 2:320–40. New York: Routledge, 2003.
Bahar, Saba. *Mary Wollstonecraft's Social and Aesthetic Philosophy: "An Eve to Please Me."* Houndmills, UK: Palgrave, 2002.
Barker, Ernest. *Essays on Government.* Oxford: Oxford University Press, 1945.
Barker-Benfield, G. J. *The Culture of Sensibility: Sex and Society in Eighteenth-Century Britain.* Chicago: University of Chicago Press, 1992.
———. "Mary Wollstonecraft: Eighteenth-Century Commonwealthwoman." *Journal of the History of Ideas* 50, no. 1 (1989): 95–115.
Berry, Christopher J. *The Idea of Luxury: A Conceptual and Historical Investigation.* Cambridge: Cambridge University Press, 1994.
———. *Social Theory of the Scottish Enlightenment.* Edinburgh: Edinburgh University Press, 1997.
Blakemore, Steven. *Burke and the Fall of Language: The French Revolution as Linguistic Event.* Hanover: University Press of New England, 1988.
———. *Intertextual War: Edmund Burke and the French Revolution in the Writings of Mary Wollstonecraft, Thomas Paine, and James Mackintosh.* Madison: Fairleigh Dickinson University Press, 1997.
Botting, Eileen Hunt. *Family Feuds: Wollstonecraft, Burke, and Rousseau on the Transformation of the Family.* Albany: State University of New York Press, 2006.
Boucher, Richard. "The Character of the History of the Philosophy of International Relations and the Case of Edmund Burke." *Review of International Studies* 17 (1991): 127–48.
———. *Political Theories of International Relations: From Thucydides to the Present.* Oxford: Oxford University Press, 1998.
Boulton, James T. *The Language of Politics in the Age of Wilkes and Burke.* London: Routledge and Kegan Paul, 1963.

Bourke, Richard. "Edmund Burke and Enlightenment Sociability: Justice, Honour, and the Principles of Government." *History of Political Thought* 21, no. 4 (2000): 632–56.

———. "Liberty, Authority, and Trust in Burke's Idea of Empire." *Journal of the History of Ideas* 61, no. 3 (2000): 453–71.

———. "Sovereignty, Opinion, and Revolution in Edmund Burke." *History of European Ideas* 25 (1999): 99–120.

Bowles, Paul. "John Millar, the Four-Stages Theory, and Women's Position in Society." *History of Political Economy* 16, no. 4 (1984): 619–38.

Boyd, Richard. *Uncivil Society: The Perils of Pluralism and the Making of Modern Liberalism.* Lanham, Md.: Lexington Books, 2004.

Brace, Laura. "'Not Empire, but Equality': Mary Wollstonecraft, the Marriage State, and the Sexual Contract." *Journal of Political Philosophy* 8, no. 4 (2000): 433–55.

Brewer, John. "Rockingham, Burke, and Whig Political Argument." *Historical Journal* 18, no. 1 (1975): 188–201.

Broadie, Alexander, ed. *The Cambridge Companion to the Scottish Enlightenment.* Cambridge: Cambridge University Press, 2003.

———, ed. *The Scottish Enlightenment: An Anthology.* Edinburgh: Canongate Books, 1997.

———. *The Scottish Enlightenment: The Historical Age of the Historical Nation.* Edinburgh: Birlinn, 2001.

———. *The Tradition of Scottish Philosophy: A New Perspective on the Enlightenment.* Savage, Md.: Barnes & Noble, 1990.

Bromwich, David. *A Choice of Inheritance: Self and Community from Edmund Burke to Robert Frost.* Cambridge: Harvard University Press, 1989.

———, ed. *Edmund Burke: On Empire, Liberty, and Reform.* New Haven: Yale University Press, 2000.

———. "Wollstonecraft as a Critic of Burke." *Political Theory* 23, no. 4 (1995): 617–34.

Browne, Ray R., ed. *The Burke-Paine Controversy: Texts and Criticism.* New York: Harcourt, Brace & World, 1963.

Bryson, Gladys. *Man and Society: The Scottish Inquiry of the Eighteenth Century.* Princeton: Princeton University Press, 1945.

Buchan, James. *Crowded with Genius: The Scottish Enlightenment; Edinburgh's Moment of the Mind.* New York: HarperCollins, 2003.

Buckle, Henry. *A History of Civilization in England.* 2 vols. London: J. W. Parker and Son, 1857–61.

Burke, Edmund. *The Correspondence of Edmund Burke.* Edited by Thomas W. Copeland. 10 vols. Chicago: University of Chicago Press, 1958–78.

———. *Empire and Community: Edmund Burke's Writings and Speeches on International Relations.* Edited by David P. Fidler and Jennifer M. Welsh. Boulder, Colo.: Westview Press, 1999.

———. *A Note-Book of Edmund Burke.* Edited by H. V. F. Somerset. Cambridge: Cambridge University Press, 1957.

———. *A Philosophical Enquiry into the Origin of our Ideas of the Sublime and Beautiful.* 1757. Edited by James T. Boulton. Notre Dame: University of Notre Dame Press, 1968.

———. *Pre-Revolutionary Writings*. Edited by Ian Harris. Cambridge: Cambridge University Press, 1993.
———. *Reflections on the Revolution in France*. Edited by J. G. A. Pocock. Indianapolis: Hackett, 1987.
———. *The Works of the Right Honourable Edmund Burke*. 8 vols. Bohn's British Classics. London: Bell & Daldy, 1872.
———. *The Writings and Speeches of Edmund Burke*. Edited by Paul Langford. 8 vols. to date. Oxford: Clarendon Press, 1981–.
Burke, Edmund, and Will Burke. *An Account of the European Settlements in America*. 2 vols. London: J. Dodsley, 1757. Reprint, New York: Arno Press, 1972.
Butler, Marilyn, ed. *Burke, Paine, Godwin, and the Revolution Controversy*. Cambridge: Cambridge University Press, 1984.
Cameron, David R. *The Social Thought of Rousseau and Burke: A Comparative Study*. London: Weidenfeld and Nicolson, 1973.
Campbell, R. H., and Andrew S. Skinner, eds. *The Origins and Nature of the Scottish Enlightenment*. Edinburgh: John Donald Publishers, 1982.
Campbell, T. D. *Adam Smith's Science of Morals*. Totowa, N.J.: Rowman and Littlefield, 1971.
———. "Francis Hutcheson: 'Father' of the Scottish Enlightenment." In *The Origins and Nature of the Scottish Enlightenment*, ed. R. H. Campbell and Andrew S. Skinner, 167–85. Edinburgh: John Donald Publishers, 1982.
Canavan, Francis. *Edmund Burke: Prescription and Providence*. Durham, N.C.: Carolina Academic Press and Claremont Institute for the Study of Statesmanship and Political Philosophy, 1987.
———. *The Political Reason of Edmund Burke*. Durham: Duke University Press, 1960.
Carpenter, Mary Wilson. "Sibylline Apocalyptics: Mary Wollstonecraft's *Vindication of the Rights of Woman* and Job's Mother's Womb." *Literature and History* 12, no. 2 (1986): 215–28.
Chapman, Gerald W. *Edmund Burke: The Practical Imagination*. Cambridge: Harvard University Press, 1967.
Chitnis, Anand C. *The Scottish Enlightenment: A Social History*. Totawa, N.J.: Rowman and Littlefield, 1976.
Clark, J. C. D. "Introduction." In Edmund Burke, *Reflections on the Revolution in France*, ed. J. C. D. Clark. Stanford: Stanford University Press, 2001.
Cobban, Alfred, ed. *The Debate on the French Revolution, 1789–1800*. London: Nicholas Kaye, 1950.
———. *Edmund Burke and the Revolt Against the Eighteenth Century*. 1929. London: Allen & Unwin, 1960.
Cole, Lucinda. "(Anti)Feminist Sympathies: The Politics of Relationship in Smith, Wollstonecraft, and More." *English Literary History* 58, no. 1 (1991): 107–40.
Condren, Conal. *The Status and Appraisal of Classic Texts: An Essay on Political Theory, Its Inheritance, and the History of Ideas*. Princeton: Princeton University Press, 1985.
Cone, Carl B. *Burke and the Nature of Politics: The Age of the American Revolution*. Lexington: University of Kentucky Press, 1957.
———. *Burke and the Nature of Politics: The Age of the French Revolution*. Lexington: University of Kentucky Press, 1964.

———. *Torchbearer of Freedom: The Influence of Richard Price on Eighteenth-Century Thought.* Lexington: University of Kentucky Press, 1952.
Conger, Syndy McMillen. *Mary Wollstonecraft and the Language of Sensibility.* Rutherford: Fairleigh Dickinson University Press, 1994.
———, ed. *Sensibility in Transformation: Creative Resistance to Sentiment from the Augustans to the Romantics.* Rutherford: Fairleigh Dickinson University Press, 1990.
Conniff, James. "Edmund Burke and His Critics: The Case of Mary Wollstonecraft." *Journal of the History of Ideas* 60, no. 2 (1999): 299–318.
———. *The Useful Cobbler: Edmund Burke and the Politics of Progress.* Albany: State University of New York Press, 1994.
Copeland, Thomas W. "Edmund Burke and the Book Reviews in Dodsley's *Annual Register.*" *Publications of the Modern Language Association* 57, no. 2 (1942): 446–68.
Corlett, William. *Community Without Unity: A Politics of Derridian Extravagance.* Durham: Duke University Press, 1989.
Courtney, C. P. *Montesquieu and Burke.* Oxford: Basil Blackwell, 1963.
Cox, Stephen D. "Sensibility as Argument." In *Sensibility in Transformation: Creative Resistance to Sentiment from the Augustans to the Romantics,* ed. Syndy McMillen Conger, 63–82. Rutherford: Fairleigh Dickinson University Press, 1990.
———. *"The Stranger Within Thee": Concepts of the Self in Late-Eighteenth-Century Literature.* Pittsburgh: University of Pittsburgh Press, 1980.
Crowe, Ian, ed. *The Enduring Edmund Burke: Bicentennial Essays.* Wilmington, Del.: Intercollegiate Studies Institute, 1997.
Davie, George E. *The Scottish Enlightenment and Other Essays.* Edinburgh: Polygon, 1991.
Deane, Seamus F. "Burke and the French Philosophes." *Studies in Burke and His Time* 10, no. 2 (1968–69): 1113–37.
———. *The French Revolution and the Enlightenment in England, 1789–1832.* Cambridge: Harvard University Press, 1988.
De Bruyn, Frans. "Edmund Burke's Natural Aristocrat: The 'Man of Taste' as a Political Ideal." *Eighteenth-Century Life* 11, no. 2 (1987): 41–60.
———. *The Literary Genres of Edmund Burke: The Political Uses of Literary Form.* Oxford: Oxford University Press, 1996.
Dickinson, H. T. *British Radicalism and the French Revolution, 1789–1815.* New York: Blackwell, 1985.
Dinwiddy, J. R. "Utility and Natural Law in Burke's Thought: A Reconsideration." *Studies in Burke and His Time* 16, no. 2 (1974–75): 105–28.
Dishman, Robert B. *Burke and Paine on Revolution and the Rights of Man.* New York: Scribner, 1971.
Dreyer, Frederick. *Burke's Politics: A Study in Whig Orthodoxy.* Waterloo, Ontario: Wilfrid Laurier University Press, 1979.
———. "The Genesis of Burke's *Reflections.*" *Journal of Modern History* 50 (September 1978): 462–79.
Dwyer, John. *The Age of the Passions: An Interpretation of Adam Smith and Scottish Enlightenment Culture.* East Lothian: Tuckwell Press, 1998.

———. *Virtuous Discourse: Sensibility and Community in Late Eighteenth-Century Scotland*. Edinburgh: John Donald Publishers, 1987.
Eagleton, Terry. "Aesthetics and Politics in Edmund Burke." *History Workshop Journal* 28 (1989): 53–62.
Einaudi, Mario. "The British Background of Burke's Political Philosophy." *Political Science Quarterly* 49, no. 4 (1934): 576–98.
Eisenstein, Zillah R. *The Radical Future of Liberal Feminism*. New York: Longman, 1981.
Engster, Daniel. "Mary Wollstonecraft's Nurturing Liberalism: Between an Ethic of Justice and Care." *American Political Science Review* 95, no. 3 (2001): 577–88.
Fennessy, R. R. *Burke, Paine, and the Rights of Man: A Difference of Political Opinion*. The Hague: Martinus Nijhoff, 1963.
Ferguson, Adam. *An Essay on the History of Civil Society*. Edited by Fania Oz-Salzberger. Cambridge: Cambridge University Press, 1995.
Ferguson, Frances. *Solitude and the Sublime: Romanticism and the Aesthetics of Individuation*. London: Routledge, 1992.
———. "Wollstonecraft Our Contemporary." In *Gender and Theory: Dialogues on Feminist Criticism*, ed. Linda Kauffman, 51–62. New York: Basil Blackwell, 1989.
Ferguson, Moira. *Colonialism and Gender Relations from Mary Wollstonecraft to Jamaica Kincaid*. New York: Columbia University Press, 1993.
———. "The Discovery of Mary Wollstonecraft's *The Female Reader.*" *Signs* 3, no. 4 (1978): 945–57.
Forbes, Duncan. *Hume's Philosophical Politics*. Cambridge: Cambridge University Press, 1975.
———. "Sceptical Whiggism, Commerce, and Liberty." In *Essays on Adam Smith*, ed. Andrew S. Skinner and Thomas Wilson, 179–201. Oxford: Clarendon Press, 1975.
———. "'Scientific' Whiggism: Adam Smith and John Millar." *Cambridge Journal* 7, no. 11 (1954): 643–70.
Fordyce, James. *Sermons to Young Women*. 2 vols. 9th ed. London: T. Cadell and J. Dodsley, 1778.
Freeman, Michael. *Edmund Burke and the Critique of Political Radicalism*. Oxford: Basil Blackwell, 1980.
Frisch, Morton J. "Burke on Theory." *Cambridge Journal* 7, no. 5 (1954): 292–97.
Frohnen, Bruce. *Virtue and the Promise of Conservatism: The Legacy of Burke and Tocqueville*. Lawrence: University Press of Kansas, 1993.
Fuchs, Michel. *Edmund Burke, Ireland, and the Fashioning of the Self*. Oxford: Voltaire Foundation, 1996.
Furniss, Tom. *Edmund Burke's Aesthetic Ideology: Language, Gender, and Political Economy in Revolution*. Cambridge: Cambridge University Press, 1993.
———. "Gender in Revolution: Edmund Burke and Mary Wollstonecraft." In *Revolution in Writing: British Literary Responses to the French Revolution*, ed. Kelvin Everest, 65–100. Milton Keynes: Open University Press, 1991.
———. "Mary Wollstonecraft's French Revolution." In *The Cambridge Companion to Mary Wollstonecraft*, ed. Claudia L. Johnson, 59–81. Cambridge: Cambridge University Press, 2002.

Gerson, Gal. "Liberal Feminism: Individuality and Oppositions in Wollstonecraft and Mill." *Political Studies* 50, no. 4 (2002): 794–810.

Gibbons, Luke. *Edmund Burke and Ireland: Aesthetics, Politics, and the Colonial Sublime*. Cambridge: Cambridge University Press, 2003.

Godwin, William. *Memoirs of the Author of A Vindication of the Rights of Woman*. Edited by Pamela Clemit and Gina Luria Walker. Toronto: Broadview Literary Texts, 2001.

Goodhart, Michael. *Democracy as Human Rights: Freedom and Equality in the Age of Globalization*. New York: Routledge, 2005.

Goodwin, Albert. *The Friends of Liberty: The English Democratic Movement in the Age of the French Revolution*. Cambridge: Harvard University Press, 1979.

Gordon, Lyndall. *Vindication: A Life of Mary Wollstonecraft*. New York: HarperCollins, 2005.

Grave, S. A. *The Scottish Philosophy of Common Sense*. Oxford: Clarendon Press, 1960.

Griswold, Charles L., Jr. *Adam Smith and the Virtues of Enlightenment*. Cambridge: Cambridge University Press, 1999.

Gunther-Canada, Wendy. "The Politics of Sense and Sensibility: Mary Wollstonecraft and Catharine Macaulay Graham on Edmund Burke's *Reflections on the Revolution in France*." In *Women Writers and the Early Modern British Political Tradition*, ed. Hilda L. Smith, 126–47. Cambridge: Cambridge University Press, 1998.

———. *Rebel Writer: Mary Wollstonecraft and Enlightenment Politics*. DeKalb: Northern Illinois University Press, 2001.

Hamowy, Ronald. *The Scottish Enlightenment and the Theory of Spontaneous Order*. Carbondale: Southern Illinois University Press, 1987.

Hampsher-Monk, Iain, ed. *The Impact of the French Revolution: Texts from Britain in the 1790s*. Cambridge: Cambridge University Press, 2005.

———. "Rhetoric and Opinion in the Politics of Edmund Burke." *History of Political Thought* 9, no. 3 (1988): 455–84.

Harle, Vilho. "Burke the International Theorist—or the War of the Sons of Light and the Sons of Darkness." In *European Values in International Relations*, ed. Vilho Harle, 58–79. New York: Pinter Publishers, 1990.

Herman, Arthur. *How the Scots Invented the Modern World*. New York: Three Rivers Press, 2001.

Herzog, Don. *Poisoning the Minds of the Lower Orders*. Princeton: Princeton University Press, 1998.

Hindson, Paul, and Tim Gray. *Burke's Dramatic Theory of Politics*. Aldershot, England: Avebury, 1988.

Hont, Istvan, and Michael Ignatieff, eds. *Wealth and Virtue: The Shaping of Political Economy in the Scottish Enlightenment*. Cambridge: Cambridge University Press, 1983.

Hume, David. *Political Essays*. Edited by Knud Haakonssen. Cambridge: Cambridge University Press, 1998.

———. *A Treatise of Human Nature*. Edited by L. A. Selby-Bigge. Oxford: Clarendon Press, 1896.

Hunt, Eileen M. "The Family as Cave, Platoon, and Prison: The Three Stages of Wollstonecraft's Philosophy of the Family." *Review of Politics* 64, no. 1 (2002): 81–119.
Johnson, Claudia L. *Equivocal Beings: Politics, Gender, and Sentimentality in the 1790s: Wollstonecraft, Radcliffe, Burney, Austen.* Chicago: University of Chicago Press, 1995.
Jones, Chris. "Mary Wollstonecraft's *Vindications* and Their Political Tradition." In *The Cambridge Companion to Mary Wollstonecraft*, ed. Claudia L. Johnson, 42–58. Cambridge: Cambridge University Press, 2002.
Jones, Peter, ed. *The 'Science of Man' in the Scottish Enlightenment: Hume, Reid, and Their Contemporaries.* Edinburgh: Edinburgh University Press, 1989.
Juengel, Scott. "Countenancing History: Mary Wollstonecraft, Samuel Stanhope Smith, and Enlightenment Racial Science." *English Literary History* 68 (2001): 897–927.
Jump, Harriet Devine. "'The cool eye of observation': Mary Wollstonecraft and the French Revolution." In *Revolution in Writing: British Literary Responses to the French Revolution*, ed. Kelvin Everest, 101–19. Milton Keynes: Open University Press, 1991.
———. *Mary Wollstonecraft: Writer.* New York: Harvester/Wheatsheaf, 1994.
Kaufman, Robert. "The Madness of George III, by Mary Wollstonecraft." *Studies in Romanticism* 37, no. 1 (1998): 17–25.
Kay, Carol. "Canon, Ideology, and Gender: Mary Wollstonecraft's Critique of Adam Smith." *New Political Science* 15 (1986): 63–76.
Kelly, Gary. *Revolutionary Feminism: The Mind and Career of Mary Wollstonecraft.* London: Macmillan, 1992.
Kilcup, Rodney W. "Burke's Historicism." *Journal of Modern History* 49 (September 1977): 394–410.
———. "Reason and the Basis of Morality in Burke." *Journal of the History of Philosophy* 17, no. 3 (1979): 271–84.
Kirk, Russell. "Burke and Natural Rights." *Review of Politics* 13, no. 4 (1951): 441–56.
Klein, Lawrence E. *Shaftesbury and the Culture of Politeness.* Cambridge: Cambridge University Press, 1994.
Kramnick, Isaac. "The Left and Edmund Burke." *Political Theory* 11, no. 2 (1983): 189–214.
———, ed. *The Portable Edmund Burke.* New York: Penguin Books, 1999.
———. *The Rage of Edmund Burke: Portrait of an Ambivalent Conservative.* New York: Basic Books, 1977.
———. *Republicanism and Bourgeois Radicalism: Political Ideology in Late Eighteenth-Century England and America.* Ithaca: Cornell University Press, 1990.
———. "Skepticism in English Political Thought: From Temple to Burke." *Studies in Burke and His Time* 12, no. 1 (1970): 1627–60.
Lambert, Elizabeth R. *Edmund Burke of Beaconsfield.* Newark: University of Delaware Press, 2003.
Landes, Joan B. *Women and the Public Sphere in the Age of the French Revolution.* Ithaca: Cornell University Press, 1988.

Lecky, William. *A History of England in the Eighteenth Century.* 8 vols. London: Longmans, Green, 1883–90.

Lehmann, William C. *John Millar of Glasgow, 1735–1801.* New York: Arno Press, 1979.

Lenman, Bruce P. "'From Savage to Scot' via the French and the Spaniards: Principal Robertson's Spanish Sources." In *William Robertson and the Expansion of Empire*, ed. Stewart J. Brown, 196–209. Cambridge: Cambridge University Press, 1997.

Lenzner, Steven J. "Strauss's Three Burkes: The Problem of Edmund Burke in *Natural Right and History.*" *Political Theory* 19, no. 3 (1991): 364–90.

Lester, John A., Jr. "An Analysis of the Conservative Thought of Edmund Burke." Ph.D. diss., Harvard University, 1942.

Lock, F. P. *Edmund Burke.* Vol. 1, *1730–1784.* Oxford: Oxford University Press, 1998.

Lovejoy, Arthur O. *The Great Chain of Being: A Study of the History of an Idea.* Cambridge: Harvard University Press, 1964.

Lucas, Paul. "On Edmund Burke's Doctrine of Prescription; or, An Appeal from the New to the Old Lawyers." *Historical Journal* 11, no. 1 (1968): 35–63.

MacCunn, John. *The Political Philosophy of Burke.* London: Edward Arnold, 1913.

Macpherson, C. B. *Burke.* Oxford: Oxford University Press, 1980.

Mansfield, Harvey C., Jr. *Statesmanship and Party Government: A Study of Burke and Bolingbroke.* Chicago: University of Chicago Press, 1965.

Marx, Karl. *Capital: A Critique of Political Economy.* Vol. 1 Introduction by Ernest Mandel, translated by Ben Fowkes. New York: Vintage Books, 1977.

McCue, Jim. *Edmund Burke and Our Present Discontents.* London: Claridge Press, 1997.

McLoughlin, T. O. *Edmund Burke and the First Ten Years of the 'Annual Register,' 1758–1767.* Salisbury: University of Rhodesia, 1975.

———. "Edmund Burke's *Abridgment of English History.*" *Eighteenth-Century Ireland* 5 (1990): 45–59.

Meek, Ronald L. *Social Science and the Ignoble Savage.* Cambridge: Cambridge University Press, 1976.

Mehta, Uday Singh. *Liberalism and Empire: A Study in Nineteenth-Century British Liberal Thought.* Chicago: University of Chicago Press, 1999.

Mellor, Anne K. *Romanticism and Gender.* London: Routledge, 1993.

Millar, John. *The Origin of the Distinction of Ranks.* 3d ed. London: J. Murray, 1779.

Monk, Samuel H. *The Sublime: A Study of Critical Theories in Eighteenth-Century England.* New York: Modern Language Association of America, 1935.

Moore, James. "The Two Systems of Francis Hutcheson: On the Origins of the Scottish Enlightenment." In *Studies in the Philosophy of the Scottish Enlightenment*, ed. M. A. Stewart, 37–59. Oxford: Oxford University Press, 1990.

Moran, Mary Catherine. "Between the Savage and the Civil: Dr. John Gregory's Natural History of Femininity." In *Women, Gender, and Enlightenment*, ed. Sarah Knott and Barbara Taylor, 8–29. New York: Palgrave Macmillan, 2005.

———. "'The Commerce of the Sexes': Gender and the Social Sphere in Scottish Enlightenment Accounts of Civil Society." In *Paradoxes of Civil Society: New*

Perspectives on Modern German and British History, 2d ed., ed. Frank Trentmann, 61–84. New York: Berghahn Books, 2003.
Morley, John. *Edmund Burke: A Historical Study*. 1867. New York: Knopf, 1924.
Mosher, Michael. "The Skeptic's Burke." *Political Theory* 19, no. 3 (1991): 391–418.
Mullan, John. *Sentiment and Sociability: The Language of Feeling in the Eighteenth Century*. Oxford: Clarendon Press, 1988.
Myers, Mitzi. "Mary Wollstonecraft's Literary Reviews." In *The Cambridge Companion to Mary Wollstonecraft*, ed. Claudia L. Johnson, 82–98. Cambridge: Cambridge University Press, 2002.
———. "Politics from the Outside: Mary Wollstonecraft's First *Vindication*." *Studies in Eighteenth-Century Culture* 6 (1977): 113–32.
———. "Reform or Ruin: 'A Revolution in Female Manners.'" *Studies in Eighteenth-Century Culture* 11 (1982): 199–216.
———. "Sensibility and the 'Walk of Reason': Mary Wollstonecraft's Literary Reviews as Cultural Critique." In *Sensibility in Transformation: Creative Resistance to Sentiment from the Augustans to the Romantics*, ed. Syndy McMillen Conger, 120–44. Rutherford: Fairleigh Dickinson University Press, 1990.
Neill, Anna. "Civilization and the Rights of Woman: Liberty and Captivity in the Work of Mary Wollstonecraft." In *Mary Wollstonecraft and the Critics, 1788–2001*, ed. Harriet Devine Jump, 2 vols., 2:418–35. New York: Routledge, 2003.
Neocleous, Mark. "The Monstrous Multitude: Edmund Burke's Political Teratology." *Contemporary Political Theory* 3 (2004): 70–88.
O'Brien, Conor Cruise. *The Great Melody: A Thematic Biography of Edmund Burke*. Chicago: University of Chicago Press, 1992.
O'Brien, Karen. *Narratives of Enlightenment: Cosmopolitan History from Voltaire to Gibbon*. Cambridge: Cambridge University Press, 1997.
———. "Robertson's Place in the Development of Eighteenth-Century Narrative History." In *William Robertson and the Expansion of Empire*, ed. Stewart J. Brown, 74–91. Cambridge: Cambridge University Press, 1997.
Offen, Karen. "Was Mary Wollstonecraft a Feminist? A Contextual Re-Reading of *A Vindication of the Rights of Woman*, 1792–1992." In *Quilting a New Canon: Stitching Women's Words*, ed. Uma Parameswaran, 3–24. Toronto: Sister Vision, 1996.
O'Gorman, Frank. *Edmund Burke: His Political Philosophy*. Bloomington: Indiana University Press, 1973.
O'Neill, Daniel I. "Burke on Democracy as the Death of Western Civilization." *Polity* 36, no. 2 (2004): 201–25.
———. "Shifting the Scottish Paradigm: The Discourse of Morals and Manners in Mary Wollstonecraft's *French Revolution*." *History of Political Thought* 23, no. 1 (2002): 90–116.
O'Neill, Daniel I., and Margaret Kohn. "A Tale of Two Indias: Burke and Mill on Empire and Slavery in the West Indies and America." *Political Theory* 34, no. 2 (2006): 192–228.
Osborn, Annie M. *Rousseau and Burke: A Study of the Idea of Liberty in Eighteenth-Century Political Thought*. London: Oxford University Press, 1940.
Pagden, Anthony. *Peoples and Empires*. New York: Modern Library, 2003.

Paine, Thomas. *The Rights of Man*. Edited by Gregory Claeys. Indianapolis: Hackett, 1992.

Pappin, Joseph L., III. *The Metaphysics of Edmund Burke*. New York: Fordham University Press, 1993.

Parke, Catherine N. "What Kind of Heroine Is Mary Wollstonecraft?" In *Sensibility in Transformation: Creative Resistance to Sentiment from the Augustans to the Romantics*, ed. Syndy McMillen Conger, 103–19. Rutherford: Fairleigh Dickinson University Press, 1990.

Parkin, Charles. *The Moral Basis of Burke's Political Thought*. Cambridge: Cambridge University Press, 1956.

Pateman, Carole. "Democracy, Freedom, and Special Rights." In *Social Justice: From Hume to Walzer*, ed. David Boucher and Paul Kelly, 215–31. New York: Routledge, 1998.

———. *The Disorder of Women: Democracy, Feminism, and Political Theory*. Stanford: Stanford University Press, 1989.

———. "The Rights of Man and Early Feminism." *Swiss Yearbook of Political Science* (1994): 19–31.

———. *The Sexual Contract*. Stanford: Stanford University Press, 1988.

———. "Women's Writing, Women's Standing: Theory and Politics in the Early Modern Period." In *Women Writers and the Early Modern British Political Tradition*, ed. Hilda L. Smith, 363–82. Cambridge: Cambridge University Press, 1998.

Paulson, Ronald. *Representations of Revolution, 1789–1820*. New Haven: Yale University Press, 1983.

Phillipson, N. T. *Hume*. New York: St. Martin's Press, 1989.

———. "James Beattie and the Defense of Common Sense." In *Festschrift für Rainer Gruenter*, ed. Bernhard Fabian, 145–54. Heidelberg: Carl Winter Universitätsverlag, 1978.

———. "Providence and Progress: An Introduction to the Historical Thought of William Robertson." In *William Robertson and the Expansion of Empire*, ed. Stewart J. Brown, 55–73. Cambridge: Cambridge University Press, 1997.

———. "The Scottish Enlightenment." In *The Enlightenment in National Context*, ed. Roy Porter and Mikuláš Teich, 19–40. Cambridge: Cambridge University Press, 1981.

———. "Towards a Definition of the Scottish Enlightenment." In *City and Society in the Eighteenth Century*, ed. Paul Fritz and David Williams, 125–47. Toronto: Hakkert, 1973.

Philp, Mark, ed. *The French Revolution and British Popular Politics*. Cambridge: Cambridge University Press, 1991.

Pocock, J. G. A. *Barbarism and Religion*. Vol. 2, *Narratives of Civil Government*. Cambridge: Cambridge University Press, 1999.

———. *Barbarism and Religion*. Vol. 4, *Barbarians, Savages, and Empires*. Cambridge: Cambridge University Press, 2005.

———. "Burke and the Ancient Constitution: A Problem in the History of Ideas." *Historical Journal* 3, no. 2 (1960): 125–43.

———. "Cambridge Paradigms and Scotch Philosophers: A Study of the Relations Between the Civic Humanist and the Civil Jurisprudential Interpretation of Eighteenth-Century Social Thought." In *Wealth and Virtue: The Shaping of Political Economy in the Scottish Enlightenment*, ed. Istvan Hont and Michael Ignatieff, 235–52. Cambridge: Cambridge University Press, 1983.

———. "The Concept of a Language and the *métier d'historien:* Some Considerations on Practice." In *The Languages of Political Theory in Early-Modern Europe*, ed. Anthony Pagden, 19–38. Cambridge: Cambridge University Press, 1987.

———. "Edmund Burke and the Redefinition of Enthusiasm: The Context as Counter-Revolution." In *The French Revolution and the Creation of Modern Political Culture*, vol. 3, ed. François Furet and Mona Ozouf, 19–43. Oxford: Pergamon Press, 1989.

———. "Introduction." In Edmund Burke, *Reflections on the Revolution in France.* Edited by J. G. A. Pocock. Indianapolis: Hackett, 1987.

———. *Politics, Language, and Time: Essays on Political Thought and History.* Chicago: University of Chicago Press, 1989.

———. *Virtue, Commerce, and History: Essays on Political Thought and History, Chiefly in the Eighteenth Century.* Cambridge: Cambridge University Press, 1985.

Poovey, Mary. *The Proper Lady and the Woman Writer: Ideology as Style in the Works of Mary Wollstonecraft, Mary Shelley, and Jane Austen.* Chicago: University of Chicago Press, 1985.

Porter, Roy. *The Creation of the Modern World: The Untold Story of the British Enlightenment.* New York: W. W. Norton, 2000.

Reiss, Timothy J. "Revolution in Bounds: Wollstonecraft, Women, and Reason," In *Gender and Theory: Dialogues on Feminist Criticism*, ed. Linda Kauffman, 11–50. New York: Basil Blackwell, 1989.

Rendall, Jane. "'The grand causes which combine to carry mankind forward': Wollstonecraft, History, and Revolution." *Women's Writing* 4, no. 2 (1997): 155–72.

———. *The Origins of Modern Feminism: Women in Britain, France, and the United States, 1780–1860.* New York: Schocken Books, 1984.

———, ed. *The Origins of the Scottish Enlightenment, 1707–1776.* New York: St. Martin's Press, 1978.

Robertson, William. *The Progress of Society in Europe.* Edited by Felix Gilbert. Chicago: University of Chicago Press, 1972.

Robinson, Daniel. "Theodicy Versus Feminist Strategy in Mary Wollstonecraft's Fiction." *Eighteenth-Century Fiction* 9, no. 2 (1997): 183–202.

Roper, Derek. "Mary Wollstonecraft's Reviews." *Notes and Queries* 203 (1958): 37–38.

Ryan, Vanessa L. "The Physiological Sublime: Burke's Critique of Reason." *Journal of the History of Ideas* 62, no. 2 (2001): 265–79.

Sapiro, Virginia. *A Vindication of Political Virtue: The Political Theory of Mary Wollstonecraft.* Chicago: University of Chicago Press, 1992.

———. "Wollstonecraft, Feminism, and Democracy: 'Being Bastilled.'" In *Feminist Interpretations of Mary Wollstonecraft*, ed. Maria J. Falco, 33–45. University Park: Pennsylvania State University Press, 1996.

———. "A Woman's Struggle for a Language of Enlightenment and Virtue: Mary Wollstonecraft and Enlightenment 'Feminism.'" In *Perspectives on Feminist Political Thought in European History: From the Middle Ages to the Present*, ed. Tjitske Akkerman and Siep Stuurman, 122–35. New York: Routledge, 1998.

Schneider, Louis, ed. *The Scottish Moralists on Human Nature and Society*. Chicago: University of Chicago Press, 1967.
Sebastiani, Silvia. "'Race,' Women, and Progress in the Scottish Enlightenment." In *Women, Gender, and Enlightenment*, ed. Sarah Knott and Barbara Taylor, 75–96. New York: Palgrave Macmillan, 2005.
Shanley, Mary Lyndon. "Mary Wollstonecraft on Sensibility, Women's Rights, and Patriarchal Power." In *Women Writers and the Early Modern British Political Tradition*, ed. Hilda L. Smith, 148–67. Cambridge: Cambridge University Press, 1998.
Sher, Richard B. *Church and University in the Scottish Enlightenment: The Moderate Literati of Edinburgh*. Princeton: Princeton University Press, 1985.
Skinner, Quentin. *Liberty Before Liberalism*. Cambridge: Cambridge University Press, 1998.
Smith, Adam. *Correspondence of Adam Smith*. Edited by E. C. Mossner and I. S. Ross. Indianapolis: Liberty Fund, 1987.
———. *An Inquiry into the Nature and Causes of the Wealth of Nations*. Edited by R. H. Campbell and A. S. Skinner. 2 vols. Indianapolis: Liberty Fund, 1981.
———. *Lectures on Jurisprudence*. Edited by R. L. Meek, D. D. Raphael, and P. G. Stein. Indianapolis: Liberty Fund, 1982.
———. *The Theory of Moral Sentiments*. Edited by D. D. Raphael and A. L. Macfie. Indianapolis: Liberty Fund, 1984.
Smith, Bruce James. *Politics and Remembrance: Republican Themes in Machiavelli, Burke, and Tocqueville*. Princeton: Princeton University Press, 1985.
Smith, Olivia. *The Politics of Language, 1791–1819*. Oxford: Oxford University Press, 1984.
Spadafora, David. *The Idea of Progress in Eighteenth-Century Britain*. New Haven: Yale University Press, 1990.
Spence, Gordon. "Mary Wollstonecraft's Theodicy and Theory of Progress." *Enlightenment and Dissent* 14 (1995): 105–27.
Stanlis, Peter. *Edmund Burke and the Natural Law*. Ann Arbor: University of Michigan Press, 1958.
———. *Edmund Burke: The Enlightenment and Revolution*. New Brunswick, N.J.: Transaction Publishers, 1991.
Stephen, Leslie. *English Thought in the Eighteenth Century*. 2 vols. 1876. New York: Harcourt, Brace & World, 1963.
Stewart, M. A., ed. *Studies in the Philosophy of the Scottish Enlightenment*. Oxford: Oxford University Press, 1990.
Stewart, Sally N. "Mary Wollstonecraft's Contributions to the *Analytical Review*." *Essays in Literature* 11 (1984): 187–99.
Strauss, Leo. *Natural Right and History*. Chicago: University of Chicago Press, 1953.
Taylor, Barbara. "Feminists Versus Gallants: Manners and Morals in Enlightenment Britain." In *Women, Gender, and Enlightenment*, ed. Sarah Knott and Barbara Taylor, 30–52. New York: Palgrave Macmillan, 2005.
———. *Mary Wollstonecraft and the Feminist Imagination*. Cambridge: Cambridge University Press, 2003.
Todd, Janet. *Mary Wollstonecraft: A Revolutionary Life*. New York: Columbia University Press, 2000.

———. *Sensibility: An Introduction.* New York: Methuen, 1986.
Trevor-Roper, Hugh. "The Scottish Enlightenment." *Studies on Voltaire and the Eighteenth Century* 58 (1967): 1635–58.
Tully, James. "Political Philosophy as a Critical Activity." *Political Theory* 30, no. 4 (2002): 533–55.
Vincent, R. J. "Edmund Burke and the Theory of International Relations." *Review of International Studies* 10 (1984): 205–18.
Wardle, Ralph. "Mary Wollstonecraft, Analytical Reviewer." *PMLA* 62, no. 4 (1947): 1000–1009.
———. *Mary Wollstonecraft: A Critical Biography.* Lawrence: University of Kansas Press, 1951.
Welsh, Jennifer M. *Edmund Burke and International Relations: The Commonwealth of Europe and the Crusade Against the French Revolution.* New York: St. Martin's Press, 1995.
Weston, John C., Jr. "Edmund Burke's View of History." *Review of Politics* 23 no. 2 (1961): 203–29.
Whelan, Frederick G. *Edmund Burke and India: Political Morality and Empire.* Pittsburgh: University of Pittsburgh Press, 1996.
White, Stephen K. *Edmund Burke: Modernity, Politics, and Aesthetics.* Thousand Oaks, Calif.: Sage Publications, 1994.
Wilkins, Burleigh Taylor. *The Problem of Burke's Political Philosophy.* Oxford: Clarendon Press, 1967.
Winch, Donald. *Adam Smith's Politics: An Essay in Historiographic Revision.* Cambridge: Cambridge University Press, 1978.
———. *Riches and Poverty: An Intellectual History of Political Economy in Britain, 1750–1834.* Cambridge: Cambridge University Press, 1996.
Wolin, Sheldon S. *Politics and Vision: Continuity and Innovation in Western Political Thought.* Exp. ed. Princeton: Princeton University Press, 2006.
Wollstonecraft, Mary. *Collected Letters of Mary Wollstonecraft.* Edited by Ralph Wardle. Ithaca: Cornell University Press, 1979.
———. *Maria, or the Wrongs of Woman.* Introduction by Anne K. Mellor. New York: W. W. Norton, 1994.
———. *A Vindication of the Rights of Men and A Vindication of the Rights of Woman.* Edited by Sylvana Tomaselli. Cambridge: Cambridge University Press, 1995.
———. *A Vindication of the Rights of Woman.* Edited by Miriam Brody. New York: Penguin, 1992.
———. *The Works of Mary Wollstonecraft.* Edited by Janet Todd and Marilyn Butler. 7 vols. New York: New York University Press, 1989.
Wood, Neal. "The Aesthetic Dimension of Burke's Political Thought." *Journal of British Studies* 4, no. 1 (1964): 41–64.
Zerilli, Linda M. G. *Signifying Woman: Culture and Chaos in Rousseau, Burke, and Mill.* Ithaca: Cornell University Press, 1994.

Burke, Edmund (*continued*)
    on aesthetics, 56–59, 129–34, 135–36, 139, 141–43, 145–48, 155–56, 224–25
    on ambition, 58n. 31, 77–78, 135
    Annual Register and, 55, 63–64, 66, 67–70, 79–80
    An Appeal from the New to the Old Whigs, 136–37, 202–5
    on barbarism, 72–78
    on bastards, 212
    on beauty, 129–31, 132–34, 135–36, 145–48, 155–56
    on chivalry, 135–36, 146–47
    on the church, 12, 14–15, 74–77, 128–29, 140–43, 215–16, 221–22
    on civilization, 9–10, 15–16, 217–25
    on the civilizing process, 14, 72–78, 84–87, 128–29, 134–43, 140–41
    on colonialism, 82–87, 137–38
    on common sense, 140
    conservatism of, 1–4, 52, 62–63, 257–61
    on constitutionalism, 76
    death of, 220–21, 225–26
    on democracy, 9–10, 15–16, 127, 142, 152–56
    on divorce, 212–13
    on duty, 203–4
    on education, 143, 207–8
    on equality, 134–40, 220–21
    An Essay towards an Abridgment of the English History, 70–78, 79, 81, 128–29, 134–35
    on family, 203–5, 207–13
    on feudalism, 77–78, 134–36
    on French Revolution, 4–10, 125–26; agents, 154–55, 196–202; and democracy, 9–10, 152–56, 200–202, 213–25; and history, 127–29; and moral philosophy, 127–29, 144–51, 202–17, 211–13; and social theory, 139–40, 202–13
    on God, 58–59, 59–61, 62, 132, 141–42, 147
    on history, 11–15, 70–87, 127–29, 140–41
    on human nature, 56–63, 81–87, 144–45, 149–50
    on imitation, 58n. 31
    on instinct, 58–62, 64–65, 140
    on international relations, 222–23
    on Jacobinism, 219–20
    Letters on a Regicide Peace, 196–97, 211–17, 222–25
    A Letter to a Member of the National Assembly, 205–8
    Letter to a Noble Lord, 213, 218
    on liberty, 137
    on love, 130–31, 132–33, 134, 206–7, 209
    on manners, 65–66, 72–78, 83–87, 135–36, 144, 146–51, 200–201, 202–3, 211, 213–17, 222–23
    on Marie Antoinette, 145–48
    on marriage, 211–13
    on men, 132, 139
    on moral philosophy, 11–15, 56–70, 127–29, 144–51
    on natural law, 138–39
    on nobility, 12, 14–15, 128–29, 134–40, 145–48, 208, 215–16, 221–22
    Note-Book, 59–61
    "On Taste," 69–70
    on people, 136–37, 154–56, 221–22
    on philosophers, 154–55, 196–202
    A Philosophical Enquiry into the Origin of our Ideas of the Sublime and Beautiful, 56–59, 60–61, 64–65, 69, 129–34, 147, 209
    on politicians, 197, 199–202
    on power, 131–32, 133, 136, 141–43, 148, 209–11
    Preface to Brissot's Address to his Constituents, 220
    on prejudice, 149–51, 219–20
    on prescription, 150–51
    on the press, 214–16
    on property, 73, 78–79, 150–51, 200
    on the Protestant Reformation, 221
    on reason, 56–63, 64, 66–67, 144–45, 149–50, 203–6
    Reflections on the Revolution in France, 4–5, 14–15, 84, 125–26, 135–36, 141–43, 144–51, 152–56, 209–11, 217–18
    on religion, 73–77, 84–87, 140–43, 197–200
    Remarks on the Policy of the Allies, 221
    on savagery, 10, 15–16, 84–85, 86, 126–27, 137, 152–56, 210–11, 216–25
    Scottish Enlightenment, connections to, 8–10, 53–56
    secondary literature on, 51–52
    on sensibility, 108–9, 145–48
    on sex, 130–31, 132, 208

social theory of, 78–87, 134–43
  on the state, 141–42, 149–51
  on sublimity, 129–32, 134, 135, 141–43, 148, 155–56, 209, 224–25
  on sympathy, 58, 64, 66, 69, 147, 222–23
  on taste, 69–70
  Thoughts on French Affairs, 221
  A Vindication of Natural Society, 61–62
  on Wollstonecraft, 195–96
  on women, 126, 136, 139, 154
Burke, Richard, 125
Burke, Will, 59, 81–87
Butler, Marilyn, 6n. 13, 111

Caesar Augustus, 72
Campbell, T. D, 26
Canavan, Francis, 57n. 26, 62n. 44, 63n. 45
Capital (Marx), 121n. 103
The Castle of Mowbray, 115
Catherine the Great, 240
character, 229–32, 243–44, 247, 248–49, 250
Characteristics of Men, Manners, Opinions and Times (Shaftesbury), 23
The Child of Woe (Norman), 113
chivalry, 135–36, 146–47, 234–37, 243
Christie, Thomas, 111
church. *See also* God; religion
  aesthetics and, 141–43
  Burke on, 12, 14–15, 74–77, 128–29, 140–43, 215–16, 221–22
  civilization and, 221–22, 240
  civilizing process and, 74–77, 140–43, 179, 234–35
  democracy and, 142
  education and, 143, 168–69, 170
  equality and, 170, 179
  French Revolution and, 173–74, 221–22, 248
  history and, 74–77, 140–41, 167–70, 234–35
  moral philosophy and, 128–29
  power and, 141–43, 167–68
  the press and, 215–16
  social theory and, 140–43, 140–43, 179
  the state and, 141–43
  sublimity and, 141–43
  Wollstonecraft on, 167–70, 173–74, 179, 234–35, 240, 248
civilization. *See also* civilizing process
  barbarism and, 260–61
  Burke on, 9–10, 15–16, 217–25
  the church and, 221–22, 240

democracy and, 9–10, 15–16, 217–25, 254–56, 259–61
equality and, 220–21
French Revolution and, 9–10, 217–25, 254–56
in Great Britain, 239–40
liberty and, 239–42
nobility and, 221–22, 240
prejudice and, 219–20
savagery and, 217–25, 260–61
in Scottish Enlightenment, 10
Wollstonecraft on, 9–10, 16, 239–42, 254–56
civilizing process. *See also* civilization; history
  in aesthetics, 141–43
  Burke on, 14, 72–78, 84–87, 128–29, 134–43, 140–41
  chivalry in, 135–36, 234–37
  the church and, 74–77, 140–43, 179, 234–35
  commerce and, 40–49
  democracy and, 238–39
  equality and, 134–40, 170, 238–39
  feminism in, 235–36
  feudalism in, 77–78, 134–36
  French Revolution and, 230–31
  in Great Britain, 72–78
  manners in, 72–78, 235–39
  military and, 179–81
  moral philosophy and, 176–81, 230–31
  nobility and, 134–40, 169–70, 234
  religion and, 73–77, 84–87, 179
  in Scottish Enlightenment, 9, 10, 38, 40–49
  sublimity and, 141–43
  Wollstonecraft on, 18–19, 161–62, 166–70, 176–81, 230–31, 232–39
  women and, 176–81
Cobban, Alfred, 4
colonialism, 41–42, 45, 82–87, 137–38
commerce
  civilizing process and, 40–49
  French Revolution and, 231
  manners and, 237
  moral philosophy and, 42–49, 92, 105–6, 231, 237
  reason and, 237
  in Scottish Enlightenment, 10, 38, 39–49
  slavery and, 84–85
  Wollstonecraft on, 105–6, 231, 237
  women and, 91–92

common sense, 30–32, 66–70, 112–13, 140, 164–65. *See also* sensibility
A Comparative View of the State and Faculties of Man with those of the Animal World (Gregory), 95–96
Condren, Conal, 2
Cone, Carl B., 85
Conger, Syndy, 108–9, 113n. 84
Conniff, James, 79n. 85
conservatism, 1–4, 10, 34–35, 52, 62–63, 257–61
constitutionalism, 76, 166–67. *See also* state
Cooper, Anthony Ashley, 23
Copeland, Thomas, 67, 79n. 86
Corlett, William, 142n. 31
Courtney, C. P., 71
coverture, 186–87
Crewe, Mrs. John, 195
Crusades, 234–35

Dalrymple, Sir John, 38–39
Deane, Seamus F., 207n. 33
de Bolla, Peter, 56
Declaration of the Rights of Man and the Citizen, 4, 185–86, 254–55, 258
democracy
    aesthetics and, 155–56
    barbarism and, 260–61
    beauty and, 155–56
    Burke on, 9–10, 15–16, 127, 142, 152–56
    the church and, 142
    civilization and, 9–10, 15–16, 217–25, 254–56, 259–61
    civilizing process and, 238–39
    conservatism and, 10, 257–61, 260–61
    education and, 207–8
    equality and, 173–75, 238–39, 254–56, 259–60
    family and, 207–13
    feminism and, 10, 257–61
    French Revolution and, 9–10, 152–56, 173–75, 200–202, 213–25, 232, 251–56
    manners and, 174–75, 184–94, 238–39
    moral philosophy and, 173–75, 213–17, 232, 238–39, 259–60
    the press and, 214–16, 245–46
    reason and, 238–39, 251–54
    rights and, 184–94, 259
    savagery and, 10, 15–16, 127, 152–56, 216–25, 260–61
    sex and, 208
    social theory and, 202–13
    sublimity and, 155–56
    the Terror and, 253, 255–56
    Wollstonecraft on, 9–10, 16, 18–19, 102, 113, 173–75, 238–39, 251–56
    women and, 102, 113, 154, 184–94
Depont, Charles-Jean-François-, 125–26, 151
Desmoulins, Camille, 220
A Discourse on the Love of our Country (Price), 4
A Discourse on the Origin of Inequality (Rousseau), 179
division of labor, 105–6
divorce, 212–13
Dodsley, Robert, 55, 81n. 95
Druids, 73–74
The Duke of Exeter, an Historical Romance, 114
duty, 203–4
Dwyer, John, 66n. 55, 92, 94, 96, 99–100

Eaton, Daniel Isaac, 5
Edmund Burke and Ireland (Gibbons), 13n. 24
Edmund Burke's Aesthetic Ideology (Furniss), 13n. 24
education
    Burke on, 143, 207–8
    the church and, 143, 168–69, 170
    democracy and, 207–8
    equality and, 187–89
    family and, 207–8
    moral philosophy and, 207–8
    rights and, 187–89
    in social theory, 143
    Wollstonecraft on, 116, 168–69, 170, 182–83, 187–89
    of women, 96, 116, 182–83, 187–89
Edward and Harriet, or the Happy Recovery, 113–14
Edward III, 166
Elliot, Sir George, 218–19
employment, 190–91
English, Thomas, 55
An Enquiry Concerning Human Understanding (Hume), 25
equality. *See also* liberty; rights
    Burke on, 134–40, 220–21
    the church and, 170, 179
    civilization and, 220–21
    civilizing process and, 134–40, 170, 238–39

democracy and, 173–75, 238–39, 254–56, 259–60
education and, 187–89
employment and, 190–91
family and, 191–93
French Revolution and, 173–75, 220–21, 254–56
history and, 170
income and, 189–90
manners and, 187–89, 238–39
in marriage, 191
military and, 179–81
moral philosophy and, 238–39
nobility and, 170
parenthood and, 191–93
property and, 190
religion and, 179
of rights, 184–94
savagery and, 84–85
in social theory, 178–94
Wollstonecraft on, 18–19, 170, 173–75, 178–94, 238–39, 254–56
women and, 178–94
Essay Concerning Human Understanding (Locke), 22–23
An essay on the Causes of the Variety of Complexion and Figure in the Human Species (Smith), 117–19
Essay on the History of Civil Society (Ferguson), 33–34, 35–36, 79–80, 110
Essay on the Nature and Immutability of Truth (Beattie), 32, 67–70
Essays and Treatises on Several Subjects (Hume), 106–7
Essays on the Principles of Morality and Natural Religion (Kames), 30–31, 39
Essay Towards a General History of Feudal Property in Great Britain (Dalrymple), 38–39
An Essay Towards an Abridgment of the English History (Burke), 70–78, 79, 81, 128–29, 134–35
Estates General, 247–48
Europe, 239–42. *See also individual states*
executive power, 251–52
The Exiles (Reeve), 113n. 85

family, 191–93, 203–5, 207–13. *See also* marriage; parenthood
A Father's Legacy to his Daughters (Gregory), 95–96, 102

The Female Reader (Wollstonecraft), 100–101, 106
feminism
in civilizing process, 235–36
democracy and, 10, 257–61
French Revolution and, 257–61
moral philosophy and, 170–73
rights and, 185
of Wollstonecraft, 1–4, 157–58, 170–73, 175, 185n. 24, 257–61
"Feminists Versus Gallants" (Taylor), 20n. 28
Ferguson, Adam
Burke and, 79–80
Essay on the History of Civil Society, 33–34, 35–36, 79–80, 110
on history, 38
social theory of, 33–34, 35–36, 44, 138–39
Wollstonecraft and, 110
feudalism, 77–78, 134–36, 235–36, 248
Filmer, Robert, 192
Fitzwilliam, Earl, 125, 210n. 35, 216, 218
Fordyce, James, 94–95, 101–2
Fortescue; or, the Soldier's Reward, 114
Fox, Charles James, 153, 202, 211n. 35, 224
Francis, Philip, 147n. 35
Francis I, 235
Franklin, Benjamin, 109–10
Frederick the Great, 241
French Revolution
aesthetics and, 139, 145–48, 155–56, 224–25
agents of, 154–55, 196–202, 245–46
Bastille taken in, 248
Burke on, 4–10, 125–26; agents of, 154–55, 196–202; democracy and, 9–10, 152–56, 200–202, 213–25; history and, 127–29; moral philosophy and, 127–29, 144–51, 202–17; social theory and, 139–40, 202–13
the church and, 173–74, 221–22, 248
civilization and, 9–10, 217–25, 254–56
civilizing process and, 230–31
commerce and, 231
conservatism and, 257–61
democracy and, 9–10, 152–56, 173–75, 200–202, 213–25, 232, 251–56
equality and, 173–75, 220–21, 254–56
Estates General in, 247–48
family and, 203–5, 207–13
feminism and, 257–61
history and, 127–29, 232–33

French Revolution *(continued)*
    human nature and, 144–45
    manners and, 144, 146–51, 174–77, 200–201, 202–3, 211, 213–17, 222–23, 230–31, 242–50
    modernity and, 3–4
    moral philosophy and, 127–29, 144–51, 173–77, 202–17, 229–32, 242–50
    National Assembly in, 248
    nobility and, 139–40, 145–48, 173–74, 221–22, 248
    October Days in, 126, 163
    people and, 154–56, 221–25
    prejudice and, 219–20
    property and, 173–74, 200
    reason and, 144–45, 227–28, 246–54
    religion and, 197–200
    Revolution controversy, 4–7, 108–9
    savagery and, 126, 152–56, 216–25
    social theory and, 139–40, 202–13, 246–50
    sympathy and, 222–23
    the Terror in, 18–19, 229–32, 242–43, 247–50, 253, 255–56
    Wollstonecraft on, 5–10, 227–28; character and, 229–32, 247, 248–49, 250; democracy and, 9–10, 173–75, 232, 251–56; history and, 232–33, 242–50; moral philosophy and, 173–77, 229–32, 242–50; social theory and, 246–50
    women in, 154
Fuchs, Michel, 138n. 23
Furniss, Tom, 13n. 24

Gauls, 72–73
Germany, 241
Gibbons, Luke, 13n. 24, 138n. 23
God. *See also* church; religion
    Burke on, 58–59, 59–61, 62, 132, 141–42, 147
    human nature and, 58–59, 59–61, 62
    in moral philosophy, 65, 147
    power and, 132, 167–68
    reason and, 167–68
    Wollstonecraft on, 167–68
Godwin, William, 5, 229
Great Britain
    civilization in, 239–40
    civilizing process in, 72–78
    colonialism of, 82–87, 137–38
    constitutionalism of, 166–67
    history of, 70–78
    liberty in, 239–40
    manners in, 148–49
    Revolution controversy in, 4–7
    war with France, 221–25
    Wollstonecraft on, 239–40
Gregory, John, 95–96, 102
Gunther-Canada, Wendy, 108

Hamowy, Ronald, 35, 80
Hardy, Thomas, 5
Harris, Ian, 65
Henrietta of Gerstenfeld, 114
The Hermit of Snowdon, 115
Herzog, Don, 16n. 26, 152–53
An Historical and Moral View of the Origin and Progress of the French Revolution; and the Effect It Has Produced in Europe (Wollstonecraft)
    Christie in, 111
    on civilization, 239–42
    on commerce, 105–6
    on democracy, 251–56
    on history, 232–39, 242–50
    Hume in, 106
    on moral philosophy, 242–50
    overview of, 227–28
    in Revolution controversy, 6
    on social theory, 246–50
Historical Law Tracts (Kames), 39
history. *See also* barbarism; civilization; civilizing process; savagery
    aesthetics and, 167–69
    in *Analytical Review*, 115–23
    Burke on, 11–15, 70–87, 127–29, 140–41
    the church and, 74–77, 140–41, 167–70, 234–35
    commerce in, 10, 38, 39–49
    constitutionalism in, 76
    equality and, 170
    feudalism in, 77–78, 235–36
    French Revolution and, 127–29, 232–33
    of Great Britain, 70–78
    human nature and, 37, 38, 81–87
    manners in, 72–78, 83–87, 235–39
    materialism in, 40–42, 44–47
    moral philosophy and, 39–40, 42–49, 65–66, 89–100, 116, 122–23, 127–29, 161–62, 176–81, 242–50
    nobility and, 169–70, 234, 246–47
    power and, 167–68
    property and, 47, 73, 78–79, 91–92, 233

race in, 117–19
reason and, 36–38, 246–50
religion and, 73–77, 84–87, 140–41, 167–70
in Scottish Enlightenment, 9, 10–11, 36–49, 89–100, 115–23
sensibility in, 89–100, 116
social theory and, 10, 38, 40–49, 140–41, 246–50
stages of development in, 10, 38–49
sublimity and, 167–69
Wollstonecraft on, 16–19, 115–23, 161–62, 166–70, 176–81, 232–39, 242–50
women and, 89–100, 116, 176–81
History of America (Robertson), 44–45, 80, 83–84
History of England (Hume), 79, 106
History of Scotland (Robertson), 80, 89, 100
History of the Reign of the Emperor Charles V (Robertson), 42–43, 80, 100–101
human nature
Burke on, 81–87, 144–45, 149–50
French Revolution and, 144–45
God and, 58–59, 59–61, 62
history and, 37, 38, 81–87
instinct in, 120–22
of men, 172–73
Montesquieu on, 37
moral philosophy and, 22–32, 56–63, 144–45, 149–50, 171–73
race in, 117–19
reason and, 56–63, 120–22, 144–45
in Scottish Enlightenment, 22–32, 33–34, 37, 38
in social theory, 33–34
Wollstonecraft on, 171–73
of women, 84, 89–100, 101–9, 171–73
human rights, 258–59. *See also* rights
Hume, David
Beattie and, 67–70
Burke and, 53, 66–70, 79
on commerce, 43–44
conservatism of, 34–35
on democracy, 253
An Enquiry Concerning Human Understanding, 25
Essays and Treatises on Several Subjects, 106–7
History of England, 79, 106
moral philosophy of, 25–27, 29, 34, 43–44, 66–70
"Of Refinement in the Arts," 43–44

"Of the Rise and Progress of the Arts and Sciences," 98–100
Political Discourses, 106
on prescription, 151n. 40
on race, 117–18
on Science of Man, 21
skepticism of, 66–70
Smith and, 53
social theory of, 34–35
A Treatise of Human Nature, 25, 29, 34–35, 69
Wollstonecraft and, 106–7, 253
on women, 98–100, 106–7
Hutcheson, Francis, 23–24, 65

imitation, 58n. 31
Imlay, Gilbert, 229
Inchbald, Elizabeth, 114
income, 189–90
Inquiry into the Human Mind on the Principles of Common Sense (Reid), 31–32
An Inquiry into the Origin of our Ideas of Beauty and Virtue (Hutcheson), 65
instinct, 58–62, 64–65, 120–22, 140. *See also* affect
intelligence, 96, 103
international relations, 222–23
Italy, 240–42

Jacobinism, 219–20
Jardine, Alexander, 116
Jesuits, 86
Johnson, Joseph, 17, 109
Johnson, Samuel, 184
Juengel, Scott, 119, 119n. 99
Julia, a Novel (Williams), 115

Kames, Lord, 30–31, 39, 89–90, 117–18
Kant, Immanuel, 25–26
Kilcup, Rodney, 59, 62n. 44

ladies, 181–84
Langrishe, Hercules, 199
language, 7–11, 22, 48–49, 90–91
law, 186–87, 211–13
Lectures on Rhetoric and Belles Lettres (Blair), 96–97, 100
legislative power, 252–54
Letter on the Present Character of the French Nation (Wollstonecraft), 229–32
Letters from Barbary, France, Spain, Portugal, etc. (Jardine), 116

Letters on a Regicide Peace (Burke), 196–97, 211–17, 222–25
Letters on the Revolution in France (Christie), 111
Letters to a young Lady (Bennett), 116n. 92
Letters Written during a Short Residence in Sweden, Norway, and Denmark (Wollstonecraft), 112
A Letter to a Member of the National Assembly (Burke), 205–8
Letter to a Noble Lord (Burke), 213, 218
liberty, 84–85, 137, 239–42. *See also* equality; rights
literature, 243–44. *See also* novels
Lock, F. P., 55, 62n. 42, 67, 81–82, 83n. 102, 85
Locke, John, 22–23
London Corresponding Society (LCS), 5
Louis XIV, 243, 244
Louis XV, 244
Louis XVI, 145, 198, 221, 244
Lounger, 97, 100, 107
love, 130–31, 132–33, 134, 160, 206–7, 209

Mackenzie, Henry, 97, 100, 107
manners. *See also* moral philosophy
  aesthetics and, 181–82
  barbarism and, 233–39
  Burke on, 65–66, 72–78, 83–87, 135–36, 144, 146–51, 200–201, 202–3, 211, 213–17, 222–23
  chivalry and, 235–37
  in civilizing process, 72–78, 235–39
  commerce and, 237
  democracy and, 174–75, 184–94, 238–39
  equality and, 187–89, 238–39
  family and, 211
  in feudalism, 135–36
  French Revolution and, 144, 146–51, 174–77, 200–201, 202–3, 211, 213–17, 222–23, 230–31, 242–50
  in Great Britain, 148–49
  in history, 72–78, 83–87, 235–39
  language of, 48–49
  Marie Antoinette and, 244–45
  men and, 177, 180–81
  reason and, 176–78, 181–84, 227–28, 236–39
  revolution in, 184–94
  rights and, 187–89
  savagery and, 233–39
  sensibility and, 184
  Smith on, 65, 103–5
  in social theory, 135–36
  Wollstonecraft on, 103–5, 122–23, 161–62, 174–88, 184–94, 187–89, 227–28, 230–31, 235–39, 242–50
  women and, 175–88, 187–89, 249
The Man of Feeling (Mackenzie), 97
Maria, or The Wrongs of Woman (Wollstonecraft), 112
Maria Harcourt, 114
Marie Antoinette, 135–36, 145–48, 164, 244–45
marriage, 186–87, 191, 193, 211–13. *See also* family; parenthood
Marx, Karl, 121n. 103
materialism, 40–42, 44–47
Meek, Ronald, 36, 39, 42
Mehta, Uday, 137, 138n. 23
Mellor, Anne, 107
men
  Burke on, 132, 139
  human nature of, 172–73
  manners and, 177, 180–81
  military and, 180–81
  in moral philosophy, 172–73, 249
  in nobility, 139
  parenthood and, 191–93
  power and, 132, 181
  reason and, 183
  rights of, 184–94
  sublimity and, 132
  Wollstonecraft on, 172–73, 177, 180–81
Menonville, François-Louis-Thibault de, 205
Mercer, Thomas, 150n. 38
Mercy-Argenteau, comte de, 219
military, 179–81
Millar, John, 35, 45–46, 54, 90–92, 94, 238
Mirror, 97, 100, 107
modernity, 3–4
Molière, 243–44
monarchy, 251, 253. *See also* nobility
monasteries, 75
Monboddo, Lord, 121–22
Monk, Samuel, 130
Montesquieu, 37, 71–72, 78
moral philosophy. *See also* manners; reason; sensibility; social theory
  aesthetics and, 56–59, 145–48, 160, 164, 181–82
  affect in, 28, 30, 60–62, 64–65

anarchy in, 66–67
barbarism and, 233–39
beauty and, 145–48, 160, 171–72
Burke on, 11–15, 56–70, 127–29, 144–51
the church and, 128–29
civilizing process and, 176–81, 230–31
commerce and, 42–49, 92, 105–6, 231, 237
common sense in, 30–32, 66–70, 164–65
democracy and, 173–75, 213–17, 232, 238–39, 259–60
division of labor in, 105–6
duty in, 203–4
education and, 207–8
equality and, 238–39
family in, 203–5, 207–13
feminism and, 170–73
French Revolution and, 127–29, 144–51, 173–77, 202–17, 229–32, 242–50
God in, 65, 147
history and, 39–40, 42–49, 65–66, 89–100, 116, 122–23, 127–29, 161–62, 176–81, 242–50
human nature in, 22–32, 56–63, 144–45, 149–50, 171–73
instinct in, 58–62, 64–65
language of, 48–49
love in, 206–7, 209
Marie Antoinette and, 145–48, 244–45
men in, 172–73, 249
natural law in, 56–57, 62–63
nobility and, 128–29, 145–48, 208, 243–46, 246–47
power and, 148
prejudice in, 149–51, 160–61, 165, 219–20
prescription in, 150–51, 173–74
property and, 48–49, 150–51
religion in, 96
savagery and, 233–39
in Scottish Enlightenment, 9, 10–11, 22–32, 34, 39–40, 42–49, 63–70, 89–107
skepticism in, 66–70
social theory and, 34, 42–49, 65–66, 161, 246–50
the state and, 149–51
sublimity and, 148, 160, 209
sympathy in, 26, 27–28, 29–30, 58, 64, 66, 69, 93, 103, 147, 164–65
taste in, 68–70
truth in, 68

wealth in, 104–5
of Wollstonecraft, 16–19, 100–109, 111–15, 116, 122–23, 158–66, 170–84, 227–28, 229–32, 242–50
women in, 89–109, 111–15, 116, 170–73, 249
Moran, Mary Catherine, 89, 90, 91–92, 95
Myers, Mitzi, 113

National Assembly, 248
Native Americans, 82–85, 86, 119, 126, 138
natural law, 56–57, 62–63, 138–39
Neill, Anna, 227n. 1
Newton, Sir Isaac, 22–23, 58
New World, 78–87
nobility. *See also* monarchy
Burke on, 12, 14–15, 128–29, 134–40, 145–48, 208, 215–16, 221–22
civilization and, 221–22, 240
civilizing process and, 134–40, 169–70, 234
equality and, 170
family and, 208
French Revolution and, 139–40, 145–48, 173–74, 221–22, 248
history and, 169–70, 234, 246–47
men in, 139
moral philosophy and, 128–29, 145–48, 208, 243–46, 246–47
the press and, 215–16
sex and, 208
social theory and, 134–40, 246–47
Wollstonecraft on, 169–70, 173–74, 234, 240, 243–46, 246–47, 248
women and, 139
Norman, Elizabeth, 113
Normans, 76–77
Note-Book (Burke), 59–61
novels, 7, 97, 107, 111–15, 171. *See also* literature

O'Brien, Conor Cruise, 85
O'Brien, Karen, 45
October Days, 126, 163
Offen, Karen, 185n. 24
"Of Refinement in the Arts" (Hume), 43–44
"Of the Rise and Progress of the Arts and Sciences" (Hume), 98–100
"On Taste" (Burke), 69–70
Optics (Newton), 22–23
Of the Origin and Progress of Language (Monboddo), 121–22

The Origin of the Distinction of Ranks
    (Millar), 45–46, 90–92, 94
Orléans, duc d', 244
overview, chapter, 11–20
Owen, John, 215

Pagden, Anthony, 85
Pappin, Joseph L., III, 62n. 44
parenthood, 191–93
Pateman, Carole, 185, 189
people, 136–37, 154–56, 221–25
Phillipson, N. T., 43, 45
philosophers, 154–55, 196–202, 245–46.
    See also *individual philosophers*
A Philosophical Enquiry into the Origin of our Ideas of the Sublime and Beautiful (Burke)
    on aesthetics, 56–59, 129–34
    on affect, 60–61
    on family, 209
    on moral philosophy, 56–59, 64–65, 147
    on taste, 69
The Philosophy of Natural History (Smellie), 119–21
Pocock, J. G. A.
    on Burke, 11, 12
    on chivalry, 235
    on language, 7, 48–49
    on *philosophes*, 196, 200, 201
    on Robertson, 45
    on Scottish Enlightenment, 10, 127–28
Poisoning the Minds of the Lower Orders (Herzog), 16n. 26
Political Discourses (Hume), 106
Political Disquisitions (Burgh), 110
Political Justice (Godwin), 5
politicians, 197, 199–202
poor, 174
power
    aesthetics and, 167–68
    beauty and, 133
    Burke on, 131–32, 133, 136, 141–43, 148, 209–11
    chivalry and, 136
    the church and, 141–43, 167–68
    executive, 251–52
    family and, 209–11
    God and, 132, 167–68
    history and, 167–68
    legislative, 252–54
    men and, 132, 181

military and, 180
moral philosophy and, 148
religion and, 141–43, 167–68
in social theory, 141–43
sublimity and, 131–32, 167–68
Wollstonecraft on, 180, 181
women and, 132, 181
Preface to Brissot's Address to his Constituents (Burke), 220
prejudice, 149–51, 160–61, 165, 219–20
prescription, 150–51, 161–62, 173–74
press, 214–16, 237, 245–46
Price, Richard, 4, 109–10
Priestley, Joseph, 110
property
    Burke on, 73, 78–79, 150–51, 200
    equality and, 190
    French Revolution and, 173–74, 200
    history and, 47, 73, 78–79, 91–92, 233
    moral philosophy and, 48–49, 150–51
    rights and, 190
    in Scottish Enlightenment, 91–92
    in social theory, 47
    Wollstonecraft on, 173–74, 190, 233
    women and, 91–92, 190
Protestant Reformation, 221, 234–35

race, 117–19
Racine, Jean, 243–44
reason
    Burke on, 56–63, 64, 66–67, 144–45, 149–50, 203–6
    commerce and, 237
    common sense contrasted, 68, 112–13
    democracy and, 238–39, 251–54
    family and, 203–5
    French Revolution and, 144–45, 227–28, 246–54
    God and, 167–68
    history and, 36–38, 246–50
    human nature and, 56–63, 120–22, 144–45
    instinct contrasted, 120–22
    manners and, 176–78, 181–84, 227–28, 236–39
    men and, 183
    in Scottish Enlightenment, 24, 25, 28–29, 96
    sensibility and, 111–15
    social theory and, 246–50
    Wollstonecraft on, 111–15, 120–22, 160–62, 163–66, 172, 173, 176–78,

181–84, 227–28, 236–39, 246–50, 251–54
women and, 111–15, 172, 173, 176–78, 181–84, 249
Reeve, Clara, 113n. 85
Reflections on the Revolution in France (Burke)
    on chivalry, 135–36
    on the church, 141–43
    on civilization, 217–18
    on democracy, 152–56
    on family, 209–11
    on the French Revolution, generally, 125–26
    on Marie Antoinette, 145–48
    on moral philosophy, 144–51, 209–11
    in Revolution controversy, 4–5
    in Scottish Enlightenment, 14–15
    women in, 84
Reid, Thomas, 31–32
religion. *See also* church; God
    aesthetics and, 141–43
    Burke on, 73–77, 84–87, 140–43, 197–200
    civilizing process and, 73–77, 84–87, 179
    common sense and, 140
    equality and, 179
    French Revolution and, 197–200
    history and, 73–77, 84–87, 140–41, 167–70
    instinct and, 140
    in moral philosophy, 96
    power and, 141–43, 167–68
    sensibility and, 96
    social theory and, 84–87, 140–43, 179
    sublimity and, 141–43
    Wollstonecraft on, 167–70, 179
    women and, 96
Remarks on the Policy of the Allies (Burke), 221
Rendall, Jane, 16, 89, 115–16
respect, 160
Revolution controversy, 4–7, 108–9
Richard II, 166–67
rights. *See also* equality; liberty
    Declaration of the Rights of Man and the Citizen, 4, 185–86, 254–55, 258
    democracy and, 259
    education and, 187–89
    employment and, 190–91
    equality of, 184–94
    family and, 191–93
    feminism and, 185
    income and, 189–90

manners and, 187–89
of men, 184–94
parenthood and, 191–93
property and, 190
Wollstonecraft on, 184–94, 254–55
of women, 184–94, 258–59
Rivarol, Claude-François de, 206n. 31
Robertson, William
    Burke and, 54, 80–81, 82–83
    on history, 42–43, 44–45
    History of America, 44–45, 80, 83–84, 89
    History of Scotland, 80, 100
    History of the Reign of the Emperor Charles V, 42–43, 80, 100–101
    Wollstonecraft and, 100–101, 234–35
    on women, 89, 91–92
Roman Empire, 72, 73, 74
Rousseau, Jean-Jacques, 179, 205–8, 230
Russia, 240
Ryan, Vanessa L., 59n. 32

Sapiro, Virginia, 19n. 28, 179
savagery
    Burke on, 10, 15–16, 84–85, 86, 126–27, 137, 152–56, 210–11, 216–25
    civilization and, 217–25, 260–61
    democracy and, 10, 15–16, 127, 152–56, 216–25, 260–61
    equality and, 84–85
    family and, 210–11
    French Revolution and, 126, 152–56, 216–25
    liberty and, 84–85, 137
    manners and, 233–39
    moral philosophy and, 233–39
    of Native Americans, 84–85, 86, 119, 126, 138
    slavery and, 138
    Wollstonecraft on, 10, 233–39
    women and, 91–92, 126
Saxons, 76–77
Science of Man, 8, 14, 21–22, 25–30, 66
Scottish Enlightenment
    Burke's connections to, 8–10, 53–56
    civilization in, 10
    civilizing process in, 9, 10, 38, 40–49
    commerce in, 10, 38, 39–49
    conservatism of, 34–35
    history in, 9, 10–11, 36–49, 89–100, 115–23
    human nature in, 22–32, 33–34, 37, 38
    language of, 8–11, 22, 48–49, 90–91

Scottish Enlightenment *(continued)*
    moral philosophy in, 9, 10–11, 22–32, 34, 39–40, 42–49, 63–70, 89–107
    property in, 91–92
    reason in, 24, 25, 28–29, 96
    Science of Man in, 8, 14, 21–22, 25–30, 66
    social theory in, 10, 33–36, 38, 40–49
    sympathy in, 26, 27–28, 29–30
    Wollstonecraft's knowledge of, 8–10, 100–107, 109–11, 115–23
    women in, 17, 89–107
sensibility. *See also* common sense
    Burke on, 108–9, 145–48
    common sense and, 112–13
    in history, 89–100, 116
    language of, 90–91
    manners and, 184
    novels and, 97, 111–15, 171
    reason and, 111–15
    religion and, 96
    in Revolution controversy, 108–9
    sympathy and, 93
    Wollstonecraft on, 100–102, 107–9, 111–15, 116, 158–66, 170–73, 184
    women and, 89–102, 107–9, 111–15, 116, 170–73, 184
Sermons (Blair), 96–97, 100
Sermons to Young Women (Fordyce), 94–95, 101–2
sex, 130–31, 132, 208
Shaftesbury, third earl of, 23
Shanley, Mary Lyndon, 108
skepticism, 66–70
Sketches of the History of Man (Kames), 30–31, 39, 89–90, 117
slavery, 82, 84–85, 85–87, 138, 193, 242
Smellie, William, 119–21
Smith, Adam
    Burke and, 53–54, 63–66
    on commerce, 105–6
    conservatism of, 35
    on division of labor, 105–6
    on history, 39–42
    Hume and, 53
    on instinct, 64
    on manners, 65, 103–5
    moral philosophy of, 26–30, 39–40, 63–66, 93, 97–98, 102–6
    on parenthood, 191
    on reason, 64
    on sensibility, 97–98
    on sympathy, 58, 66, 93, 103
    The Theory of Moral Sentiments, 26–30, 39–40, 53–54, 63–66, 93, 97–98, 102–5, 191
    The Wealth of Nations, 39–42, 43, 94, 105–6
    Wollstonecraft and, 102–6
    on women, 94, 98
Smith, Charlotte, 114–15
Smith, William, 219–20
social theory. *See also* moral philosophy
    aesthetics and, 135–36, 139, 141–43
    of Burke, 78–87, 134–43
    the church and, 140–43, 140–43, 179
    colonialism in, 137–38
    common sense in, 140
    democracy and, 202–13
    education in, 143
    equality in, 178–94
    French Revolution and, 139–40, 202–13, 246–50
    history and, 10, 38, 40–49, 140–41, 246–50
    human nature in, 33–34
    instinct in, 140
    manners in, 135–36
    military and, 179–81
    moral philosophy and, 34, 42–49, 65–66, 161, 246–50
    natural law in, 138–39
    nobility and, 134–40, 246–47
    people in, 136–37
    power in, 141–43
    property in, 47
    reason and, 246–50
    religion and, 84–87, 140–43, 179
    in Scottish Enlightenment, 10, 33–36, 38, 40–49
    stages of development in, 10, 38
    the state in, 141–43
    sublimity in, 141–43
    the Terror and, 247–50
    Wollstonecraft on, 161, 176–94, 246–50
    women in, 176–94
Some Remarks on the Apparent Circumstances of the War in the Fourth Week of October 1795 (Auckland), 211
Spence, Thomas, 5
Spirit of the Laws (Montesquieu), 72
Stanhope Smith, Samuel, 117–19
Stanlis, Peter, 57n. 26, 57n. 27, 163n. 11

state, 141–43, 149–51. *See also* constitutionalism
Stewart, Dugald, 31, 32, 35, 38, 54, 81
"The Story of La Roche" (Mackenzie), 97, 100
Strictures on Female Education (Bennett), 116n. 92
sublimity
   Burke on, 129–32, 134, 135, 141–43, 148, 155–56, 209, 224–25
   the church and, 141–43
   in civilizing process, 141–43
   democracy and, 155–56
   family and, 209
   feudalism and, 135
   French Revolution and, 224–25
   history and, 167–69
   love and, 134
   men and, 132
   moral philosophy and, 148, 160, 209
   power and, 131–32, 167–68
   religion and, 141–43
   in social theory, 141–43
   Wollstonecraft on, 160, 167–69
sympathy
   Burke on, 58, 64, 66, 69, 147, 222–23
   French Revolution and, 222–23
   in Scottish Enlightenment, 26, 27–28, 29–30
   sensibility and, 93
   Smith on, 58, 66, 93, 103
   Wollstonecraft on, 103, 164–65

Talleyrand, 6, 176, 185–86, 257
taste, 68–70
Taylor, Barbara, 19n. 28, 168n. 15, 179
Terror, 18–19, 229–32, 242–43, 247–50, 253, 255–56
theater, 243–44
Thelwall, John, 5
The Theory of Moral Sentiments (Smith)
   Burke and, 53–54, 63–66
   on history, 39–40
   on moral philosophy, 26–30
   on parenthood, 191
   on sensibility, 93, 97–98
   Wollstonecraft and, 102–5
   on women, 98
Thomas Aquinas, Saint, 61, 63
Thoughts on French Affairs (Burke), 221
Todd, Janet, 110–11
Tooke, John Horne, 5

Travels in the United States of North America (Brissot), 122–23
A Treatise of Human Nature (Hume), 25, 29, 34–35, 69
truth, 68

"A View of the Progress of Society in Europe" (Robertson), 42–43
A Vindication of Natural Society (Burke), 61–62
A Vindication of Political Virtue (Sapiro), 19n. 28
A Vindication of the Rights of Men, in a Letter to the Right Honorable Edmund Burke (Wollstonecraft)
   on French Revolution, generally, 173–75
   history in, 166–70
   Hume in, 106
   moral philosophy in, 158–66, 170–73
   overview of, 157
   in Revolution controversy, 5
   on women, 108, 170–73
A Vindication of the Rights of Woman (Wollstonecraft)
   equality in, 178–94
   feminism founded by, 157–58
   history in, 176–81
   Monboddo in, 121
   overview of, 176–77
   in Revolution controversy, 5–6
   rights in, 184–94
   social theory in, 176–94
   on women, 101–2, 103–5, 106–7, 108, 175–94

wealth, 104–5
The Wealth of Nations (Smith), 39–42, 43, 94, 105–6
Weddell, William, 153
White, Stephen K., 56
The Widow of Kent, 114
Williams, Helen Maria, 115
Windham, William, 223n. 49
Wollstonecraft, Mary
   on aesthetics, 160, 164, 167–69, 171–72, 181–82
   on agriculture, 233
   Analytical Review and, 109–23
   on barbarism, 166–67, 233–39
   on the Bastille, 248
   on beauty, 160, 171–72

Wollstonecraft, Mary *(continued)*
  on character, 229–32, 243–44, 247, 248–49, 250
  on chivalry, 234–37, 243
  on the church, 167–70, 173–74, 179, 234–35, 240, 248
  on civilization, 9–10, 16, 239–42, 254–56
  on the civilizing process, 18–19, 161–62, 166–70, 176–81, 230–31, 232–39
  on commerce, 105–6, 231, 237
  on common sense, 112–13, 164–65
  on the Crusades, 234–35
  death of, 256
  on democracy, 9–10, 16, 18–19, 102, 113, 173–75, 238–39, 251–56
  on education, 116, 168–69, 170, 182–83, 187–89
  on employment, 190–91
  on equality, 18–19, 170, 173–75, 178–94, 238–39, 254–56
  on Estates General, 247–48
  on Europe, 239–42
  on executive power, 251–52
  on family, 191–93
  The Female Reader, 100–101, 106
  feminism of, 1–4, 157–58, 170–73, 175, 185n. 24, 257–61
  on feudalism, 235–36, 248
  in France, 229–32
  on French Revolution, 5–10, 173–75, 227–28; and character, 229–32, 247, 248–49, 250; and democracy, 9–10, 173–75, 232, 251–56åd history, 232–33, 242–50; and moral philosophy, 173–77, 229–32, 242–50; and social theory, 246–50
  on God, 167–68
  on Great Britain, 239–40
  An Historical and Moral View of the Origin and Progress of the French Revolution; and the Effect It Has Produced in Europe, 6, 105–6, 111, 227–28, 232–56
  on history, 16–19, 115–23, 161–62, 166–70, 176–81, 232–39, 242–50
  on human nature, 171–73
  on income, 189–90
  on instinct, 120–22
  on ladies, 181–84
  on law, 186–87
  on legislative power, 252–54
  Letter on the Present Character of the French Nation, 229–32

  Letters Written during a Short Residence in Sweden, Norway, and Denmark, 112
  on liberty, 239–42
  on love, 160
  on manners, 103–5, 122–23, 161–62, 174–88, 184–94, 187–89, 227–28, 230–31, 235–39, 242–50
  Maria, or The Wrongs of Woman, 112
  on Marie Antoinette, 164
  on marriage, 186–87, 191, 193
  on men, 172–73, 177, 180–81
  on military, 179–81
  on monarchy, 251, 253
  moral philosophy of, 16–19, 100–109, 111–15, 116, 122–23, 158–66, 170–77, 176–81, 181–84, 227–28, 229–32, 242–50
  on National Assembly, 248
  on nobility, 169–70, 173–74, 234, 240, 243–46, 246–47, 248
  novels and, 7, 107, 111–15, 171
  on parenthood, 191–93
  on philosophers, 245–46
  on the poor, 174
  on power, 167–68, 180, 181
  on prejudice, 160–61, 165
  on prescription, 161–62, 173–74
  on the press, 237, 245–46
  on property, 173–74, 190, 233
  on the Protestant Reformation, 234–35
  on race, 118–19
  on reason, 111–15, 120–22, 160–62, 163–66, 172, 173, 176–78, 181–84, 227–28, 236–39, 246–50, 251–54
  on religion, 167–70, 179
  on rights, 184–94, 254–55
  on savagery, 10, 233–39
  Scottish Enlightenment, knowledge of, 8–10, 100–107, 109–11, 115–23
  on sensibility, 100–102, 107–9, 111–15, 116, 158–66, 170–73, 184
  on slavery, 242
  on social theory, 161, 176–94, 246–50
  on sublimity, 160, 167–69
  on sympathy, 103, 164–65
  on the Terror, 18–19, 229–32, 242–43, 247–50, 253, 255–56
  A Vindication of the Rights of Men, in a Letter to the Right Honorable Edmund Burke, 5, 106, 108, 157, 158–66, 166–70, 170–73, 173–75

A Vindication of the Rights of Woman, 5–6, 101–2, 103–5, 106–7, 108–9, 121, 157–58, 176–94
   on women, 17, 18, 100–109, 111–15, 116, 170–73, 175–94, 249
Woman (Adams), 115–16
women
   aesthetics and, 181–82
   beauty and, 133, 171–72
   Burke on, 126, 136, 139, 154
   civilizing process and, 176–81
   commerce and, 91–92
   democracy and, 102, 113, 154, 184–94
   education of, 96, 116, 182–83, 187–89
   employment and, 190–91
   equality and, 178–94
   in French Revolution, 154
   history and, 89–100, 116, 176–81
   human nature of, 84, 89–100, 101–9, 171–73
   income and, 189–90
   intelligence of, 96, 102, 103
   as ladies, 181–84
   manners and, 175–88, 187–89, 249
   moral philosophy and, 89–109, 111–15, 116, 170–73, 249
   nobility and, 139
   in novels, 111–15
   oppression of, 91–92, 94–95, 96, 97, 99–100, 101–2, 104–5, 106–7, 171–73, 176–84
   parenthood and, 191–93
   power and, 132, 181
   property and, 91–92, 190
   reason and, 111–15, 172, 173, 176–78, 181–84, 249
   religion and, 96
   rights of, 184–94, 258–59
   savagery and, 91–92, 126
   in Scottish Enlightenment, 17, 89–107
   sensibility and, 89–102, 107–9, 111–15, 116, 170–73, 184
   in social theory, 176–94
   Wollstonecraft on, 17, 18, 100–109, 111–15, 116, 170–73, 175–94, 249
Woodford, Captain, 219

Young, G. M., 71

Zerilli, Linda, 154
Žižka, John, 225–26